LIAM LYNCH was born near Anglesboro in County Limerick on 9 November 1893, the fifth of a family of seven.

When the organisation of the Volunteers commenced in November 1913, nearby Mitchelstown was one of the first towns to form a corps and Liam became a member. Though the Cork companies obeyed 1916 cancellation orders and did not take part in the fighting, Easter Week was for Liam Lynch 'a flame that illuminated the past and showed the way into the future'.

From then on, he prepared himself for the battle he knew lay ahead. He was elected Adjutant of the Fermoy Battalion in 1917, Brigade Commandant of the Cork No. 2 Brigade in 1919, and Divisional Commandant in 1921. After the Treaty he was offered a commission commanding the 1st Southern Division.

After the split between pro- and anti-Treaty forces, he was appointed Chief of Staff of the Irish Republican Army.

FLORENCE O'DONOGHUE was born in Rathmore, County Kerry on 21 July 1894. He was Brigade Adjutant and Intelligence Officer of the Cork No. 1 Brigade of the Irish Volunteers, and transferred to the same posts in the 1st Southern Division in 1921. He took no part in the Civil War.

He served in the Defence Forces, 1940–45, as Intelligence Officer First Division and was a member of the Advisory Council of the Irish Bureau of Military History.

Major O'Donoghue was an exceptionally competent and diligent military historian whose writings are distinguished by minute accuracy and exhaustive research. He wrote two major works on aspects of the Irish national struggle 1916–1922; *No Other Law* (1954) and *Tomas MacCurtain* (1955). He edited Karl Spindler's *Mystery of the Casement Ship* (1965) and Diarmuid Lynch's *The IRB and the 1916 Rising* (Cork nd).

He died in 1967, a year after the death of his wife Jo, who had been one of his most confidential collaborators in pre-truce IRA Intelligence. He is survived by two sons and two daughters.

FLORENCE O'DONOGHUE

NO OTHER LAW

ANVIL BOOKS

Published by Anvil Books Limited 1986
90 Lower Baggot Street, Dublin 2

First published in 1954 by *The Irish Press*

Copyright © Executors Florence O'Donoghue 1954

ISBN 0 947962 12 3

Printed in Great Britain by
Richard Clay, Bungay, Suffolk

CONTENTS

INTRODUCTION

THIS is my humble tribute to the memory of a brave man who died for an ideal. The simple patriotism which Liam Lynch understood was measured in terms of service to the cause of national freedom. He set it above everything in his life, and finally above life itself.

In the years of national resurgence and under the searching strain of warfare he bore his share of heavy responsibility with courage and honour, unswayed by envy or anger. His life's work is inseparable from the vision of freedom which inspired him, and from the great national movement which was the arena of his labours.

This slight record is, however, no more than a small contribution to one aspect of the history of that movement; but within its limits I have spared no effort to make it accurate.

Of the errors and omissions which those who work the same field after me will find in it, I desire only to put on record that nothing has been included which I do not believe to be true and which has not been tested as fully as the limited means at my disposal permitted. My hope is that others better qualified, having more ample leisure and access to a wider range of historical material, will ensure that men like Liam Lynch do not die a second death by fading from the memory of their nation.

They have left us a heritage of faith, courage and loyalty—part of a greater heritage which will continue to inspire the generations that are yet to be, and guide them in the achievement of that part of the task which remains unfinished.

Cork, December, 1953.   F. O'D.

ACKNOWLEDGMENT

No work of this kind, however slight, is possible to-day without the assistance of a large number of collaborators. Much of the material required by anybody working on the military aspect of the 1916–1923 period, still exists only in the dimming memories of a dying generation.

I have been fortunate in receiving in the most generous measure the good will, co-operation and active assistance of a very large number of men and women who were associated with the national struggle for freedom, or who have made some study of the period. I am indebted to so many for vital information, for rare documents, for criticism and advice, that it is not possible to make individual acknowledgments, however much I would like to do so.

With one notable exception, every person whose name occurs in the text who participated in the military aspect of the movement on the Irish side, and who was living during the three years the work has been in progress, has contributed to it in one way or another, irrespective of any division caused by the Civil War. To each and all of them I offer sincere and grateful thanks.

To the small group who initiated and sustained the onerous task of collecting material, George Power, Liam Deasy and Maurice Twomey, I am especially indebted for generous and unfailing co-operation; to the surviving officers of Liam Lynch's old commands, Cork No. 2 Brigade, First Southern Division and G.H.Q. Staff and to the members of his family, I offer sincere appreciation and thanks for invaluable co-operation and assistance.

CHAPTER I

TRADITION AND THE FLAME OF INSURRECTION

No Rising must begin in the country. Dublin streets for that.

MITCHEL.

NEAR Anglesboro, in the County Limerick, five miles north of Mitchelstown, the townland of Barnagurraha shelters under the western slopes of the Galtee mountains. Here, on 9th November, 1893, a son was born to Jeremiah Lynch and Mary Kelly, the fifth of a family of seven children. He was baptised William Fanaghan Lynch—Fanaghan in honour of the patron Saint of Mitchelstown, whose feast day is 24th November. He grew to manhood in the years of national awakening, and in the notable part he played in the armed struggle for the establishment of the Irish Republic he was known to everybody as Liam Lynch.

His people were farmers. The house where he was born overlooks the vale that cradles the infant Aherlow river, flowing northwards here before turning east at Galbally through its lovely glen. Paradise Hill rises in a gentle slope between Barnagurraha and the towering Galtees.

With Gleann na gCreabhar—the ancient and lovelier place-name for which some invader substituted Anglesboro—and with all the vast plain between the Galtees and the Blackwater, numerous families bearing the name Lynch have had a long association. There were Lynches here when Geoffrey Keating was writing his history of Ireland in the nearby Glen of Aherlow, nearly three and a half centuries ago. In earlier historical records the name occurs. An O'Loingsigh derived from the illustrious race of Heremon ruled the Kingdom of Ireland for eight years from 685 to 693. Lynches were lords of Dalradia from 985 to 1156, and are frequently mentioned in the Annals. Mailmaire O'Loinsigh, a Bishop of Lismore, died in 1159. Seven clans of the name are recorded in history, one of which, a branch of the Corca Laoighe, inhabited a part of south-west Cork, almost co-extensive with the present diocese of Ross.

Family tradition suggests that from this clan came the first ancestor of Liam Lynch, of whom we have some historical record. He was John Lynch, who lived from 1696 to 1758, and is buried at Castlehyde. His wife's name was Bourke and they had a son, also John, born in 1724.

This John Lynch married Ellen Joyce of Ardpatrick, County
Limerick and they had a large family consisting of at least Philip,
John, James, Dorothy, a daughter who became Mrs. Roche and
another who became Mrs. Fitzgibbon. In his will, John Lynch
made provision for a child then unborn, who was to lead a romantic
life and die a tragic death.

This child was James Lynch. He was born in the year of his father's
death, 1785, and from him are descended the many present-day
Lynches of Anglesboro, Ballinamona and Broomhill, as well as the
Lynches of Barnagurraha. Though born at Castlehyde, he was reared
at Broomhill, about two miles west of Mitchelstown where the
family had a farm, and spent some time at Tully, between Mitchelstown and Kilfinane, where one of his brothers had a holding. His
wife was an aunt of Edward O'Meagher Condon, one of the prisoners
tried with Allen, Larkin and O'Brien, the Manchester Martyrs, in 1867,
whose cry of, "God Save Ireland," from the dock became the title
of T. D. Sullivan's popular rebel ballad.

James Lynch acquired from the landlord, Maxwell Lowe, title
to "all Barnagurraha for his lifetime," and thus became himself a
landlord in a small way, receiving rents from the other six or eight
farmers in the townland. Whether this comparative affluence, or the
jealousy it aroused, contributed to his death is not quite clear. It
was a time when killers could be hired to avenge an injury, real or
imaginary. On 12th November, 1847, when walking alone towards
his own house from Barnagurraha where his son lived, he was shot
down and killed by a gang of local bandits called "Black Boys."
He was buried in Brigown.

When he was killed, at the age of sixty-two years, James Lynch
had a son, also James, who had married Johanna Mary O'Donnell.
Their six children were John, Jeremiah, James, Martin, Hannah and
Ellen. James and Martin became Christian Brothers. Hannah married
Matthew Cranitch of Anglesboro and Ellen married Robert Walsh of
Corderry, Galbally. John, the eldest of the family, married Margaret
Casey and their nine children were John, James, Tadhg, Martin,
Eugene, Hannah, Mary, Jeremiah and Joseph.

Jeremiah, the second youngest of this family, born in 1845, was
the father of Liam Lynch. His wife was Mary Kelly, daughter of
James Kelly, Ballyduff, and they had seven children, John, Jeremiah,
Margaret, Martin, Liam, James and Thomas. John lives at Knockadea,
Ballylanders, Jeremiah was accidentally drowned while bathing in
London in 1904. He was in the Civil Service, and his fellow-country-
men erected a fine cross to mark his grave in St. Pancras cemetery.
Margaret married Patrick Mullins and lives at the old home at
Barnagurraha. James lived there until his death in 1933 at the age of

39. Martin is Reverend Brother Placidus, of the Christian Brothers Kilrush, and Thomas became Very Reverend Dean Lynch, P.P., of Bega, New South Wales. He died in a Sidney hospital on 28th March, 1950.

The Lynches had deep roots in this fertile plain, anciently known as Feara Muighe Feine. It was once a territory of great importance, Glanworth at its centre being for centuries the royal seat and capital. Later, it was all Desmond land, parcelled out after the confiscations in thousands of acres to Elizabethan adventurers, on condition that it should be planted with English settlers. It was so planted, and yet some few of the old Gaelic families, driven from the rich plain into the foothills of the Galtees, but holding on tenaciously generation after generation, managed to survive and preserve their most precious traditions.

Three hundred years of Irish history is reflected in miniature in what happened in this locality. An Arthur Hyde was granted six thousand acres of rich land from which the mere Irish had been driven by the sword. He paid one penny per acre on the undertaking that he would plant them with English subjects. For nearly three centuries the Hyde family ruled these estates, and at the end the land went back to the descendants of those whose patrimony it was before the invasions, and one branch of the Hyde family gave Ireland a man who set a land-mark in her history by founding the Gaelic League, and who became the first President of Ireland—An Craoibin. One of the dispossessed was a Lynch. We know little of the miracle by which families such as his survived the terrible seventeenth century, but survive they did, and five generations after him, Liam Lynch led the men of South Munster in the fight which finally destroyed all that the plantations aimed to achieve.

Had the clearances been absolute no Irish names would have survived in these rich lands. A remnant of the old stock somehow evaded the universal sentence of banishment beyond the Shannon, and gradually attained to a precarious tenancy of small holdings from the new lords of the land. The planters found it necessary to tolerate a limited number of former owners in a state of menial servitude, without rights, without property and for a time without even a legal existence. These families are the slender thread by which the tradition of nationhood survived through the centuries of persecution and proscription. With them survived the old Faith, the native tongue and something of Gaelic culture. In them a tradition lived, a tradition sufficiently vital and enduring to exist despite the loss of almost all the marks of separate nationhood—except itself. Liam Lynch was reared in that tradition.

At the age of four-and-a-half years he began to attend at Anglesboro

School, where he continued as a pupil until October, 1909. His teacher, Mr. Patrick Kiely, remembers him as a mild, gentle boy, above the average in intelligence. It is remarkable how many of those who knew him in manhood, were struck first by that same trait of gentleness, and spoke of it in their recollection of his character. One day when he was eight or nine years of age, he burst into tears in class because he had failed in some lesson. Investigation revealed that his failure was due to a slight defect in his eyesight. He had to leave school for a short time and have treatment in Cork. Thereafter he wore glasses almost continuously.

Around his early youth the Galtee countryside wove a spell that never lost its magic to the day of his death. He had a sense of the indefinable spirit which inheres in a place rich in history. The country-side has a long memory, and in Gleann na gCreabhar the tradition of local associations with the many phases of the struggle for freedom, had transmitted down the generations songs and stories of courage and endeavour. He heard them with a receptive heart.

As he grew older he developed a taste for reading. His natural preference for books on Irish history was sharpened by local and family contacts with some of the events of the past. No boy of his spirit could fail to be thrilled by the story of the fight at Kilclooney Wood, not far from his native place. He had heard many times how Peter O'Neill Crowley, having captured the coast-guard station at Knockadoon, and waited in vain for the reinforcements which were to join him at Killeagh, marched north with two companions, McClure and Kelly, to Kilclooney Wood at the end of March, 1867. He had heard how they were surrounded there by British troops, and how the last episode of that attempt to achieve freedom was enacted in the fight made by these men, before O'Neill Crowley was shot down and killed.

Or, touching more closely his family pride, he had listened to the story of how his uncle, John Lynch, and William Condon, rode on horseback to Kilmallock for the Rising, only to find the town surrounded and their companions scattered. In Gleann na gCreabhar, as in all rural Ireland, stories of the land war were a fireside topic. He had heard of the worthy part played by his mother, Mary Kelly, in those difficult years, when she worked as joint secretary of the Ballylanders Branch of the Ladies' Land League.

His godmother, Mrs. Hannah Cleary, was a daughter of William Condon. Often she told him the story of her father's fight for his land, and showed him the warrant for William Condon's arrest signed by "Buckshot" Forster in 1882. The Black-and-Tans attempted to burn that document later, but Hannah Cleary saved it and still treasures it, only slightly damaged, in her possession.

Even in his schooldays, Liam appears to have been particularly attracted by deeds of bravery and daring. Patrick Sarsfield was one of his heroes. A fellow-pupil at Anglesboro School, Liam O'Cathain, recalls that on a climb to the top of Galteemore he pointed northwards to Ballyneety, and gave his companions an accurate account of Sarsfield's famous night ride and of his destruction of the Williamite siege train. He was to refer to it again many years later in one of his letters to his brother Tom.

In 1910, when he was seventeen years old, Liam left his home under the Galtees and entered upon a term of three year's apprenticeship to the hardware trade with Mr. P. O'Neill, Baldwin Street, Mitchelstown. He was then a rather shy, quiet lad, but of striking physique. He was beginning a commercial career in a prosperous country town, and there was nothing in his circumstances or prospects to forecast the revolutionary changes which the next twelve years held for him and for his generation.

But, unknown to him, the beginning of a new national movement, destined to dominate the whole of his adult life, was just then arising from the confluence of many small streams of national resurgence. In the preceding twenty years a number of organisations had come into existence which, while they had no ostensible political aims, prepared the ground for Sinn Féin and the Irish Volunteers. The Gaelic League, the Gaelic Athletic Association, the Irish Literary Society, the Abbey Theatre and the Feis Ceoil, all contributed to the creation of a more vigorous and self-reliant national spirit. A spark in the embers of Fenianism was being nursed into new flame. It was the year in which Tom Clarke, who had returned from the United States in 1907, became a member of the Supreme Council of the Irish Republican Brotherhood. Once again there was an organised body of Irishmen working for the achievement of national independence in arms. From that day an Insurrection was inevitable.

In Mitchelstown Liam came into an atmosphere that was national, but not at that time, revolutionary. He joined the Gaelic League and the Ancient Order of Hibernians, and returned to his home at Barnagurraha almost every Sunday. He continued his education by joining a technical class and by much reading.

The town, of which Arthur Young has said that it had " a situation worthy of any capital in Europe," was once dominated by Mitchelstown Castle, where that tyrannical landlord the first Earl of Kingston ruled. In his day, material from the demolished Catholic Church at Kilcoughlan, was used in the building of the White Knight's Tower. Time has brought changes. Now, nothing of the Tower, and scarcely anything of the Castle, remains ; stone from its ruined walls went into the building of the new Cistercian Church at Mount Melleray,

where Liam Lynch's surviving comrades have erected an altar to
the memory of all those who died in the fight for freedom. Mitchelstown was a storm centre in the land war of the '80's. There the Plan
of Campaign had been perfected, and the shooting of three men by
Crown forces at a great public meeting originated the slogan,
" Remember Mitchelstown."

When the organisation of the Irish Volunteers commenced in
November, 1913, Mitchelstown was one of the first towns to form a
corps. Standing at the junction of three counties, the town became
an important centre in the subsequent rapid development of the
organisation in the surrounding countryside. By the summer of
1914, 2,000 men had been enrolled in the eight companies of the
Galtee regiment. Liam became a member of the Mitchelstown
company.

Having completed his term of apprenticeship in 1913, he remained
at O'Neill's for a further year, after which he went to similar employment in Millstreet for a short time. He returned again to O'Neill's
late in 1914. In the Autumn of 1915 he transferred to Messrs. J.
Barry & Sons, Ltd., Fermoy, where he continued to be employed
until he took up whole-time active service duty with the Army. He
had, by then, acquired a sound knowledge of commercial life, and
was a keen student at Gaelic League classes.

Since he had joined the Mitchelstown Company of Irish Volunteers
two years earlier the whole political situation in Ireland had been
transformed. For many years before 1913, the Irish Parliamentary
Party, under the leadership of John Redmond and commanding the
support of the great majority of Nationalists, had waged a constitutional
battle in the British House of Commons for a limited measure of
legislative independence. The passing of the third Home Rule Bill
by the British Parliament seemed assured in 1913. The Unionists of
North-east Ulster became alarmed. In opposition to even a shadowy
form of Irish freedom, they organised the Ulster Volunteer force,
and set up an Ulster Provisional Government under the Chairmanship
of Sir Edward Carson. Preparations were made to resist Home Rule
by force of arms ; 35,000 rifles, a number of machine-guns and a large
quantity of ammunition were imported into Ulster, and a " Solemn
League and Covenant " signed by over 470,000 men and women.

A weak British Government was intimidated. When certain British
Army officers, stationed at the Curragh decided, with the active
support of Sir Henry Wilson, then Director of Military Operations
at the War Office, that they would not serve against the Ulster
Unionists, and when the British Government failed to punish their
indiscipline, it was clear to all Nationalist Ireland that the Asquith
Administration could not be relied upon to enforce Home Rule.

But the Ulster Volunteers had given a lead which the Separatist elements were not slow to follow. The founding of the Irish Volunteers, in November, 1913, aroused national enthusiasm and general support from all classes except the pro-British Unionists. The rapid growth of the organisation into a widespread national movement, in which large numbers of his own followers were enrolled, induced John Redmond, who had hitherto looked on the new development with a resentful and unfriendly eye, to take steps to control it. In May, 1914, the Irish Party decided to give its support to the Volunteer movement, and in June, a majority of the original Committee agreed to Redmond's demand for the inclusion of a number of his nominees on the Committee, sufficient to give him control. The original body had been, in the main, representative of the Separatist elements which had been gathering a little strength since the turn of the century, but were still only a small fraction of the population. By July, 1914, about 150,000 men had been enrolled in the Volunteers.

The outbreak of war in Europe, in August, 1914, divided Ireland into two well-defined sections—those who supported the British war effort, and those who held that Ireland was not at war, but should utilise the international situation to gain her freedom from British rule. In the ranks of the Volunteers, as elsewhere, opinion was divided. But when Redmond, at Woodenbridge on 20th September, advised Volunteers that it was their duty to serve " wherever the firing extends, in defence of right, freedom and religion, in this war," he took a decision which split the Volunteers and sealed the political doom of his own party. The expulsion of his nominees from the Volunteer Executive, and the creation of a new organisation—the National Volunteers—from his own supporters, followed rapidly. The large majority followed Redmond. Of the 180,000 enrolled Volunteers only eleven or twelve thousand remained with the minority. For a time there were two rival organisations, but during 1915 the National Volunteers crumbled, and the Irish Volunteers commenced to rebuild their strength in a much clearer atmosphere.

In County Cork they made better progress in the country districts, particularly in places supporting William O'Brien's All-For-Ireland League, than they did in the towns. The organisation was almost non-existent in Fermoy when Liam Lynch went there immediately after the Split. In Mitchelstown he had made an instinctive response to the appeal of soldiering, but he was politically immature. Now he began to think, to study and reflect. Fermoy was a garrison town. Its two barracks held a larger concentration of British troops than any other town in the county. Adjacent to it, Kilworth and Moore Park camps contained other strong elements of British units. Union Jacks, khaki and recruiting oratory were much in evidence. Large numbers of young men, with evident public approval, had joined the British forces. Men in high places had assured them that they were fighting for the freedom of small nations—including their own.

Yet there was a minority of young men who doubted, who questioned the wisdom of reinforcing the military strength of the foreign power whose troops occupied their country. Liam was one of them. Intensely now he " watched everything and everybody, to see where was truth and where was sincerity." Not until Easter Week was he sure. Standing on the bridge at Fermoy on the morning of 2nd May, 1916, he saw the Kents rushed over it by scared British soldiers, after their heroic defence of Bawnard House; Thomas, in his bare feet, William and their mother prisoners, and then the galloping horse drawing a cart on which Richard and David lay wounded. Richard was to die two days later in the hands of his captors, and Thomas to face a British firing squad in Cork within a week. That scene, associated as it was in his mind with the slow horror of the executions in Dublin, was something he never forgot. For him all doubts, all questionings were at an end.

That night he made a resolution and a vow. He would, God helping him, atone, as far as the dedicated life of one man could atone, for the sacrifices of the martyred dead. He would exact retribution for the long years of tyranny and injustice, he would do his part in making a reality the Irish Republic for which heroic men died. From that day he was a man " of one allegiance only." Nor was he troubled by any doubts as to the morality of his methods of working for freedom. At a time when many doubted the wisdom of armed challenge to the might of England, and when those doubts appeared to be justified by the military failure of the Rising, he was unperturbed and confident that force could be countered successfully only by force; that it was in arms, and only in arms, Ireland would achieve liberty. No nation had then achieved it otherwise. The course of his life subsequently will show with what single-minded devotion and tenacity of purpose he pursued his aim without the slightest deviation from it to the end.

The Rising was for him, as for so many other young Irishmen, a flame that illuminated the past and showed the way into the future. In its light he saw clearly that English rule in Ireland, rooted in conquest, depended then as always upon force for its continued existence. The past acquired a fresh and potent meaning; the duty of the future was clear.

He saw the history of our long struggle for liberty with a new vision. '98 was no longer merely a story of " battles long ago." He knew where Doheny and Stephens had come over the Comeraghs after the heartbreaking failure at Ballingarry in '48, where they had

slipped past Kilworth on their hunted journey, and where they had
crossed the Blackwater at Castlehyde. Now he knew that they were
kin to the men who died in Dublin. Peter O'Neill-Crowley, dying
of British bullets in Kilclooney Wood in a later and equally
unsuccessful effort, was of the same gallant company. All of it had
unity, continuity and the indelible stamp of truth. Everything that
was generous, noble and passionate in his nature responded with
eager gladness to the call of patriotic duty. " Will no day of vengeance
come, O God ? " Doheny had prayed in the bitterness of defeat.
With a glowing heart Liam promised himself that the day would
come.

Many and many a time in the years that followed he would in
intimate conversation with his brother Tom, then a clerical student in
Thurles, recall those days after Easter Week—the burning anger
he could not repress, the ecstasy of pride that brave men had risen
in his own day to challenge again in arms the long usurpation of
Ireland's right to freedom, the great happiness of seeing the day when
an Irish Army was again in process of formation. But neither anger
nor ecstasy could blind him to realities—then or subsequently.

He had a logical mind with a stubborn hardness at its core. And
now he began to think seriously, and to some purpose, not on dying
for Ireland—for that he thought of as too easy and as a thing he was
prepared to do without question whenever it became necessary—
but of so fitting himself to live and work for Ireland, that his service
might help to strike the last blows which would drive the invader
from her shores for ever.

As a boy, he was an excellent draughts-player, quick to see the
weakness in an opponent's position and take swift advantage of it,
skilful in forestalling attack, cool and consistent in planning his own
moves. These were, in embryo, the characteristics of his command
of Volunteer forces, strategically and in action, in the kind of warfare
which developed in the subsequent years—a type of warfare in which
he was a pioneer in Ireland. There was little to be learnt about it in
the literature available to him in 1916; it was some time in the
following year that he discovered books on the Boer struggle in South
Africa, and on the Peninsular war.

Even at this early stage, however, thoughts were stirring which
had the stamp of originality and vision. Thinking over the task
which he saw as an inescapable obligation on the Volunteers after
1916, he deemed it to be of paramount importance that the nation
should not relapse into the despair that had followed the failure of
previous armed efforts to achieve freedom, that the nostalgic swan-
song of defeat which had become almost a national anthem should
not again infect us. His manhood rose in violent protest against the

attitude of mind which, while cherishing and admiring the fortitude
and nobility of our soldiers and martyrs, regarded their cause as a
lost cause and their sacrifices a waste of valuable lives. " 'Tis slaves
we'll ever be" was a sentiment he rejected utterly.

Too many of us he thought, had died, and to too little purpose. Others,
too, must die, but that was merely incidental if the struggle was going
forward on a plan that gave hope of ultimate victory. In the Volunteers
he saw the material from which a powerful weapon could be forged.
How it was to be wielded he did not know, but he had an extraordinary confidence that an effective way would be found.

Meanwhile, if the Volunteers were to honour the sacred trust they
had inherited from the dead generations and from the leaders who had
proclaimed the Republic, they must look ahead, determine their
strategy and tactics with coolness and deliberation, and be prepared
not merely to fight resolutely and to a conclusion, not merely to be
brave and honourable, but also to be masters of their weapons and
their methods, to be tough and wily and enduring. For those who
would lead them, loyalty and idealism were not enough ; they must
divest themselves of all anger against England ; they must be cool
and relentless ; they must plan an approach to the military problem
different from those of 1798, 1803, 1865 or even 1916. All these had
failed ; he and his comrades must not fail.

With these thoughts exercising his mind, it is not surprising to
learn that Liam was at this time a silent and serious young man.
His father had died in 1914, and he was intensely devoted to his
mother. Every Sunday, up to the time his Volunteer duties wholly
claimed his attention, saw him at his home in the Galtees. Even
there by the fireside on these quiet Sundays he was thinking. " Glory
be to God," his mother would say, " he is the queer visitor. I haven't
got three words out of him."—

> " So many an Irish mother
> Has seen her boy go from her
> As if they had bewitched him
> Those fierce old Irish dead."

At Easter, 1916, there were in Cork City and County, forty-six
organised companies of Irish Volunteers, many of them not exceeding
twenty men, and almost all poorly armed. They, in common with all
other units of the organisation in Munster, were denied participation
in the Rising through the confusion and uncertainty which followed
a number of conflicting orders from Dublin. The Cork leaders in
good faith, accepted MacNeill's cancellation of all parades on Easter
Sunday, although they had worked ceaselessly in the previous two
years to organise, train and arm their forces for whatever action they

might be called upon to take. The Cork City and County Companies mobilised on Easter Sunday and marched to the destinations determined for them in the general plan for the country. The cancellation order caused disappointment and a certain amount of resentment, but was obeyed in the belief that it represented the united decision of all the Dublin leaders. Thus it happened that in the County it was only at Bawnard House the British forces met armed resistance.

Thomas and David Kent had been active in the organisation of the Volunteers in East Cork, and with their brothers, Richard and William, they had not been sleeping at home after the Rising. The night of 1st May was the first they spent in their own home for some time. Early next morning the house was surrounded by armed police who, in reply to a question as to what they wanted, replied that they had orders to arrest the whole family. The mens' aged mother was the only other occupant of the house at the time. The Kents, armed with a rifle and three shot guns, decided to resist. The police opened fire on the house and a conflict ensued which lasted until the defenders had exhausted their ammunition and the police had called in military reinforcements. Head Constable Roe was shot dead, and some of the other attackers wounded. When the Kents surrendered after a three hours' defence of their home the house was partially wrecked and David was seriously wounded. He had lost two fingers in the fight and received a wound in the side.

Thomas was not allowed to put his boots on when taken prisoner. He was immediately handcuffed. Before Richard, a famous athlete, could be similarly treated he made a gallant bid to escape, but was shot down and mortally wounded. He died two days later in Fermoy Military Hospital. Thomas was sentenced to death by a British Courtmartial and executed in Cork on 9th May.

The organisation of the County was not complete at that time. In many areas no Volunteer company existed. The nearest companies to Fermoy were those at Glanworth, Mitchelstown, Castletownroche and Dungourney. The immediate aftermath of Easter Week almost disintegrated the organisation in the county. Leaders were arrested and deported to internment camps. All parades and meetings, even hurling and football matches, were prohibited under the military rule of Sir John Maxwell. No open Volunteer activity of any kind was possible, and there was a period of quiescence. But in the hearts and minds of the people there was growing a sense of national pride unknown to that or the previous generation. There was a resurgence of the spirit of nationality, so long smothered and latent in many hearts. Pearse and his companions had in the popular mind joined the company of Tone and Emmet and the Fenians.

When the internees were released at Christmas, the contrast between the sullen hostility of the people through whom they had been marched away into banishment in May, and the hysterical enthusiasm of the cheering thousands who acclaimed their return, astonished and delighted them. When the sentenced prisoners were released in June, 1917, the country was ripe for the vigorous organising drives, both in the political field and for the reanimation and expansion of the Volunteer organisation, which were immediately undertaken.

Like many another young man at the time, Liam Lynch took the keenest interest in these developments, but always his thoughts were turning to the military side of the problem. He longed to meet someone who had taken part in the fighting in Dublin, and to learn from him every detail of the historic week. A farmer from the Galtees told him in Barry's shop that he had one of the men who took part staying with him. Liam made arrangements to meet the man on the run. He was delighted to discover him to be another Galtee man, a not-too-distant neighbour, Donal O'Hannigan. Liam brought him at once to Barnagurraha where he stayed for some time. Tom returned from College soon afterwards, and devoted himself zealously to the safety of their visitor. Liam visited them frequently, and there was only one subject upon which he would talk—the Irish Republic.

CHAPTER 2

THE RESURGENT NATION DEFEATS CONSCRIPTION

" From the graves of heroes dead spring living nations."

PEARSE.

1917 WAS a year of awakening. A mounting wave of national resurgence swept the country. Young Ireland, making its first exhilarating contact with the historic past, and roused to fiery enthusiasm, felt itself to be borne on the authentic stream of national destiny, whose course had often been disturbed or obstructed, but never altered. The tradition of nationhood, which had for so long lived a subordinate existence in the shadow of an alien culture broke free, and became the beacon in the light of which youth surged forward to find its own road to freedom. The spiritual potentialities of that tradition, its strength, its unifying influence, its vitality and capacity for endurance, were soon to become evident.

Liam Lynch was a product of that tradition. Loyalty to the idea of freedom was in the blood of long generations of families such as his, binding them in a great linkage of destiny, and flowering into action under propitious conditions. For such as he, it is the voices of the blood that speak in great moments of decision. That he would serve the old cause with all the single-minded devotion of his nature was pre-ordained for him. The manner in which he would serve was of his own choosing. He chose the soldier's way.

It was a springtime in the nation's life. The new bright colours of the flag of the Republic were everywhere in evidence, worn as favours, crudely painted on walls, decorating pictures of the executed leaders, and occasionally, before the police could tear it down, a genuine flag waved proudly from some pinnacle high over city or countryside. The published songs of the dead poets of Easter Week became woven into the fabric of national memory. The living poets were moved to speak of the men in quick-lime graves in words that endure. Some of those who had died had put on record the principles of their national faith. Others, less gifted but not less faithful, had left a shining deed to stand in testimony of their love. Young Ireland took them all to its heart. Youth saw its destiny and its duty. Joyfully it went forward, exhilarated, eager, the goal discernible, the way

uncertain yet. James Stephens[1] put in words the thought of many a
young man :

> " With gladness now we re-begin the quest
> That destiny commands. Though where we go,
> Or guided by what star, no man doth know.
> Unchartered is our course ! Our hearts untried !
> And we may weary ere we take the tide,
> Or make fair haven from the moaning sea.
> Be ye propitious, winds of destiny !
> On us at first blow not too boisterous, bold ;
> All Ireland hath is packed into this hold."

But, valuable and inspiring as this exuberant spirit was, it had yet
to be transmuted into organisation ; it required discipline, direction
and concentration upon the objective before it could begin to grapple
with the immense task of achieving liberty. National direction and
co-ordination of the whole effort was essential, but no small group
of leaders, however able or self-sacrificing, could create and maintain
the necessary organisations throughout the country. To the unsung
local leaders and organisers, must be given much of the credit for
welding the malleable material of the time into powerful organisations.
Liam Lynch was foremost in this work in his own area.

While he shared the hopes of many of his fellow Volunteers,
that Ireland's claim for independence might receive a favourable
hearing at the Peace Conference, which would take place at the
end of the war, he was not prepared to rely solely on that possibility.
" I, as well as thousands of others," he writes to his brother in October,
1917, " are preparing hard to mount whatever breach is allotted to us.
. . . If we do not get what is our own at the Peace Conference we will
have to fight for it." Looking forward he writes : " In a few months
we will be able to marshal an army." All over the country that army
was beginning to organise itself with no more than tenuous national
direction, cohering in groups and companies, electing its own officers,
giving itself elementary training, learning the unselfishness of voluntary discipline, always under the strong pressure of that urge towards
unity which dominated the whole national effort at the time. The
Irish Volunteer company at Fermoy was re-organised early in 1917.
Liam Lynch was elected First Lieutenant. Thus he took the first
step which was a prelude to the ever-widening scope of his activities
and responsibilities in the following years.

The foundation was laid in 1917 of that splendid national unity
which lasted until the end of 1921. The overwhelming majority
by which Eamon de Valera was returned in the Clare election in

[1] *Green Branches*

June, was the first clear indication of the temper of the people and of their endorsement of the aims of the men of Easter Week. Here, the full Republican demand for sovereign independence (a definition that Lloyd George used all his wiles to evade swallowing in 1921), was put to the electorate for the first time without equivocation. In the two earlier bye-elections, North Roscommon and Longford, where the Sinn Féin candidates had been successful, no very definite policy was put before the electors.

While the name, Sinn Féin, had come to be applied to all Republicans, the organisation itself was controlled by a National Council, formed before the sentenced prisoners were released. but on which some of them had been co-opted, and consisting of representatives of various national organisations, including the Volunteers and the Irish Republican Brotherhood. Griffith's Dual Monarchy policy of pre-1916 days was still its maximum demand, but that was not a definition of the national case for freedom which satisfied either the Volunteer or the I.R.B. representatives. The great opportunity for unity on a Republican policy came in the October Ard-fheis. This Ard-fheis, representing twelve hundred Cummain throughout the country, unanimously adopted a constitution, the preamble to which declared :

> " Sinn Féin aims at securing the international recognition of Ireland as an independent Irish Republic. Having achieved that status the Irish people may by referendum freely choose their own form of Government."

The organisation pledged itself " in the name of the Sovereign Irish people " to

"(a) deny the right and oppose the will of the British Parliament and Crown, or any other foreign government, to legislate for Ireland," and

"(b) make use of any and every means available to render impotent the power of England to hold Ireland in subjection by military force or otherwise."

Arthur Griffith " the father of Sinn Féin," and Count Plunkett, withdrew their nominations for the Presidency of the organisation in favour of Eamon de Valera. At the Volunteer Convention on 27th October, he was elected President of that body also, thereby gaining control of the two principal organisations upon which would fall the main burden of the coming struggle. The nation, gathering its strength, had found a leader.

The great national movement, then in process of formation, was unique in several ways. Never before in the long struggle for freedom, had the people grasped with so sure an instinct, the fundamental conception that they could not afford to exclude any weapon from their armoury in the coming fight. Force, under disciplined national control and allied to the greater moral and spiritual weapons, was recognised to be legitimate and necessary. Never before had there been national direction and control of a movement that embraced so many sources of potential national strength, that tended to unify these forces, and, while not restricting the activities of any one of them in its own legitimate field, canalised all into a great forward movement for Sovereign Independence.

Never before had so potentially powerful a national movement, animated by high ideals and leavened by exuberant vitality, been launched at a moment when the material resources of the people were in such a healthy condition. The war had brought prosperity to many, particularly to the farming community, and with prosperity came a greater independence of spirit, more virility, more manliness.

Powerful spiritual forces stirred the heart of the nation. There was a clearly-defined objective. The Proclamation of the Republic enshrined in lofty language the dream of the dead generations, established immutably the goal towards which all effort strained, and defined the tasks of youth and age alike. In an inspired moment, facing death, Thomas MacDonagh had said :

"From minds alight with Ireland's vivid intellect it sprang, in hearts aflame with Ireland's mighty love it was conceived. Such documents do not die."

Nor did the young men fail to cherish in their hearts his confident faith in them :

"The generous high-bred youth of Ireland will never fail to answer the call we pass on to them, will never fail to blaze forth in the red rage of war to win their country's freedom. Other and tamer methods they will leave to other and tamer men, but for themselves they must either do or die."

Had the resurgence been confined to the Volunteers the movement would have been immeasurably weaker, and the ultimate results must have been different. No unarmed body, however courageous or resolute, circumstanced as they were, could for long have sustained a conflict with the British forces without the organised assistance of a majority of the people. It was in the combination of disciplined armed force with an organised public opinion in the political field, working for a common objective, that Ireland found the secret of victory. Side by side with the expansion of the Volunteer organisation went the growth of Sinn Féin, Cumman-na-mBan, Fianna Eireann, the Gaelic League and various bodies concerned with the welfare of prisoners and their dependants. There was a place for everybody in some organisation.

Much of the leadership personnel at the top was common to both of the main organisations, and in the direction of both the I.R.B. through its members was able to exercise a considerable influence. This interlocking of leadership personnel tended to unify policy and correlate activities, but it had serious disadvantages which only became apparent later. To a lesser extent, this concentration of control of both organisations in the hands of the same men existed in County Cork, but under the stress of action, most Volunteer officers later found it increasingly necessary to devote the whole of their energies to military duties. At no time did the political side of the movement appeal strongly to Liam Lynch. He was a soldier by instinct and temperament. He could have been a great priest, but he did not possess that flexibility of character which would have made him a successful politician.

A people, like a crowd, may be moved by a common impulse, and may act strongly, even decisively, before it falls apart into its constituent elements. If leadership is lacking its effort will be short-lived. No task so immense and, for a small nation, so difficult, as that of ejecting the forces of a powerful Empire then emerging successfully from a European war, could hope to succeed without great and continued efforts, sustained in the face of defeats, losses and suffering. If the efforts necessary to achieve freedom were to be sustained and made effective, inspiring leadership, voluntary discipline, undeviating adherence to the objective and first-class organisation were vital pre-requisites. This was particularly true in the case of the Volunteers ; and to those who had the vision to see it, and the capacity to impress it upon their comrades, responsibility and leadership came rapidly. So it was with Liam Lynch. 1917 was a year in which the Volunteer organisation was gathering strength numerically, but as it was a practically unarmed force it first tentative challenges to British authority, had, of necessity, to take other forms. British proclamations on 1st August prohibited the wearing of military uniforms or the carrying of hurleys. On the 15th large-scale arrests of Volunteers took place throughout the country, and hunger-strikes, which culminated in the death of Thomas Ashe in Mountjoy on 25th September, focused public attention upon the conflict taking place in the jails all over the country.

The Volunteer Executive decided to challenge the British prohibitions by ordering parades in uniform to be held throughout the country on Sunday, 21st October. On that day Liam Lynch, in uniform, was second in command of the sixty-seven men of Fermoy

Company who marched out to meet the Glanworth Company under the observation of note-taking R.I.C. men. Proudly he writes the details of their two hours' drilling to his brother a few days later. " We are to keep drilling " he wrote, " until the last man is gone . . . we mean to break the law of illegal drilling." He warns his brother, who was then in Thurles, that letters coming to him in Fermoy are being censored in the Post Office, and urges Tom to write only on "friendly matters." Plainly he is visualising the possibility that he may be arrested.

In the next letter, written on 1st November, there is a note of disappointment that he has not yet been arrested. That seemed to be the way in which one could best serve at the time. That was a frame of mind which did not last very long ; he was quick to see the soundness of Tom's advice, " that though it was honourable and good to go to jail, it would be better for the lads stay out, work harder, and give England something livelier than jail work." But, for the moment, he is eager to join those on whom imprisonment has put the seal of service. The only cloud he sees is the worry his arrest will cause his mother. " The minute you hear of me," he exhorts Tom, " write at once to console mother, as I am only doing my duty to God and my country." The company captain, Liam O'Denn, had been arrested and Liam had taken his place in command of the company at the previous Sunday parade. That, he felt sure, would result in his own arrest, but in this he was disappointed.

The arrests of Volunteer-officers were not effective in preventing the Sunday parades. The moment an officer was arrested, another stepped into his place and carried on the exercises. The spirit which animated the whole body was expressed by Liam in one of his letters : " We have declared for an Irish Republic and will not live under any other law. . . ." There was no way, short of internment of the whole Volunteer force, by which the British authorities could defeat that spirit. On 9th November he writes :

> " Our parade was not prevented last Sunday, but we had
> made arrangements to carry on elsewhere if such happened.
> We marched to Ballyhooley . . . with about 100 Volunteers
> where we met Glanworth, Glenville, Rathcormac and Ballyhooley
> Volunteers—in all about 300, and I had the honour to be at
> their head. When we came back to town we had nearly all the
> town marching at our side, so you see even ' loyal Fermoy ' can
> be changed. We had drill in open ground during the week."

Under the mistaken impression that the prisoners in Cork Jail were able to indulge in military training, he regrets not being with them. " I would want to go there," he says " at least for a few weeks' training." That was one of his principal aims now, to get military training in any way he could, to prepare himself for the conflict he saw ahead, to fit himself for leadership. He read and studied such British text-books and manuals as he could lay hands on. He revelled in Emmet's plan for the capture of Dublin. He sought for information from any source where the conditions of the opposing forces bore any resemblance to the position in Ireland. He studied the guerilla tactics of the Boers in the South African war, but always his main preoccupation was with the immediate military problem under his eyes in the heavily-garrisoned town of Fermoy, the police posts scattered over the surrounding countryside, with which the Sunday parades were making him familiar, and the multiplication of these same problems all over the country. How could a practically unarmed Volunteer force, untrained, inexperienced, possessing no military assets beyond a sturdy manhood and a glowing faith in the justice of its cause, hope to fight the well-entrenched army of occupation and reduce it to the point of surrender or evacuation? That was the broad problem, and however mad a dream it seemed that victory for the Volunteers should be possible, it was the faith which sustained Lynch and men like him throughout the whole struggle.

Eamon de Valera spoke at a public meeting in Fermoy in mid-December. The local company paraded to welcome him, Liam Lynch in uniform, in charge of it. Thereafter, he discarded uniform as an unnecessary and foolish handicap on his activities. It had served its purpose as a gesture of defiance to British authority, and however much he desired to wear the uniform of which he was so proud, realisation of the practical needs of the position made him forego his own wishes.

1918 was a year of preparation. More and more young men were joining the Volunteers; recruiting for the British forces was almost dead. Volunteer organisation was being perfected, new companies were being organised, the frame-work on which the final territorial organisation of companies, battalions and brigades rested, was being steadily built up. In County Cork there was scarcely a parish without a local Volunteer Company. That position was reached in Fermoy district in September, 1917. The companies at Fermoy, Kilworth, Araglin, Rathcormac, Watergrasshill, Glenville, Ballynoe, Bartlemy and Castlelyons, were formed into the Fermoy Battalion. It was the sixth of the Brigade's twenty Battalions at that time. At the election of officers Martin O'Keeffe was elected Battalion Commandant, Michael Fitzgerald, Vice-Commandant, Liam Lynch, Adjutant, and George Power, Quartermaster.

The system of the election of officers, rather than their appointment by higher authority, as is the case in regular armies, was one that had

obtained in the Volunteers from their inception, and it was continued
in general until the active service conditions of late 1920 and 1921
made the normal system essential. That was only one aspect of
military organisation in which the Volunteers departed from accepted
procedure, and adopted a form more suitable to their peculiar needs
and circumstances. Indeed, the almost complete absence of anything
more than the bare minimum of regulations in the sphere of organisation was of prime importance, in securing and maintaining the great
flexibility and adaptability of the whole body throughout the struggle.
The system of electing officers proved itself sound, mainly because
of the spirit in which men served. The distinction of ranks as such
meant little more than a recognition of their necessity. But in a body
of high-spirited, intelligent men, serving voluntarily and with eager
fidelity a cause to which they were passionately devoted, election to a
post of responsibility was the highest form of honour.

Liam's election as Battalion Adjutant gave a wider scope for his
activities. In a Battalion of nine Companies having only four officers,
as was normal, the amount of work to be done was limited only by
the amount of time the officers could devote to it. It is characteristic
of him that in every post he held he set a standard by demonstrating
in his own work what could be achieved in any sphere of Volunteer
activity by a man who put his best into the effort. He was ceaselessly
active. He made it a practice to visit one company each week, making
an intensive study of every problem they had to face, always urging
the perfection of organisation, the intensification of training, and the
acquisition of arms. His capacity for work expanded with every new
call upon it. He was gaining experience at a stage in the development
of the organisation, and in his own development, when that experience
was particularly valuable. The novelty of volunteering had worn off;
the realities were being faced. One of them was the need for arms,
another was the problem of creating that spirit of unity and discipline
without which no progress could be made. Still another was the
control and reconciliation of those strong human passions and
prejudices inseparable from all great movements where a body of
ardent, young men are honestly and deeply moved. Idiosyncrasies
of character, the clash of wills, our natural bent towards individuality
and independence in thought and action, the still-surviving influence
of past political party affiliations—all these created problems in almost
every company.

Along with much else, the previous generation had lost the sense
of service to the nation as a soldier understands it, and their sons
had to relearn it, often painfully, in the Volunteers. There was
idealism, there was fidelity to a worthy objective, there was a growing
desire to render service, there was intelligent appreciation of the

practical problems but these were not yet fused into that kind of patriotism which is so unconscious of itself that its energies are not dissipated.

The threat of Conscription in April tended to further unify the national will and to harden the temper of the people against British rule. But, subtly, it altered for a time, both the military character and the unselfish spirit of the Volunteer organisation. To the Volunteers the conscription threat brought a substantial acquisition of strength, the support of elements in the population who had hitherto looked on them with hostility or indifference, and acceptance by the people as a whole. Volunteering had become respectable. The influx brought into the organisation many whose motives were not entirely disinterested and who were better politicians than soldiers. A point had been reached where the politically astute decided that the new national movement was the coming force in Irish politics. For a variety of reasons—because they had some local standing, because everyone was ready to welcome a convert, because they were loudest in vocal resistance, or simply because they had " the gift of the gab "—many were, in the undeveloped areas, elected to officer posts for which they were unfitted, and, where they did not drop out at the end of the crisis, had to be removed before their units made any military progress. That situation did not, however, obtain to any great extent in County Cork.

Compulsory military service for all men under the age of forty-six had been in force in Britain since 1915. The age limit had recently been raised to fifty, and the continued exemption of Irishmen occasioned much hostile comment in the British Press. On no great question of public policy for many years had the British Government been confronted by so unanimous and determined a body of Irish opinion.

On 9th April the Episcopal Standing Committee of the Irish Hierarchy met at Maynooth and issued a solemn protest :

> " With all the responsibility that attaches to our pastoral office we feel bound to warn the Government against entering upon a policy so disastrous to the public interest, and to all order, public and private."

The Conscription Bill passed its final stages in the British House of Commons on the 16th. An Order in Council was all that was necessary thereafter to put it into effect. A conference, convened by the Lord Mayor of Dublin and representatives of Sinn Féin, the Irish Parliamentary Party, the All for Ireland League, Labour and Independents, assembled at the Manion House on 18th April. A pledge was adopted in the following terms :

"Denying the right of the British Government to enforce compulsory service in this country, we pledge ourselves solemnly to one another to resist conscription by the most effective means at our disposal."

The Irish Hierarchy, meeting at Maynooth on the same day, received a deputation from the Conference and issued a manifesto which declared :

"We consider that conscription forced in this way upon Ireland is an oppressive and inhuman law which the Irish people have a right to resist by every means that are consonant with the law of God."

On Sunday, 21st April, public Masses of intercession were everywhere celebrated, the anti-conscription pledge was signed all over the country, most people signing at the church doors. Throughout County Cork Volunteers and Sinn Féin co-operated in the arrangements for recording signatures. On the 23rd a one-day all-Ireland general strike was held, in which organised labour registered its unanimous opposition to the proposal. Protests were made by Public Bodies and a fund of over £200,000 subscribed.

On 6th May, Lord French was appointed Viceroy, and Edward Shortt, K.C., Chief Secretary. French's appointment was an indication that the British Government had resumed the traditional policy of its predecessors in relation to Ireland and intended to employ force to operate the Act. Powerful moral and spiritual forces were being organised to defeat the imposition of such a measure against the will of the people. Nevertheless, it was obvious to the Volunteers that should the attempt be made the task of defeating it would fall mainly upon them, both because they were the men the British authorities wished to conscript, and because they alone were in some measure ready to meet force with force. A period of rather hectic preparation for armed resistance began. For the ensuing six months the conscription issue and plans for resistance dominated all other considerations for the Volunteers.

So probable did it appear to Liam that the Volunteers would take the field, and so completely was he cured of his desire for imprisonment, that when the crisis threatened in April, he left his employment immediately. With Michael Fitzgerald, Larry Condon and George Power he devoted his whole time to preparations for active service. One of his first acts was to go out to Bawnard House and tell David Kent of his decision. He had consultations also with Donncada O'Hannigan, later O/C East Limerick Brigade. The British authorities invented a mythical German Plot to justify large-scale arrests of

Volunteer and Sinn Féin leaders, designed to leave the people without leadership and weaken national morale. The arrests were made on 17th and 18th May. Seventy-three persons were deported to England. Liam, having then left his employment, escaped arrest. He was raided for on three occasions, and it was suggested to his employers that he should be dismisssed as he was a disturbing influence on the town. The suggestion was treated with the contempt it deserved.

The first mobilisation of a large number of men from the battalion for an active operation took place in the summer of 1918. Information was received that a train from Mallow to Fermoy would carry arms on a certain date. About fifty men were mobilised at a point between Ballyhooley and Castletownroche, where it was decided to hold up the train. They were under the command of Liam Tobin and Liam Lynch. Cars were on the spot to remove the expected arms capture, and arrangements for the safe disposal of the weapons were made by Araglin Company. Wires were cut, the train was held up and searched, but it contained no arms. Although futile from the point of view of increasing the armament of the battalion, the organisation of the raid provided valuable experience.

The Brigade Commandant, Tomás MacCurtain, visited the battalion and gave Liam instructions with regard to the positions which his forces were to occupy on the event of an effort being made to enforce conscription. The Volunteer Executive and General Headquarters Staff appear to have been able to do no more than to indicate the broad policy of a general plan of resistance, The many local problems and difficulties which would arise in every area had to be visualised by the brigade and battalion officers, whose responsibility it was to make plans to meet them.

An tOglac[1] ; commenting on the situation which would arise "in case of an attempt to conscript Irishmen," said :

> " Martial Law will be proclaimed *on both sides*. The military authorities of the Irish Republic will become the persons to whom *all* Irish Republicans, whether combatants or not, must look for light and leading . . . political methods will be practically suspended, and schemes of ' passive resistance,' based on the theory of normal conditions, must prove unworkable. . . . Every Volunteer officer must contemplate the possibility of finding himself called upon to act as the chief military authority in his district."

In the Cork Brigade the situation which was visualised was that the whole force would be called out on active service, that it would mobilize by companies, and even smaller groups if necessary, self-

[1] Vol. 1, No. 30, September, 1918

contained and capable of offering the maximum resistance. Detailed instructions on discipline and on the problems of billeting and feeding the force were issued. A communications system of cyclist despatch-riders was established and tested out. The appointment of officer personnel for all units was completed and substitutes nominated. Every available piece of useful equipment was secured or marked down for commandeering. Note was taken of stocks of food and cattle in all areas. Chaplains were appointed to each battalion, and detailed instructions issued to them by the brigade chaplain, Rev. Father Dominic, O.F.M.Cap. The arms position could not be improved, but the most thorough steps were taken to ensure the maximum effectiveness of what arms were available. Plans were made for the destruction of facilities which would be valuable to the British forces, e.g., telephone exchanges and railways, in so far as the limited supply of explosives permitted; thought was given to the problem of evacuating civilians liable to conscription from large centres of population, and routes were planned on which they would be moved. These plans were, I believe, as advanced as those made in any part of the country, and far in advance of what was visualised in many areas.

Lord French was confident that he could enforce conscription. Sir Henry Wilson, Chief of the Imperial General Staff, was not afraid of the consequences of taking 100,000 young Irishmen against their will and distributing them through the Imperial forces. On 3rd June, French asked for 50,000 recruits by 1st October, and 20,000 monthly thereafter. On the 26th, he said that conscription had not been abandoned, and would be enforced if he did not get the number of recruits asked for. By then over 200,000 men had joined the Irish Volunteers.

As long as the war in Europe continued no relaxation of vigilance was possible for the Volunteers, and every additional day's respite was devoted to perfecting their preparations. *An tOglac*,[1] referring editorially to the duty of the Volunteers " as agents of the national will," said it was " the unanimous decision of the Executive of the Irish Volunteers to resist conscription to the death with all the military force and warlike resources at our command." While this was valuable in consolidating the determination to resist throughout the Army, the fact remained that neither the Executive nor the Head-quarters Staff could offer much practical assistance to the brigades throughout the country. They could not supply arms or ammunition. They could not supply trained leaders. It is doubtful if they could have exercised any effective control over the national forces if a con-

[1] Vol. 1, No. 2, September, 1918

flict had commenced. Headquarters did not have the means of doing any of these things, and practical local officers recognised that position. They planned to rely mainly on their own resources, to be self-sufficient in everything their own localities could supply.

Liam Lynch had imagination and foresight. He could visualise a situation with considerable accuracy, and exercise sound judgment in making plans to meet unexpected contingencies. He was methodical and thorough. In the Summer and Autumn of 1918, his active mind was constantly applied to the many problems he foresaw if his battalion took the field. In this crisis his fellow-officers recognised the emergence of those qualities which marked him out for leadership. He became the driving force in the effort to perfect the organisation of the battalion, ceaselessly active, very sure of what he wanted and how to get it done, but amiable, kind, unselfish, and still a little shy. He was twenty-five. His capacities were only beginning to expand.

It required faith as well as courage on the part of the average Volunteer, to accept without question the policy of military resistance. He could not help contemplating the almost entire absence of weapons with which to fight, nor reflecting on the inexperience of most of the Volunteers in the use of arms. But that seemed only to make every man more determined to make the best use of what was available, to fight if need be, with " knife or pitchfork," to resist fiercely and to the death.

To practical officers, like Liam, it was clear that they would themselves have to grapple with the task of feeding, clothing, and finding shelter for their forces if they were called out in a mass effort at resistance. They would themselves have to decide how and where they would fight, how they would overcome the danger of inexperienced men becoming an unmanageable mob under the first impact of hostile fire, how they would maintain communications, care for the wounded and sustain morale. One conviction, emphasized by his pondering on these problems, impressed itself firmly on Liam's mind. The vital and paramount need was arms. Given arms, all other difficulties could be overcome. He never forgot that. It became a belief that shaped the course of his actions ever afterwards.

The war in Europe ended on 11th November. It had claimed the lives of 29,000 Irishmen fighting in the Imperial forces of Britain. The threat of conscription was ended. National unity and leadership, grim determination to resist, the effective mobilization of moral and spiritual reserves, willingness to meet force with force against any odds—these, combined into one powerful weapon of defence, had defeated the will of the Government and Parliament of Great Britain. Ireland had acted with a strength and dignity worthy of her best tradition. The people had won a significant and bloodless victory. The young Volunteer Army of the nation stood justified.

CHAPTER 3

A NATIONAL GOVERNMENT AND ARMY ARE FORMED

*" On a wider fighting field . . . must we close for our final struggle
with England, or sink and surrender."*

FINTAN LALOR.

THE original purpose and principal duty of the Army remained.
An tOglac[1] promptly reminded Volunteers that " the Army of Ireland
was not established to resist conscription," and that its function was
to fight for the rights and liberties of the people of Ireland. " That
fighting might be in the nature of an offensive, as in Easter Week,
1916, or it might be of a defensive nature." This was, indeed, the
vaguest kind of prospect. No one, except, perhaps Dublin Castle,
thought another Easter Week probable in 1918, and all talk of
defensive action seemed meaningless except as a prelude to something
more positive. There was little point in Volunteers defending their
arms at the risk of their lives, as Donncada McNeilus had done in
Cork, unless they were preserving them for a day of action.

The carrying of arms had been prohibited since February. From
June onwards a series of proclamations were issued by the British
authorities, designed to intimidate the people and disrupt the growing
solidarity of the national organisations. All the Munster Counties
except Waterford, and several others as well as the cities of Cork and
Limerick, were made " proclaimed districts," other districts were
declared to be " special military areas " under the Defence of the Realm
Act. On 4th July, the Irish Volunteers, Sinn Féin, Cumann-na-mBan
and the Gaelic League were proclaimed. Their meetings were prohibited and declared illegal. On the following day the holding of
meetings, processions or assemblies in public places anywhere in
Ireland was prohibited.

These were intolerable restrictions and the people, in a new-found
exhaltation of spirit, proceeded to reduce them to nullity. On 4th
August, fifteen hundred prohibited G.A.A. matches took place all
over the country. On the 15th, under national direction, hundreds
of public meetings were held. Police efforts to enforce the British
prohibitions not infrequently provided some amusement. A public
meeting or an aerideacht would be announced for a particular venue,
police would assemble in force to break it up, while at the same

time it was taking place perhaps half-a-mile away. That was general. Such wholesale outwitting of the forces of the Crown gave an added zest to participation in prohibited activities. There was a spice of danger which contributed to the lifting of national morale. But there was also a grimmer side. Arrests were fairly numerous, raids on houses by police were frequent, meetings were broken up by force, newspapers were suppressed or placed under censorship. Arrests of Volunteer officers created many problems for their units as well as for their dependants. Resistance and hunger strikes in the jails were continuous.

The numerous arrests of Volunteers made it imperative that the conflict should be continued in the jails in a disciplined manner, and that a uniform policy of resistance should be pursued which would reflect the general attitude of the Army to the occupation forces. To this end, G.H.Q. issued an order on 20th August, 1918, which defined the line of action to be taken by prisoners :

> " Irish Volunteers must as heretofore refuse to recognise the jurisdiction of the Court when brought to trial. They must enter no defence, nor are they to be legally represented. If the option of bail is given to a Volunteer he must only exercise same by direction of his commanding officer, and in case of an officer by direction of his superior officer. In all cases the direction to give bail can only be issued after authority has been obtained from the Brigade Commandant."

At mid-1918 the whole of County Cork had been reorganised under the vigorous direction of Tomás MacCurtain, the Brigade Commandant. The brigade then consisted of twenty battalions, having an average of eight companies each, and a total strength of about eight thousand men. It could not be said that all were fit for military service. In some company areas almost every man of military age, and a few above and below it, were Volunteers, but the large majority were of the stamp that had given Ireland its character as a military nation down the ages. The conscription threat had expanded many companies to abnormal strengths, but most of the recruits which it drove into the ranks disappeared again when the crisis was over.

Except for a negligible minority, the Volunteers were then untrained in the use of modern arms. While many men in country districts were familiar with shot guns, and a lesser number with miniature rifles and small arms, the great majority had never handled or fired a service rifle. It was only the very exceptional Volunteer, usually one who had served in the British forces, who had even a theoretical knowledge of machine-guns, mortars or heavier weapons. Arms

training for all Volunteers was not possible for the simple reason
that the arms did not exist. There were, at most, one hundred rifles
and carbines of various kinds in the brigade. They had to be kept
singly or in twos or threes in places of absolute security, often only
sporadically accessible, and in the custody of the most reliable men.
To make a rifle available to a company for training, even for a few
hours, was an event. To fire a round of service ammunition was an
experience that not one Volunteer in a thousand found possible at
that time. The brigade did not possess a single machine-gun or heavier
weapon.

Training was almost entirely training without arms. Parades
were held on one, or sometimes two, nights each week and almost
every Sunday. Few officers at this time were devoting their whole
time to Volunteer work. There were few instructors and fewer
manuals. Rarely were any facilities available for indoor training.
Most Volunteers acquired such proficiency as they attained in the
long Sunday marches and the week-night drills in the open. There
was much eager and earnest activity, which to the superficial observer
might have appeared futile or mere exhibitionism. It was neither
one nor the other. It produced two things of great subsequent
value—an acute and widespread sense of the value of and need for
voluntary discipline, and a steadily growing capacity for acting
effectively in combination.

It was not possible for brigade officers to maintain constant contact
with such a large number of battalions dispersed over a county the
size of Cork. Of necessity, much of the initiative in the development
of efficient organisation in any area remained with the local officers of
battalions and companies. Where there were good local officers,
there were good units. Where the company and battalion officers
failed in determination to prepare, morally and materially, for a
conflict, or where they failed to appreciate the strength and weakness
of the Volunteer position, no amount of direction or nursing from
higher levels could make their slack units fully efficient. This need
for local initiative and self-reliance imposed by the voluntary nature
of the organisation in the peculiar circumstances under which it
expanded at this time, was a significant factor in creating in sufficient
volume the high quality of local leadership which emerged in the
stress of the following years.

The potency of the desire to obtain arms was so strong that it
threatened to endanger discipline. The Volunteer Executive and the
Headquarters Staff were unable to arm the rapidly expanding forces
under their nominal control. While there was an agreed objective,
there was as yet no agreed policy, beyond the declaration of the use
of " any and every means," as to the rôle of the Volunteers in the

effort to attain it. But throughout the Volunteer organisation there was a growing conviction, emphasized by the conscription crisis, that an unarmed body organised on military lines was futile and ridiculous. If it was to be an army it should have arms. There were only three ways in which its meagre armament could be increased without fighting—by importation from outside the country, by capture or surreptitious purchase from the occupation forces, or by seizure of such arms as were held in the country by civilians whose loyalty to the British connection was not in doubt. The first was outside the province and the capacity of local units. In the second a lead had been given in County Cork, by the capture of rifles and other equipment in a daring and well-planned raid on the Grammar School in the city in September, 1917, by the disarming of two R.I.C. men at Newmarket on 17th March, 1918, and by the attack on armed police at Bealagleanna, between Ballingeary and Ballyvourney, on 8th July, 1918, in which police carbines and ammunition were captured. The third presented opportunities to a greater or lesser extent in almost every company area.

Some raids on private houses had taken place, and some arms had been obtained in this way, before Headquarters issued, on 2nd March, an order prohibiting such raids. That order closed one potential source of supply, and for the next eighteen months the arms position in the county remained almost static, consisting of such arms as had been in the hands of a much smaller organisation before 1916, such shot guns as were voluntarily given to the Volunteers by their owners, some small arms imported through the crews of trading vessels, and the occasional purchase or capture of a rifle or revolver from an individual British soldier. In every company there were some shot guns, and in most, one or more .22 miniature rifles, which were used for target practice. Relatively large quantities of shot gun ammunition had been loaded with heavy slug; efforts to manufacture explosives and grenades were in the embryonic stage.

After the European war ended large numbers of Irishmen were demobilised from the British forces. They returned to homes where, in many cases, political opinions had undergone a change since 1914. Some of these men joined the Volunteers. The numbers were not large—less than one hundred for County Cork—but they brought into the force an invaluable asset until then lacking—a leaven of men with combat experience. They did excellent work as training instructors, and in the subsequent conflict they played a worthy part. Arms, brought home by them as souvenirs from France, were a significant contribution in some poorly-armed areas.

The Volunteer organisation was subject then only to the control of its own Executive. Neither the Executive nor the Headquarters

Staff was in a position to supervise activities throughout the country. They could do no more than issue general directives on policy and organisation, and mould as far as possible the fiery but malleable material under their command into the shape of an army which would act as a single strong weapon and be responsive to direction and control.   But that function had a remarkable significance.

That the value of such a development was recognised at an early stage, and that the idea of national direction was accepted without question throughout the country, is one of the factors which made for subsequent success.   Had its importance not been recognised and accepted before the conflict became intense, it is doubtful if it would have been possible to create any such conception of a national force in 1920–21, when the exercise of any detailed control by General Headquarters became extremely difficult.   But, by then, the idea had become part of the philosophy of the army, and its spirit continued to operate.

Since organised military resistance on a national scale was broken in 1601, no Irish army had fought under a single command directed from the capital.   What had happened in 1916, providential though it may have been for the future development of the national military effort, was a sharp reminder of how difficult and hazardous it was to establish and maintain effective control over a widespread territorial organisation in a country occupied by a hostile army and police force, under the direction of centralised Government, controlling absolutely the whole civil and administrative machinery.   How much more difficult and hazardous that task was likely to be in conditions of sporadic warfare was beginning to be realised.

But it was essential that the effort should be made.   In the circumstances of 1918, one effective method of fostering the idea of a National Army under the control of a properly constituted Headquarters Staff, and of securing the acceptance of that idea amongst the Volunteers generally, was the issue of a small monthly journal devoted exclusively to matters of interest to Volunteers as soldiers.   It had of course, to be printed and distributed secretly.   The first issue of *An tOglac*, a four-page, quarto publication, printed for the Headquarters Staff, is dated 15th August, 1918.   Three or four copies per month were distributed to each company through the communications channels operating within the organisation.   The companies, out of the weekly subscriptions of their members, even paid for the journal, just as they paid for their equipment, and for such arms as they were able to purchase.

In September an order was issued by the brigade requiring the battalions to collect complete information in regard to the police barracks in their area, giving ranks, strength and armament, together with an indication of the reactions of the police to recent developments.

With the ending of the conscription threat a period of great potential danger to the Volunteer organisation commenced. The rhythm which marks the growth and decline of all human co-operative effort was, after the sustained fever of the anti-conscription activities, slowing to a feebler tempo. This almost inevitable ebbing of enthusiasm had to be counteracted by immense labour and unflinching determination on the part of those who saw in this loosely cohering body a potential weapon for the achievement of liberty in their day. There were no obligations, other than those of conscience and patriotism, on any man to remain in the ranks, or to continue to devote his time and energy to an organisation having an objective— the establishment of an Irish Republic as a freely functioning State —which seemed to many impossible of achievement, and having a policy so nebulous as to be incapable of being grasped by the average Volunteer.

There was then no other objective having the same magnetic attraction for Volunteers, as the idea of achieving that freedom for which so many generations had worked and fought in vain. For Liam Lynch it had become a conviction that his generation was destined to achieve liberty. But militarily no way forward seemed to be open, the means available appeared insignificant and wholly inadequate, the obstacles in the path impregnable. It required faith to go on. Many dropped out, but numbers were never a problem. There was always more men available and willing to fight than there were weapons with which to arm them.

The immediate problem was not to prevent the defection of those lacking in spirit, but to maintain the organisation until a policy for achieving its objective was evolved. All that could be done in the meantime was to arm, to improve the standard of training which had been reached, to continue it without interruption, and to increase the general efficiency of the whole organisation. The extent to which the morale of the Volunteers was maintained in any area depended very largely upon the outlook and exertions of local officers. In this matter, Fermoy Battalion was fortunate. Neither Liam Lynch nor the other officers were unduly distracted by engagement in political activities. They were very strongly imbued with the conviction, always dominant in Liam's mind, that if the army crumbled all hope of attaining the Republic in that generation was vain.

The results of the General Election in December, 1918, transformed the whole political situation, and marked a turning point in Irish history. The Volunteers, as the most compact body of Republican opinion in the country, had intervened effectively, though not as an organisation, to ensure that the full Republican programme was the issue put before the electors. For the Volunteer there was here no conflict between his duty as a citizen and his duty as a soldier. Many Volunteers, officers and men alike, were members or officers of Sinn Féin Cumainn. The Army did not restrict the freedom of decision which was every man's right as a citizen, and many Volunteer officers were selected to contest the Parliamentary elections as Sinn Féin candidates.

The Army as such, had, however, definite duties and responsibilities in the election. Volunteers acted as protecting forces for public and private meetings and for the Committee Rooms of Republican candidates. They acted as peace patrols during the election campaign, as guards on polling booths to prevent intimidation or molestation of voters, as escorts for ballot boxes, and as guards over the places where the boxes were deposited between polling-day and the conclusion of the counting of the votes.

The following general order was issued by Headquarters Staff:

OGLAIG NA hEIREANN

To   GENERAL HEADQUARTERS,
Tomas MacCurtain,   DUBLIN, 19/11/'18.
    Commandant,
        Cork Brigade.

General Instructions with Reference to the Duties of Irish Volunteers in the General Election

1. You will immediately make the following arrangements for providing protection by Volunteers in connection with the impending General Election:

(*a*) You will appoint a Volunteer Officer in each constituency within your Brigade Area to take entire charge of all Volunteer activities therein. In making these appointments it will be advisable to leave the Brigade Staff free for general supervision and inspection.

(*b*) You will arrange, *for election purposes only*, that all Battalions and odd companies in each Constituency will respond to the orders and carry out the requests of the Officer so appointed.

(*c*) Where any Constituency covers portion of two or more separate Brigade Areas the respective Brigade Commandants will co-operate to place an officer in charge and arrange for the different units within the Constituency to carry out (*for election purposes only*) the orders of this Officer.

2. Volunteers to carry out the duties hereafter outlined will be supplied only on the application of the Director of Elections. This application to be made to you either in writing or in person.

3. To ensure the smooth working of this provision you should notify the Directors of Elections for the Constituencies in your Brigade that you are the officer to be applied to.

(Names of Directors enclosed herewith.)

4. You will hand in a list of the attached duties to all officers appointed.

N.B.—It must be clearly understood that instructions and orders to Irish Volunteers are to be issued from Brigade Headquarters only through the officers appointed under this scheme, and that on all occasions when Irish Volunteers are acting as such, they will be under the command of their own officers to whom alone they shall be responsible.

Issued by Order of the EXECUTIVE,
From HEADQUARTERS STAFF.

Polling in the general election took place on 14th December, and the complete results were available on the 28th. Of the one hundred and five seats in the whole country, Republicans had captured seventy-three, an overwhelming vote in favour of Sovereign Independence, and a solemn endorsement of the action of the men of Easter Week. The Irish Parliamentary Party was almost annihilated, retaining only six seats. The remaining twenty-six were held by Unionists. In Munster every constituency except one, Captain Redmond's in Waterford, was represented by a Republican.

The election results immensely strengthened the moral authority of the Volunteers. Hitherto they had been acting as an expression of the will of the Irish people, without the sanction of a formal declaration of the opinions which they believed to be generally held. Having availed of the machinery of a British ordered general election, the people had now declared themselves for an Irish Republic in the most explicit and democratic way. To that extent the road was clear.

There was, however, no trace of a plan of action for the Army, nor indeed any indication that the national leaders contemplated the use of force at that time. There was a school of thought within the organisation which visualised the creation of a well-trained military force, brought to a standard of strength and efficiency which would give it some hope of challenging with success in the field the occupation forces maintained in the country by Britain. They were, of course, thinking in terms of previous insurrections. How it was to be armed was an unsolved problem. How far the British Government would hesitate before attempting to smother such a development was equally problematical. There were those who thought that a strong, disciplined, nation-wide Volunteer organisation would constitute a potential threat strong enough to force Britain to concede our demand for freedom, and there were those whose eyes were turned hopefully on the Peace Conference. The policy of guerilla warfare which emerged in the following year had not yet been evolved.

Official Volunteer policy was still balanced precariously between the defensive and now unrealistic role defined in its original objective—" To maintain and defend the rights and liberties common to all the people of Ireland "—and the growing need for a forward offensive policy. Officers, like Liam Lynch, who took a realistic view and were in daily contact with the spirit of the organisation, were fully conscious of the danger that inertia and inactivity would sap its virility. A voluntary body of high-spirited men could not be kept indefinitely on the kind of training then available to them, almost entirely without arms as it was. Morale was in serious danger of deteriorating in the absence of some positive activities on which substantial numbers of men could be engaged. Election duties had provided a brief outlet for the growing urge to action of some kind, but much more was needed. A number of men from Liam's Battalion had been on duty in the Waterford constituency, where the election had been contested with much bitterness, and where some of them had received physical injuries. At the end of 1918 morale was high, but courage and endurace were still untried. .For the minority who were grimly determined to find a way forward the formidable question was—how?

CHAPTER 4

THE ARMY SWEARS ALLEGIANCE

" There is always a chance for brave men who challenge fortune."
THOMAS MacDONAGH.

DURING 1917 and 1918 the forty-six companies in the Cork
Brigade at Easter, 1916, had been expanded into twenty battalions,
which covered the whole county. Total strength was about 8,000
all ranks. A territorial brigade of such a size and strength was
obviously unwieldy. G.H.Q. decided to divide the county into three
brigade areas; Cork No. 1 in the centre, extending from Youghal
to the Kerry border beyond Ballyvourney, and including the city;
Cork No. 3 in the West, and Cork No. 2 in the North.

Cork No. 3 Brigade was formed at a meeting of battalion officers
from the area held at Kilnadur, Dunmanway on 5th January, 1919.
Michael Collins presided, and Tomas MacCurtain, Commandant of
the original Cork Brigade now being divided, was present accom-
panied by his Brigade Adjutant and Quartermaster. Tom Hales was
elected Brigade Commandant, Seán Hayes, T.D., Vice-Commandant,
Michael McCarthy, Dunmanway, Adjutant, and Denis O'Shea,
Skibbereen, Quartermaster. A reorganisation in the following
August created some changes in this Staff. Ted O'Sullivan, then
O/C 5th Battalion became Brigade Vice-Commandant, Liam Deasy,
Adjutant 1st Battalion, became Brigade Adjutant, replacing Michael
McCarthy, who was appointed O/C 3rd Battalion, and Pat Harte
became Quartermaster.

This meeting for the formation of Cork No. 3 Brigade was the last
occasion but one on which Michael Collins visited the South until
after the Truce. He presided at a brigade meeting at Caheragh,
Drimoleague on 16th August, 1919. At this meeting the Staff changes
mentioned above were made. Gearoid O'Sullivan, Adjutant General,
attended a Staff meeting at Hurley's, Lauragh, Bandon, in July, 1919,
to complete arrangements for a brigade training camp at Glandore in
August. That camp was under the control of Commandant Dick
McKee, O/C Dublin Brigade. Subsequent to August, 1919, no
senior member of G.H.Q. Staff visited any of the Cork Brigades
until after the Truce, but senior members of the Staffs of all the
brigades visited Dublin periodically for G.H.Q. Conferences.

On 6th January, 1919, a meeting of officers from the battalions forming the new Cork No. 2 Brigade was held at the house of Batt Walsh, Glashbee, Mallow. The brigade was formed from seven battalions, Fermoy, Mallow, Castletownroche, Charleville, Newmarket, Kanturk, and Millstreet, and they were numbered one to seven in that order. The Commandants of the Newmarket and Kanturk Battalions were not present. Due to a failure in the communications system, the notice convening the meeting did not reach either of them. Tomás MacCurtain presided at the meeting. Liam Lynch was unanimously elected Brigade Commandant, Dan Hegarty, Mallow, Vice-Commandant, Tom Barry, Glanworth, Adjutant and George Power, Fermoy, Quartermaster. About 3,500 Volunteers were included in the new brigade.

Liam's unanimous election to the position of Brigade Commandant was a remarkable tribute to the capacity for leadership which he had displayed as a battalion officer, and an expression by his fellow-officers of their entire confidence in his patriotism and ability. He was still carrying on his normal employment in Fermoy, having resumed it when the Conscription crisis ended, and he continued to work at Barry's until September. When his brother Tom visited him there after the brigade meeting, he found Liam elated and happy. Tom, a little frightened at the turn of events, asked anxiously if he realised the responsibilities and the heavy task before him. " I'll be able for it," Liam said confidently, " 'Tis great scope."

His brigade was not an easy one to administer, particularly from Fermoy, situated almost at its eastern extremity, but for the moment there was no possibility of having Brigade Headquarters elsewhere. Territorially the brigade extended from the Cork-Waterford border near Tallow on the East to the Kerry border at Rathmore in the west, and from Milford in the North almost to Donoughmore in the South. Shortly after formation the Brigade Adjutant and Quartermaster exchanged posts. This was an advantage in that the Brigade Adjutant was thereafter in daily contact with Liam, and in that it centralised most of the brigade correspondence to Fermoy. George Power began, also, at this time to build up an Intelligence Service.

On 21st January, 1919, the first Dáil Éireann assembled in the Mansion House, Dublin. Every representative elected for an Irish constituency was invited to be present, but only the Republicans attended. Of the seventy-three, thirty-six, including De Valera and Griffith, were in jail. Ireland's Declaration of Independence, promulgated by this first Dáil Éireann, having referred to the Proclamation of the Republic on Easter Monday, 1916, and its endorsement by the votes of the people in the General Election of December, 1918, went on to say :

" Now, therefore, we, the elected Representatives of the ancient Irish people, in National Parliament assembled, do, in the name of the Irish nation, ratify the establishment of the Irish Republic, and pledge ourselves and our people to make this declaration effective by every means at our command.

" We ordain that the elected Representatives of the Irish people alone have power to make laws binding on the people of Ireland, and that the Irish Parliament is the only Parliament to which that people will give its allegiance ;

" We solemnly declare foreign government in Ireland to be an invasion of our national right which we will never tolerate, and we demand the evacuation of our country by the English Garrison ;

" We claim for our national independence the recognition and support of every free nation in the world, and we proclaim that independence to be a condition precedent to international peace hereafter :

" In the name of the Irish people we humbly commit our destiny to Almighty God, who gave our fathers the courage and determination to persevere through long centuries of a ruthless tyranny, and strong in the justice of the cause which they have handed down to us, we ask His Divine blessing on this the last stage of the struggle we have pledged ourselves to carry through to freedom."

At the session of Dail Éireann on 2nd April, Cathal Brugha was appointed Minister for Defence, and thereupon Richard Mulcahy became Chief of Staff, posts which both men were to hold until the Treaty. Technically, the Volunteers were still subject to control only by their own Executive. Their President was also President of Dáil Éireann. One of the principal members of the Executive was Minister for Defence and another Chief of Staff. To the extent that both Dáil and Executive were working for the same objective, and had expressed their determination to strive for its attainment by every means at their command, a broad basis existed for satisfactory relations between them. The danger lay in the fact that, while they were travelling in the same direction, they might develop at different velocities. Moreover, if the relatively weak national forces were to be conserved and if the maximum results were to be obtained from their efforts, it was essential that the activities to be undertaken both in the military and political spheres should be planned and co-ordinated.

Otherwise, the road was now clear for the Volunteers to resume their primary task, that of striking at the foundation of British power in Ireland—the armed forces of occupation. To officers like Liam, it was entirely clear that the British Government of Ireland was still, as Joseph Chamberlain had described it in 1885,[1] "a system which is founded on the bayonets of 30,000 soldiers encamped permanently as in a hostile country," with the difference that the number of troops had increased to 58,000 reinforced by 10,000 armed constabulary men.

Seán Treacy, Dan Breen, Séamus Robinson and their comrades of South Tipperary Brigade had struck a blow at Soloheadbeg on 21st January, and the reaction to it showed that not all Volunteers were yet in the frame of mind to accept fully the needs and the consequences of a conflict such as this action presaged. But taken in conjunction with the declaration of Dáil Éireann on the same day, this blow had a quality of stark reality which braced the Volunteer mind for the task now looming ahead. Officers who saw that task clearly and appraised its difficulties with cold realism, redoubled their efforts to bring their commands to that state of efficiency which would enable them to undertake it and to create in the mass of their forces a determination and fighting spirit which would provide an inexhaustible reserve of strength. The material for an unbeatable army was in existence; what it needed was a widespread infusion of fighting spirit.

In a happy spirit of confident enthusaism Liam now began this re-conditioning of his brigade. Methodically and with unwearying zeal he utilised every afternoon and Sunday to visit his battalions. In a short time he had made personal contact with almost every officer under his command and with large numbers of Volunteers in all parts of his area. Everywhere he went men were impressed by his dignified, soldierly bearing, his sincere earnestness and intuitive understanding. It was only gradually that they sensed the steady determination and stubborn strength of will behind his quiet exterior. He was a big man, with regular, handsome features and an attractive personality. He wore rimless glasses at this time. His steep brow and broad expanse of forehead gave him a scholarly appearance. He was shrewd in his appraisal of men, but he had an innate honesty of mind which predisposed him to think the best of everybody. If he had any personal ambition it was inspired only by a desire to give himself wholly and unreservedly to the service of the cause of freedom. He had not acquired great fluency in speech or writing, and in rare angry or ecstatic moments he would stutter over a word. Because his cast of thought was original and constructive his opinions commanded respect. He had in him some intangible force, perceptible and attractive, of which he seemed to be wholly unconscious. Men felt it an honour to serve the cause he served.

[1] At West Islington, 17th June, 1885

He was a natural leader, adaptable, quick-witted, shrewd, with broad vision and balanced judgment. Although in these days somewhat diffident in asserting his own views too forcibly, there were things in which he was inaccessible to argument. Any policy for the Army except a fighting policy was one of them. At council meetings he never interrupted the programme to pursue extraneous ideas or suggestions which had emerged, but those present would find that he made notes and would discuss them dispassionately at the end of the meeting. He was always ready to make allowance for difficult circumstances, but intolerant of slackness or negligence. He initiated a system of asking for suggestions in writing from any Volunteer, officer or man, in every area, which would tend to improve the organisation or develop its fitness for battle. This created a spirit of friendly rivalry. He was always careful to give credit for good suggestions where it was due, and to put the proposals into operation whenever possible.

At these conferences he expressed, without reservation, his faith in the possibility of a resumption of the armed conflict. There was nothing turbulent or flamboyant in his approach to it. He had himself assessed the actuality and the immensity of the task calmly. He sought now to get his officers and men to see it similarly, and to foster in them that offensive spirit which would gain and retain the initiative. He directed their thoughts to the numerous practical problems which had to be faced and solved if the Army was to go forward. Relying on their patriotism, he saw the task before them simply as a duty.

His Volunteer work filled his life to the exclusion of all other interests. From the day he joined the reorganised Fermoy Company and the Sinn Féin Club, he broke away from all his commercial and social contacts and gave his whole time and his whole mind to the movement. He attended every parade and every meeting, always eager to serve in any way he could. With his shy, retiring disposition, that must have cost him a big effort at first. Later, in the last eighteen months of the struggle before the Truce, he had so concentrated all his mental faculties upon the great task that it obsessed him completely. Sometimes he would wake one of his officers in the middle of the night to discuss a problem. He used to say that his brain appeared to be on fire and he couldn't sleep.

It is typical of his outlook that from his earliest association with the Volunteers he thought in terms of the nation as a whole and visualised the organisation for the whole country as a unit. Always he was taking the broad view, making contacts and exchanging ideas with neighbouring commands, in the early days making frequent visits to the brigade officers in Cork, Limerick, Waterford and Tipperary, and from 1919 onwards maintaining, in addition, personal touch often at great risk, with the G.H.Q. Staff and officers of the Dublin Brigade.

Only those who were close to him spiritually knew that there was an element of poetic dreaming in his character, or that he looked beyond the conflict to the day when the buildings now housing a foreign army would be converted to the peaceful purposes of religion and learning. That was one way in which he saw a free Ireland using its freedom.

Most strongly marked of his characteristics were those two so consistently representative of the best in his race—soldierly spirit and missionary zeal. Because he reached manhood at the start of the greatest period of resurgence in the modern history of his country these two aspects of his character were in conflict for supremacy. The soldier won because the need for him then was greater. No other passion stirred him so deeply as this imperative call to follow an ancient quest. He had been little troubled by the unrest of adolescence. Thoughts of love and marriage he put aside so that nothing might stand between him and complete dedication in service to the duty he envisaged, although the love and prayer of a devoted lady went with him through all the days of strife, constant and faithful to the end, and he was not indifferent.

The decision he made in 1916 governed his actions for the remainder of his life. Now, with opportunity opening before him, strong in the conviction of the justice and righteousness of his cause, untroubled by any doubts concerning the morality of his means, he bent all his will and energies to the great task. He strove to cultivate a calm and unruffled disposition, so that no anger would cloud his judgment, no incidental difficulty or defeat divert him from the goal on which his eyes were fixed. The contemptible outrages against the civil population of which the occupation forces were later guilty, British official persistence in regarding our soldiers as murderers, notwithstanding their own admission of the existence of a state of war, the execution by shooting or hanging of prisoners of war taken in honourable combat, the torture of prisoners, the reign of terror, the burnings and lootings—all these things which are popularly supposed to have steeled the hearts of the Volunteers—had no more influence on his conduct of the conflict than had the summer's sun or the winter's snow upon the Galtees. He had read enough Irish history to know that the reactions of British Imperialism, challenged in arms, would not be different in 1920 to what it had been in any of the three preceding centuries. He had a high nobility of character, and believed that the service of freedom only stood below the service of God. He would not deviate from honourable methods of warfare, no matter to what depths of depravity his opponents descended.

He had a happy disposition and he was happy in these busy days and nights of 1919. Everywhere in his brigade he experienced a progressively improving state of efficiency and keenness, a growing awareness that a resumption of the armed conflict was imminent, and that it would be bitter and bloody. A considerable section of Republican opinion regarded with misgiving the prospect of a resumption of armed resistance, and that state of mind was not without its effects upon the Volunteers. The hostility of another section of public opinion may be judged from the almost unanimous condemnation by the Press of the action at Soloheadbeg, of which this editorial comment by the *Independent*[1] is representative:

"Such a cold-blooded and brutal crime will be condemned by every section of the community. For the sake merely of obtaining possession of a handful of gelegnite two policemen were wantonly murdered . . . this appalling outrage will be regarded as a blot, not only on Tipperary, but on the whole country."

As late as 11th August the Dublin Corporation passed a resolution condemning what it called "outrages."

Despite the influence of the Press and Conservative opinion, and the hopes reposed in the Peace Conference until President Wilson finally dissipated them in June, there was by mid-summer a very substantial body of opinion in the Cork Brigades which favoured and pressed for offensive action. This was neither a desperate nor an irresponsible frame of mind. It was rather a conviction reached after mature deliberation, and with an appreciation of the fact that a voluntary military organisation such as the Volunteers had to go forward or disintegrate. And, with Terence MacSwiney, they resolved:

"We shall not perish off the land in dastardly disgrace."[2]

But the strongest and most permanent impulse for the idea came from the deep and burning desire, almost frightening in its strength, not merely to strike a blow for freedom but to achieve it. Men felt that they had been cheated of an opportunity in 1916 of participating in the Rising. They were determined that nothing on earth would prevent them from contributing their share to a new effort. They were determined to be themselves a destiny, not to submit to one.

In every country there are elements in the population indifferent or insensible to national welfare. Historical causes had given us, in addition to these elements, others which were actively hostile to the whole philosophy of a free Ireland. To see the struggle in its true perspective it has to be realised that what coalesced and acquired potency in these years were minorities who were the "Voice of an

[1] 22nd January, 1919   [2] Battlecries: 1918

idea older than any Empire." The desire to achieve national independence had become for them a passion. The characteristics which these minorities, and their predecessors in the same national faith, had kept alive expressed themselves in the highest form in individual personalities—consciousness of a great mission in Pearse, a sense of duty and sacrifice in MacSwiney, honour, abnegation and heroic spirit in Lynch. These minorities were the expression of an idea that was essentially spiritual, and their mission was to translate it into historical reality. Theirs was in no way a struggle for mere personal power, individually or collectively.

There was little tendency to indiscipline or unauthorised action. Therefore when plans were made they were submitted to G.H.Q. for sanction. In the case of Cork No. 1 Brigade, sanction was withheld on the grounds that action in Cork might prejudice the chances of success of a more important action planned in Dublin—the attack on Lord French. Liam visited Dublin in April, 1919, to press some proposals for Cork No. 2 Brigade, and to endeavour to get some arms for his command. He expressed disappointment with the results. He got a few revolvers, but did not get a single rifle.

Any assessment of the contribution of the Cork Brigades to the fight must include the significant fact that they had to arm themselves by captures from the enemy. Liam's Brigade did not get more than six or seven rifles from G.H.Q. during the whole of the Tan War, notwithstanding that when it had reached a crisis early in 1921, rifles were collected from the Dublin Brigade for the ostensible purpose of arming the Southern Brigades. They did not come to the 1st Southern Division.

Dáil Éireann approved the Oath of Allegiance to the Republic on 20th August, 1919. The wording of it reflects the position at the time, when two governments struggled desperately for mastery :

"I ...., do solemnly swear (or affirm) that I do not, and shall not yield a voluntary support to any pretended Government, Authority or power within Ireland hostile and inimical thereto, and I do further swear (or affirm) that, to the best of my knowledge and ability, I will support and defend the Irish Republic, and the Government of the Irish Republic, which is Dáil Éireann, against all enemies, foreign and domestic, and I will bear true faith and allegiance to the same, and I take this obligation freely without any mental reservation or purpose of evasion, So help me God."[1]

It was administered to the Volunteers at public parades of companies

[1] General Orders, No. 11, 1920 (New Series)

or smaller units during the Autumn of 1920. This action placed the Army formally under the authority of the *de jure* government of the country. So far as the military activities of the Army were concerned, it did no more than express a little more explicitly the validity always claimed for them by Republicans. That validity had a moral and historical basis, implicit in all resistance to foreign rule, and it could neither be improved nor nullified. Any controversy which the matter engendered centered on the question of the wisdom or otherwise of surrendering domestic control of the organisation to an outside body, rather than on the moral issue. The number of Volunteers who were then members of the I.R.B. did not exceed five per cent. of total strength, and these men were instructed by the Supreme Council to take the oath.

A change of this kind should normally have been the subject of decision by a Volunteer Convention. Brigade Conventions were held in November, 1919, for the purpose of electing delegates to this national assembly, as provided for in the Constitution of the Volunteers. Liam Lynch presided at the Convention of his Brigade which was held at Glashabee Schools under the guise of a Gaelic League convention. But the risks of assembling such a large number of Volunteers in Dublin made the holding of a National Convention too dangerous. Elected delegates were asked, instead, in a letter from Seán McGarry, Honorary Secretary of the Volunteer Executive, dated 2nd June, 1920, to signify in writing their approval or otherwise of the proposed oath of allegiance. The great majority approved.

Republicanism, as a form of Government, had no more than an academic interest for Volunteers. Their inspiration was the older one—to eject the invader, to achieve freedom from foreign rule. If that could be done, the form of government was inevitable in our circumstances. As early as 1909 *Irish Freedom* had said : " Government can take only one form amongst us, a Republic." But the expression " Republic " was coming to symbolise, indeed had now come to symbolise, all the teaching, all the hopes and all the claims made for Ireland by every fighter for Irish freedom since the first Norman set a predatory foot on our soil. It was now as it had always been, the fundamental aspiration was for freedom. " For freedom they made their ranns, for freedom they stood in battle through five bloody centuries."[1] The inspiring words of the 1916 Proclamation now enshrined everything for which Irish Ireland worked, prayed and fought. Volunteers everywhere gladly pledged their solemn oaths of allegiance to the Republic it envisaged.

The first internal crisis in the Volunteer organisation after 1916

[1] P. H. Pearse : Ghosts

came in the summer of 1919, and it was not concerned with the oath.
The distraction of political activity, the hopes based on the Peace
Conference, the discouraging shortage of arms, and the absence of a
military policy comprehensible to the average Volunteer, had combined to make it difficult to maintain the organisation at all in some
areas. In all areas the tenseness which had marked the second half of
1918 had been relaxed. It is symptomatic of this time of crisis that
it is marked by the emergence of new leaders, in many cases replacing
those who had directed the local commands from the beginning.

In the circumstances of the time the organisation might have
crumbled, the creeping paralysis of inactivity might easily have killed
it. It was saved mainly because a minority of officers and men
vigorously agitated the policy of action, argued its feasibility, and
more or less convinced or coerced General Headquarters into giving
it a reluctant sanction. Liam Lynch was one of the most earnest
and far-seeing of these officers. He was one of the minority which
always inspires the multitude.

Pressure on G.H.Q. to approve a policy of attacks on British
garrison forces came mainly from the Southern Brigades. As there
appeared to the officers of these commands to be no prospects of
acquiring arms in any quantity by purchase or importation, they urged
strongly that they be permitted to attempt the capture of weapons
from enemy forces, police or military, whenever the opportunity
offered. Upon that turn of events rested the destiny of the Volunteer
movement and the fate of the cause of Irish liberty for a generation.
That is the measure of the significance of officers such as Liam Lynch.

There was nothing arrogant or overbearing in his methods, and
he had a sharp sense of the value of discipline. He was clear-sighted
enough to see that the whole organisation in every part of the national
territory should go forward on a common policy. He saw that the
alternative to that course was the deterioration of the struggle into an
unco-ordinated series of fortuitous conflicts with the occupation forces.
His approach to the task was always national, never narrow. It
depressed him that there should be a reluctance on the part of G.H.Q.
at that time to take responsibility for military actions.

Although certain actions in which arms were captured from enemy
forces had taken place without G.H.Q. sanction, in County Cork and
elsewhere, it appeared to Liam that the logical consequence of an
extension of such activities would lead ultimately to indiscipline,
unless they were sanctioned by G.H.Q. He wanted to have a policy
in that regard defined and adopted by the whole organisation. Very
creditable and successful raids had been carried out before this date :
the Grammar School, Cork, in September, 1917; Eyeries police post
in April, 1918; Bealagleanna in July, 1918; rifles captured from a

party of military at Mount Massey, Macroom, in January, 1919. If these activities were laudable the time had come when G.H.Q. should approve them and urge a more widespread adoption of them. Liam, therefore, took the course of endeavouring to convince G.H.Q. that wisdom and good policy alike, lay in giving approval to all such plans submitted to them, where it was clear that they had a reasonable chance of success.

How appropriate that policy was soon became evident. When a few of these activities, under proper sanction, had been carried out successfully, the Volunteer organisation was revitalised and sprung at once into an honoured place in the nation's defences. The Army assumed leadership, the dynamic leadership of action and example. It became the spearhead of national effort, and set a standard of service which the whole people braced itself to emulate. The exuberant but vague Republicanism of the time was concentrated into a powerful weapon. Almost unconsciously, the Army evolved for itself the method of fighting best suited to its organisation, arms, and state of training, the only method which gave it any hope of survival and success—guerilla warfare. The prime need now was arms.

Every unit in Liam's Brigade was now alertly watching every opportunity to arm itself. It was not inappropriate that the Fermoy Battalion, which had advanced rapidly to a high standard of efficiency, should be the first to see a chance and take it. The routine of the police at Araglin barracks had been carefully observed. Con Leddy, then O/C Araglin Company and later O/C Fermoy Battalion, sought permission from the Brigade Commandant to raid the barracks. Liam was then at Barry's and the request was made to him there. With George Power, he made an inspection of the locality himself, and then obtained G.H.Q. sanction for the job.

On Sunday morning, 20th April, 1919, when three of the four R.I.C. men occupying the barracks were at Mass, a small party of seven Volunteers quietly approached the building from the rere. There were no windows on that side of the barrack. When the constable, who was the only occupant of the post, took a bucket and went outside for water the Volunteers entered without being observed. When he returned he was held up by the men detailed to receive him. Dashing the bucket of water at his unexpected visitors, and shouting that if he was armed he would blow their brains out, the constable ran down the yard in an attempt to escape. He was, however, quickly overhauled and when he saw that the Volunteers were armed, his truculence evaporated.

Con Leddy recalls that Michael Fitzgerald, Commandant of Fermoy Battalion, who was in charge, was at this time looking down from an upper window of the barrack and very much enjoying the events taking place below. "It was his happy day," Con Leddy writes, "and perhaps his last happy day on this earth, although to suffer seemed to be a joy to him." He was one of those destined to die in the following year after a hunger-strike lasting sixty-seven days.

The Volunteers stripped the barracks of its arms, ammunition, equipment and documents. Everything of military value was removed but nothing else. The raid added to the battalion armament six carbines and 400 rounds of .303 ammunition, a Webley revolver and twenty rounds of ammunition. The constable was not molested. He expressed his thanks to the Volunteers for the way they had treated him, and never afterwards attempted to identify any of them. In addition to Michael Fitzgerald and Con Leddy, the following members of Araglin Company took part in the raid : Lieut. John O'Mahony, Section Commander Thomas Brennock, Company Adjutant Maurice Hyland, Volunteer Owen McCarthy and Volunteer John O'Donovan.

Seán Hogan of 3rd Tipperary Brigade was rescued from a police escort at Knocklong Railway Station on 13th May. Two Volunteers who were wounded in the course of the fight, Ned O'Brien and Jim Scanlan of Galbally, came into the Mitchelstown Company area. On the second night after the rescue, Mitchelstown Volunteers found them accommodation in the home of Mr. and Mrs. William Bailey, Ballinabrook where Dr. Jim Barry of Fermoy attended them and dressed their wounds. About a week later they moved to the Bally-poreen district, where they stayed with cousins of Ned O'Brien's, O'Farrells, O'Donnells and Sheehy's Templetenny. This was not a very safe place for them because in the intensive raiding then being carried out by British forces, all relatives of both wanted men were frequently visited.

This position was reported to Liam Lynch and he acted promptly. With Tom Cavanagh, Fermoy Company, driving, he arrived at Ballyporeen at night, and took the two wounded Volunteers to Mr. Jim Moloney's, Ballydorgan, near Tallow. Mitchelstown was avoided on the journey, but Moore Park Camp had to be passed. The sentry there challenged and called on the car to stop. Liam ordered Tom Cavanagh to drive on. The sentry fired but the car and its occupants escaped without injury. For one Volunteer at least, the driver, that was the first indication of Liam's determination. Some miles on the Tallow side of Fermoy a whistle was blown. Liam had the car stopped, and the party were joined by Michael Fitzgerald and Larry Condon, who accompanied them to Tallow.

While they remained in his Brigade area, Liam Lynch arranged for the protection of the two wounded East Limerick men, did everything necessary for their welfare, and went out himself one night with Michael Fitzgerald and a Fermoy chemist, William Ahern, who dressed their wounds.

George Power and Tom Griffin, Ballynoe, were in constant touch with them until Liam had them moved again, first to Dr. Con Molan's at Conna, where they stayed almost a month, and later to Dan Daly's at Bushy Park, Watergrasshill. Throughout the large scale continuous raiding then in progress the efficient use of the Brigade organisation and intelligence directed by Liam Lynch kept these two brave Volunteers out of the clutches of the enemy.

CHAPTER 5

LYNCH'S BRIGADE GOES INTO ACTION

*" War—the exposure of ourselves to wounds, toil and death—is as much
our duty, in a just cause, as any other mode of sustaining justice."*

THOMAS DAVIS.

TOWARDS the end of April, 1919, Liam went to Dublin and
endeavoured to get G.H.Q. sanction for activities in his Brigade
area, designed primarily to secure serviceable arms. In the following
month he had consultations in Cork with the Brigade officers of
Cork No. 1 Brigade, with the idea of co-ordinating activities—an
idea with which these officers fully concurred, and for which the
Brigade Commandant had already asked G.H.Q. sanction. Circumstances were somewhat different in the two areas. In Cork No. 1,
where the arms position was little better than in Cork No. 2, certain
police barracks offered the most favourable targets for initial attacks
designed to secure arms, and these attacks were subsequently carried
out in the opening days of 1920. In Liam Lynch's Brigade area,
some military objectives appeared to offer a more hopeful possibility.

In July he sought permission from G.H.Q. for an attack on British
military forces. This was at first refused, but subsequently a qualified
sanction was given, and he was told that if he could disarm a military
party without casualties he could go ahead. Liam now began to
plan the putting into operation of a long cherished idea. It was to
open the attack on British military forces, by striking in the heart
of the enemy's most powerful stronghold in his Brigade area—Fermoy.
The British 6th Division, under the command of Major General Sir
E. P. Strickland, which garrisoned Munster and the Counties of
Kilkenny and Wexford, then consisted of four infantry brigades,
two cavalry regiments, four brigades of field artillery, a machine-gun
battalion, coast defence forces at Berehaven and Cork Harbour,
together with the usual supply and transport, engineering, signals,
medical, legal and military police units of a division. Division
Headquarters was at Cork, as was also the headquarters of the 17th
Infantry Brigade, to which was attached one of the cavalry regiments.
Sixteenth Brigade Headquarters was at Fermoy ; 18th, with the other
cavalry regiment, at Limerick, and Kerry Brigade Headquarters at
Buttevant. One brigade of Royal Field Artillery was at Fermoy, one

at Cahir, one at Moore Park and the other at Kilkenny. The machine-gun battalion was at Ballyvonaire. The 16th Brigade comprised five battalions, the 17th, five battalions and a cavalry regiment. The 18th Brigade included four battalions and a cavalry regiment, and the Kerry Brigade, two battalions.

Liam Lynch had in his brigade area elements of the 16th and Kerry Brigades, approximating five battalions, two brigades of Royal Field Artillery, a machine-gun battalion, and two enemy Brigade Head-quarters and their Staffs. The total military garrison in his area was not less than 4,300 all ranks. There was, in addition, about 490 armed police, distributed in fifty-four posts, mainly in the towns and villages, throughout the brigade area. The police had an intimate knowledge of the population, and of every factor likely to influence the course of an armed conflict.

All these opposing forces were, of course, housed in well-fortified and comfortable barracks, many of their officers were experienced veterans of the European war, most of the troops had received adequate military training, they were armed with modern weapons and backed by administrative and supply services on a war footing. It would be difficult for them not to have regarded their grip upon the area as impregnable.

Opposed to them Liam Lynch commanded 3,800 partly-trained Volunteers, now excellently organised in a tight, efficient, disciplined body, under the control of responsible officers and with a clearly-defined chain of command. None was at that time on whole-time active service. They had neither pay, barracks nor supply services. They were not clothed, armed, or rationed by the State. Their specialised services, engineers, signallers, transport, intelligence and medical, were then of the most rudimentary nature. They had no heavy weapons of any kind. Their arms consisted of a dozen rifles, some of doubtful reliability, and less than one hundred revolvers and pistols. Poor in material resources, they were rich only in moral and spiritual qualities.

For this first trial of strength, this first matching of his wits, ingenuity and capacity for organisation, against the enemy, Liam planned with the most meticulous attention to detail. The objective was an armed party of British soldiers who, on Sundays, attended service at the Wesleyan Church about half-a-mile from their barracks, and at the eastern end of the town of Fermoy. It was not known if the rifles they carried were loaded or not. Some time previously a report had appeared in the Press of an accident in Cobh, in which a soldier on church parade was injured by the discharge of a bullet from his own rifle. Plans were made on the assumption that the rifles would be loaded.

On Sunday morning, 7th September, 1919, about 10.30, fourteen
soldiers, with a corporal in charge, left their barracks and marched
through the town towards the Wesleyan Church. They carried their
rifles at the slope. About twenty-five Volunteers from Fermoy
Company, with six serviceable revolvers between them, assembled in
groups of twos and threes in the vicinity of the church. They had to
remain well spread out along the street to avoid creating attention or
alarm on the part of the soldiers. The main attacking party, of which
Larry Condon was in charge, included John Fanning, Michael
Fitzgerald, Patrick Ahern and James Fitzgerald. Other groups were
detailed to collect the rifles and rush them to the waiting cars, the
remainder to close in from the rear and prevent any attempt by the
British to get back to their barracks. The unarmed Volunteers carried
short clubs, concealed in their coatsleeves.

One car with George Power in charge stands near the church.
Two men are attending to an imaginary defect. Another car moves
up Patrick Street behind the British party, and increases its speed so
as to arrive at the church at the same moment as they do. In it is
Liam Lynch.

A sharp whistle blast. Liam calls on the party to surrender, they
prepare to resist, the Volunteers rush them, shots are fired and for a
minute there is a confused struggle. Liam jumps for a rifle lying on
the road, slips and falls, a soldier rushed at him, swinging a rifle-butt,
but is shot down. That rifle, too, is gathered. In a minute it is all
over, fifteen rifles are loaded into one of the cars, and both move
away up the Tallow-Lismore road. Their occupants can hear the
bugle-call in the barracks sounding the alarm. The remaining Volunteers scatter on foot. One soldier had been killed and three wounded.

So quickly was the alarm raised in the barracks that within five
minutes two lorries of military were tearing out the Lismore road in
pursuit of the cars. This, of course, had been foreseen. At Carrigabrick, a-mile-and-a-quarter from the town, two trees on the roadside
were partly sawn through that morning and held in position by ropes,
while Volunteers waited under cover for the cars carrying the rifles
to pass. The moment they were through the trees came down with
a crash, and the roadblock thus created forced the military pursuit
to detour and lose the trail.

Leaving Fermoy, Liam realised that he was wounded. He had
received a bullet through the shoulder, but the injury did not appear
to be serious. At Carrigabrick, as had been arranged, William Ahern,
the Fermoy chemist's assistant who had dressed the wounds of Jim
Scanlan and Ned O'Brien after Knocklong, was waiting with a first-aid
outfit. He got on the car and gave Liam such treatment as was
possible in the speeding Buick. In his elation at having carried out

successfully the first part of the operation, Liam made light of his wound.

The security of the captured weapons was equally essential to complete success, and now the plans he had made for that came into operation. At Kilmagner, five miles from Fermoy, Larry Condon, Mick Fitzgerald and John Fanning got off the cars, and assisted by Ned and William Lane, took the rifles to a prearranged place where they were safely concealed. On the following night they were transferred to a dump in Araglin Company area.

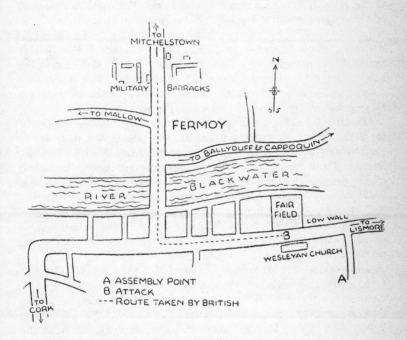

A ASSEMBLY POINT
B ATTACK
--- ROUTE TAKEN BY BRITISH

Because the raid would have to take place in daylight, during which many persons would have opportunities of observing those participating, Liam had given much thought to the selection of officers and men for the task. It was inevitable that well-known local officers and men taking part would thereafter have to go on the run to evade arrest. That was foreseen and accepted. But it was necessary to use cars, if the arms, the possible casualties and the immediate participants were to be removed quickly from the scene. Local cars and drivers would be particularly vulnerable. Speed was

essential to success ; Liam's command was then in no position to
fight any kind of action with the forces which the British could
muster at the spot within, at most, ten minutes.

The brunt of the action was borne by Fermoy Company. The
assistance which Liam looked for from outside the company was
transport. But when George Power went to Mallow to get one car,
a number of men there volunteered to come with the car and participate in the action. The car was a Buick and was driven by Leo
O'Callaghan. The Mallow men who travelled in it were Dan Hegarty,
Owen Harold, Brian Kelly and Ned Waters. The ostensible purpose
of their journey was a Sunday trip to Mount Melleray.

Jack Mulvey, of Rathcormac, had a Ford car, and when the use of
it was requested, he, too, volunteered to drive himself. On the Sunday
morning he brought with him to Fermoy other Volunteers—Pat
Leahy, John Joe Hogan, Peter O'Callaghan and Tom Griffin of
Ballynoe Company. Martin O'Keeffe and Willie O'Mahony, of the
same company, travelled to and from Fermoy on bicycles.

Liam had asked his old friend, Pax Whelan, O/C Waterford Brigade,
for a third car. Pax procured the car but was unable to travel to
Fermoy on that day. George Lennon and Mick Mansfield volunteered. Their driver, who was not a Volunteer, became suspicious
of his passengers and left Fermoy for Dungarvan before the action
took place. The two Waterford men subsequently made their way
back to Dungarvan on foot, having a number of narrow escapes
from capture during the day. On one occasion they joined a party
stooking oats in a cornfield to evade the attention of a military search
party.

All the rifles were loaded into the Buick driven by Leo O'Callaghan.
Into it also piled Liam Lynch, Owen Harold, Ned Waters, Tom
Griffin, Lar Condon, Mick Fitzgerald and John Fanning. Leaving
Fermoy, Mulvey's car, a Ford, carried Pat Leahy, John Joe Hogan,
Peter O'Callaghan, George Power and Dan Hegarty. A short distance out Power and Hegarty left the overloaded car and made their
way back into town through the fields. At Kilmagner, Tom Griffin
transferred to it and the party went on to Mount Melleray. Returning
home that evening, this group were held up by police at Lismore
and their names were taken. A few miles farther on near Tallow, they
were overtaken by an armoured car and lorry containing police and
military. They were further questioned and searched, but allowed to
proceed. It was fortunate that Tom Griffin had earlier got his companions to turn out their pockets and dispose of incriminating articles.
One had a British cap badge which he was keeping as a souvenir of
the events.

Liam's wound was not serious, nevertheless it was necessary

for him to have medical attention and rest until it healed. As the Buick sped towards Youghal after the rifles had been dumped, it was decided that Liam and William Ahern would drop off near the town, and that the car with the remaining occupants would continue to Cork City and thence back to Mallow. It reached Mallow without incident, having been allowed to pass through a military barrier at Dunkettle without search.

Leaving Liam near Furry Hill about two miles from Youghal, William Ahern walked into the town, called on a member of Cumann-na-mBan, Miss O'Keeffe, who was a native of Fermoy, and explained what assistance was required. Miss O'Keeffe promptly informed the Youghal Company officers, Jim Keogh and Mick Kelleher. They, with Michael Walsh, went at once to where Liam was and brought him on foot along the Seafield road to the house of Thomas O'Connor, Seaview Cottage, near the Mental Hospital. At this time the centre of the town of Youghal was in the grip of a large scale hold-up by the military. The most important of the men for whom they were searching was now in friendly shelter within a few hundred yards of their Youghal post.

The local company medical officer, Dr. Thomas Kennedy, was absent from Youghal that day, but at the request of the company officers, Dr. Michael Twomey, who was not a member of the Volunteer organisation, came at once to Seaview Cottage and dressed Liam's wound.

An intensive search by military and police forces continued during the day. All neighbouring police and military posts were notified of the occurrence, parties of military in lorries scoured the countryside, cars were held up and a large number of persons questioned. The military lorry baulked by the road block at Carrigabrick went to Ballynoe, where its occupants treated an innocent match-making party, which had gone out from Fermoy in a motor car, to a foretaste of the brutality so many citizens were destined to experience later. Next night the East Kent Regiment turned out in force and sacked the town of Fermoy. Two days later the district was proclaimed a military area.

Liam remained at Seaview Cottage on Sunday night. But he was anxious to move into Waterford and a message was sent to Pax Whelan, O/C Waterford Brigade, at Dungarvan. The necessary arrangements were quickly made. On Monday Pax sent a car which picked up Jim Mansfield at Old Parish and went to Youghal. Accompanied by Michael Walsh, Liam walked from O'Connor's across the bridge over the Blackwater to a point where he was picked up by Jim Mansfield in the car. They went into Ardmore, had tea at Foley's and continued towards Dungarvan.

About a mile outside the town Liam was met by Phil O'Donnell
and Paddy Lynch, who took him first to the home of Miss Broderick
and later to Cooney's, at Carrigroe.   Here he remained for about
two weeks, having his wound dressed daily by Dr. Moloney, of
Dungarvan, and nursed by Dan Cooney, then a champion Irish boxer,
and expert first-aid man.   His next move was by pony and trap,
driven by James Kirwan with armed escort and scouts, to Kirwan's,
at Graigavalla, on the slopes of the Comeraghs.   Here his wound
was attended to by Dr. Murphy of Carrick-on-Suir.   In this move,
also, he was accompanied by Paddy Lynch, Vice-Commandant, 1st
Battalion Waterford Brigade, who became a great friend of his.   At
Liam's request George Power came to tell him how Fermoy had
reacted to the raid and its consequences.   Liam came in from Kirwan's
to meet George at Miss Broderick's, Abbeyside, Dungarvan.   He
returned to Cooney's again after about three weeks at Kirwans'.

At Jerry Kirwan's hospitable house Liam had every comfort,
including a very good library.   Here Michael Doheny had rested
awhile in '48 on his hunted journey from Ballingarry and failure to
West Cork and exile.   Here Liam read again, with what must have
been a keener insight, *The Felon's Track*, in which Doheny tells the
heartbreaking story of the failure of one effort at insurrection.   He
was now a " felon " himself.   Jerry Kirwan cycled to Clonmel and
brought the news to Liam's brother Martin, Brother Placidus of the
Christian Brothers, that Liam was staying with him.   On the following
Saturday Martin visited Carrick-on-Suir, and cycled to Kirwan's.
In the house near Crotty's Lake the brothers met in a reunion that
made Liam very happy.   His devotion to all the members of his
family made him almost pathetically eager to have their approval
in the great adventure upon which he was now embarked.   In a
cheerful letter to Tom on 15th November, he expresses delight at
various items of news from home, and at having met Brother Placidus,
" who took his case so well."   " Whatever has happened now," he
writes, " after years will justify our cause."   After the absence of over
two months he returned to his own area in a car going to a funeral at
Fermoy.

Public reaction to these more vigorous Army activities was
indicative of the state of Republican feeling.   Where the actions had
been carried out without casualties, as at Eyeries, Bealagleanna,
Newmarket, Rathclarin and Araglin, there was delight and entire
approval.   Where casualties were suffered on either side, as at
Gortatlea, in Kerry, where two Volunteers were killed, or at Soloheadbeg, Knocklong and Fermoy, where deaths of British personnel
occurred, many were gravely troubled.   They viewed a continuation
and development of such a policy with considerable misgiving.

Historic causes had driven a sense of the invincibility of British might and power deep into the consciousness of the people. Admiration for the intrepid men who were challenging the Colossus was tempered by the old, troubled, sober fear that they, too, would come to the bitterness of defeat.

Moreover, neither support nor encouragement was forthcoming from the public Press or the ecclesiastical authorities. The newspaper having the widest circulation in Liam's Brigade area—the *Cork Examiner*, maintained a dreary editorial whine of despair during the three vital years of struggle. Other daily papers were equally detrimental to national morale. A few individual priests, with truly heroic fortitude, took their stand with the Volunteers, and suffered for it; but on the part of the Bishops and the majority of the clergy the reaction to the early military activities of the national armed forces was one of unqualified disapproval and public condemnation. It would be easy to quote pronouncements as unequivocal and as illogical as that of His Lordship of Cork, Most Rev. Dr. Coholan: " The killing of policemen is morally murder, and politically of no consequence."

To a force almost entirely Catholic, and in the main devout, the persistent and occasionally insensate denunciations of their Bishops and clergy were a source of pain and heart-searching. What was involved for the average Volunteer in disobedience to the teaching of his spiritual advisers must be set against that even stronger belief of his in the justice, morality and righteousness of the service in which he was engaged. It was voluntary service. No man was compelled to fight. Volunteers, generally, were not of the type that could regard lightly the moral issue so starkly raised by the developing conflict. They did not waver. Their steadiness under ecclesiastical condemnation, and, in the Diocese of Cork, even under a purported Decree of Excommunication, was not only creditable to them as a disciplined force, but was, also, one of the factors which made the progressive development of the struggle possible.

Upon the morale of the Volunteers these early actions had an almost incalculable effect. They were the first ray of light upon a military problem which had seemed insoluble. They were the beginning of a new method of attack upon the old task which had faced every revolutionary movement since Ireland's national defence forces were broken at Kinsale. They were the germ of the guerilla idea, then almost unconsciously beginning to emerge in the minds of active and determined officers like Liam Lynch. Few Volunteers made the mistake of minimising the significance of these actions merely because they were small or local. Generally the possibilities of expansion of this type of effort were quickly recognised and appreciated. That had a bracing effect upon morale. It set the whole army thinking upon new lines and eager to emulate the lead which had been given. A price had to be paid in casualties and arrests, and it is one of the tragedies of the time that some of the best fighters had to eat their hearts out in jails and internment camps, and some to die in the slow torture of hunger-strike. But there was light and hope. Never thereafter did men fight in despair.

The Fermoy action claimed its quota of sacrifice from the brigade. Arrests followed. The local Battalion Commandant and Vice-Commandant, Michael Fitzgerald and Larry Condon, and the Fermoy Company Captain, John Fanning, were amongst those taken.[1] Two months later further arrests were made at Mallow. Police intelligence was still functioning well enough at this time to direct their suspicions accurately on the Mallow men concerned. But their enquiries were somewhat confused by the fact that they were searching for three cars, two of them from Mallow. In fact a second car had left Mallow for Fermoy on the morning of the action. It carried a number of delegates to a Sinn Féin function at Fermoy, and these men were entirely unaware of the proposed action by the Volunteers. The following extracts from a report by Head Constable D. Sullivan, R.I.C., who was summarily dismissed from the force for refusing to make a deposition and arrest certain Volunteers, when in his opinion there was "no evidence whatsoever" to connect them with the affair, throws some light on police methods at the time.

Head Constable Sullivan, who had forty years service, received the usual notice of the occurrence in Fermoy, a description of three cars and instructions to make enquiries. His report goes on to say:

"About 19th Sept. I received from D. I. Lewis, Fermoy, a description of a black-looking Ford Car, dirty appearance. We were looking for this car until 7th November, when Mr. Lewis, D.I., came to Mallow and directed me to go to Mr. Thompson and get car No. 1342 to go to Mallow Railway Station, on the pretence that I was to take up a sick policeman there, as he (Lewis) had a man to identify the car. I went to Mr. Thompson and told him what the car was wanted out for. Const. Simon O'Dea and I drove in the car to the railway station. Leo O'Callaghan drove us. Const. O'Dea and I walked into the platform and after a short time Const. O'Dea introduced to me the supposed sick constable who I believe was Lieut. Haigh. I had within a short time three interviews with Haigh on the platform. Haigh left the platform

[1] Others arrested were James Fanning, John Swaine, John Joe Hogan, Martin O'Keeffe, Dick O'Keeffe, Pat Leahy, Tom Griffin, Peter O'Callaghan, and Jack Mulvey.

on foot for police station, Mallow. The car with Const. O'Dea in it left three minutes later and I walked to the police-barracks which took me about 10 minutes. When I arrived in D.I.'s office, D.I. Lewis and Lieut. Haigh were there and Mr. Lewis asked me if I went in car to the Railway Station. I told him I did with Const. O'Dea and that Const. O'Dea returned in it. Lieut. Haigh then asked me, 'Are you the man I was speaking to at the Railway Station.' I said I was. He then said 'I was not sure." He and Lewis then talked about the car and Lewis said in a loud impressive voice to Haigh—'It is a Beuc (sic) car.' Before they left the office both persuaded me there was a bridge spanning the River Blackwater between Mallow and Killavullen, which is not so. Neither of them told me that the car was identified, and later when speaking to Constable O'Dea about the matter he told me that Haigh had asked him at the Railway Station if the car at the station were No. 1342. These incidents gave me to understand that there was something wrong in the identification of the car after two months when the same man could not identify an old Head Constable after 15 minutes."

On the 11th November he received an order to arrest Daniel Hegarty, Brian Kelly, Edward Waters, Owen Harold and Leo O'Callaghan, to charge them with the murder of Pte. William Jones, of the K.L.I. Regiment at Fermoy on 7th September, to have them brought before Mr. Hardy, R.M., and remanded in custody to Cork Jail. He was to seize motor car I.F. 1342 and have it taken to Fermoy.

Promptly on the same date he refused to carry out this instruction, and wrote the following report to Mr. Smyth, D.I., Mallow :

"I beg to state that I have got no evidence whatsoever to ground a deposition to have these men remanded. I, as well as Sgt. McGill, have got no evidence to connect them with the crime and I beg to request to be armed with a warrant for their arrest to safeguard me against future consequences, as two months have now passed since the crime was committed."

D. SULLIVAN, H.C."

On a report made by County Inspector Clayton to Dublin Castle, H.C. Sullivan was dismissed, and the arrests were carried out. H.C. Sullivan was given sixteen days to get his family and furniture out of the barracks. Thus the Castle rewarded forty years of service and an unblemished record in all four ranks which this man had held. It is an interesting point that he had been instructed by the County Inspector, when taking statements on this case, to state to the persons interviewed, "That it was Mr. Carroll, Crown Solicitor, who directed him to take them and not the police authorities."

After a series of weekly remands, thirty-five in the cases of the first arrests, the prisoners were returned for trial at the Cork Assizes in July, 1920. In the meantime the Crown had got an order in the High Court on 9th June transferring the trials to Derry, but this order was discharged on 24th June at a hearing before the Lord Chief Justice, Mr. Justice Kenny and Mr. Justice Gibson, and the trials fixed for the City of Cork. Mr. Patrick Lynch, K.C., Mr. J. Fitzgerald, and Mr. Joseph O'Connor, instructed by Mr. John S. Troy, Solicitor, Fermoy, represented the prisoners. At Cork the Grand Jury found true bills against Fitzgerald, Hogan and Hegarty. The remainder were released.

One of the numerous difficulties which the British had in endeavouring to prevent the complete breakdown of their civil and judicial administration at the time was that jurors refused to attend their courts, despite heavy penalties. No jury could be empanelled to try the prisoners, and they remained in custody in Cork Jail. In a letter written to Father Tom from the Comeraghs, Liam expressed his concern for the fate of his comrades, and the hope that they would soon be released.

In August, 1920, Commandant Michael Fitzgerald, with a number of other untried prisoners in Cork Jail, decided to hunger-strike for release. This was Fitzgerald's second experience of imprisonment, and his ardent spirit yearned for the freedom which would enable him to rejoin his comrades in the fight. About two weeks after his successful capture of Araglin R.I.C. barracks he was arrested at Clondulane. Some ammunition was found in the house in which he lived, and he was sentenced to two months' imprisonment. He was released about the end of August and took part in the action at Fermoy on 7th September. He was a man of estimable character, temperate and a non-smoker. His outstanding soldierly qualities gained quick recognition in his appointment as O/C 1st Battalion. He was Secretary of the Glandulane Branch of the Irish Transport and General Workers' Union, of which Attie Hallinan, who took part in the action, was President. Liam Lynch was deeply attached to him, and while gravely concerned about his fate was not without hope that it would be impossible for the British to procure any evidence connecting him with the Fermoy raid.

Once more only did Liam see his old friend alive, and that was when he himself was a prisoner for a short time in Cork Jail. When Fitzgerald's body was in the mortuary in Fermoy church on the night before his burial, Liam came in quietly and had the coffin lid removed to look for the last time on the dead face of the man to whom he was

most deeply attached.   For sixty-seven days Fitzgerald endured the
ordeal of hunger, and then death came as a merciful relief from his
suffering on 17th October, 1920.

His funeral from S.S. Peter and Paul's Church in the city was made
the occasion of one of those arrogant displays of force and disregard
for the piety and devotion of the people, who had come to pay their
last tribute to a dead soldier.   After the Mass, British military in war
equipment, wearing steel helmets and carrying fixed bayonets, invaded
the church and walked over the seats to the altar rails.   An officer,
with a drawn revolver, handed a notice to the priest to the effect that
only a limited number of persons would be allowed to take part in
the funeral.   A machine-gun was mounted at the church gates and
armoured cars toured the vicinity.   Notwithstanding the threats and
the menacing attitude of the military, thousands took part in the
funeral procession.   Armoured cars and tenders carrying heavily-
equipped forces accompanied the cortege to the city boundary.
Similar scenes were witnessed in Fermoy next day when Michael
Fitzgerald was buried at Kilcrumper.   A few hours after the grave
had been closed some of his comrades assembled above it to pay
their last tribute to a heroic soldier and a good man.   Those shots
must have been heard by the military in their barracks in Fermoy.

In all the strain and cares of the following years Liam never forgot
Michael Fitzgerald.   When his own hour came to die, after that
tragic running fight over the Knockmealdowns, his last request was
to be buried beside his old comrade at Kilcrumper.   And there he
sleeps.

In the letter to Tom from the Comeraghs, previously mentioned,
Liam wrote : " The Republic is now within our grasp, at the most
eighteen months."   How near that came to being prophetic !   Just
nineteen months afterwards Britain asked for a Truce.   In the letter
to which this is a reply Tom had evidently made a reference to
Sarsfield's ride to Ballyneety.   Liam writes :   " I always thought
Sarsfield made a daring ride—yes, but he burned the guns ! "

That reflects his reaction to his own military problem.   He would be
the first to recognise how impossible it was for Sarsfield to have dealt
otherwise than he did so brilliantly with the Williamite siege train,
but if the Irish Army of 1920 was to fight successfully, destruction
of enemy weapons was not enough.   It had to capture sufficient
war material from its opponents to enable it to fight, and it had to
prevent recapture of what it acquired.

The very intense police search for him did not deter him at any time
from keeping his contacts and carrying out his duties as fully as if
he had been entirely free of the danger of capture.   In the police

description of the men taking part in the Fermoy action he was one of two identified by name. He is described as being :

> " 28 years of age, fresh complexion, long thin face, 5 ft. 10 ins., in height, high cheek bones, smart appearance, light brown hair, wears gold rimmed glasses, rarely ever seen without glasses."

As a police description it is reasonably accurate. A rumour emanated from police sources in Fermoy that he had died as a result of his wound. If that was an oblique effort to get information it did not succeed. Nothing was said to discourage the possibility, but it cannot have been many months before the British authorities became aware that he was alive and active.

With the Fermoy attack Liam began the period of whole-time active service which terminated only at his death. When he returned to his brigade area he set up headquarters at Glenville, about ten miles South-west of Fermoy. Some changes took place in his staff. Dan Hegarty, the Brigade Vice-Commandant, then under arrest, was replaced by George Power; Maurice Twomey, then Adjutant of Fermoy Battalion, became Brigade Adjutant. Tom Barry, Glanworth, the Brigade Quartermaster, was unanimously elected O/C of the 3rd Battalion, Castletownroche, and was replaced by Jeremiah Buckley, Mourneabbey, who held the post until arrested in August, 1920. He was then replaced by Paddy O'Brien of Liscarroll, who had Michael O'Connell, of Lombardstown, as Assistant. In spite of all difficulties Liam maintained the closest contacts with his staff, and, now free to give the whole of his time and energy to the work, toured the brigade area giving special attention to the battalions at the Western end which he had not hitherto been able to visit so frequently. These activities occupied him until Christmas, 1919.

As Christmas approached his thoughts turned to Barnagurraha. That love of the Galtee homestead breaks out in all his letters. He feared that this would be the first Christmas he would not spend there, and clearly he was considering whether his people should be subjected to the anxiety and strain which his visit would entail.

He had written to Tom asking advice about whether he should go home for Christmas. Tom had replied promptly urging him to come and assuring him that the necessary precautions could be taken to ensure his safety while at home. Thus his brother describes that Christmas Eve in the home at Barnagurraha under the Galtees :

> " Darkness set in and no Liam. The old home was so strange without him. We were all trying to be happy at supper, I being the only one to know he would surely attempt to come. How often I walked out into the darkness and listened sadly. At 8.30

a knock at the door, and rushing out to receive another rebel—Dinny Hannigan, afterwards Brigade General of East Limerick—Liam was waiting behind the pier of the gate lest some of the neighbours be in the house. At that time people had not learned to keep their tongues quiet. That was a great night. Three of us brothers watched the boreen, each his turn of an hour till dawn. . . . Nobody knew he was home that Christmas. After dark each night I strolled with him for hours down the old boreen, and he was happy. He would talk on one subject only—the Irish Republic."

The longest continuous period during which Liam remained in Dublin during the Tan War was after Christmas, 1919. About 7th January, 1920, he went there, accompanied on the journey by Tadhg Crowley and Eamonn Tobin, of Ballylanders. He remained until 7th March. During these two months he was in frequent consultation with the officers of the G.H.Q. Staff, particularly with Richard Mulcahy and Michael Collins. With Dan Breen and Seán Treacy he had many an animated discussion about plans for developing the fight. It was during this visit to Dublin that he underwent a slight operation for the removal of a troublesome tooth. He feared that he might talk under the anaesthetic, and he arranged that Dan Breen would be present during the operation. He was happy when Dan was able to assure him afterwards that he had been satisfactorily silent.

While in Dublin, on this and on later occasions, Liam stayed at the home of Mr. and Mrs. John O'Mahony, De Courcy Square, where there was always a cordial welcome for him. Once during his first visit the home was raided in the day time, but the raid did not appear to be specially for him. On another occasion when he was at the Abbey Theatre with Miss O'Mahony (now Mrs. Florence Burke), they met Seán Treacy there. As a result of a warning, all left before the performance ended, and they had only reached O'Connell Street when the Abbey was surrounded.

A proposal was now put to him which, if he had accepted it, might have changed the whole course of his subsequent activities. He was offered the post of Deputy Chief of Staff. There is nothing that I know of on record to indicate the reasons which influenced him in declining to accept this promotion. There is only a guarded reference to it in a letter to his mother on 28th March. Having told her that there was a position he could take up in Dublin any time he wished, he went on to say : " I intend remaining in the country to help the boys while things remain at their present pressure." It is reasonable to assume that he preferred the active warfare of the field, which he knew would develop in the South, to the wider but no less dangerous duties of a G.H.Q. staff officer.

On 7th March he travelled to Cork with the Tipperary hurling team, amongst whom he had many friends. From the city he went to his own brigade area. Two weeks later he was back in Cork again to take his place publicly in the ranks of his fellow-officers from all parts of Ireland who marched behind the remains of Tomás MacCurtain, Commandant of Cork No. 1 Brigade and Lord Mayor of Cork, who had been murdered by R.I.C. men on 19th March.

In the letter to his mother referred to above, he wrote:

> "You have heard, I expect, that I attended the Lord Mayor's funeral—yes, I and several like me risked anything and everything to see the last of a noble soldier. He was one of my best friends in the cause, and I have indeed felt terribly over him. He was foully murdered by the enemy, but the hour is at hand when they shall rue the moment they did so."

These were no empty words. When a man like Liam comes to this, only one consequence is possible—action against the enemy, fearless, determined, ruthless action.

CHAPTER 6

REPRESSION BY MURDER AND TERROR

*Our Patriotism is measured, not by the formula in which we
declare it, but in the service which we render.*

PEARSE

IN the Spring of 1920, when Liam was very fully occupied with
plans for activities in the brigade area, his attention was diverted
for a short time to deal with a serious problem which had developed.
He became concerned about the implications of certain crimes which
had been committed in the area under his command. The R.I.C. had
practically ceased to carry out the normal police duties of peace
officers, leaving a small criminal element in the community free to
exploit a situation favourable to lawlessness.

As part of the general policy of supplanting British institutions by
governmental machinery under national control, Dáil Éireann, had
in June, 1919, decreed the establishment in every county of national
Arbitration Courts. To enforce the authority of these Courts and to
enable them to function completely, a Police Force was essential.
This force was drawn from the ranks of the Volunteers, and in each
brigade and battalion area remained under the discipline and control
of the commanding officers. In the early months of 1920 selected
Volunteers were detailed in each company to act as Republican police.
Brigade and battalion police officers were appointed, and the force
became one of the special services then being organised in the Army.
This force contributed valuable service to the national movement
in the ensuing eighteen months. One of its most striking achievements
was in Cork No. 2 Brigade area.

In the early hours of the morning of 17th November, 1919, two
bank officials travelling in cars from Millstreet to open their branch
offices at Knocknagree for a fair on the same date, one carrying
£10,000 and the other £6,700, were held up at Ballydaly by armed and
disguised men and robbed of the whole sum. The crime was reported
to the R.I.C., but beyond arresting a local Volunteer officer who had
no connection whatever with the matter, they took no serious steps
to trace the criminals or bring them to justice. In the British press
it was freely stated, without a shred of evidence, that the crime had
been committed by Sinn Féin. Rumours circulated in the district to

the effect that persons connected with the national organisations were involved in the occurrence.

So seriously did Liam regard these reflections upon the national organisations, and the menace of a criminal element in the community capable of carrying out robbery on this scale, that he took the most vigorous steps to investigate the occurrences and bring the perpetrators to justice. The case was a difficult one. The robbers had made their plans circumspectly and with thoroughness. The normal facilities available to a police force in the investigation of a crime of this kind were not at the disposal of the newly organised Republican police. Up to the middle of March no clue had been discovered which threw any light on the mystery of the identity of the gang, and no evidence was available to justify action against any individuals.

Liam then moved to Drishanebeg, near Millstreet, and personally supervised the inquiries upon which he concentrated all the locally available resources of the Army. He was completely successful. The local officers were deeply impressed by the methodical thoroughness he exercised in assembling and assessing the little scraps of information which finally led to the discovery of the criminals. A complete check of the population in the Ballydaly neighbourhood convinced him that the robbery had not been committed by local men. He widened the scope of his inquiries. And then a few small events emerged—a light seen on a mountain six miles from the scene in the early hours of the morning of the robbery, an armed man on horseback at a place where no armed men should be without the knowledge of the local Company Captain, an apparent search, as if for something hidden, made suspiciously in an old graveyard—these things pointed the way to a solution of the crime.

On 24th April, 1920, warrants were issued for the arrest of the ten men who composed the gang which carried out the robbery. On the same night detachments of the Millstreet Battalion, in support of the local Republican police, entered the town of Millstreet and eight of the wanted men were arrested. The search which these arrests involved occupied several hours. The R.I.C. forces in their fortified barracks in the town did not dare to interfere.

The Army had no jails or other places of detention for prisoners. Prisoners were in fact an embarrassment and a nuisance. They had to be fed and guarded in the houses of Republicans. Nevertheless, these prisoners were held in custody pending trial, and Liam gave orders that they were to be treated as well as the conditions would permit. He even ensured for them supplies of tobacco and cigarettes.

On 27th April he himself presided over a special Court before which the eight prisoners were tried. At the second interrogation preceding the Court the ringleader had broken down, made a full confession and disclosed the hiding place of his share of the money. Four of his confederates did likewise, and a total sum of £9,208, had been recovered before the sitting of the Court. Seven of the prisoners were found guilty. Five were sentenced to deportation from Ireland for terms varying from fifteen years downwards, and two were sentenced to exclusion from the brigade area. The sentences were carried out by armed escorts. Later the ringleader returned, but was again arrested, brought before a Court, and had five years added to his sentence, after which he was again deported. All the money recovered was returned to the banks.

In thus turning aside for a while from his principal duties and ridding the area of a criminal gang, Liam Lynch had demonstrated the integrity of the Army and its ability to detect and punish evil-doers, at a time when these functions were crimes in the eyes of British law, and when the officers and men who thus vindicated justice were themselves in many cases fugitives from the vengance of the occupation forces. Moreover, he had raised the prestige of the whole organisation throughout the country, and set an example which put an effective end to any similar acts of crime. For this meritorious action he and his brigade were complimented by G.H.Q. What was more important, they earned the respect and approval of every law-abiding citizen.

The matter had also a wider significance. It demonstrated the extent to which the armed Royal Irish Constabulary had abdicated its normal police duties, and that at a moment when the force, was, for the first time in its history, being shaken to the core by discontent and resignations. No impartial observer, looking at the facts of the Millstreet bank robbery, could any longer accept the British con-tention that the organisation which concerned itself with the detection and punishment of the perpetrators of this crime, that concerned itself with the administration of justice and the protection of the com-munity from a criminal element, was merely a murder gang. It must also have been clear to any person seeking the truth about the situation as it then was that the men who controlled this organisation had acted with creditable efficiency and with a sense of public responsibility.

The events of the first six months of 1920 determined the final character and course of the struggle. The first important factor was the widespread and persistent efforts of the occupation forces to arrest or otherwise eliminate the most active officers and men of the I.R.A. thereby forcing substantial numbers of them to abandon their normal occupations and devote their whole time to Army duties. The second determining factor was the collapse of R.I.C. morale.

That collapse had resulted from the attacks made upon their posts by the I.R.A., from the policy of social ostracism operated against them by general consent of a large majority of the people, from large scale resignations from the force and the virtual cessation of recruitment to it. That position forced upon the British Government the necessity of recruiting Englishmen into the R.I.C. and of creating another and a new pseudo police force—the Auxiliary Division. That procedure was dictated by British reluctance to admit the existence of a state of war in Ireland, and by their frantic endeavours to maintain the fiction that they were dealing with a small gang of criminals who had terrorised the population into acquiescence with their extreme views.

All the measures of repression so far taken by the British Government had failed utterly to stem the mounting tide of determination which now animated every section of the people engaged in the struggle for freedom. In the three years ended December, 1919, 174 proclamations under the Defence of the Realm Act had been issued in Ireland. Dáil Éireann had been declared prohibited and suppressed. Similar edicts of suppression had been made against the Irish Volunteers, Sinn Féin, Cumann-na-mBán and Gaelic League. Raids by military and police at all hours of the day and night had become commonplace. Arrests were numerous. The jails in Ireland were full. Towards the end of January over sixty persons were arrested and deported to England. A murder campaign, under the cloak of official secrecy, was being pursued by a blood-thirsty element which was an integral part of the occupation forces. These measures had not been effective.

British reactions to that situation followed the pattern of the worst tradition of British Government in Ireland. Irish national aspirations were to be beaten out in blood and terror. General Sir Nevil Macready, the instrument of this policy, accepted appointment as G.O.C. British Forces in Ireland on 23rd March, 1920, and took up duty on 14th April. Shortly afterwards Sir Hamar Greenwood replaced Mr. Ian Macpherson as Chief Secretary. Macready had recorded in the bluntest terms his own view of the policy which should be pursued. Referring to discussions between Sir Henry Wilson, Chief of the Imperial General Staff, and himself, he says :[1]

> " Before I crossed to Dublin we had several long talks on the general situation, from which it was clear that he firmly held to a policy of stamping out rebellion with a strong hand, a policy with which I was in absolute agreement on the understanding that the government would provide the necessary means, a

[1] *Annals of an Active Life*, Vol. 2, p. 428

vital condition on which I was by no means sanguine, even then."

As an indication of the vigour with which he proceeded to use the " strong hand " he records that, by the end of April, 1920, 241 known or suspected officers of the I.R.A. had been dealt with, a third of whom came from County Cork.[1] It may be said however that the incipient breakdown of police intelligence had resulted in the inclusion amongst the internees of a substantial number of men who were not Army officers, and of some who were not Volunteers. Nevertheless this is an indication both of the organisation and of the area from which Macready feared the greatest threat to his mission of " stamping out rebellion."

As part of the "necessary means," the British Government recruited 8,000 men for the R.I.C. in Great Britain. A high percentage of them were as unprincipled a lot of ruffians as ever wore uniform. The majority were unfit for employment as peace officers. Some were convicted criminals, many had criminal tendencies. But they were fit material for the work contemplated by their paymasters. It was not police work. They were joining an armed force. The fact that the R.I.C. was armed was the rock upon which it foundered. Sir Joseph Byrne, the Inspector-General of the force who had been removed from office to clear the way for the new policy of murder and terror, had stated in a report to the British Government : " If we had no rifles we should be quite safe . . . we do not need rifles for the discharge of our ordinary duties."

The R.I.C. had now ceased to perform the ordinary duties of a police force. Because of the fact that it was armed, the logic of events had driven it steadily in the previous three years into active opposition to the national will. Its members were now faced with the alternatives of resignation or participation in a policy of ruthless repression against their own people. Many resigned, some joined the I.R.A., a few remained in the force to work for us, thereby risking not only their livelihood but their lives.

Attacks on police and on their barracks became general in the early months of the year. In County Cork, Carrigtwohill barracks was captured on 2nd January, 1920, after a fight in which the walls were breached by explosives. The arms and ammunition which it contained fell into the hands of the attackers, but the garrison were set free after surrender. It was the first barracks in Ireland to be captured by attack since 1916. Many similar actions had taken place, not all of them so successful. In Cork No. 2 Brigade three R.I.C.

[1] *Ibid.*, p. 241

men on patrol had been disarmed at Aghern on 31st January. On 16th February Aghern barracks was attacked. The action was unsuccessful owing to failure of the explosive. The I.R.A. had one man seriously wounded by grenades thrown from the building. He was Volunteer Michael Condon, of Bartlemy Company. Three or four others were slightly wounded.

The first reaction of the British authorities to these attacks was to close down a number of the smaller police posts, and concentrate their garrisons in the towns and larger villages. Amongst those evacuated in Cork No. 2 Brigade area were Araglin, Aghern, Ballynoe, Ballyhooley, Glanworth, and Glenville. These were amongst the 258 police barracks burned down and 44 otherwise destroyed all over the country on 3rd April, in the most widespread single action so far undertaken by the I.R.A.[1] Apart from the good effect which this had upon the morale of the Volunteers, it was valuable in that it cleared substantial areas completely of hostile forces. These areas thereafter constituted islands of relative safety in which conferences could be held, training carried out, and in which officers and men on the run were to some extent relieved of the perpetual strain which the conditions of their service imposed.

The incorporation into the R.I.C. of the British element popularly known as the Black and Tans destroyed whatever was left of the morale of that force. A new cadre of officers was introduced, designated Divisional Commissioners, and drawn from high ranking ex-officers of the British Army. The Commissioner appointed for Munster was Lieut. Col. Gerald Brice Ferguson Smyth, D.S.O., King's Own Scottish Borderers. In his brief service in that post he earned for himself an unenviable reputation and met a fate he deserved. But he revealed the murderous policy to which the R.I.C. was being incited.

On 19th June, accompanied by other high ranking officers, including General Tudor, later Commandant of the Auxiliary Division, Divisional Commissioner Smyth visited Listowel barracks, where already trouble had arisen between the old members of the force and the newly recruited Englishmen. He made a speech which epitomised the new policy:

> " Well men, I have something of interest to tell you : something I am sure you would not wish your wives to hear. Sinn Féin has had all the sport up to the present and we are going to have the sport now. . . . I am promised as many troops from England as I require, thousands are coming daily. I am getting 7,000 police from England. . . . Police and military will patrol

[1] Cmd. 709. H.M. Stationery Office, 1920.

the country at least five nights a week. They are not to confine themselves to the main roads but to take across the country, lie in ambush, and when civilians are seen approaching shout, ' Hands Up.' Should the order not be immediately obeyed, shoot, and shoot with effect. If persons approaching carry their hands in their pockets and are in any way suspicious-looking shoot them down. . . . The more you shoot the better I will like it, and I assure you no policeman will get into trouble for shooting any man . . . we want your assistance in carrying out this scheme and wiping out Sinn Féin."

There were men in that barrack who, despite the worst that Depot training had done to them, were still Irishmen. Their leader, Jeremiah Mee, answered Smyth's peremptory, " Are you prepared to co-operate," by stripping off his uniform cap, belt and arms. " By your accent," he said, " I take it you are an Englishman, and in your ignorance you forget you are addressing Irishmen." Tossing his equipment on the table, he continued, "These, too, are English—take them. . . ." So menacing was the attitude of the eighteen policemen assembled in the dayroom that the officers had to leave the barracks without being able to take any action against the men who had defied them so contemptuously. Later, there was a similar occurrence in Killarney barracks. On 9th July the *Irish Bulletin* published a circumstantial account of the events. Acting on good intelligence, Cork No. 1 Brigade struck swiftly. On the evening of 17th July Divisional Commissioner Smyth was shot dead in the Country Club, South Mall, Cork. It was a blow equivalent to a major victory in the field for the I.R.A.

Meanwhile the most infamous of all the forces of the Crown in Ireland was being recruited—the Auxiliary Division of the R.I.C. Composed mainly of ex-officers of the Army, Navy and Air Force, most of these men had seen service in the recent European War. They were a tough lot, potentially good fighting material, and they were paid the then attractive remuneration of one pound per day. The conditions under which they served accentuated an inherent laxity of discipline, amounting to licence. Eight companies of the force, each about one hundred strong were eventually recruited under the command of Brigadier-General Crozier. The first contingents arrived in Ireland in July, and later one company was stationed in a commandeered house, Mount Leader, near Millstreet, in Liam Lynch's brigade area.

Upon the morale of the Irish forces the events of the first half of 1920 had an exhilarating effect. The mere resumption of the struggle would have been heartening. But the resumption of it on a new plan which offered great possibilities of development and expansion, which had achieved moderate success, and which had above all provided a means of securing some modern arms, was the most significant event in the life of the young army. Morale is a sensitive, elusive thing, hard to define. But no one who experienced the high and gallant spirit which animated the I.R.A. in 1920 and 1921 could ever afterwards be unconscious of its presence or absence in an organisation. It was not a unit morale, such as mercenary armies take great pains to build up for its fighting value. It was national in fibre and content, embracing the whole Army, binding it into a strong brotherhood of unity, defiant of death or despot. Liam's letters at this time reflect his happiness. " It's a grand generation to live in," he wrote in one of his letters to Tom.

Once taken, the decision to resume the struggle was irrevocable. It had been taken only after mature deliberation and with full appreciation both of the hazards of such a policy and of the very limited means available to sustain it. The minority responsible for the decision were inspired by a spirit of extraordinary determination to succeed against all odds. The idea had matured slowly during the two previous years, in the course of which a large body of men had adjusted themselves mentally to a new concept of the historic struggle, and now when that concept began to be given expression in action it evoked a resurgence of self-sacrifice, loyalty, ingenuity and daring such as this nation had not known for many a day.

The national effort of 1920-21 had three significant features in its military aspect which distinguish it from all previous attempts to attain liberty. In the first place it was a radical departure from the traditional mode of previous insurrections. 1798, 1803, 1848, 1867, and even 1916 had all been dominated by the idea of remaining in the field under arms as long as possible after an insurrection began. They committed the whole available force to the conflict at the first blow, and stood or fell by the result. The guerilla idea was a fundamental departure from that policy. Secondly, previous efforts had been much influenced by the hope of foreign aid. In 1920-21, the I.R.A. had no thought or hope of obtaining any military assistance from outside the country, except to the extent that it might be possible to purchase and import arms. Thirdly, the I.R.A. had an advantage not possessed by any Irish Army since the Confederate War—the approval of a national government constitutionally elected by the votes of an overwhelming majority of the people.

Apart from the moral effects of that position it was valuable in that it assured a certain, though limited, financial support for Army needs. In one sense it was an added responsibility for in the last analysis everything else depended upon the ability of the Army to

remain on the offensive and strike effectively. It had created the Irish
Republic ; it was the force upon whose continued existence the
functioning of Government depended ; it was the main instrument
and security of the Government's executive power. The departments
of State operated to the extent, and only to the extent, that it was able
to protect them from molestation.

The arrests of officers and men created no serious disruption of
Army organisations or activity. There was everywhere a sufficient
reservoir of personnel unhesitatingly prepared to step into the shoes
of everybody removed by arrest. The widespread and continuous
raiding by British Forces had, however, the effect of compelling a
growing number of Volunteers to abandon their normal employments
and go on whole-time service. They received no remuneration, and
lived on the generosity of the people until towards the end of the
year when Brigade and Column Quartermasters had developed plans
for feeding and to some extent clothing them. As far as their duties
permitted these officers and men at first combined in small groups,
and remained continuously armed. They were the nuclei of the
Flying Columns.

At mid-1920 the I.R.A. was in effect on active service and in the
field. Brigade Staffs in Munster and in a few other active areas were
devoting their whole time and attention to Army duties. Some
Battalion Staffs were in a similar position. A number of men were
on whole-time training duties. All Volunteers carrying on their
normal occupations were aware that they might be called upon at
any time to leave their employment and come out on active service
for such periods as might be necessary. Such calls increased in
frequency as the struggle intensified, but because of the shortage of
arms, the general policy aimed at keeping the number of men on
whole-time service down to those who could be armed. Wherever
possible, therefore, men returned to work in field, factory or office
when the particular operation for which they were called out was
completed. This was generally possible in the country Battalions.
Where it was not possible, they joined the expanding groups on
whole-time active service. That development was in the pattern of
all I.R.A. organisation. It was not rigid, and adapted itself very
readily to the changing needs of a fluid situation.

This flexibility is evident in the ease with which the organisation
was expanded during 1920 to embrace new services made necessary
by greater activity. When Liam returned to his brigade at the
beginning of March, 1920 and set up his headquarters at Mourne
Abbey—a position more centrally situated than Glenville—the
importance of what were known as the special services was becoming
apparent. He appointed additional officers on the Brigade Staff

with definite responsibility, each for his own service—Tadgh Burns for Intelligence, Charles O'Connor for Engineering, Jack Barrett for Communications, Patrick Healy for Police, Con Moylan for Munitions. In each battalion and company officers and men were detailed for duty with these services. Liam always upheld the principle of giving an officer the maximum amount of authority and freedom of action, and of holding him absolutely responsible for the results. His ready delegation of authority and responsibility tapped new sources of energy, and increased still further the resilient strength of the basic organisation.

Men still vividly remember the infectious enthusiasm with which he nursed the development of the guerilla idea in his own brigade, and eagerly watched its growth in others. First, while his force was acquiring a mental adjustment to combat, activities were directed mainly towards acquiring serviceable arms; secondly, these arms were used for attacks on police posts and small patrols, with the result that the small posts were driven in, leaving substantial areas clear of enemy forces; thirdly, the continuous sniping and minor attacks on all enemy strongholds, creating a state of nervous uncertainty extremely destructive of enemy morale; and finally the organisation of flying columns for larger operations from the best trained, fittest and keenest officers and men.

The whole development was built on captured arms. Incidentally, that is one of the causes of the uneven development of the conflict over the country as a whole. Brigades that depended on any sources outsides themselves for arms remained unarmed. They found themselves in the later stages of the struggle unable to capture arms from the occupation forces because the conditions which obtained in 1919 and the first half of 1920 were no longer operative. One of the important results of the adoption of the guerilla idea was to put the initiative into the hands of the I.R.A. It became thereafter a question of their own ability and resourcefulness whether or not they retained it in any particular area.

While his own brigade was developing its capacity for progressively larger actions, Liam, always seeing the whole Army and the whole fight as a unit, became sensitive to another aspect of the problem which was beginning to loom up. I.R.A. activity over the country as a whole was uneven and in many areas merely spasmodic. Indeed, despite all efforts, that continued to be the position down to the Truce. Liam became concerned about the possibility that the absence of continued activity over the whole country would enable the British Forces to concentrate against the active areas. In May, 1920, *An tOglac*[1] expressed official concern about this tendency.

[1] 1st May, 1920.

"Those places where guerilla warfare against the enemy has been waged with great activity and effectiveness represent only a small portion of the country. In some parts there has been marked inactivity. Officers who are neglecting their duty must get on or get out."

It could not be said of Liam and his officers that they possessed a technical proficiency in the trade of arms equivalent or superior to that of officers of similar ranks in a modern regular army. But they had something at least equally valuable, a very practical appreciation of the military situation, a sense of where strength and weakness lay on both sides, and a concept of striking effectively while conserving their limited resources in arms and trained men. In the early days of the Volunteers their training came largely under the influence of British Reservists or ex-service men. Whatever danger may have existed then that the force would have become a bad copy of a mercenary army it was completely dissipated by the Rising and the subsequent reorganisation which threw the Volunteers entirely on their own resources for planning and training. From that point onwards the I.R.A. had all the attributes of natural growth.

Liam had studied military text-books and had acquired a sound general knowledge of tactics. He had undergone a course of training at G.H.Q. when he was there in January and February. But his most consistent mentor in planning his strategy and tactics was his intense practical study of his own military problem on the ground. Out of that he developed a sound appreciation of the principles of guerilla warfare, and always behind all his plans and actions lay that cool, fierce, unwavering determination to succeed. The meagre military resources at his disposal were handled with a skill rarely equalled and never surpassed in similar circumstances.

The success of I.R.A. operations depended very largely upon the initiative of local Commanders, particularly at brigade and battalion level. There was not in 1920 any higher formation than a brigade. Brigades were then so well integrated and organised that they were generally responsive to the will and example of their commanders. In 1920 their situation was without military precedent in the historic struggle for liberty. The plans upon which they were operating, the difficulties they had to overcome, the methods forced upon them by inadequate and insufficient arms, all combined to demand originality and vision at every level of command, but particularly in the local leaders. These officers had considerable freedom of decision and action. They, and they alone, could avail of unforseen opportunities to act effectively. A chance allowed to slip through their hands rarely recurred.

Liam had a very acute appreciation of that position, so strongly in contrast to what obtains in large scale modern warfare. He had the kind of vision which saw the war as a whole, reached into the future and visualised its developments. From the beginning he had a keen appreciation of the value of leadership and example. As his fighting forces grew progressively larger and better armed he continued to encourage local initiative, to develop the policy of ceaseless pressure on the enemy and the widest possible distribution of the fighting, constantly using the elements of speed and surprise to strike effectively while conserving his force and retaining freedom of action.

The success of such a policy called for constant vigilance, excellent organisation, swift decision and bold action. The decisive year which followed found Liam and his brigade fit and competent to take a leading part in the fight.

CHAPTER 7

CAPTURE OF GENERAL LUCAS

Our independence must be had at all hazards.
TONE.

TOWARDS the end of April, 1920, when investigation of the Millstreet bank robbery had been successfully concluded and the criminals punished, Liam returned to his headquarters at Mourne Abbey. The Mourne Abbey Stores, owned by Batt Walsh and Jeremiah Buckley, became the clearing house for all despatches to and from brigade headquarters while it remained in this area. The stores were subsequently burned down by British Forces as a reprisal after the ambush which took place nearby.

Here Liam was joined by his Vice Commandant, George Power, who was then beginning his own term of whole-time active service. George had been evading arrest for some time. On 1st April he was surprised on a visit to his parents' home at Fermoy and arrested by a combined force of military and police. Receiving permission from the officer in charge to go upstairs to collect some clothing, he went into a bedroom, locked the door, escaped through a window and got clear away.

At no time during the previous eight months, in which the shadow of the hangman's noose hung over the heads of Michael Fitzgerald and his comrades in Cork Jail, did Liam forget them or become resigned in his inability to rescue them. Several rescue schemes were considered, but no plan could be worked out which promised success. Worrying at the problem in his persistent way, Liam pioneered a new phase of the struggle. If the British could take our officers and men prisoner, why should we not take theirs ? True, we had no jails to hold them, consequently we should be selective, and take only prisoners of high rank. Could a few senior enemy officers be taken and held, possibly used as hostages ? Liam thought their capture was feasible. Holding them might be a difficult and troublesome problem, but the very fact of their capture would have a good effect upon Volunteer morale.

The brigade intelligence organisation was beginning to operate that systematic observation of enemy movements and activities which gave such valuable results later. The Fermoy Battalion, asked to report on the movements of enemy senior officers, very quickly turned in the information that a few of them permitted themselves occasional relaxation by fishing on the Blackwater. Liam considered them a fair target. He worked out a careful plan which was kept a closely guarded secret. Basing his decision upon reports of observed routine at Fermoy Barracks, and the movements of senior officers, Liam fixed Saturday, 26th June, as the date for the attempt to capture them.

He selected two of his best officers—Commandant Seán Moylan, Newmarket Battalion and Commandant Patrick Clancy, Kanturk Battalion to act with George Power and himself in taking and escorting the prisoners. Moylan and Clancy travelled from their own areas in a Ford car the property of Mr. D. D. Curtin, Newmarket, which that staunch supporter of the I.R.A. had lent without questioning the purpose for which it was to be used. Some days before the 26th Liam and George Power moved into Fermoy Battalion area, and made a final check on the details of their arrangements.

On Saturday scouts were posted to observe the fishing pools, and from Kilbarry, five miles east of Fermoy, a report came in the afternoon that General Lucas with two other officers had arrived and that all three were fishing. They were accompanied only by the General's personal servant. The four I.R.A. officers and the others immediately engaged assembled near the fishing hut and waited until evening. Then the hut was quietly occupied and the General's personal servant placed under arrest. The party then proceeded to round up the three British officers. One was encountered a short distance from the lodge to which he was returning. Taken completely by surprise, he offered no resistance and was led back a prisoner. Shortly afterwards a second officer was found and treated likewise. Coming through a small wood George Power came suddenly face to face with Lucas, and after a moment of mutual scrutiny, George ordered him to put his hands up. Lucas hesitated slightly then dropping his fishing rod he complied. He was disarmed and marched back to the lodge. Brigadier General Cuthbert Henry Tyndall Lucas, commanding the British 18th Brigade was a prisoner in the hands of the I.R.A.

When the prisoners were assembled in the fishing lodge neither Liam nor any of his companions were aware of the identity of the two officers acompanying the General. George Power than gave Lucas the names and ranks of the I.R.A. officers and asked him if he had any objection to giving similar information of his fellow officers. General Lucas replied that he had none, and thereupon pointed out Colonel Danford of the Royal Artillery and Colonel Tyrell of the Royal Engineers. He then enquired what the I.R.A. officers proposed to do with them. He was informed that all three would be held prisoners pending instructions from General Headquarters, and that in the meantime the facilities usually accorded to such prisoners would as far as possible be granted to them. They were allowed to have a meal at the lodge before being removed. Some hours later when Lucas' servant was released he was given a letter for delivery to the officer commanding the British post at Fermoy. In this letter Liam notified the capture of the three officers and repeated that they were being held and would be treated as prisoners of war.

The more difficult part of the project lay ahead. It was necessary to remove the prisoners to some safer area a considerable distance from Fermoy, and it was necessary to do it promptly because it was realised that the reactions to their capture would be swift and very probably violent. The brigade had no facilities for holding prisoners. Any person held in custody was an additional burden on our own people in whose homes they had to live and at whose tables they had to look for their daily bread. Liam was quite determined to treat his prisoners honourably and humanely, giving them the best accommodation that detention and security would permit.

The British officers had come to Kilbarry in a motor car. Volunteer Owen Curtin of Fermoy Company now took his place as driver of this car. Lucas and Danford, with Lynch and Clancy, took their seats in it, Liam sitting in front with the driver and Clancy between the two prisoners at the back. Power and Moylan took Tyrell in the Ford. The party set out in the direction of Mourne Abbey. The arrangment was that both cars would keep in touch as far as possible, with the Ford travelling fifty to one hundred yards ahead of the other car. The route had been settled.

For a time all went well. The cars headed south to avoid passing through Fermoy and maintained contact until approaching the main Cork-Fermoy road about two miles south of Rathcormack. The captured officers had now fully realised their position. Instinct and training alike urged them to make a bid for freedom. Lucas and Danford held a brief conversation in a language then unknown to Liam Lynch but subsequently discovered to be Arabic and, evidently by pre-arrangement, they sprang simultaneously on Lynch and Clancy. The attack was so sudden that the I.R.A. officers were at first at a disadvantage, being reluctant to use their arms, and they were in fact almost disarmed in the first onset. In the furious fight going on inside the speeding car the driver lost control, crashed into the roadside ditch and was rendered unconscious. The struggle between Liam Lynch and General Lucas was particularly severe both being athletic and trained men nearly six feet in height and evenly matched. In the first onslaught Lucas had got on top of Lynch, making frantic efforts to wrench the gun from him, and had almost succeeded when the door of the touring car gave away. Both were

thrown on to the roadway where the struggle continued until finally
Liam's superior strength and fitness wore Lucas down and he was
overpowered. Meanwhile Danford and Clancy, now also on the
roadside, were fighting desperately with Danford getting the
better of the encounter. He had almost succeeded in throttling
Clancy, and when Liam looked around after having overpowered
Lucas he saw at a glance that Clancy's situation was desperate. He
shouted to Danford, " surrender or I shoot," but Danford ignored
the command and maintained his grip on Clancy's throat, whereupon
Liam fired, the bullet striking Danford on the face causing him to
collapse over his opponent.

Meanwhile George Power and Seán Moylan in the Ford car had
gone some little distance before they noticed that the other car was
not following. They realised that something was amiss and turned
back. On rounding a bend of the road they saw the big touring car
lying in the ditch with the driver still unconscious at the wheel.
Nearby on the grass verge Colonel Danford was lying in a pool of
blood, with General Lucas bending over him rendering first aid,
while Liam was attending to Paddy Clancy.

A hurried conference was held on the roadside at which Liam
decided to release Colonel Tyrrell in order that he might attend to
Colonel Danford, and to send the Volunteer driver of the wrecked
car, who had now regained consciousness, to the nearby village of
Rathcormack for a doctor. It was further decided that Lynch,
Moylan and Clancy would take Genral Lucas in the Ford car and drive
to Brigade Headquarters. George Power was instructed to proceed
to Dublin and report the capture to General Headquarters. He
narrowly escaped capture himself that night when the house in which
he stayed was surrounded by a raiding party. He travelled to Dublin
by train next day and reported to Michael Collins and Cathal Brugha
who questioned him closely about the captured officer, the problem
of his safe custody and the general position in the brigade.

Meanwhile, the Ford car turned west near Rathcormack and went
on to Mourne Abbey. Here they picked up Jerry O'Hanlon and
Jerry Buckley who guided them to the house of Patrick O'Connell,
Lackandarra, Lombardstown, on the southern slope of the Blackwater
valley, where Lucas was detained during his first night as a prisoner
in the hands of the I.R.A. " When General Lynch's escort and
prisoner entered the house," John O'Connell writes, " two of the
party were unknown to me, namely Lynch and the prisoner, Lucas—
two very reserved personalities in my opinion. I did not even know
captive from captor until the prisoner was put to bed." They had
travelled some distance on the main Cork-Mallow road before taking
to the bye roads again in the direction of Lombardstown. When they

arrived at O'Connell's it was found that the house held another
prisoner, a railway official from Mallow who had been arrested by the
I.R.A. for co-operating with the British Forces by dismissing railmen
who refused to work trains carrying troops and equipment. Railway-
men generally were at the time, refusing to operate trains on which
armed members of the occupation forces attempted to travel or which
carried munitions of war. Many of these men had lost their employment as a result, but the boycott continued. The rail official prisoner
was transferred to Buckley's at Lackandarra, and Lucas remained at
O'Connell's.

On the same afternoon one of the O'Connell family, who was a
student at St. Colman's College, Fermoy, arrived home on holidays
and informed Liam that reports in Fermoy credited the British with
the intention of carrying out reprisals for the capture of General
Lucas. Liam thereupon wrote a further intimation to the British
Headquarters in Fermoy that he held Lucas as a prisoner of war, and
was treating him as such. Michael McCarthy cycled to Fermoy with
the message. That did not save the town. For the second time
British forces turned out in strength on the night of 28th and indulged
in a prolonged orgy of looting and destruction. The grim ordeal to
which the people of Fermoy were subjected had one ludicrous aspect.
Above the crash of breaking glass as shop windows were smashed in,
the cockney accents of drunken soldiers rose in intermittent shouts :
" We want our ——— General back " : " Give us back our ———
General."

Intensive searches over a wide area, in which aircraft and large
forces of infantry in lorries were used, followed the capture. Mrs.
O'Neill, the caretaker of the fishing lodge, was very closely questioned
by the police as to the identity of those who took part. In the hope
of breaking down her refusal to give information they arrested her
son Patrick, who was a Volunteer. That action availed them nothing ;
like many another Irish mother at the time she refused to be
intimidated.

On the night of the 28th Lucas was moved to McCarthy's at
Greggane near Lombardstown, and next day he was transferred to
the West Limerick Brigade area. After a few days there he was taken
across the Shannon and placed in the custody of Commandant
Michael Brennan, O/C East Clare Brigade. While in that area he
was accommodated at Mrs. Horgan's, Cratloe, Ernest Corbett's,
Bunratty (now the Castle Hotel), Corney Brennan's, Smithstown
House, and Hastings, Tullyvarrigo, where Shannon Airport now
stands. A report of a projected British raid on that area made it
necessary to transfer the prisoner to John Hartigan's Waterpark,
Castleconnell. After a little over a month in custody, on 30th July,

while being transferred from East Clare to Mid-Limerick Brigade, General Lucas escaped from his escort near Oola, eighteen miles from Limerick city, and was able to rejoin his own forces.

Immediately after his capture Liam Lynch asked his prisoner to name a place where letters coming to him from his relatives could be collected and undertook to have all communications of a personal nature delivered to him. Lucas selected a shop in Fermoy, and this shop was used for the purpose during the period of his detention. On the night of 1st December following, a party of Auxiliaries from Tipperary, probably on their way to the funerals of their comrades who had been killed in the Kilmichael ambush a few days previously, stopped at Fermoy and indulged even more freely than usual in drink. Late that night some of the party wantonly murdered a British Army ex-officer named Prendergast and threw his body into the Blackwater. They seized a man named Dooley whom they also threw into the river, and at whom they fired several shots, but he fortunately escaped with his life. Not satisfied with these activities they proceeded, for no apparent reason, to burn a number of shops in the town. One of those destroyed was O'Keeffe's, the place selected by General Lucas for the collection of his mail. Whether this was deliberate or merely a piece of indiscriminate villainy on the part of these gentlemen is not known.

At a time when the exploits of the I.R.A. were beginning to acquire the characteristics of surprise, unexpectedness, efficiency and success, the capture of General Lucas was a first class sensation. When so many of our own people were suffering imprisonment, there was jubilant approval of Liam's action, which submitted even one highly placed enemy officer to the same restriction of liberty, though perhaps under more congenial conditions. It was a gift to the ballad-makers, and one popular piece of doggerel, to the air of " The Blarney Roses," was sung all over Munster.

By the summer of 1920 the issue between the Irish people and the occupation forces was very sharply defined. The activities of the Army, loyally supported by the people, had stripped off the last shreds of sham legality under which British rule in Ireland had for so long masqueraded, leaving the country, as Mitchel said in '48, " as naked of all law and government (save the bayonet) as on the day when she first rose from the sea." For those who still retained some faith in British professions of high principles, it was a salutary experience. The situation provoked some plain speaking on the part of British leaders, and of the Press, which had an excellent effect upon Irish morale. Speaking on 31st March, Lloyd George said :

"If you asked the people of Ireland what plan they would accept, by an emphatic majority·they would say: 'We want independence and an Irish Republic.' There is absolutely no doubt about that. The elected representatives of Ireland now, by a clear, definite majority have declared in favour of independence—of secession."

But such a declaration by the Irish people, made in the most democratic and emphatic manner, could not be permitted to become a functioning reality so long as a British Government considered that it ran counter to Imperial designs. Traditional British policy was expounded by other leaders in terms which left no doubt of their determination to flout the peoples' will and put down their national aspirations with a Cromwellian hand. Speaking in the House of Lords on 19th May, Lord Birkenhead said :[1]

"It is the policy of the Government, whether the struggle is long or short, to employ the whole available forces and the whole resources of these islands to restore law and order and to render utterly impossible the campaign with the object of secession."

In the *Sunday Pictorial* of 13th June Winston Churchill wrote :

"We can never concede to Irishmen the means of setting up an independent republic, nor can we ever compel Ulster by force of arms to participate in a Dublin Parliament."

Sir Hamar Greenwood was petulant but not less emphatic :[2]

"We won't stand for independence, we won't have a republic. Short of that, if this campaign of violence and anarchy ceases, the Irish people can have any measure of Home Rule they can agree on."

If there was at the time on the part of the British Government any accurate assessment of the determination of the Irish forces and of the Irish people to make their declared freedom effective and their Republic a functioning State, it is not evident in the public statements of responsible Ministers. After his escape General Lucas had made a report to his own authorities, a copy of which was secured by General Headquarters Intelligence. In this report he had included his impressions of I.R.A. organisation as he had seen it through contact with officers and men during the month he was a prisoner. He was

[1] *Hansard*, p. 430
[2] Interview, *Chicago Tribune*, Paris edition, 24th May, 1920

F

impressed by their standards of discipline, determination and efficiency. In his opinion the British Forces in Ireland were confronted with a much graver military situation than was generally realised. He foresaw a long and bitter struggle, in which it would be necessary to employ much larger forces than those then garrisoning the country if the Army of the Republic was to be exterminated.

Extermination of the Irish armed forces, openly in the field, by midnight murder, or by shooting or hanging prisoners under the contorted legality of Martial Law, was in fact the policy decided upon by the British Cabinet. Voices which raised doubts of the efficiency of such a policy were ignored. In the House of Lords on 26th April Lord R. Cecil said :

> " We are drifting through anarchy and humiliation to an Irish Republic . . . we will never settle the Irish question except in accordance with the wishes of the Irish people."

The Cabinet decision was an obvious and base abandonment of the principles of freedom for which Britain had ostensibly fought a great war. The ruthless use of force to bludgeon a people into submission against their will had nothing to recommend it except that it had succeeded in Ireland in the past. He would be a bold prophet who would say it would fail in 1920. To the cynical Lloyd George and the Cromwell-minded Sir Henry Wilson it must have appeared utterly incredible that a great Empire's resources would be insufficient to obliterate a comparatively small and poorly armed guerilla force. Both were realists enough to appreciate that that little force was the kernel of the situation. And yet, as Wilson records :[1]

> " The Cabinet were frankly frightened, and agreed that all Macready's proposals must be acceded to."

The British Army of occupation in Ireland at that moment exceeded in strength the first British Expeditionary Force sent to France to fight the Germans in 1914.

Sections of the British Press began to display a refreshing clarity in discussing the issues involved in the struggle. The Irish demand for freedom could no longer be ignored, nor could the plain facts of the situation be confused or clouded by specious argument. National unity and national determination had put Ireland in an almost impregnable position. In justice, her case for complete sovereign independence was unanswerable. Her armed forces, however

[1] *Diary of Sir Henry Wilson*, p. 237

inadequate, could not be talked out of existence, intimidated by British prestige or purchased by British gold. They had the Fenian faith and believed, with James Stephens, that "Ireland's trained and marshalled manhood alone can *ever* make—could ever have made—Ireland's opportunity."

Moreover, they did not fight pitched battles as their fathers had done, they did not oblige the army of occupation by pitting their puny military resources against it in the open and being annihilated. They were ubiquitous and silent and deadly. Irishmen in the service of their own country had at last begun to utilise some of those fighting qualities which they had so often displayed in the service of foreigners. The British Government was no longer confronted merely by a political problem. They had on their hands the necessity for a military reconquest of Ireland as grim as any which faced Elizabeth Tudor.

"It is clear," wrote the *Morning Post* of 7th May, "that if the Government do not intend to lose Ireland they must set about the task of reconquest immediately." The London *Globe* of 13th May was no less outspoken : "Southern Ireland is rapidly becoming a Sinn Féin Republic bitterly hostile to England. . . . Sinn Féin is winning all along the line and if England does not rapidly bestir herself in earnest Ireland will be lost." On the same day the *Daily Herald* said : "General Macready's plans for Ireland are much on the lines of a reconquest of the country. Hundreds of blockhouses are to be established and strongly garrisoned by troops."

In an interview given to the *Daily Express* early in April, Lord French had admitted that the Volunteers were an Army, "properly organised in regiments and brigades, led by disciplined officers." What was more significant was that this voluntary army had taken the initiative, and was confronting the occupation forces with a whole series of new problems. Tactics were adopted which kept the occupation forces under a perpetual strain, speculating where the next blow would fall, and sure of nothing except that it would be different to anything which had happened previously. In that situation normal routine was disrupted in a thousand ways, continuity of training became impossible, recreational facilities were severely restricted, and the whole occupation force became infected with the conviction that it was a hated imposition on a hostile country.

"A close and constant watch," Macready records,[1] "was kept by the staff on every fresh phase of tactics employed by the rebels, in order to forestall them, or to counter as rapidly as possible the new development, the information being always at the service of the

[1] *Annals of an Active Life*, Vol. 2, p. 445

police forces whose legitimate duties gradually approximated more and more towards purely military operations, for which they had little experience or training."

Early in June the British Government began to give effect to the policy of reconquest by military force upon which they had decided. Through every port reinforcements were poured into the country. "Four fresh battalions arrived."[1] There were then forty British battalions in Ireland, but Macready estimated that he required nine more before he could attempt the enforcement of Martial Law. Much of the energy and strength of his forces were of necessity dissipated fruitlessly on activities and duties which contributed little to the solution of the military problem. For instance, the equivalent of six or seven battalions was eventually detailed for guarding prisoners in internment camps.

In the disposition of the new reinforcements the British authorities had to decide whether they would attempt a re-occupation of the areas from which their forces had been driven, or whether their additional strength would be used to reinforce existing posts. Suitable billeting accommodation presented some difficulties. Generally, no attempt was made to re-occupy villages or posts evacuated by the R.I.C., but frequently existing R.I.C. posts in towns were reinforced by the establishment of new military posts in close proximity.

Since these military outposts were equipped with wireless, they gave the R.I.C. posts a more secure means of communication with their headquarters, which made prolonged attacks upon them by the I.R.A. more difficult, and their capture virtually impossible. All R.I.C. posts were now diluted by a percentage of British personnel, wireless installations were not infrequently operated by men of the Marine Service, so that it was not unusual to see in the occupation forces of any town, the khaki of the regular soldier, the dark bottle green of the R.I.C. men, the motley of the Black and Tan, the blue of the Marine Service and the glengarry bonnets of the Auxiliaries. Barracks and posts had steel shutters, barbed wire and sand bag defences. The forces occupying them were on a war footing. Referring to the month of June Macready writes : " Orders were issued that all troops when on duty were to consider themselves as on active service, and to use their weapons with effect regardless of results."[2]

Liam Lynch's brigade area, already heavily garrisoned, received its quota of British reinforcements. New military posts were established at Mitchelstown, Castletownroche, Liscarroll, Banteer and Kanturk—

[1] *Ibid.*, p. 478
[2] *Annals of an Active Life*, Vol. 2, p. 469

points already occupied by R.I.C.—and later an Auxiliary Company was billeted at Mount Leader, a large house half a mile from Mill-street. The brigade area included two of the most extensive British posts outside the Curragh—Buttevant and Fermoy—and two of the largest training camps—Kilworth and Ballyvonaire. Moreover, the brigade did not possess any large area containing natural defence facilities, and it was cut, through its whole extent from west to east, by the river Blackwater. Every bridge from Mallow eastwards was covered by an adjacent enemy post.

For each individual I.R.A. Brigade Commander his own area presented a series of problems peculiar to itself. The extent to which he was successful in first partly arming his forces, then preserving them from annihilation and finally using them to strike effectively at the enemy, was the measure of his capacity and of the extent to which he had studied his problems uninfluenced by extraneous conditions. It is doubtful if any brigade area in Ireland presented greater difficulties from the I.R.A. point of view than those which Liam Lynch faced and overcame in Cork 2.

Being in command of one of the few brigades then pioneering the offensive against British occupation forces, he had not merely to solve his local problems but also, somehow, to carry G.H.Q. along with him. His national concept of the struggle and his sense of discipline demanded that. How cautious the G.H.Q. attitude was (rightly so perhaps, taking the position all over the country into account) may be judged from the text of General Order No. 4 issued on 26th May, 1920.

" No action of anything like a military nature shall be taken or ordered to be taken by any Volunteer except in so far as this is covered by definite orders or permission actually received from his superior officer. The fact that action of a certain type has taken place in one brigade or battalion area does not con-stitute such an order or permission."

Although this was described as being designed to preserve the offensive spirit by preventing it from running riot in hasty action to its own detriment, there was in fact little danger of such a result, and the practical effect of the order was a prohibition of any military activity of an offensive nature without specific G.H.Q. sanction. Liam continued to press his views on G.H.Q. by correspondence and visits, but it was not until the end of July, at a conference which representatives of some southern brigades had with the Chief of Staff and other G.H.Q. officers, that a limited and conditional sanction to ambushing was given. Even then the Chief of Staff was anxious to insist that in all cases British Forces so attacked would be called on to surrender before being fired upon.

In an earlier visit to Dublin at the beginning of July Liam had discussed with the Headquarters Staff a proposal to exchange General Lucas for Robert Barton who was then a prisoner. The project did not materialise. In a letter to Tom, referring to this visit, he mentions that he had been out at Ireland's Eye with Michael Collins and Harry Boland on a Sunday afternoon. Boland, he said, gave glowing accounts of developments in America. President de Valera was then in the United States, where he had organised a powerful section of public opinion in favour of recognition of the Irish Republic, and successfully floated a national loan. The active support of Irish exiles in America, Australia, Britain, and many other countries was then being organised to finance and encourage the national struggle and that support was a significant factor in determining the final issue.

While Liam kept a friendly eye on the development of the political side of the movement, and felt that it was an essential factor in the conflict, he was convinced that its role was secondary, that " the young men at home should stick to the one and only course " and that their place was in the Army. " The Army," he wrote to Tom, " has to hew the way to freedom for politics to follow."

CHAPTER 8

LYNCH AND MACSWINEY CAPTURED

We must be prepared for casualties in the last battle for Irish Independence
TERENCE MACSWINEY.

ONCE only did Liam Lynch fall into the hands of his enemies. He was arrested at the City Hall, Cork, with Terence MacSwiney and a number of other officers, on the night of Thursday, 12th August, 1920. Of all the thousands of similar raids carried out by British Forces at the time there was none in which the element of chance played a larger part. Nor was there any more highly charged with consequences which influenced, perhaps decisively, the course of the national struggle in that crisis. Events, both before, during, and after the raid, moved on a course which seemed predestined to create a combination of dramatic circumstances, all contributing to and setting the stage for one of the most heroic challenges to tyranny ever made by a single man. The raid marked the beginning of the hunger strike in which Terence MacSwiney sacrificed his life and captured the imagination of the world. The two or three hundred British troops in lorries and armoured cars, who concentrated on the City Hall that August afternoon, flashed upon public notice one scene in a dramatic series of events, some of which had gone before and the gravest of which were to follow.

It has not been possible to determine with any certainty why Liam decided to come to Cork on 12th August. It seems possible that he came to attend an I.R.B. meeting called for the City Hall on that night, but this is not certain. MacSwiney was unaware of his intention and did not expect a visit from him just then. They had met little more than a week before. Liam, Terry and Liam Deasy had represented the three Cork Brigades at a G.H.Q. conference in Dublin on 31st July. Liam Lynch had gone to Dublin via Limerick, where he had passed the night of the 29th, and had returned to his own area immediately after the conference.

On the morning of the 12th Liam sent for Patrick McCarthy, Lackanineen, and instructed him to get a car as quickly as possible and be ready to travel with him to Cork. On the way to the City from Mourne Abbey he told McCarthy that he wanted to see Terry MacSwiney and had brought Paddy with him as he himself did not

know the city very well. They drove to Con Twomey's house at
Dublin Hill, outside the city. There Liam remained while Paddy
McCarthy went into the city to make an appointment for him with the
Lord Mayor. After some difficulty, and with the assistance of Joe
O'Connor, Brigade Quartermaster, Paddy McCarthy saw Terry and
arranged that he would be available to meet Liam at the City Hall at
7 o'clock.

Except on the occasions when his public duties required his
presence eleswhere, Terence MacSwiney had spent most of his days
and nights at the City Hall in the previous four months. Various and
onerous duties fell upon him as T.D. for Mid-Cork, Lord Mayor of
the City and Commandant of Cork No. 1 Brigade. In the two last
named posts he had succeeded his friend and colleague, Tomás
MacCurtain, who had been brutally murdered by Crown Forces in
March. His brigade maintained an armed guard on him day and
night. This was protection against the possibility of assassination
rather than with a view to resistance in the event of a raid for him
in force by the enemy. It was almost inevitable that sooner or later
an attempt would be made either to assassinate him or to silence him
by arrest on some pretext.

On the occasion of his acceptance of the office of Lord Mayor he
had made a speech which must rank amongst the great patriotic
utterances of all time. In the course of it he said :

> " I come here more as a soldier stepping into the breach than
> as administrator to fill the first post in the municipality. At a
> normal time it would be your duty to find for this post the
> Councillor most practised and experienced in public affairs.
> But this time is not normal. We see in the manner in which our
> late Lord Mayor was murdered an attempt to terrify us all.
> Our first duty is to answer that threat in the only fitting manner
> by showing ourselves unterrified, cool and inflexible for the
> fulfilment of our chief purpose—the establishment of the
> Independence and integrity of our country—the peace and
> happiness of our country. To that end I am here. . . . I wish
> to point out again the secret of our strength and the assurance of
> our final victory. This contest of ours is not on our side a rivalry
> of vengeance, but one of endurance—it is not they who can
> inflict most, but they who can suffer most, will conquer—though
> we do not abrogate our function to demand and see that evil
> doers and murderers are punished for their crimes. . . . Those
> whose faith is strong will endure to the end and triumph. The
> shining hope of our time is that the great majority of our people
> are now strong in that faith."

Having referred to those who had yet no vision and who cried out that the sacrifice was too great, he went on :

" But it is because they were our best and bravest that they had to die. No lesser sacrifice could save us. Because of it our struggle is holy—our battle is sanctified by their blood, and our victory is assured by their martyrdom. We, taking up the work they left incomplete, confident in God, offer in turn sacrifice from ourselves. It is not we who take innocent blood but we offer it, sustained by the example of our immortal dead and that divine example which inspires us all for the redemption of our country. Facing our enemies we must declare our attitude simply. We ask for no mercy, and we will make no compromise."

It had been arranged to hold a Brigade Council meeting of Cork No. 1 Brigade at the City Hall on the night of 12th August. The venue was not normal for such meetings. It had been selected on this occasion to facilitate the Brigade Commandant. The usual time would have been 8 o'clock, and this probably explains why MacSwiney fixed the time of interview with Liam Lynch at 7. Liam was not aware, before he came to Cork, that a Brigade Council meeting was to be held that night. A small number of I.R.B. officers from the County had also arranged to meet there on the same night. Terence MacSwiney had no knowledge of the intention to hold this meeting, and Liam Lynch would have known of it only if he was one of those summoned to attend, which is not established.

So tense had the struggle then become that each side was straining every nerve to gain even the slightest advantage. Behind the open military activities by both sets of opponents a silent, ceaseless, deadly Intelligence battle was being fought out by unseen forces day and night. I.R.A. Intelligence had developed to the point where it was beginning to utilise all the resources available under the conditions which existed. Mails were a potential source of information to both sides. Our raids upon them, which earlier had been somewhat indiscriminate, were now under complete control, and were made only with a specific objective in view. Raids on mails by British Forces were not general. They recurred periodically and appeared to follow no set pattern.

But a British raid on local mails at one point on 9th August gave them an indication of the possibility that some officers would meet at the City Hall three days later. There was not in the manner in which this information fell into British hands any question of treachery, or even of culpable negligence, on the part of anybody concerned ; it was an accident of war which gave the astute Intelligence officer of the British 6th Division at Cork a slight lead which he fully utilised.

He had a stroke of luck, and he made the most of it. The raid on the City Hall was decided upon, apparently without consultation with the R.I.C., as no police took part in it.

A Dáil Éireann Court for the city was in session in the Council Chamber that night, at which an important action listed for hearing was one in which a prominent English Insurance Company was plaintiff. Published statements to the contrary notwithstanding, Terence MacSwiney was not concerned with its proceedings in any way. The Court was in session when the raid began. Judges, lawyers, witnesses and members of the general public were amongst the mixed bag of prisoners. The military raiding party were in sufficient strength to surround the whole block of buildings, including the City Hall and the Corporation stores and Cornmarket to the rere of it. They dropped off their lorries on three sides of the buildings, climbed over the railings or forced their way in where necessary, and quickly over-ran the whole area.

Terence MacSwiney should have been in possession of a key to a camouflaged door giving egress from the City Hall to the Cornmarket and Stores. He had inadvertently left it at Belgrave Place, and it is doubtful if he could have made any effective use of it, so quickly was the whole area surrounded. With the other I.R.A. officers he did in fact get out into the sheds at the rere of the City Hall before he was placed under arrest.

One of the main charges against MacSwiney at his Courtmartial was that of being in possession of the key to the police cipher then in current use. It was sworn that this document was found in his desk at the City Hall. That was untrue. The facts are as follows. The police cipher key was normally in my custody. In the early afternoon of the day of the raid, the Brigade Commandant sent for me and said that it was essential I should attend a meeting of the 8th Battalion Council on that night. I should leave immediately for Kilnamartyra. I do not now remember what had arisen in the 8th Battalion to occasion this decision, but I left the city almost at once, and did not return until next day.

In my absence from Brigade Headquarters the police cipher key was in the custody either of Joe O'Connor, the Brigade Quartermaster, or of Miss Nora Wallace, St. Augustine Street, whose shop was in effect Brigade Headquarters during the whole period of the struggle. It was Joe O'Connor who brought the cipher key to the City Hall on the night of 12th August. He had it in his possession when he was placed under arrest after the military over-ran the buildings. The guard on the prisoners was watching them closely, and some who had attempted to destroy documents were prevented from doing so. Joe O'Connor found it impossible to destroy the sheet of paper containing the cipher key, but he managed to dispose of it in a crevice of the woodwork in the shed where the prisoners were first held. The document could not therefore have been found anywhere except where Joe O'Connor disposed of it. The Brigade Quartermaster wished at the time of the Courtmartial to make a public statement of these facts, and take responsibility for the document. This was not sanctioned, as it was believed that it would have no influence whatever on the Lord Mayor's sentence. It was, nevertheless, a remarkable coincidence that a cipher should have figured in his first trial and in his last. Five years earlier he stood in the dock of the Cork Police Court to answer a number of charges, one of which was unlawful possession of a cipher. On that occasion he was acquitted.

About 9 o'clock, one and a half hours after the raid had started, the raiding party had sorted out their prisoners. They released all with the exception of the following twelve:

Terence MacSwiney, O/C Cork No. 1 Brigade.
Seán O'Hegarty, Vice O/C Cork No. 1 Brigade.
Joseph O'Connor, Quartermaster, Cork No. 1 Brigade.
Daniel Donovan, O/C 1st Battalion, Cork No. 1 Brigade.
Michael Leahy, O/C 4th Battalion, Cork No. 1 Brigade.
Liam Lynch, O/C Cork No. 2 Brigade.
Patrick McCarthy, M.C.C., Lackanineen, Mourne Abbey.
Michael Carey, 18 Ninety Eight Street, Cork.
Laurence Cotter, 30 Abbey Street, Cork.
Thomas Mulcahy, 28 Marlboro Street, Cork.
Patrick Harris, 11 St. Nessan Street, Cork.
Thomas McCarthy, Nicholas Street, Cork.

The British Forces had made the most important capture of the war in Munster. It included besides Liam Lynch almost the entire staff of Cork No. 1 Brigade as well as two of the ablest and most active of the Battalion Commandants, the O/C's of the 1st and 4th Battalions. The O/C 2nd Battalion, Commandant Michael Murphy, had the narrowest of escapes. He was in Anglesea Street on his way into the Brigade Council meeting when the British Forces appeared on the scene. All the prisoners, with the exception of Liam Lynch and Michael Leahy, gave correct names and addresses, believing that they would be identified in any event. Liam gave his name as James Casey, and his address as 25 Camden Street, Dublin, and these are the particulars which appear in the prison record. Michael Leahy gave his name as Thomas Power.

While under military guard in a shed at the rere of the City Hall the Army officers had a brief exchange of views about their position.

Terence MacSwiney was the last to join the group, and he immediately proposed to his fellow prisoners that they should hunger-strike from that moment. Neither Liam Lynch nor any of the other officers expressed any strong views for or against the proposal, though some at least amongst them were not enthusiastic about hunger strike as a weapon. It was clear that MacSwiney had determined his own line of action. No one opposed the suggestion, and all refused food from the time of their arrest. Even if they had not done so then, the matter would almost certainly have been determined for them when they were brought to Cork Jail. The untried prisoners there led by Maurice Crowe of Tipperary, with Liam's 1st Battalion Commandant, Michael Fitzgerald as deputy leader, had started a hunger-strike on the previous day, in which the new prisoners would undoubtedly have joined.

The prisoners were taken to the waiting lorries and removed to the military detention barracks, where they were detained on the first night. Next day they were removed to Cork Jail. There Liam met for the last time his old friend and comrade, Michael Fitzgerald. Another prisoner who met him there was a relative of his, Tom Crawford, who had taken a prominent part in activities in the East Limerick Brigade.

Three days later, on the 16th the British authorities did an extra-ordinary thing. They released all those taken in the City Hall raid except Terence MacSwiney. It would be fruitless now to speculate upon the reasons for this action. It has been suggested that it was an error, and that a cancellation of the release order came to the jail after the prisoners had left. It seems incredible that if men like Liam Lynch and Seán O'Hegarty had been identified they would be released. It will be remembered that no police took part in the raid, and no police were brought in at any later stage to identify the prisoners. What is certain is that if all the officers captured had been recognised and detained it would have been a staggering blow to two of the Cork brigades. In concentrating their action against one man the British took the final step which set that man upon the road to martyrdom and immortality. His death, seventy-three days later, was an event which rang around the world, carrying into the hearts of freedom loving people everywhere appreciation of his ideals, sympathy for the cause he served so nobly, and detestation of the power which sought in vain to crush his heroic spirit.

No explanation of Liam's release seems feasible except that his captors did not recognise him or take the normal precaution of having a police check on the identity of the prisoners. There is little doubt that the British authorities were savagely determined to remove from the arena an opponent named Lynch. Two men of his name met sudden deaths about this time in circumstances which illustrate the excesses to which the actions of the Crown Forces were carried by faulty intelligence and murderous intent. Both of the victims were natives of localities close to Liam's birth-place—one of Hospital and the other of Kilmallock, County Limerick. The absence of co-operation between two sections of the occupation forces which created the accident of his release, unidentified and obviously without check on the fictitious name which he gave, was in the same pattern as the purblind activity which resulted in these two tragic deaths. When R.I.C. espionage broke down the Crown Forces had lost the first round of the battle.

On 4th August the home of a man named James Lynch, living at Hospital, County Limerick, was raided at night by military forces. Lynch was questioned closely while being eyed intently by two or three soldiers. No attempt was made to arrest him and the party left. The family knelt down to say the Rosary. Before it was finished two or three soldiers returned, beckoned to Lynch and told him the officer wished to speak to him outside. Lynch went out and walked about two hundred yards from the house. There a volley was fired into his body and he fell dead.

On the night of 22nd September John Lynch of Kilmallock, a County Councillor, Gaelic League enthusiast and Republican Court Registrar for East Limerick, retired to his bedroom in the Exchange Hotel, Dublin, where he was staying for a few days. Later in the night a party of men called to the hotel and asked the boots for Councillor Lynch's room saying they were friends of his. Two of them wore British uniform. A few of them went up to the room, came down soon afterwards and the whole party left. About an hour and a half later a party of police arrived, saying they had been sent by the British Military Command as a murder had been committed in the hotel. They knew who had been murdered, they asked for Councillor Lynch's room. The astonished boots took them there. Stretched on the bed was the body of Councillor Lynch. He had been shot at close range with a revolver carrying a silencer.

Within the next day or two the British Authorities evidently discovered that they had got the wrong man. The most astonishing efforts were made to hush up the murder. On the 26th it was officially announced that no inquest would be permitted, neither would a public funeral be allowed. Three separate official reports were issued, all differing in certain essential points. Councillor Lynch, they said, had fired on Crown Forces who went to arrest him, and had to be shot in self defence. But independent doctors saw the body as it lay in the hotel bedroom; they saw that the revolver had been held so close to his face that powder had burnt his chin. There was no sign of a struggle in the room. All the resources of Government attempting to conceal the truth were ineffective in hiding from the people the grim fact that official murders were being perpetrated and the murderers shielded by the highest authorities. There is no conclusive evidence that these two men were shot in mistake for Liam Lynch, but the circumstances appear to suggest it.

On the night of his release from Cork Jail Liam remained in the city and stayed in a house at Richmond Hill where Joe O'Connor found accommodation for him. He was anxious to get back to his own command, and despite the effects of four days' hunger strike he left for Mourne Abbey early next day. There bad news awaited him. Commandant Patrick Clancy, who had taken part with him in the capture of General Lucas, and Commandant Seán O'Connell, both of Kanturk Battalion, had been killed at Derrygallon near the town on the 16th. The background of that disaster is a good illustration both of the difficulties which an inexperienced and poorly armed force had to contend with in fighting regular troops, and of the risks to which all officers and men were exposed in the active areas just before the formation of the flying columns.

On 14th August a British military plane made a forced landing owing to engine trouble at Drominagh, Banteer. Twenty British soldiers were brought to the scene and set as a guard on the grounded aircraft. The local battalion officers decided to attack this party. Surprise or stratagem may have given them success. A set battle could not. They had no weapons to match twenty rifles and an ample supply of ammunition. They had spirit and the same courage as the unremembered pikemen who charged into the muzzles of Walpole's Artillery at Tubberneering in '98. But the I.R.A. had to learn by experience that valour alone does not win battles in their circumstances. The fight lasted two hours, a number of men were wounded on both sides, but the attack was not a success, and the attackers had to withdraw without capturing the position or adding any arms to their meagre supplies.

All that could be said for the action was that it was a valuable lesson for the officers and men engaged. It gave a much needed opportunity of mobilising men from almost all of the battalion's ten companies and giving large numbers of them experience of protection and scouting duties. Enemy posts at Kanturk, Newmarket, Banteer and Millstreet were all within easy striking distance of the scene, so that any of the protection parties could have found themselves engaged at any time. The lessons of the attack itself could not be lost upon anybody participating.

In reprisal for this attack British Forces made a surprise raid on Kanturk on the following night. In resisting capture Clancy and

O'Connell were killed. Despite the risks involved Liam attended the funerals at Kanturk. As an interim measure of protection, pending other developments which he had in mind, he issued an order to his brigade that all known officers being sought for by the enemy should be permanently armed.

The development of the special services at this time illustrates the manner in which facilities existing in the area were utilised to bring the brigade to a higher state of efficiency. Communications—a vital service in every army—may be taken as an example.

The railway system provided some natural arteries of communication for the internal correspondence of the brigade, as well as the speediest and most reliable method of maintaining contact with G.H.Q., and it was used extensively. All railway employees who were Volunteers were so efficiently organised that there was a daily collection and delivery of despatches. Very rarely even in the most difficult times did a letter take more than two days between G.H.Q. and Brigade Headquarters.

In the early days of the brigade all despatches going through the railway service were cleared at Fermoy Station. When headquarters was moved to Mourne Abbey, Mallow became the vital centre of collection and distribution. When a second step westward had to be taken—an involuntary one, unlike the move from Glenville— Lombardstown became the point on which the daily routine of communications revolved. The stationmaster and all the members of his family rendered splendid service.

But these arteries had to be fed and at times supplemented. From both Mallow and Fermoy a service of cyclist despatch riders radiated on established routes to the various Battalion Headquarters, and in a few cases these routes were extended to give contact with adjoining brigades. Despatch riders operated day and night from company to company in relays. For the exceptionally urgent or important message members of Cumann-na-mBán were always available.

When the use of bicycles was prohibited except under permit from the British Forces, other means had to be found in some parts of the brigade area. Horse drawn transport was largely used for a time. In an effort to discloate the service, which they knew was operating under their noses, the British adopted in 1921 a system of cavalry patrols on roads, holding up and searching all travellers. This was a particular menace in the Fermoy area. It was circumvented by using despatch riders on horseback. Some hunters were com- mandeered for the purpose.

At no time were the British successful in dislocating the routine of the communications service for more than a few days, and then only at times and in places where they had concentrated very large forces for extensive raids and searches of a locality. The additional traffic resulting from the presence of brigade headquarters in any area, the comings and goings of officers and despatch riders, the duties of guards and sentries, no matter how unostentatiously carried out, occasionally resulted in attention being focussed on a particular locality. That caused the gradual movement of brigade headquarters westwards as the conflict developed in intensity, from Glenville to Mourne Abbey, from Mourne Abbey to Lombardstown, from Lombardstown to Nadd.

The Restoration of Order in Ireland Act became law on 9th August, and regulations under it were issued on 21st. From the British point of view the reign of terror was now legalised. Courts-martial and military courts could now try persons for treason, treason felony, felony and lesser offences. They could compel the attendance of witnesses. Coroners' inquests were suppressed, and military courts of inquiry substituted. Uncontrolled powers of arrest and internment were placed in the hands of the military authorities. They could restrict motor traffic, prohibit the holding of fairs and markets and impose curfew at will. Trials under the Act could be held in secret. This facade of legality was the last British effort to maintain the fiction that a state of war did not exist. The next step was Martial Law. And the weapon which was to defeat both was being forged by the Army—the Flying Column.

CHAPTER 9

THE FLYING COLUMNS FIGHT SUCCESSFULLY

Thank God for it, the game is afoot at last.

MITCHEL.

EARLY in August, 1920, immediately after his return from the G.H.Q. Conference, Liam Lynch took the first step towards the creation of a brigade flying column. A brigade council meeting consisting of the staff and officers from each of the seven battalions met at O'Callaghan's, Quartertown. Its principal business was to select a number of officers and men from each battalion who were prepared to undertake whole-time active service and whose absence would not disrupt battalion organisation. It was decided that they would form a striking force to operate whenever opportunity presented itself within the brigade. It was found to be unnecessary to order anybody to join the column. There were far more Volunteers from each battalion that could be armed, conveniently assembled or rationed at one point at the same time. Commandant Patrick Clancy was appointed Column Commander, and training was to begin on 15th August.

Events, however, upset this programme. Liam himself was arrested and Paddy Clancy was killed. The column assembled at Mrs. Hickey's, Badger's Hill, Glenville, on 15th September. Ernie O'Malley, then a G.H.Q. Staff Captain and later O/C 2nd Southern Division, arrived in the area and undertook the training of this first column. Its members were :—

Newmarket Battalion : Patrick McCarthy, Michael O'Sullivan, Dan Browne.

Fermoy Battalion : Larry Condon, John O'Mahony, Daniel Daly, John Fanning.

Castletownroche Battalion : Daniel Shinnick, Jeremiah Donovan, James O'Neill, Michael O'Halloran.

Charleville Battalion : Patrick O'Brien, Thomas Coughlan.

Kanturk Battalion : Daniel Vaughan.

Millstreet Battalion : Patrick Healy, John Healy.

Liam himself, his Vice Commandant, George Power, George Lennon, Vice O/C Waterford Brigade and M. Creed also took the two weeks course of training. The provision of food, equipment and some necessary clothing for the column was made possible by the very generous action of the North Cork Executive of Sinn Féin, which voted a sum of £400 for the purpose.

The column went into position near Bartlemy in the hope of attacking a police patrol, and also occupied a position at Keim in the Glenville area, but no action took place in either case. During the whole period of hostilities that was a frequent experience. An ambush position could not be occupied with safety for more than a few days. If the anticipated enemy party did not arrive the column had to be withdrawn.

Liam visualised the brigade column as an initial effort which would ensure uniformity of training methods and inculcate the idea of aggressive offensive tactics everywhere that an opportunity presented itself. He outlined to his staff and the members of the brigade column his intention of creating an active service unit in each battalion for such operations as a column of eighteen to thirty men could undertake with the arms available to them. Two or more of these columns should at all times be capable of combined action for larger operations. In this way he proposed to secure the widest possible distribution of the fighting in his area, the security of his forces, the maximum utilisation of the basic company organisation on scouting and protection duties, and the solution of the problem of housing and feeding a number of men on continuous active service.

At the conclusion of the two weeks course of training the battalion officers with the column returned to their own commands and began to put these ideas into effect. Meanwhile the brigade staff were watching intently for a suitable opportunity for action.

One item of information with regard to the barracks occupied by the 17th Lancers at Mallow appeared to offer possibilities. Two Mallow Volunteers, Richard Willis and John Bolster, were employed on the civilian maintenance staff of the barracks as painter and carpenter respectively. In the course of their employment they had ample opportunity of observing troop movements, the routine of training, and the rotation of guard duties. From these observations they thought that the capture of the barracks was possible. They reported their opinions, and these were transmitted to the brigade. The garrison consisted of one officer and thirty-eight non-commissioned officers and men. The officer and part of the garrison normally left the barracks each morning for the purpose of exercising the horses. During these periods the remainder of the garrison appeared to be a force well within the capacity of the brigade column to deal with. Willis and Bolster were ordered to report to brigade headquarters. They came out to Tadgh Looney's, Island, Burnfort where they gave a full account of their information in regard to the barracks to Liam Lynch and his staff and produced a sketch map of the post. Owen Harold, who had been billeted for some days previously in a house facing the barracks was able to give corroboration in regard to the movement of troops and the routine of the post.

A decision to attempt the capture of the barracks was made. The post was in a narrow side street off the main street, and one of the difficulties was that of bringing the attacking force within striking distance without attracting the attention of the strong R.I.C. contingent in the town. This difficulty was surmounted by moving the men into the Town Hall under cover of darkness on the night before the attack. The Volunteers did not move through the town but came in through the Park after crossing the bridge over the Blackwater near the town. The Town Hall was occupied without incident.

On the morning of the 28th September, 1920 no change took place in the routine of the garrison, the Lieutenant and part of his command leaving as usual for exercise. Jack Bolster and Dick Willis arrived at work at the usual hour but they brought with them this morning a man who masqueraded as a contractor's overseer. He was Captain Patrick McCarthy, Quartermaster of the Newmarket Battalion, who had been specially selected for the dangerous job of holding up the guard-room as soon as the attacking party arrived at the gate. Captain McCarthy, Willis and Bolster were armed with revolvers. The "contractor's overseer" went through the routine of measuring doors and windows while he waited for his comrades outside to begin the operation. About 9.30 a.m. the sentry on duty answered a knock on the small door beside the main gate. This door had a loophole covered by an iron grille. When the sentry pushed back the slide over the loophole a man presented an envelope, which he said was for the barrack warden, who was then in the barracks. The man carrying out this apparently innocent errand was Ernie O'Malley. The sentry opened the door slightly to take the envelope, and O'Malley said he wanted to give it to the barrack warden personally. While the sentry hesitated over this request he made the fatal mistake of allowing O'Malley to come close to him. O'Malley grabbed the sentry's rifle and wrested it out of his hands. Commandant Paddy O'Brien and another Volunteer immediately behind O'Malley pushed the door open. Liam Lynch and a small party were on their heels. The attackers were in.

The guard room was situated about thirty yards from the entrance gate and about midway in the block of buildings. McCarthy, Willis and Bolster, who were waiting beside it on the pretext of examining some defects, came into action the moment they saw their comrades at the gate. They rushed into the guard room and held up the guard

Immediately inside the main entrance on the left was an open shed where the senior N.C.O., Sergeant Gibbs, was at that moment supervising the shoeing of a horse. On seeing the first man of the raiding party come through the door, he rushed towards the guard room. He was called upon to halt but ignored the order. A shot was fired over him, but he did not stop. He was fired on point blank and fell mortally wounded at the guard room door.

The members of the guard were then marched out on to the square where they were held until the remainder of the garrison was collected from the various apartments. First Aid was given to the wounded Sergeant, and one of the garrison was left to attend to him. The remainder were locked into one of the stables.

While this was happening Liam had given the pre-arranged signal and three waiting motors cars were driven into the barrack. All the arms, ammunition and useful equipment was piled into them. The arms consisted of two Hotchkiss light machine guns, twenty-seven rifles, a revolver, Very light pistols, 4,000 rounds of ammunition and a quantity of bayonets and lances. Some petrol and hay from the barracks stores were set alight with the intention of burning down the buildings, but the fire went out after the departure of the Volunteers.

No rifles had been brought in by the attackers. They were armed only with revolvers to avoid attracting attention. Leaving the barracks each man carried a rifle and two bandoliers of ammunition, prepared to fight their way out of the town if necessary. The whole operation was carried out with great speed and precision. A time limit of twenty minutes had been put on it, and when the pre-arranged whistle signal was given at the end of that time the job had been completed. The R.I.C. post in the town was unaware of the occurrence until it was all over.

The three motor cars, driven by Leo O'Callaghan, Mallow and Seán and Paddy Healy of Millstreet, took the road to Glashbee, where the Ahadillane Company took over local protection of the material for that night. All the members of the raiding party got back to their base without interference or casualties. The captured arms were not dumped ; they were distributed to the battalions and thereafter were in daily use all over the brigade. About two hundred men of the Mallow Battalion were engaged on various protection duties.

Liam was jubilant at the result of the operation. He regretted the death of Sergeant Gibbs, a brave man who died doing his duty. The final instruction which Liam had given before the attack was, in fact, that no shots should be fired except in case of absolute necessity. This highly successful first action of the column was unique in that it was the first occasion on which the enemy military post was captured and stripped of its arms and equipment in daylight. The

effect of the capture of arms was particularly significant. The two
Hotchkiss guns helped somewhat to redress the balance hitherto
so heavily against the brigade. Willis and Bolster, who now joined
the column, were quickly trained in their operation and maintenance
by Volunteer Matt Flood of Fermoy, who had served in a machine gun
battalion of the British Army.

The aftermath of the raid was in the pattern now becoming familiar
to the civil population. In Mallow, however, it had a new feature.
Hitherto looting and destruction carried on by Crown Forces in
towns appeared to be wanton and spontaneous outbursts of lawlessness
on the part of indisciplined troops. The forces which descended on
Mallow from their barracks at Buttevant and Fermoy on the night
of 28th September, 1920 were under the control of officers, and they
set about the business of burning and looting public and private
property as an organised military operation. They created a night of
terror for the inhabitants of the town. The local creamery and the
Town Hall were burned to the ground. Drunken troops roamed the
streets, firing indiscriminately and throwing petrol-filled bottles into
any house showing a light.

A further sequel to the capture of Mallow barracks took place
eight months later. On 23rd May, 1921 a Courtmartial opened at
Victoria Barracks, Cork before which six men were charged with
the murder of Sergeant Gibbs. They were John Murphy, Fair Street,
Mallow; David Buckley, Farran, Mourne Abbey; Owen Harold,
42 Bank Place, Mallow; Denis Barter, Kilquane, Mourne Abbey;
Daniel McCarthy, Lackanineen, Mourne Abbey and Timothy Breen,
Brittas, Lombardstown. Five were later sentenced to death, and of
the five one was not a Volunteer. In connection with the sentences
Liam issued the following public statement in June:

"It is reported that four citizens of the Irish Republic have
been sentenced to death by a British Courtmartial on the grounds
that they took part in the successful raid on the enemy military
barracks at Mallow on 28th September, 1920. Their names are
John Murphy, Fair Street, Mallow; Denis Barter, Kilquane,
Mourne Abbey; Owen Harold, Bank Place, Mallow; and
Daniel McCarthy, Lahakineen, Mourne Abbey.

As the officer in charge of the operation in question I desire
to state publicly that none of these men had any part in it.

Furthermore, I wish to state that I alone am responsible for
all that was done on that occasion. The raid on the barracks was
carried out as a military operation on my orders by a body of
Republican troops acting under my direction, and I acted by
virtue of my commission as an officer of the Irish Republican

Army, under the authority of my superior officers and the Government of the Irish Republic, in accordance with the laws of regular warfare.

(Signed) Liam O'Loingsigh,
O/C Cork No. 2 Brigade."[1]

In a further statement published in the 16th July issue of *An tOglach* Liam says that the name of Denis Buckley, Farran, Mourne Abbey, who had also been sentenced to death, was inadvertently omitted from the list given in his previous letter, and that Denis Buckley was not a member of the I.R.A. and had nothing whatever to do with the attack. No comment is necessary now upon the type of procedure and evidence which could produce so grave a miscarriage of justice as the conviction and sentences on these men indicate. It was what passed for British law in Ireland in 1920. None of the sentences were carried out.

From Lombardstown, where the column had billeted after the capture of Mallow barracks, it moved on 30th September to Ardglass in the Charleville battalion area. Here an attack was planned on Churchtown R.I.C. barracks, but was cancelled at the last moment when information was received that the post was aware of the proposed attack. Later it was found that this information was false. The column then moved to Freemount and got in touch with officers of the Drumcollogher Battalion of West Limerick Brigade. An attack on an R.I.C. patrol was planned but did not take place. Commandant Patrick O'Brien of Liscarroll was appointed Column Commander. The Brigade Commandant, who had been in charge since its formation, devoted himself to the general duties of his own post although he remained with the column for some time longer.

At Freemount, Seán Moylan came to him with a proposal for an attack on a military party which travelled in lorries between Kanturk and Newmarket. These two towns, four miles apart, had strong garrisons of military and police. Here again the value of continuous observation and good intelligence reporting became evident. The reports of Jack O'Connell, the Newmarket intelligence officer, indicated that two lorries of military passed between Newmarket and Kanturk at least once weekly. Seán Moylan was convinced that a well concealed ambush party on this road would get action within a day or two. He urged on Liam also the value of close co-operation with the local units. Next day Liam, O'Malley and Moylan inspected the position suggested by the latter at Ballydrochane, and while doing so saw two lorries containing about twenty-four British soldiers pass along the road.

[1] *An tOglach*, 1st July, 1921.

The column was marched to Drominarigle the night before the attack. At 3 a.m. on 6th October it moved out across country to occupy the position at Ballydrochane before dawn. Silent and motionless, the men had to wait concealed until after 11 o'clock. Then came the long awaited sound of a lorry. Two were expected. It was planned to let the first one well into the position before the four men holding a farm cart inside an open gate rushed it out to create a road block. These men were signalled into action at the last minute ; they pushed the cart out and scuttled for cover. The lorry stopped ; no second one followed it, and the elaborate pre-parations were unnecessary. In five minutes the fight was over. The driver had been killed and all the remainder of the party wounded. Members of the column collected their rifles, equipment and ammunition. As the column withdrew they could hear a Lewis gun firing from the post at Kanturk.

Apart from its good effect on the arms position, this action was valuable for the experience it gave large numbers of men. The proximity of two enemy posts, and the possibility that the force which it was planned to attack might be larger than anticipated, gave Liam Lynch the opportunity of mobilising strong contingents of the Kanturk and Newmarket Battalions and employing them on protective duties. These men were armed only with shot guns and revolvers, since no rifles could be spared for them. They dispersed without casualties at the conclusion of the action.

In view of what happened in Mallow Liam decided that the British Forces would not find Kanturk undefended should they decide upon similar reprisals there. The column was therefore marched to Drominarigle after the ambush, and moved in that night to occupy Kanturk. British activities there had been closely watched by the local company during the day. Units were posted to cover the creamery and the main business portions of the town. No reprisals were attempted that night. The column withdrew at dawn. It was billeted near Keale Bridge in the Millstreet Battalion area for about a week. While there it co-operated in the capture of one of the Millstreet bank robbers, who had successfully evaded all previous efforts to arrest him.

About the end of October, 1920 the brigade column was de-mobilised and its component units reverted to their own battalions. Thence forward each Battalion began to build its own column of fifteen to thirty men, always keeping in mind the possibility of combining two or more of these forces for a large operation. By meetings of the brigade council, which were attended by the Commandant of each battalion and by visits to the battalions themselves Liam Lynch nursed the incipient development and training of the battalion columns. He was gratified to find that there emerged in every one of his seven battalion officers and men competent and eager to undertake any actions possible with the arms which they possessed. Anything less than twelve or fourteen rifles, supported by shotguns, offered only slight hope of success against the average type of enemy target available in the brigade area. From the point of view of the objective which they presented there was no longer any difference between the enemy police and military forces. " From the Spring of 1920 " Macready states,[1] " until the Truce of 1921 the police in Ireland were to all intents and purposes carrying out, or attempting to carry out, purely military duty, and the remains of the R.I.C. would have been amply sufficient to uphold the illusion of the civil power for the purpose of carrying out the policy of the Government."

At the western end of the brigade the Millstreet Battalion began getting together the nucleus of a column. The town of Millstreet, focal point of the battalion area, had for some time been subjected to bouts of wild night firing by its R.I.C. and Black and Tan garrison. An attempt had been made on the life of Father Joe Breen, C.C. He had been a member of the Irish Volunteers in Tralee before 1916, and, on his transfer to Millstreet after Easter Week, he had continued to give valuable services unsparingly to the Army. Compelled by the threat to his life to abandon his normal sacred duties for a time he maintained close contact with the I.R.A. and was always at the service of the fighting men.

Some members of the small battalion column took up positions in the town on the night of 22nd November with the intention of attacking an R.I.C. patrol. In the fight which ensued, and in which two Black and Tans were wounded, the brigade suffered a severe blow. Captain Patrick McCarthy was killed at Upper Mill Lane. A native of Meelin, he had joined the Volunteers immediately after 1916. He was arrested early in 1918, took part in the Belfast hunger strike under Austin Stack, was transferred to Strangeways Jail, Manchester, and succeeded in escaping from there in September, 1919. From his return to Ireland he devoted the whole of the remainder of his short life to the fight against the invader. He had taken a dangerous and decisive part in the capture of Mallow Barracks and again at Ballydrochane he had displayed that initiative and intrepidity so characteristic of him.

On the night of his death he was attended to by Father Joe Breen. Later that night his comrades removed his body to the house of Eugene O'Sullivan at Gortnavehy, where, guarded by the whole column, it was waked with the mournful reverence paid to dead

[1] *Annals of an Active Life* Vol. 2, p. 482

chieftains of old. On the following night Liam Lynch took charge of the funeral procession which set out for his family burial ground at Lismire where he was buried with full military honours.

Anticipating British reprisals for the shooting of the Black and Tans on the previous night Liam Lynch decided to occupy the town of Millstreet and afford its inhabitants protection against the expected actions of the garrison. He himself took charge of the I.R.A. forces in the town on that night. British forces did not however leave their fortified posts, and the members of the column were sent to billets before dawn after an uneventful night. Speaking to Captain Con Meany on that occasion Liam said: " No matter who is killed or captured by the British now, thank God there are plenty of men left to lead and carry on the fight."

The fog of uncertainty which clouds all insurrection was dissipating. He knew now what strength was with him, and what against him. He was confident that the fight would go on despite losses and sacrifice. Now, as always, he was thinking nationally, and although he knew that certain brigades in other counties were not fighting effectively, he had hopes that men would yet emerge in them of the calibre of those he led, and that they too would contribute their potential strength in achieving final victory. In the method of warfare now being developed by leaders like Liam, an inconclusive action, or even a local defeat, was not disastrous. The loss of trained officers and men was serious, and any diminution of the scanty supply of arms heartbreaking, yet there remained the great reservoir of eager men in the companies which covered every square mile of his territory, and behind them a brave people, steadfast and undaunted by terror.

The deaths of young, intrepid officers like McCarthy, Clancy and O'Connell in action, and later that of Michael Fitzgerald on hunger strike, were severe blows to the brigade. To officers and men alike they emphasised the grim reality of the price which had to be paid for freedom. Everywhere it was the best and most gallant of our fighters who were destined to make the supreme sacrifice. These men did not live to see the end of the struggle, nor taste the fruits of such success as was achieved; but their deaths were, above all else, the immediate and vital influence which steeled the hearts of their comrades and urged them on to heroic endeavour. This voluntary army, which the professional ranks of its opponents regarded with unintelligent scorn, had evoked in it by these sacrifices a spirit of high daring and disregard for death which was the core of its invincible strength thereafter.

Liam spoke for them all when in a letter to his mother a few months later he said: " I am living only to bring the dreams of my dead comrades to reality, and every moment of my life is now devoted to that end. . . . Thank God, I am left alive to still help in shattering the damned British Empire." In these days of ceaseless activity and movement he was transmuting the dreams of generations into sharp-edged weapons, tempering these weapons in the fire of conflict, and using them with a cool determination and skilful effectiveness which set a standard for the whole army.

A few days after Ballydrochane, while inspecting a proposed ambush position at Keimcarriga on the Macroom-Millstreet road with George Power, Paddy O'Brien and Captain Con Meany, he and his party had a narrow escape from capture when British forces came upon them unexpectedly. A few days later again he made one of his very few public statements. The occasion was the funeral of Liam O'Connell of Lackandarra who had been shot in an attack on an armoured car in Dublin on 14th October. He was buried at Glantane, and there Liam spoke briefly. " We are here," he said, " at the grave of one of our Volunteers whose young life is given for the freedom of Ireland. We will avenge his great sacrifice, and will continue the fight until it is brought to a successful conclusion. Many more may follow Liam O'Connell before this country obtains its Independence."

Curfew was being imposed generally on the towns and cities of Munster under the authority of the euphemistically styled Restoration of Order in Ireland Act. It was a further restriction of civil liberty which hardened public feeling against the occupation forces. More-over, as curfew duties were undertaken mainly by troops, enforcement of the regulations represented a wasteful dissipation of military strength without imposing any serious inconvenience on the I.R.A. Curfew was primarily a punitive measure against the whole population, the varying hours of enforcement at different times and in different localities being a regular barometer of I.R.A. activity. At one period it operated from as early as 5.30 p.m. in Cork City. It could not be enforced in the country. Except in a few of the principal cities, the vital nerve centres and unit headquarters of the I.R.A. were now in the country districts, so that as a curb on Army activities curfew was almost worthless.

But if the people in country districts were spared the restrictions imposed by the curfew regulations they were subjected to many other hazards and losses which tested severely their loyalty to the cause of freedom. The attempted destruction of the economic life of the country by the burning of creameries, the prohibition of fairs and markets and the indiscriminate shooting of persons pursuing their ordinary peaceful avocations, combined with the sporadic night raiding of fear-ridden and often drunken Auxiliaries and Black and Tans, made the lives of defenceless people a daily adventure.

Nor were the regular troops exempt from acts of wanton terrorism.

One example from the brigade area may stand as typical of the indiscriminate shooting by Crown Forces taking place all over the country.
One evening in July, 1920 a party of boys and girls had gathered at
Coracunna, about a mile from Mitchelstown for the customary
cross-roads dance. They were chatting in a group when a military
lorry came along on the road from Cahir. Without reason or warning
its occupants opened fire on the group at the cross-roads. A short
distance from the cross the lorry halted, the soldiers dismounted,
lined the road-side fence and continued to pour a hail of bullets in
the direction in which most of the group had run for shelter. Without
investigating the results of their action, the soldiers entrucked and
drove away. Two young men, McDonnell and McGrath had been
shot dead. At the subsequent inquest, the soldiers swore that they
had been attacked and had fired in self-defence. This was not true.
The jury, despite the intimidation of British bayonets, found a verdict
of murder against the soldiers.

The Army itself, of necessity, added burdens to the backs of its
friends. The destruction of bridges and the trenching of roads,
now widely used to hinder and restrict enemy movement, created
serious inconvenience for the people everywhere, involved them in
financial loss, and exposed many of them to the vengeance of the Crown
Forces. The women rendered heroic service. Even outside the ranks
of the young and active girls organised in Cumann-na-mBan, who
carried despatches, nursed the sick and wounded, provided clothing,
first-aid equipment, funds, and risked their lives as freely as the men,
there were women and girls who kept many a long vigil, who cooked
and washed and provided shelter, and who were, when the tests came,
splendidly silent, immune alike to threats and blandishments. It
is a truism to say that without the voluntary and intelligent co-
operation of the people, amongst whom they lived, the men of the
I.R.A. could not have sustained the fight for a single month in the
conditions existing in County Cork in 1920.

The widespread aggressive tactics which Liam Lynch had advocated
for his brigade, were beginning to be put into operation at every
opportunity that offered in each of his seven battalions. Charleville
Battalion had information that a patrol of police operated between
Milford and Drumcollogher, and Commandant Paddy O'Brien laid
an ambush for them within 300 yards of Milford Barracks on the last
day of October. The patrol did not appear, and on 3rd November,
the Milford post was evacuated. After the evacuation, Commandant
Seamus Brislane, the Battalion O/C, with Commandant O'Brien,
took a party there with the intention of burning down the building.

After nightfall both officers made a careful search of the evacuated
post for booby traps. Finding none, O'Brien remained in the building

alone, while Brislane went to collect his party and a supply of paraffin oil. O'Brien had reached the front door on his way out of the building when he was fired upon from the darkness outside, and then ordered to put his hands up. A party of Black-and-Tans who had arrived from Dromcollogher were his assailants. He had noticed earlier that the door was backed by a steel plate and had a crank bar for securing it in the closed position. Though wounded in the jaw, he drew behind the door, closed it, and threw the bar into position before fire was resumed. Brislane and his party returned, but hesitated to open fire for fear of hitting O'Brien. After about five minutes the Tans captured one of Brislane's party, Volunteer Tim Crimmins, brought him up to the barred door, and threatened to shoot him if the door was not opened. O'Brien opened the door slightly, fired over Crimmins' head and shut the door again. The Tans immediately outside scattered and in the confusion Crimmins escaped back to his own party. Brislane, learning the position from him, opened fire on the Tans who retreated precipitately towards Drumcollogher. Recovering from his wound in a Cork hospital, Commandant O'Brien read in an English newspaper the death of a Black-and-Tan who had been wounded in Milford. The Milford Dairy Society's Creamery was burned down by British Forces on the 26th.

Castletownroche Battalion, of which Commandant Thomas Barry had been O/C since January, 1920, now had a small column in the field under his command. They had planned a number of activities which did not materialise. Their first action was at Kildorrery on 7th August, 1920. It was an attack on a patrol of Black-and-Tans, which left the barracks on foot on certain days. When preparations were being made Commandant Donnchadh O'Hannigan, O/C East Limerick Brigade Column arrived in the area with some of his men and volunteered to participate in the action. Fourteen of his column and eleven of Tom Barry's took part. The police patrol numbered six on the occasion. One was killed and the remaining five wounded. Six rifles and 250 rounds of ammunition were captured by the attackers.

The next action of Castletownroche Battalion Column was at Labacally near Glanworth on 26th November. The ambushed military party had been holding an inquiry at Glanworth into the shooting of a lad named O'Donnell by Black-and-Tans. It was decided that the main effort of the column would be concentrated on the staff car, and that the first of the two lorries escorting it would be allowed to pass. The staff car carried a number of military officers and an R.I.C. officer. The ambush position was on a very steep hill, and, inadvertently, fire was opened on the leading lorry. The result was that three of the occupants were killed and four wounded. An officer was blown out of the lorry by a grenade thrown by one of the attacking party. He was found on the road subsequently badly wounded. The staff car did not, however, come into the ambush position; the officers abandoned it and escaped across the fields to their barracks at Fermoy. The only captures were the wounded officer's revolver, ammunition and equipment. The Column Commander and one member of his party received slight wounds.

A very successful action was fought at Glencurrane, in the East Limerick Brigade area, and near Liam Lynch's birthplace, on 19th December, 1920. Commandant Donncada O'Hannigan, O/C East Limerick Brigade Column, was in command of the combined forces from his brigade and from Castletownroche Battalion of Cork No. 2 Brigade. Commandant Tom Barry's Column had one of the Hotchkiss guns captured at Mallow. Scouting and protection elements were

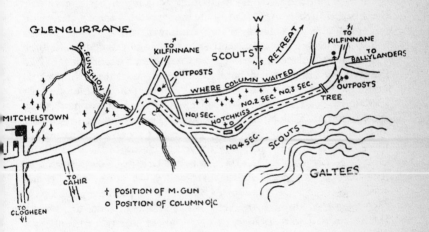

provided by the local battalion of East Limerick Brigade, and by Mitchelstown Company of Cork No. 2 Brigade. Men from both these formations took part in the actual fight. The action was an excellent example of co-operation between adjoining brigades.

The columns went into position about 8 a.m. The expected target was a military convoy which used this road on journeys between Tipperary and Kilworth Camp. An armoured car normally escorted the lorries. It was decided that the attack would be made when the convoy was on the return journey to Tipperary, as prisoners were frequently carried to Kilworth. About noon, two lorries of troops passed through the ambush position going south. Later it was learned that the armoured car accompanying the lorries had broken down at Galbally.

A tree had been partly sawn through at the northern end of the ambush position and when, about 4 p.m., the scouts signalled the approach of two lorries from the south, it was felled. The first lorry pulled up quite close to the tree and fire was opened on both lorries. The leading one reversed in an effort to get clear of the ambush position. The second one came forward, with the result they both collided directly under the fire of the Hotchkiss gun. After about five minutes the British party surrendered. Of the eighteen men in the two lorries, two had been killed and three wounded. The columns captured eighteen rifles, five or six hundred rounds of ammunition, two dozen Mills grenades and some sacks of mails. The lorries were burned. Amongst the mails were found three silver medals, addressed respectively to a lieutenant, a sergeant and a corporal of the British forces, and inscribed : " For gallant conduct in Ireland."

On the following day both columns took up a position on the Kilfinnane-Mitchelstown road, but the expected enemy party did not travel and the columns were withdrawn.

On 10th December the recently-formed Fermoy Battalion Column had a successful action at Leary's Cross, near Castlelyons. Two unsuccessful attempts had been made during the previous week to find a target. On this date a section of ten men of the column under Captain Patrick Egan, O/C Bartlemy Company, were crossing through the country to a billetting area south of Fermoy, when they saw a lorry of British troops approaching Leary's Cross. Anticipating the route the lorry would take, they arrived at a bend of the road almost simultaneously with it. As there was not time to make dispositions they attacked at once. At the first volley the driver was hit and crashed his lorry. The occupants, although outnumbering the I.R.A. party, scattered through the fields on the opposite side of the road. In the ensuing pursuit nine British soldiers surrendered and were disarmed.

As the year drew to a close the mounting tension of the struggle increased daily, particularly in Dublin and in the Munster counties. In July, 1920, there were forty British battalions in Ireland, of which sixteen were in Munster. By the end of the year eleven fresh battalions had arrived, making a total of fifty one. Troops and police aggregated 40,000 men.[1]

At the beginning of 1920, the serviceable arms in Liam's Brigade consisted of the fifteen rifles captured at Fermoy, the few carbines from Araglin Police Barracks, three or four rifles procured from G.H.Q., and about a dozen weapons of older vintage and doubtful reliability. Now his brigade was armed with two Hotchkiss guns,

[1] Macready, *Annals of an Active Life*, Vol. 2, pp. 480, 533

about eighty-five serviceable rifles, a sufficient number of revolvers and pistols to arm all officers, and a large supply of shot guns. He had a small number of grenades and some progress had been made in the manufacture of land mines. Most of the arms had been captured from the occupation forces. It was, in truth, still a small, an almost insignificant, armament with which to confront the forces opposed to him. Consider that just a fraction of the British troops occupying his brigade area, was a complete machine-gun battalion at Bally-vonaire. Only by the most skilful tactics and resolute action could he hope to preserve what he had won in fighting, and use his arms to capture further supplies, while continuing to maintain and extend the struggle.

At the beginning of 1920 only a few members of the brigade were on wholetime active service. At the close of the year, seven columns, each varying in strength from fourteen to thirty men, were in the field, all capable of reinforcement from their own battalions at short notice, by any required number of men armed with shot-guns and revolvers, and any two or more of them capable of efficient co-operation for large operations. They were disciplined, seasoned, tough, capable of great endurance, and animated by a fine offensive spirit.

Behind them, the basic company and battalion organisation had been brought to a state of considerable efficiency, and maintained at a high level despite the disruption of arrests, changes of officer personnel, as a result of the formation of the columns, imprisonments and deaths, and the difficulties, even the impossibility in many areas, of carrying on normal training. Liam's foresight in devoting part of his energies always to the maintainence of this basic organisation in a high state of efficiency is evident. It kept enemy activity and movement in every part of his brigade under constant vigilant observation, it organised billeting and protection for the columns, it maintained his lines of communication.

The year closed with the imposition of Martial Law on the Counties of Cork, Kerry, Tipperary and Limerick, a measure for which Macready had been clamouring. On 14th December, proclamations were issued by the military governors of these counties to the effect that after 27th December, any person convicted by a Military Court of certain offences would be liable to suffer death. The offences included, possession of arms, ammunition or explosives, wearing of Irish Volunteer uniform or " clothing likely to deceive," " harbouring and aiding and abetting rebels." On the 18th, Brigadier General Higginson, a British military governor of the martial law area, issued a notice giving warning that captured officers of the " rebel forces " would, in future, be carried in Government motors and lorries. The mask was off. The pretence that a state of war did not exist could no longer be maintained.

The inclusion of only part of the British 6th Division area under martial law created administrative and other difficulties, which at once became apparent. On 4th January, it was found necessary to include the remaining Counties of Clare, Waterford, Kilkenny and Wexford, so as to make the martial law area co-extensive with that garrisoned by the 6th Division, although, if Macready is a reliable witness, it was to be applied in these counties, particularly Wexford, with a lighter hand.

For the Army of the Republic, this last desperate effort of British Imperialism in Ireland had little significance. Prisoners of war taken in arms could now be brought before " drum-head " courts of British officers, sentenced to death and executed forthwith, but the time was long past when that situation could have diverted even the youngest and least responsible of them from carrying out their duties. Ample proof of that fact was given by men of Liam's Brigade, and by men all over Ireland, in the six months of supreme effort and sacrifice which followed.

CHAPTER 10

INTELLIGENCE AND COUNTER INTELLIGENCE

Notice is taken of every person that is able to do either good or hurt. It is known, not only how they live and what they do, but it is foreseen what they purpose or intend to do.

SIR JOHN DAVIES, 1602.

IN estimating the factors which contributed to the success of the I.R.A. in its operations against the Crown Forces, the admitted superiority of its intelligence services, particularly in the eighteen months before the Truce, must be taken into account. That superiority was not an accidental circumstance, but rather the result of creating two complementary pieces of organisation specially designed for a specific purpose, and imposing on each only tasks within its capacity to perform. Like all other branches of I.R.A. organisation, the intelligence services were developed to cope with a particular situation. Before that situation began to emerge there was no general appreciation of the need for such services. One result was that the organisation created was practical and utilitarian.

But it started with a long handicap as compared with the British services opposed to it. England, in her long struggle for supremacy in Ireland, always had a better appreciation of the value of political intelligence than we had, and for centuries had been able to suborn some Irishmen from their natural allegiance. Previous armed efforts to achieve liberty had often been weakened and sometimes frustrated by the activities of spies and informers. Much of our history since the Union had been influenced by the adroit manner in which our rulers had managed the delicate business of purchasing the espionage services of Irishmen, whose information was useful in helping to secure and maintain a prying, secret supervision over every aspect of national activity. The men who directed British policy in Ireland were never content with that alone. It was necessary, in addition, to keep a finger on the national pulse in every city and town and parish. In this aspect of espionage they had been well and faithfully served by the R.I.C., since the establishment of the force. From its country-wide net-work of stations, manned by a body of men generally conscientious and intelligent in the discharge of their duties, having an unrivalled knowledge of the inhabitants and a shrewd understanding of Irish character, a constant flow of information reached Dublin

Castle through the filter of R.I.C. organisation. Up to a point, it was sufficient to keep the Castle authorities well informed, even if they did not always evaluate very accurately the significance of the information.

British espionage in Ireland suffered its first striking reverse in many years when it failed completely to penetrate the reorganised Irish Republican Brotherhood in the decade before 1916. The incident which gave the authorities a belated indication of the project to import arms from Germany was fortuitous, and not attributable to the activities of their own organisations. Characteristically, they regarded the information with scepticism, but luck favoured them at the last minute in capturing the *Aud* in Tralee Bay. The Rising at Easter took them completely by surprise.

With an alertness sharpened by this reverse, the R.I.C., in the three years after the Rising, devoted much time and energy to the acquisition of up-to-date information on all aspects of the national movement in every part of the country. The Volunteer organisation, as the most menacing potential threat to British domination, merited and received a constant priority in that espionage. But, early in 1920, all that elaborate machinery of spying and reporting began to crumble and collapse. A number of factors contributed to its disintegration. General Order No. 6, issued on 4th June, 1920, directed that:

"Volunteers shall have no intercourse with the R.I.C., and shall stimulate and support in every way the boycott of this force ordered by the Dáil."

From the conscription crisis in 1918, there had been within the R.I.C. a group of men, ably led by T. J. McElligott (Pro Patria), who sought to confine R.I.C. duties to those of a normal police force, and to align the body more closely with national aspirations. The activities of this group had got a majority of the force to join the British National Union of Police and Prison Officers, and at a National Conference in London, early in 1919, after an address by Mr. McElligott, there was complete unanimity on a resolution demanding the disarmament of the R.I.C. When this and other efforts to prevent the force from being used as an armed section of the occupation forces failed, attention was concentrated upon the effort to secure large-scale resignations, coupled with a boycott of those who refused to resign. Sinn Féin issued a national call to its members to co-operate with parents and relatives of R.I.C. men to secure these resignations, and to give every assistance possible to resigned men.

In view of the magnitude of the sacrifice thus being demanded from men, many of whom had family and other responsibilities, this effort was reasonably successful in its direct object, and completely successful indirectly because it dried up the normal flow of Irish recruits into the force.

The closing down of a large number of stations all over the country, and the consequent cooping up of the garrisons in larger barracks in cities and towns, broke the local contacts so valuable to a police force. The social ostracism operated against those remaining in the force after mid-1920, reduced still further its ability to discharge what had been one of its primary functions. The infusion of an incompatible, vulgar, foreign element in the persons of British recruits, created internal stresses and dissensions which completed the demoralisation of what had once been a highly-disciplined and efficient organisation.

Quite suddenly, and with shattering finality, the mainstay of British espionage in Ireland had become almost worthless. Political intelligence, and that falling normally within the security sphere, had once been its almost exclusive province. Now, there was a gaping void. It was not a situation in which the British authorities could be expected to remain inactive, and they did not remain inactive. The hasty schemes they improvised to replace the coldly efficient R.I.C. system suffered from two grave defects. In the first place they were not, and never became, completely co-ordinated between the civil authorities, the army, the R.I.C. and the Auxiliary forces. Secondly, the British authorities had, of necessity, to rely largely on the very poorest sources of information when dealing with a nation in revolt— paid spies; loyal subjects of the Crown who, though living in the country were alien to its people in mind and spirit; information extracted by threats and terror; ordinary soldiers sent into the country in the guise of deserters; " stool pigeons " in jails and internment camps; and, finally, the brave though misguided efforts of individual officers. All these were used.

Normal British Army organisation, as it then existed in Ireland, did not include any intelligence formation well fitted to grapple with the guerilla type of warfare which developed. Their formations had a combat intelligence complex, influenced by the trench warfare experience of the European war. Nothing could have been less useful to them in Ireland.

On the British side there were a number of advantages. There was in the Castle a corpus of information, a legacy from the activities of the R.I.C., which up to a point had considerable value. They had unlimited funds at their disposal for the purchase of information. They had still sufficient of the prestige of power and patronage to influence into their service here and there persons not susceptible to a cruder approach, persons who still believed that defeat for the national forces was inevitable, and that the old days of British supremacy would return. They had, scattered in every part of the country, persons fanatically loyal to the British connection, who would and did risk their lives to serve it, and who would scorn any reward. Finally they had officers and officials of long experience and training, who knew Ireland and the Irish mind, and who were still prepared to serve them with unquestioning loyalty.

On the Irish side Intelligence organisation was built up from nothing, by inexperienced personnel who had no rigid ideas about the kind of organisation needed, but who were entirely clear about what results they wanted from any organisation set up. To derive the maximum benefits from whatever system was adopted, it was essential that, while it was uniform for the whole army, it should have sufficient flexibility to make it readily adaptable to the varying conditions in different brigades. In this sphere, as elsewhere, success or failure depended largely on the vision and energy of the responsible local officers.

In his own spehre, Liam was one of the first to realise the value of accurate and timely information, and to take steps to put the acquisition of it on a well organised, practical basis. An order[1] which he issued later expresses his view of this aspect of the struggle :

> "On an efficient Intelligence system will, to a large extent, depend our success against the enemy. . . . The importance of reliable Intelligence should be impressed on all Volunteers of all ranks, as each man can help in this matter. The value of Intelligence will be much enhanced . . . by having it conveyed without the least loss of time to the H.Q. of the nearest unit."

In its ultimate development, I.R.A. Intelligence had two main branches, an observation and reporting formation in each Army unit, and an espionage service inside British organisations and institutions, wherever it could be created. One observed the opposing forces from outside, the other watched their machinery and methods from inside. It was closely integrated because, both at G.H.Q. and in the brigades, all sources of information were under unified control, at G.H.Q., that of the Director of Intelligence, and in the brigades, where most of the local work was done, under that of the Brigade Intelligence Officer. For most of the formative period, and continuously up to the Truce, the Director was Michael Collins, and to his initiative, energy and resourcefulness, much of the success of the service is due. Nevertheless, he would have been largely powerless outside Dublin, were it not for the work done in the local brigades.

[1] Operation Order No. 10—30th August, 1922

Early in 1920, intelligence organisation in Cork No. 2 Brigade, was put upon a regular basis by the appointments of brigade and battalion intelligence officers, and the detailing of picked men in each company under an N.C.O. for the work. The numbers of men in the company sections varied according to local needs, two or three in country districts, four to six in towns or in companies in close proximity to British posts. There were no battalion intelligence sections, nor was there any need for them. In action, protection and scouting duties were carried out by local companies. The main duties of this brigade organisation were to ensure the security of our own forces, and gather by observation the maximum of information on the organisation, strengths, tactics, routine, and intentions of the British garrison. A subsidiary duty was observation of the activities, contacts and movements of persons in their areas suspected of being actively hostile to our forces. The company section reported, through the company captain, to the battalion intelligence officer, whose duty it was to assemble and co-ordinate these reports and transmit to the brigade everything of more than purely local significance.

The second branch of I.R.A. Intelligence, consisted of a relatively small body of intrepid workers, employed in a civilian capacity in the various British organisations, in places frequented by British personnel, and in the Post Office service. The efficient organisation of the work of these invidivuals and groups, the maintenance of regular contacts with them, and the arrangements necessary for a prompt and uninterrupted delivery of such documents as they could obtain and such information as they had to transmit, were all matters which required the exercise of tact, patience and the utmost discretion. For these workers themselves, no mere words of praise would be adequate.

The Post Office side of this branch had been in operation in a limited way before the formation of Cork No. 2 Brigade. At Mallow Post Office, Siobhan Creedon (Mrs. Seamus Langford), had been active on behalf of the Cork Brigade as early as 1917, and she continued to work for Cork No. 2 Brigade after its formation, with great efficiency and success during the whole period of the struggle. In 1919 she had secured some very valuable information in regard to the British plans for conscription, and these had been promptly transmitted to Richard Mulcahy, Chief of Staff. Gradually, under the skilful direction of George Power and Maurice Twomey, almost all the post offices in the brigade area were included in the intelligence net, and contacts were established at the British posts at Buttevant and Ballyvonaire, and in the two military barracks at Fermoy. The post office organisation was of the greatest value to the brigade. The telephone and telegraph systems were extensively used by the British forces, although they had radio equipment at their disposal. Nearly all R.I.C. and Auxiliary force messages of an urgent nature were sent over the telegraph system, in cipher. I.R.A. intelligence operators in the post offices copied these messages and transmitted the copies to the brigade, where they were deciphered from a key supplied regularly by the Director of Intelligence.

The successful and uninterrupted achievement of such a task, in post offices where all the staff were not prepared to co-operate, and where the usual rotation of duty hours made it a difficult problem to cover messages going through during the whole of any twenty-four hours, called for the utmost ingenuity and perseverance. The post offices at Mallow and Fermoy became of paramount importance as the struggle developed, and the workers for Army Intelligence in these offices, earned for themselves the highest appreciation of Lynch and his Staff.

The intelligence battle was abnormal, and the methods evolved on both sides had only this in common, that they were original and devised to meet a situation of which neither side had any previous experience. Referring to the British difficulties and their effort to over-come them, Macready says :[1]

"As soon as the rebels began to attack and molest the troops there was no dearth of volunteers for Intelligence work, and when during the summer of 1920, authority was obtained from the War Office to enlarge and improve the whole organisation little difficulty was found in obtaining keen volunteers who were already well acquainted with the localities in which they were stationed.

"The principle upon which the reorganisation was built up was that the Army Intelligence Service should be pushed forward as rapidly as possible, until such time as the police system had been remodelled by the new Police Adviser or Chief of Police, General Tudor, who had brought with him over to Ireland an officer for the special purpose of reorganising the moribund Intelligence branches of the two police forces."

These "volunteers for intelligence work" were courageous men. Those of them who were encountered in the Cork Brigades were officers, some of senior rank. They left their posts in civilian attire, sometimes very poorly dressed, and penetrated the coutryside in an effort to obtain information or establish contacts for the purpose. Creditable as it was to their sense of duty, this type of activity dis-closed a boy scout mentality, and a complete absence of any sense of

[1] *Annals of an Active Life*, Vol. 2, p. 462

reality of the situation which then existed. Moreover, their contacts were of necessity limited to a narrow circle of persons antipathetic to the Army and the national struggle, whose information could rarely be more than general and belated.

Practically every brigade in the active areas had experience of the efforts of these " volunteers for intelligence work." In Liam Lynch's area a British officer from the Fermoy garrison, Lieutenant Vincent, was captured near Watergrasshill while engaged in this duty. He was disguised as an ordinary tramp. In his possession was found a note-book containing a list of names of persons known to be loyal to the British connection. It had been evident for some time that loyalists in some parts of the brigade area were supplying information to the British forces. Liam Lynch had stayed at a number of houses in the area south-east of Fermoy in January, 1921, usually not more than one night at any one house. A series of British raids on these houses followed, in each case only a day or two after the date on which he had been there. The manner in which information in regard to his movements was transmitted came to light later.

Lieutenant Vincent was removed to the Glenville area under guard and arrangements were being made for his trial. On the morning of the day following his capture, British forces began a round-up of the area in which he was held, and the prisoner made a desperate attempt to escape. He was shot down and killed.

Individual soldiers sent into the country from British posts in the guise of deserters, presented a difficult problem for the brigade, particularly in the Charleville Battalion area where the practice was frequent. There were a number of genuine deserters, and for a time it was hard to distinguish between them and the men masquerading as deserters. As there were no facilities for detaining prisoners, the practical alternatives were release or execution, and for a time deserters and pseudo deserters alike, were released and warned to get out of the country. They were even escorted to the ports and given their fares to England. There is little doubt that amongst them some who were engaged in spying escaped the penalty of their crimes. But, when it was found that men posing as deserters returned as members of raiding parties to houses where they had been befriended, sheltered and fed, sterner measures became necessary. It was only after five or six of these men had been executed, that the practice of sending them out from British posts ceased.

The Army was singularly free from any taint of disloyalty within its own ranks. Only in one isolated case had a Volunteer in Liam's Brigade turned informer. That case and its consequences are dealt with later.

As both branches of Army Intelligence developed, the staffs of all the Cork Brigades began to acquire a more accurate knowledge of the forces opposed to them, although this knowledge was never at any time as complete as it might have been. The British genius for improvisation, and the lack of uniformity in their army organisation, were often a source of confusion and puzzlement. Where a British brigade appeared, we were inclined to look for three battalions, not appreciating the fact that it was quite as likely to be two or five. Fortunately this was not an aspect of the work which had a vital importance for us.

As the work of those operating inside the British machine became organised a steady flow of documents resulted. Cork No. 1 Brigade had established a most valuable contact at British 6th Division Headquarters, a lady who has not been persuaded to abandon the anonymity of the pseuodonym " G " under which she operated. From this source came much material of value not alone to the local brigade but to the whole Army, a fact to which Michael Collins paid frequent tribute. There was, at all times, a regular and reasonably speedy exchange of information between the three Cork Brigades and between each of them and the Director of Intelligence. When necessary, on a particular matter, daily communication was maintained. There were cases in which communications issued by Major General Strickland did not reach his Brigade Commanders more than a day before they were in the hands of the I.R.A. Brigade Commanders opposing them. There was a case, in May of 1921, in which a document issued from British 6th Division Headquarters, transmitted to Cork No. 1 Brigade by their operator there, was circulated, in part, and with some observations, to the Brigade Commandants of the 1st Southern Division. A copy of the circular was captured by the British, again issued with their observations, and the new circular once more came into our hands, this whole series of incidents taking place within a week.

The extent to which British Intelligence had succeeded in delineating the I.R.A. organisation opposed to its forces in the South, its knowledge of I.R.A. personnel, and its information on I.R.A. methods and intentions, may be judged from an official document[1] captured by the East Limerick Brigade Column in May, 1921, and made available through the courtesy of Lieut.-Col. J. M. McCarthy. This is a British 6th Division Weekly Intelligence Summary, dated 17/5/21, less than two months before the Truce, issued from Division Headquarters at Cork to all British formations in the area including the police forces, and signed by Major General Sir E. P. Strickland. The document bears internal evidence that it is a composite assembly of police and military intelligence, and may, therefore, be taken as representing

[1] See Appendix 1

both the type of information available to the Crown forces at that period, and the best results of the pooled efforts of all British agencies in the area of the 6th Division.

The statement, over General Strickland's signature, by which the document is prefaced, is in its general tendency propagandist rather than factual. Reviewing a list of Army activities in this period, it is difficult to find justification for the opening sentence : " The long expected rebel offensive took place on Saturday," unless it is a reflection of what was a rather persistent British obsession—that the I.R.A. was not playing the game according to the best Imperial rules. It was not fighting large-scale pitched battles. There was widespread activity in this particular week, but no actions comparable to earlier engagements at Crossbarry, Kilmichael or Clonbanin, or later ones such as at Rathcoole.

The second paragraph assures its readers that " no military skill or courage was shown by the rebels, who evidently find it more profitable to shoot down unarmed men—and women, than to take the field." No woman had been shot by the I.R.A. in the period referred to, but this is probably an oblique reference to the execution of Mrs. Lindsay of Dripsey, some months earlier. In her case the death sentence followed a flagrant and deliberate action against the Army, that of conveying information to the occupation forces in regard to the Dripsey ambush. Even after sentence had been passed, an official letter from Cork No. 1 Brigade to General Strickland indicated that the sentence would not be carried out if the prisoners taken at Dripsey were treated as prisoners of war. The communication was ignored and Mrs. Lindsay was shot. If one turns to the other side of the picture it will be seen that in the previous month alone, thirty unarmed men and at least five women had been shot down by Crown Forces, including prisoners of war and inoffensive civilians. This summary itself contains a gloating reference to one of the foulest of these deeds—the murder of Captain Jeremiah Lyons at Gortha- glanna, County Kerry, in the previous week.

The naive optimism of the next sentence will be amusing to any- body with a knowledge of conditions at the time : " The appearance of large numbers of pamphlets addressed to the members of the I.R.A. may have acted as a deterrent to many who have not yet actually committed murder." This solitary British army pamph- leteering effort (aeroplanes were used for distribution), did no more than provide a little light relief against the grim background of the time. The sentence which follows is curiously ill-informed for the period : " The recent heavy losses among their leaders, by arrest or decease (sic.) had undoubtedly hampered their operations, which were probably planned by organisers in their G.H.Q." There had been some, but not "heavy," losses by arrests, and none at all from disease. The planning of all operations had always been a local function in the brigades of the South.

The final paragraph displays a remarkable absence of appreciation of one aspect of the situation : " There has been no recurrence of counter-reprisals by the rebels, who appear to have been stopped by our determination to increase the ratio of destruction indefinitely." That was written at a time when the section of the population loyal to the Crown was imploring the British Government to stop the futile policy of reprisals, the reactions to which threatened to annihilate the faithful civil garrison. General Strickland had to wait less than a week to see the residences of four loyalists burned down within sight of his own headquarters.

Finally, the vague and groundless optimism of this general statement, prefacing the summary, may be contrasted with the British official statistics for the same week. Sixty attacks on Crown forces had taken place. The casualties numbered fifty-five, including twenty-three deaths, and were the highest for any week since 1916. It may be concluded that absence of accurate information and the need for propaganda to bolster up the sagging morale of the occupation forces combined to give its character to the document. This is borne out by an examination of typical items of alleged information.

British Intelligence had acquired fairly accurate information on the territorial areas covered by the brigades, and in some cases by the battalions. This is in no way surprising because I.R.A. organisation was simple and uniform and delimitation generally had been completed before the collapse of R.I.C. espionage. Captured documents would also have assisted to some extent in enabling trained personnel to work out our organisation. On the other hand, British information on the officer personnel of the units, and on the more recent developments in organisation is wildly inaccurate. What appears to be indicated is that after the R.I.C. espionage system had been undermined and its effectiveness destroyed nothing had been found to replace it which could produce even a modicum of accurate or reliable information.

An item concerning Cork No. 1 Brigade illustrates this :

> " Information received from several sources goes to show that there is no Flying Column for Cork No. 1 (Mid) Cork Brigade, and that Hales' Column is spoken of as the Flying Column of both No. 1 and No. 3 Brigades. There are a certain number of active service men who go around in small bands, but these appear to spend their whole time in attempting to avoid capture. Their numbers, when reported by civilians, are greatly exaggerated."

Another reference to this column states : " It is now established that the Flying Column collects all the best men and material from the two brigades." Both of these items of information are wholly contrary to the facts in two respects. Cork No. 1 Brigade had then, and for six months previously, a brigade column of forty to sixty men and two battalion columns of about thirty men each in the field, as well as a whole time active service unit of twelve men in the city. What is referred to as " Hales' Column " is the Cork No. 3 Brigade Column, then under the command of Commandant Tom Barry. Tom Hales, who had been O/C Cork No. 3 Brigade up to the date of his capture, was then a prisoner, and it is evident that the reference is to Sean Hales whom the British believed to be in charge of the West Cork Column.

Much of the material in this summary suggests that certain British sources of information were either extremely credulous or so well aware of the ignorance of their employers that they were confident of the acceptance of any story, however fantastic. A few examples may be cited.

" James Brislane, Commandant of Charleville Battalion is believed to have gone to Clare, and one of the Clare leaders is reported to have taken his place."

" Pat Whelan, who was relieved of his command in Waterford Brigade, is now somewhere in the west of Ireland undergoing a course of Intelligence work."

" John Linehan is reported to be in command of Cork No. 1 (Mid) Cork Brigade in the place of Sean Hegarty who is in Kanturk at present. This is not confirmed."

Apart from the fact that these things were simply untrue, they reflect an apparent acceptance of the belief that transfers of officers between the brigades were normal. This was not so. Except Commandant Andy Cooney, who had been put in charge of Kerry No. 1 Brigade by G.H.Q. during a period of reorganisation, all the officers in the 1st Southern Division area continued up to the Truce to operate in the brigades and battalions to which they were attached when the period of active operations began. These were usually their native districts.

In regard to the three items quoted above it may be said that Commandant Brislane was with his battalion column at the time ; Commandant Whelan was capably leading his brigade and continued to do so until his command was extended to the whole of County Waterford during the Truce ; Commandant O'Hegarty was not in Kanturk, he was with his brigade column. There was, in fact, no one named John Linehan associated with Cork No. 1 Brigade in any post of responsibility.

Two further statements, which were completely unfounded, will suffice to indicate the kind of information which was being supplied by touts in Cork City to the British Forces.

> " Frank McCarthy . . . is on the Brigade Staff."
> " Tim O'Neill, the new Brigade Intelligence officer, is sleeping somewhere in the Curragh Road, Cork."

Frank McCarthy was not on the Brigade Staff, and no one named " Tim O'Neill " was concerned with the intelligence services of Cork No. 1 Brigade.

The extent to which the credulity of the occupation forces had been imposed upon, may be judged from an item under the head of Communications :

> " Every kind of communication is now used for notifying the rebels of the approach of Crown Forces. Post office and Railway telephones are made free use of. The column of smoke from chimneys is now a warning throughout County Cork."

One aspect of this intelligence summary merits attention, because it reports a typical activity of Crown forces, and discloses the manner in which lying accounts of murders were fabricated for official use. It should be borne in mind that, at this time, martial law was in force in the area garrisoned by the British 6th Division, and that all Crown forces in that area were under the control of the military governor, General Strickland, the man who set his signature to this summary. The case to which reference is here made is the murder by Crown forces of Captain Jeremiah Lyons at Gortaglanna, Co. Kerry on 12th May, 1921.

There are two separate references to it in the summary. The first, under the head, " I.R.A. movements, 1st (West Kerry Brigade)," and the second under the head " General (d) Kerry Brigade area." The " Kerry Brigade " in this context is a British force.[1]

The first reference is : " The Duagh Column attempted their anticipated ambush with unfortunate results to themselves, for their leader Jerry Lyons and 2 others were killed and a number wounded."

The second reference is more elaborate : " The Crown Forces have met with success both in North Cork and in Kerry, the most notable achievement being that of a small patrol of Listowel police who encountered a gang of about 80 rebels and put them to flight

[1] See p. 49

and killing their leader and two others and wounding several more. This operation was doubly successful in that the dead leader has been recognised as Jeremiah Lyons of Duagh, the commander of the Flying Column which has been active in N. Kerry for some time past."

These two accounts of the same event, with their obvious discrepancies, may well stand as typical of many of the official reports of events published on the highest British authority at the time and defended and relied upon by leading members of the British Government. Having embarked upon a policy so infamous as that operated by the Crown forces in Ireland, it became a practical necessity for the authors of that policy not to seek to ascertain the truth in relation to such revolting crimes as it inevitably produced, but rather to grasp at and bolster up any explanation, however illogical or mendacious, furnished by the lawless instruments of tyranny. When, as in the case of Jeremiah Lyons, a number of policemen conspired to give their version of an occurence, the whole powerful official machine was set in motion to convince the world that their shameless lying was the truth. Almost the only truth in either of these two reports is that Jerry Lyons was killed. Let us look at the manner of his death. It will be sufficiently clear from these extracts from a sworn statement made by Cornelius Dee, one of his companions who was fortunate enough to escape from the murderers :

" About 9.30 a.m. on Thursday, May twelfth, 1921, I, Cornelius Dee, accompanied by Patrick Dalton and Patrick Walsh, left Athea, unarmed, where we had been attending a mission given by the Redemptorist Fathers. We were walking along the road leading to Listowel when at Gortaglanna Bridge we met Jerry Lyons ; he was cycling. He dismounted and began talking about various happenings. After a few minutes Paddy Walsh suggested that we should go into a field as it would be safer than the roadside. We moved and were just inside a fence when we heard the noise of a lorry . . . we tried to conceal ourselves as best we could. . . . Very soon we were surrounded by men in the uniforms of the Royal Irish Constabulary . . . we were asked our names and gave them correctly ; we were searched and found unarmed, having nothing but a copy of the *Irish Independent*. We were then compelled to undress and while we were fastening our clothes again we were beaten with rifles, struck with revolvers and thrown on the ground and kicked in trying to save ourselves. Then we were separated some distance from each other ; four or five men came round each of us and my captors continued to beat me with their rifles and hit me with

their fists. After about twenty minutes we were marched towards
the road and then to the lorries. Paddy Walsh and Paddy Dalton
were put on the first lorry. I was put on the second and Jerry
Lyons on the third. The lorries were then driven for about half
a mile towards Athea. They were then stopped and turned
round. Paddy Walsh and Paddy Dalton were changed to the
lorry in which I was, Jerry Lyons was not changed out of the
last lorry, which was now leading. The lorries were then driven
the same road about a mile. We were then ordered out of them.
I saw blood on Jerry Lyons' face and on Paddy Walsh's mouth.
Paddy Dalton was bleeding from the nose. We were then asked
to run but we refused. We were again beaten with rifles and
ordered into a field by the roadside. We refused but were forced
into the field. We asked for a trial but the Black and Tans laughed
and jeered and called us murderers. We were put standing in
line facing a fence about forty yards from the road. . . .   Then
a Black and Tan with a rifle resting on the fence was put in front
of each of us. . . . I looked straight into the face of the man in
front of me. He delayed about twenty seconds as if he would
like one of his companions to fire first. The second Black and
Tan fired. Jerry Lyons flung up his arms, moaned and fell
backwards. I glanced at him and saw blood coming on his
waistcoat, I turned and ran. I was gone about twelve yards
when I got wounded in the right thigh. My leg bent under me
but I held on running although I had to limp. I felt I was being
chased and I heard the bullets whizzing past me. One of the
lorries was driven along the road on my front and fire was
maintained from it. . . .   When too exhausted to run further
I flung myself into a drain in an oats garden. I was there about
forty five minutes when two men came along. They assisted me
to walk . . . and I was taken to a house.

I recognised Head Constable Smith, Listowel, along with the
Black and Tans present at the massacre ; also Constable Raymond,
and there was one in the uniform of a District Inspector of the
Royal Irish Constabulary."

These four Volunteers were the " gang of about 80 rebels " which
figure in one report ; the deliberate and cowardly murder of three
of them is the " notable achievement " referred to with such evident
satisfaction in the same account. The accidental capture of these
four unarmed men is the " anticipated ambush " of one report, and
Cornelius Dee is the " several more " who were wounded and put to
flight in the other account.

An analysis of almost any item in this intelligence summary would give results similar to the foregoing. If there be excluded from it the mere post factum reporting of occurrences common at the time, which had no particular value except in a propaganda sense, what remains is a confused hotch-potch of rumour, gossip, inaccuracies, plain untruths and mendacious reports. Under martial law in the south of Ireland in May, 1921, British intelligence had come to this. All the resources of a trained and permanent divisional staff, under the direction of an energetic officer, who was an Irishman, aided by a police force which, up to eighteen months earlier, had operated for years one of the most efficient espionage systems in any European country, commanding the services of large forces, armed with unlimited powers of search and interrogation, served by an intelligent pro-British element in the population, purchasing the contemptible aid of pimps and touts, and assisted by the efforts of the " volunteers for Intelligence Work" amongst its own personnel, had failed utterly in May, 1921 to obtain such information of the Volunteer Army opposed to it as would enable the British forces to make effective use of their immense superiority in strength and arms. The creation and maintainence of that remarkable state of affairs reflected the highest credit, not alone upon those who risked their lives in the service of the Army, and the prisoners who withstood all threats and tortures, but also upon the great body of faithful people whose loyalty and reticence remained unshaken after a year of terror. Without their active participation and steadfast refusal to help the occupation forces in any way no such results would have been possible.

Out of thousands of similar interrogations, one remembers the typical encounter between an old farmer and a truculent Auxiliary officer during a raid. Under a rapid fire of questions the old man seized on one : " Did you see any Shinners around here ? " " I did then," he replied, " they were here yesterday." Sensation ! " An' 'tis a curious thing," he continued, " but, 'twas ye they were looking for." And then, with reflective good humour, " Maybe 'twas as good ye didn't meet."

CHAPTER II

THE STRUGGLE INTENSIFIES UNDER MARTIAL LAW

Try your valour and your strength on those who have banished you and resolve to destroy you, bud and branch.

OWEN ROE O'NEILL, at Benburb.

THE year 1921 witnessed the final effort of a British government to effect a reconquest of the resurgent nation by terror—and it saw the failure of that ruthless design.

When the year opened the counties of Cork, Kerry, Tipperary and Limerick were already under martial law. On 6th January the counties of Waterford, Kilkenny, Wexford and Clare were included in the martial law area. General Strickland became military governor.

Three proclamations were issued on the 3rd. The first required all householders to keep affixed to the doors of their houses a list of the occupants. The second prohibited all meetings in any public place (six adults constituting a meeting), forbade the use of carrier pigeons, telegrams in code or cipher and wireless telegraphy, and made it an offence to stand or loiter in a public place. The third commanded the public to refuse food or shelter to the Volunteers, and to report to the occupation forces any person suspected of being in possession of arms.

Commenting next day on this new phase of repression the *Westminster Gazette* said :

> " This proclamation really orders the Irish to risk their lives for an administration they have consistently opposed, and which has so far been unable to guarantee that orderly well behaved people should be left unmolested. Technically, General Strickland is in the right, but in view of the existing circumstances in Ireland, his order in our opinion exposes the people to an ordeal which is critically severe."

A proclamation issued on the 12th prohibited the use of motor cars, motor cycles, or pedal cycles between 8 p.m. and 6 a.m.

The policy of official reprisals came into operation. At Midleton, seven houses were destroyed by being burned down by Crown forces in reprisal for an attack on police there by the 4th Battalion of Cork No. 1 Brigade. At Fermoy, a fine of £100 was imposed on the

town for tearing down of a copy of the military governor's proclamation. When the fine remained unpaid, crown forces collected it
in kind from four traders, half the goods seized being wines and
spirits. Commenting on the Midleton reprisal, the *Daily Express* of
4th January, said:

> "This is of course Martial Law. It is legal and disciplined.
> It is, we must believe necessary. But it is horrible."

For the Army the only difference which the British imposition of
martial law made was that any Volunteer captured under arms, might
now be tried by drumhead courtmartial and executed forthwith. The
first official execution under martial law was that of an officer of
Liam's brigade, Captain Cornelius Murphy of Ballydaly, Rathmore,
Co. Kerry. He had taken part in the attack on Rathmore R.I.C.
barracks in the previous June, and in the fight with Black and Tans
at Millstreet in November. He was one of the foundation members
of the Millstreet Battalion Column. In his character and military
service he was typical of that large body of company officers without
whose unremitting and zealous labour the organisation could not
have been maintained in a state of efficiency. " It is no exaggeration
to say that, as a class, they represented all that was best in the countryside."[1] On 4th January, whilst on leave from the column, to visit
his parents, he was captured near his home by Auxiliaries and Black
and Tans. He was taken to Cork military barracks, tried by courtmartial on a charge of being in possession of a loaded revolver, and
sentenced to death. He was shot on the 1st of February.

The Newmarket Battalion, under Commandant Seán Moylan,
carried out an attack on British troops at Meelin on 4th January.
As occasionally happened at the time, the target was a different one
from that for which plans were made. In this case the British forces
had been trying to give their troops, cooped up behind sandbags and
barbed wire defences in their barracks at Newmarket, some exercise
by marching them out of the town a few evenings each week. They
had occasionally used the Meelin road and the ambush was laid with
the intention of attacking a party on foot. Most of the I.R.A. arms
for this action were shot guns, and it was therefore necessary that the
fight should be at close quarters. Scouts had been posted in positions,
to give warning of the approach of Crown forces from any direction.
While the ambush party waited for the expected marching patrol
the scouts signalled the approach of a strong party in lorries, not
from the south as expected, but from the west. The ambush party
was not in a good position to deal with this problem and were

[1] *A Soldier in Ireland*: Lieut. General Sir H. Lawson.

hurriedly moved towards a more suitable one. Before reaching it however, the lorries were too close to permit of its being occupied and the Volunteers had to take such cover as immediately offered. Nevertheless they opened fire and succeeded in stopping the lorries. The British dismounted quickly and a duel commenced which lasted until dusk and the arrival of British reinforcements. The I.R.A. party withdrew, without casualities, but without having achieved any success. The experience was valuable however as a number of men were engaged who had not previously been under fire. In this case Commandant Moylan's column was unlucky in having chosen a day on which the Newmarket garrison was relieved, and when reinforcements with adequate motor transport were consequently available. The following day British troops visited Meelin, burned a half dozen houses and treated the inhabitants with that brutality now becoming a regular feature of their activities. They shot an inoffensive youth, Morgan Sweeney. He died on the following day.

In the Charleville Battalion area a trench was cut on the road near Shinanagh Cross and an outpost stationed covering it on the Charleville side. A staff car containing Colonel Hope, O/C Ballyvonaire, came along after the trench digging party had left. The car drove through two carts, attempted to jump the trench, broke both rear wheels and was put out of action. The I.R.A. outpost came into action and the exchange of fire continued for some time. Colonel Hope and his party got away across country to Ballyvonaire.

On the 28th the Newmarket Battalion brought off a very successful ambush at Tureengarriff, two miles west of Ballydesmond. A few days earlier they had been in position west of Newmarket and would have attacked a British party in four lorries were it not for the fact that civilian hostages were being carried, including one of the principal supporters of the I.R.A. in Newmarket. Now they learned that two cars had gone in the direction of Castleisland and in the hope of taking them on their return the ambush was laid. At the same time Seán Moylan had notified the Commandant Kanturk Battalion of his intention, and suggested that as there was a possibility that these cars might return through Killarney and Rathmore he should lay an ambush at Clonbanin.

The Tureengarriff ambush did not come off on the first day the men were in position. They had occupied it from 6 a.m. to well after dark on a day of thick wet fog and penetrating cold. A trench was dug across the road. Next morning again at 6 a.m. the party was in position. It was a clear dry day. About mid-day when some of the men were about to be relieved to get food, two cars were sighted approaching from the west. The ambush party had excellent observation and cover from view, but there was practically no cover from fire and it had to be a fight to a finish. If the cars came into the position there was no escape for the Crown forces, because men of the local companies, armed with shot guns, had been mobilised and placed in positions to cut off any possible retreat. The first car skidded to a halt when the driver saw the trench. The second car pulled up behind it. The ambush party opened fire. The occupants of the cars leaped to cover behind a loop in the fence and fought back gallantly. A whistle blast was blown, firing on the I.R.A. side ceased, and the Column Commander called upon the Tans to surrender. Their reply was a further volley of fire. The fight was resumed until two of the party had been killed—one of them Divisional Commissioner Holmes —and practically every man wounded. They then surrendered.

Their arms, including six rifles, automatic shot guns, twelve grenades, revolvers and ammunition, were collected by the I.R.A. and loaded into one of the cars which was driven away. The other car was returned to the Crown forces to permit them to remove their dead and wounded. The captured car was not traced, the I.R.A. having taken the precaution of obliterating its tracks. The search party which scoured the area subsequent to the ambush were further misled by the felling of several trees along a road which the I.R.A. had not taken.

Divisional Commissioner Holmes, who was killed in this action, had replaced Divisional Commissioner Smyth, who had been shot dead in the Country Club, Cork, on 19th July, 1920, a short time after he had made his outrageous proposals to the police at Listowel.

To Listowel also his successor had gone on this occasion, one reason at least for his visit, as papers found on him proved, being the collection of evidence against some prisoners then detained in Cork, seeking to connect them with the shooting of a District Inspector Sullivan at Listowel. Sullivan had been the inspiration of the defence of Kilmallock R.I.C. barracks, where he was Sergeant in charge, when this barracks, although reduced to a ruin, successfully resisted the efforts of the I.R.A. to capture it in a night long battle on 27th May, 1920. The Sergeant had been promoted Inspector and transferred to Listowel where he met his death.

The Millstreet Battalion, under Commandant C. J. Meany, had been studying the possibility of bringing off an attack on British troops using trains passing through the area. Various plans were made and men were in position on a number of occasions during January, but for one reason or another the projected attack did not materialise. The battalion column, under Commandant Jerh. Crowley, examined the possibility of the proposal again. The essential features for the success of any such attack were that the train containing the troops should be brought to a halt at a point where the column was already in a position, that an attack should be made only on an occasion when the troops travelling were armed, and where the party was neither too small to be worth while or too large to risk the failure of the operation. There was the further point that civilian passengers on the train had to be protected as far as possible from injuries. Trains travelling east or west were both potential targets. A position was selected at Drishanebeg about a mile west of Rathcoole station, between Millstreet and Banteer. On a few occasions the trains were allowed to pass unmolested, because the soldiers they carried were unarmed, but finally on the evening of 11th February the attack came off. About 6.30 p.m. when it was nearly dark the column went into position. The plan which had been made for bringing the train to a halt came into operation.

One of the Volunteers, whose duty it was to inspect the train and board it if it contained a suitable party of British forces, this evening saw that the party of troops travelling was such as could be dealt with by the column. He boarded the train and travelled to Rathcoole where two armed Volunteers were waiting. At his signal they boarded the engine as the train was leaving the station and on arrival at the ambush position compelled the driver to bring the train to a halt. A long whistle blast was blown sometime in advance as a pre-arranged signal to the attacking party. A lighted bicycle-lamp placed on the track indicated the exact position at which the engine should stop. The Column Commander called upon the military in the train to surrender and was answered with a rifle shot. Fire was then opened upon the carriages containing the military party and the fight continued for about fifteen minutes. The slopes of the cutting were lit by oil torches prepared in advanced by the column and thrown down outside the target carriages when the fight began. The fight was one-sided from the start, the attackers having the advantage of cover and darkness. The British party surrendered. One had been killed and practically all were wounded. The column collected fifteen rifles and 700 rounds of ammunition. They had no casualties.

The dangers to which the civil population were exposed were tragically illustrated at Mallow on the night of 31st January, 1921. About 10.20 p.m. on that night an attack was made on Captain W. H. King, R.I.C., in the vicinity of Mallow railway station. Captain King was accompanied by his wife and in the exchange of fire Mrs. King was killed. At the time there were about 100 workers on duty at Mallow railway station. British military and Black and Tans turned out in force, entered the station premises, indulged in a good deal of indiscriminate firing and arrested all the men they could find. A little later a party of Black and Tans, under a Head Constable, entered the station as the Thurles goods train arrived. They opened fire on the engine driver and his fireman. They broke into the saloon bar and helped themselves liberally to drink. Meanwhile such of the workers as had escaped arrest were carrying on their normal duties when this party of police re-emerged and commenced firing at every man they saw carrying a lamp. Many had narrow escapes. In the waiting-room attached to the locomotive department a number of railway men were preparing for work when the place was raided by the police. All the men were ordered out on to the road outside the station, with their hands over their heads. They were then told to run for their lives. Fire was opened on them and most of them were wounded. Three died subsequently of wounds, a seventeen year old lad named Bennett, Patrick Devitt, father of eight children, and Daniel Mullane, a twenty-three year old fireman who, having escaped himself went back to assist a wounded driver, Harry Martin, and received three bullet wounds through the hips, from which he died early on the following morning.

A military court of enquiry was held by the British into this occurence. Its President was Colonel Commandant H. R. Cumming, D.S.O. who himself was killed at Clonbanin before its sittings were concluded. The findings of this enquiry while admitting that :

> " The R.I.C. did remove signal men from their respective cabins without previously having provided suitable or any reliefs . . . that a member of the R.I.C. did forcibly enter the railway refreshment room and obtain stimulant for Mrs. King, that his action, in the circumstances, is considered justifiable, that thereafter such refreshment room remained opened and was entered by some members of the R.I.C. and the railway staff, but that there is no evidence to show who is guilty of the alleged heavy depredations." [1]

The findings blandly allege that the railway men were mistaken in thinking that their wounds had been inflicted by members of the Crown forces, and implies that the men killed and wounded were the victims of rebel fire. The report is typical of the kind of mendacity to which the British authorities were driven by occurrences of this kind.

The sustained ordeal of the civil population was not confined to the men. The following extract from the *Cork Examiner* of 25th January indicates how the women were treated :

> " Extraordinary and unprecedented were the scenes in Glanworth on Sunday when a wholesale search by military took place and roads from all quarters were controlled. The National Schools were commandeered, as were also the premises of

[1] Cmd. 1220, H.M. Stationary Office, 1921

Mr. P. Walsh and Mr. J. O'Connor, corn merchant. The women were all rounded up at the National Schools and minutely searched by English women searchers, but one lady, Miss Gallagher, refused to submit." She was arrested.

A few days earlier, in an interview given to a special correspondent of the *Manchester Guardian*, General Strickland had been protesting : " The Army was not making war on women, and soldiers never interfered with women, unless they had direct evidence against them." In the same interview he admitted that " the formations of the Republican force were almost as well organised as those of the British Army," but he was still unrealistic enough to suggest that the citizens of Cork should form some sort of unarmed vigilance committee " to police the town." This, in a city crawling with " police " under his own control ! The fact that any such force would have to be unarmed, would not in his opinion " prevent it from assisting in intelligence work—the collection of information, which was the first condition of any success in putting down crime." Truly, his intelligence staff had confessed its complete failure.

In another interview given to the *Evening Standard* special correspondent a week later, General Strickland said :

> " What we are doing at present is—we are taking their officers locally, commanders here, Intelligence officers there, somebody else in another place, and so on. That breaks their communications.

> " If you will recall, say, the fight for Kilmallock police barracks last year, and compare it with these recent attacks you will observe a vast difference. You will notice that nothing is accomplished in these recent attacks. In all cases they are easily beaten off, and the attackers withdrew after half an hour or so. It is complimentary to suggest that improved communications and the mobility of our own patrols and reinforcements compel the early abandonment of these attacks, but I think rather it is due to a lack of brawn of the other side."

That was a superficial estimation and a misreading of the situation in the areas of the active southern brigades. All recent attacks on barracks had been no more than sniping by a few men, designed to inflict casualties, damage British morale, or draw out forces which could be attacked in the open. What was lacking on " the other side " was not brawn but weapons suitable for attack on fortified posts. Granted good organisation, which Strickland admits, a more reliable test of Army strength at the time was the quantity of serviceable arms

in its possession, and the use it was making of these arms. As has
been shown, there had been a progressive improvement in this
respect since the active campaign opened in Liam's brigade. A
similar improvement in the arms position had taken place in the other
Cork brigades, in the Kerry and East Limerick brigades and in the
Tipperary brigades. It was due almost entirely to captures from the
occupation forces in action.

But the ammunition supply for these arms was always woefully
precarious, so much so indeed that it was frequently the determining
factor in deciding what actions could be undertaken. In the best
days, there was no possibility of sustaining a fight involving more than
the expenditure of twenty to thirty rounds per man. Actions therefore
had to be short and sharp, and had to be broken off if not successful
at an early stage. Explosives and equipment were in very short
supply, and not always of reliable quality. These were the Army's
most difficult problems. General Strickland's singularly inapt
suggestion of " lack of brawn " is a reflection of one aspect of
British military opinion on the forces opposing them in Ireland—
unintelligent professional scorn for the efforts of amateurs—and it
was a state of mind that contributed something to the failure of the
policy of coercion and terror.

The most serious reverse suffered by Liam's brigade occurred at
Mourne Abbey on 15th February. Information had been received
that a conference of senior British officers in the martial law area
would be held at division headquarters in Cork about that time.
Liam decided to occupy positions on the two roads through his
brigade area most likely to offer targets, the Fermoy-Cork road and
the Mallow-Cork road, with the intention of attacking a convoy on
the way to or returning from the conference. Liam assembled a
conference at Lombardstown on Sunday, 13th, and detailed the
Mallow Battalion Column to occupy a position at Mourne Abbey.
Kanturk Battalion Column was ordered to stand ready to reinforce
the Mallow men if that course was deemed necessary as a result of
any later information. It did not in fact, participate in the action.

Mallow Battalion Column, under Commandant Jack Cunningham,
occupied a position about a mile south of Mourne Abbey. The
Battalion Commandant, Tadg Byrne, was with them. The largest
section, thirteen riflemen, was posted on the rising ground west of
the main road. Sections armed with shotguns were posted on the
flanks of the position, but on the eastern side of the road. The usual
signalling and protective elements were posted and preparations were
complete in the early hours of the morning of 15th February.

Cycling into Mallow that morning on the Burnfort road Siobhan
Creedon (Mrs. Seamus Langford) met two lorries of troops and police.

She knew that some I.R.A. operation was planned at Mourne Abbey, having been stopped by a sentry after leaving her home at Clogheen, and she became immediately suspicious of the mission of the two enemy lorries on this unfrequented bye-road. Reaching Mallow at 9.15 a.m., she went at once to Daniel McDonnell, the Mallow Company I.O., told him what she had seen and asked him to go to Mourne Abbey and warn the officers there.

McDonnell cycled to Mourne Abbey along the main road and located Commandant Byrne near the southern end of the ambush position. He gave him the information. Together they crossed the Clydagh, a stream flowing parallel to and beside the road, to the position where Commandant Cunningham was with the riflemen.

Within a few minutes firing started, not on the main road but to the north east. The protective sections there were engaged. Other reports came in indicating the presence of British forces in strength on three sides of the position. Suddenly, in the most disquieting and inexplicable manner, the column found that it was itself in the role of ambushed rather than ambusher. The British forces had adequate transport, machine guns and armoured vehicles. In this unforeseen and unexpected situation the column had to withdraw, fighting its way out as best it could. The sections to the west of the road were favoured by an apparent error made by one British detachment in taking up its position. It left a gap through which they withdrew westward towards Dromahane. The sections on the eastern side, where the first shots were fired, fared worse. Three men were killed: Patrick Flynn, Monee, aged 25; Patrick Dorgan, Island, aged 22; and Eamon Creedon, Clogheen, aged 20. One man died subsequently of wounds, Michael Looney, Island, aged 30. Eight prisoners were taken, of whom two were subsequently executed at Cork, after trial by courtmartial. They were Patrick Ronayne, aged 24, of Greenhill and Thomas Mulcahy, Toureen, aged 18. Both were members of the Burnfort Company.

Was this successful British action due to chance or luck? It appears otherwise. The Crown forces had quite effectively assembled detachments so as to surround completely this particular patch of terrain at the right time and on the right day. It was, in their circumstances, an intricate operation requiring organisation, time, and above all fore knowledge. Nothing like it had ever happened before in the brigade. Information, easily accounted for, the British had frequently about the general location of the columns, but this operation of theirs had a certainty and assurance in its execution which could not be attributed to chance. It pointed to one, and only one, disquieting conclusion—that the Crown forces were on this occasion acting on accurate information. How did they get it? This was an aspect of the struggle which had never caused Liam any difficulty in his brigade up to now, nor indeed was it one that gave serious trouble in any brigade at any time. The Army as a whole was singularly free from traitorous elements. But now it disquieted him to have to contemplate the possibility that some one who knew of the arrangements for Mourne Abbey, some one who knew the date and the time and the position, had deliberately passed that information to his enemies. He set enquiries going at once, but it was nearly a month later, when a similar though less disastrous event occurred, that the probable explanation came to light.

In January, 1921 the Fermoy Battalion was under considerable pressure and had suffered severely through arrests of officers. The battalion had not found it possible to send any officers to the training camp then being conducted at Nadd. Liam and Commandant Paddy O'Brien visited the area, and at a meeting held in Ballynoe appointed officers. Tom Griffin was appointed Battalion O/C, but was arrested early next morning. That incident illustrated one of the difficulties with which all battalions had to contend, although it was rather worse in Fermoy area than elsewhere. Liam was determined that activities should be undertaken which would take some of the pressure off the Fermoy Battalion. Having discussed the matter with Paddy O'Brien, on their way back to headquarters at Lombardstown, it was decided that O'Brien would go to the Charleville Battalion area and carry out certain activities there.

The largest British posts, Fermoy, Kilworth, Moore Park, Buttevant and Ballyvonaire, were situated in the areas of the battalions at the eastern side of Cork No. 2 Brigade. British strength was so overwhelming in the areas of the Fermoy, Castletownroche and Charleville battalions that the uninterrupted prosecution of the conflict in these areas was highly creditable to the officers and men who maintained it under almost insuperable difficulties. Most of the actions were of necessity on a smaller scale than those undertaken in the relatively less heavily garrisoned areas of the battalions on the western side of the brigade.

On 12th February a constable was killed at Churchtown near Buttevant On the 15th, Churchtown barracks was sniped. On the 18th an ambush was laid between Charleville and Buttevant and sniping attacks opened on the Charleville military and R.I.C. posts in the hope of drawing out from Buttevant relief forces which could be attacked in the ambush position. The sniping attacks however failed to draw out any reinforcements and the ambush party had to be withdrawn. On the 21st a British party was fired on near Doneraile. A military patrol investigating this occurrence was attacked near Kilbrack and four soldiers wounded. On 1st March an R.I.C. patrol was attacked in Charleville. On the same date Seán O'Brien, Chairman of the Rural District Council, was murdered by British forces as a reprisal. Two Black and Tans called to his home. When he opened the door, one fired revolver shots at him, the other threw a bomb, which inflicted the injuries from which he died.

Towards the end of February a British soldier was captured by the Liscarroll Company. He pleaded that he was a deserter and was released. A short time later every house in which he had stayed was raided. Not long afterwards another alleged deserter was captured between Liscarroll and Freemount. He was taken to Freemount, tried and sentenced to death. He was taken back to the vicinity of Buttevant where the sentence was carried out. If proof was needed that this man and others shot in similar circumstances were not deserters, but rather some of those whom Macready has described as " volunteers for Intelligence work," it was provided by the fact that they were accorded military funerals. Reprisals followed and O'Brien's and Regan's houses in Liscarroll were bombed.

On 3rd March Fermoy Battalion Column attacked a police patrol at Macollop, five miles east of Fermoy on the Ballyduff road. The patrol surrendered after a loss of one killed and one wounded. On the 18th soldiers were fired on in Fermoy, and police attacked in Castletownroche, in which three were wounded. Moore Park camp and the aerodrome at Fermoy were sniped. On 10th April two policemen were killed at Kildorrery, and two sniping attacks were subsequently made on their barracks. On the 15th Fermoy aerodrome, Kilworth camp and Moore Park were again sniped. On the 21st there was an exchange of fire between police at Castletownroche and a party in position to attack the barracks. Later in the month a military patrol was attacked at Pall on the Mallow road. On the 30th a police patrol was fired on in Charleville.

On 23rd May police were ambushed near Rockmills and two of them killed. On the 29th another attack on the Castletownroche police post resulted in one Black and Tan being killed and one wounded. Fermoy aerodrome, Kilworth Camp and Kildorrery barracks were sniped. On 1st June a policeman was killed at Ballinrush, Kilworth. On the 5th Rathcormack barracks was sniped. During the month two police were killed in an attack on Kildorrery barracks, three wounded at Castletownroche, and one at Grange, Glanworth. Crown forces were attacked at Ballindangan, a train was raided at Ballyhooley and mails captured, a despatch rider was held up at Skeheenarinka and relieved of his revolver, ammunition and despatches. There was another attack on Crown forces at Glanworth, in which two revolvers were captured. In an ambush at Drumdeer, Doneraile, two soldiers were disarmed. Ballyhooley post was sniped, a mail car was raided between Buttevant and Churchtown. These harrassing activities continued up to the Truce in what was probably the most heavily garrisoned area in Ireland. Nothing that the British forces were able to do could stop them. The I.R.A. battalions concerned lost few men and no arms.

Seán Moylan, Commandant of the Newmarket Column, had been in contact with Kerry No. 2 Brigade and had arranged to co-operate with companies of the Rathmore Battalion, for an attack on British forces passing between Mallow and Killarney. They lay in ambush for two days at the Bower, four miles west of Rathmore, without result. He then decided to move east into County Cork, lay an ambush on the Rathmore-Mallow road, and await a British party

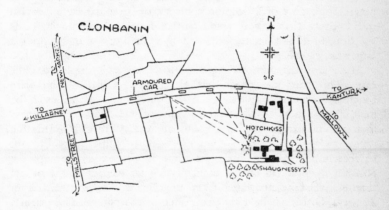

accompanying senior officers then on an inspection tour in Kerry on the way back to Buttevant. The position selected was at Clonbanin, five miles east of Rathmore. The position was about six miles from Kanturk, where there was a strong military post and about the same distance from Millstreet, then garrisoned by a force of Black and Tans and R.I.C. On the night of the 2nd March, Seán Moylan moved his column from the Bower to Ummeraboy, in the parish of Knocknagree. He had already detailed Denis Galvin and three men to select a position and to arrange for the co-operation of the Millstreet Battalion Column in the projected action. At 3 a.m. on the morning of the 3rd, Moylan's column moved out for Clonbanin and were in position by 6 a.m. They were joined by a section of the Kerry No. 2 Brigade Column, under Commandant Tom McEllistrim, and a detachment from Charleville Battalion Column, under Commandant Paddy O'Brien. The Newmarket and Charleville units occupied positions on the northern side of the road. The Kerry men and a section of the Millstreet Column had positions on the south side of the road. They had one of the Hotchkiss guns captured at Mallow, manned by Bill Moylan and Denis Galvin. The remainder of the Millstreet Column occupied a position covering the roads from Kanturk to deal with expected reinforcements from that direction. The local companies provided scouting and protective elements.

Commandant Paddy O'Brien detailed the sections to their positions and Commandant Moylan arranged for the laying of the half dozen road mines which the force had. And at 7 a.m. the column was ready for action.. Strict instructions had been given to the section commanders that fire was not to be opened on any target until a mine was exploded, the explosion being the signal for attack. This was necessary because of a decision come to by Commandants Moylan and O'Brien that a very small British force passing through the position would not be attacked, as long as the hope of intercepting a larger target existed.

At 10 a.m. the outposts signalled three lorries coming from the east. This was unexpected, but Moylan and O'Brien, who were together, decided to attack. When the leading lorry came over the mine controlled by Moylan he pressed the switch. Nothing happened, there was no explosion. At the same moment, O'Brien covering the driver, pressed the trigger of his rifle. The round failed to go off. In that minute of anticlimax the three lorries passed through the position, a soldier in one of them playing an accordion, the others singing, blissfully unaware of the mishaps that saved them from disaster. Discipline held the remainder of the column from firing. When the lorries had passed the tense silence of the groups was broken by excited questioning of men who had lain out in wet ditches for several days awaiting such an opportunity as that which had now slipped through their hands.

They were reassured however by the hope that, as it was still early in the day, the expected convoy from the west would duly make an appearance. The men settled down again to the long wait. It was later found that the reason for the mine failure was that high tension wires were being used with a low tension battery. The Cork Brigades were all handicapped by lack of expert knowledge of road mines. Successful use of this weapon later was the result of a slow process of trial and error.

At 2.15 p.m. the patience of the waiting column was rewarded; a convoy was signalled coming from the west. It consisted of three lorries, an armoured car and a touring car. The vehicles were spaced, as had been anticipated, at such intervals as to cover half a mile of

road. No attempt was made now to use the mines. Fire was opened
on the leading lorry, the driver was hit and it was ditched. A burst
from the Hotchkiss penetrated the slit in front of the driver of the
armoured car; the driver was wounded and it too was ditched.
The remaining vehicles halted, their occupants dismounting rapidly
and seeking whatever cover was available. A tall man in officer's
uniform was seen to jump from the touring car and run for cover
on the north side of the road. He was shot down before reaching
there and was later discovered to be Brigadier-General Cumming.

The action now became general and developed into a long duel
that ended only at dusk. About five minutes after the armoured
car was ditched its heavy machine-gun came into action and continued firing during the whole course of the fight. The opposing
forces were about equal in strength but the British had the advantage
of heavier weapons and an incomparably better supply of ammunition.
The armoured car commanded the road and prevented two efforts
made by the I.R.A. to drive in the flanks of the British position.
The British forces, too, attempted an outflanking manoeuvre but it
was defeated by I.R.A. fire. The British had the advantage also of a
deep ditch and several houses which gave them cover from the fire
of the Kerry and Millstreet units on the south side of the road.

The fact that the armoured car continued in action was the key
to the position and decided the fate of the ambush. The I.R.A.
had no means of putting it out of action and they had always to
consider the advent of reinforcements to the British. The sound of
firing could be heard distinctly in Kanturk, Newmarket and Millstreet, and reinforcements from these posts could be expected.
General Cumming's Brigade Headquarters at Buttevant was only
twenty-five miles away, and the fight had now continued for over
two hours. As dusk began to fall it was decided to withdraw, the
Kerry and Millstreet units to the west, and the Newmarket and
Charleville units north to Kiskeam. It was learned later that the
British casualties were thirteen killed and fifteen wounded. The
columns suffered no casualties.

On 8th March, Kanturk Battalion ambushed a party of Black-and-
Tans at Father Murphy's Bridge, Shronedaha, near Banteer. One
R.I.C. man was killed and the remainder disarmed. This action took
place within a mile of Banteer Barracks, and it curbed the very
aggressive system of patrols then being operated from this post.
Relays of Volunteers had occupied the position for several days before
the action.

Towards the end of February, British activity in the Lombardstown
area forced Liam to move Brigade Headquarters further west into the
area then occupied by sections of the Mallow and Kanturk Columns

around Nadd. A training camp had also been in progress there for some months, and David Herlihy's farmhouse had come to be known as "the barracks." The columns were widely dispersed amongst the farmhouses in the district. It was a base to which columns or sections of them returned after actions. The ambush at Father Murphy's Bridge had been carried out by a section of the Kanturk Column, which afterwards returned to Nadd.

Here, in the driving rain and fog of a raw March morning, the British forces staged one of their most elaborate and well planned efforts to annihilate the brigade staff and the columns. Large forces drawn from Cork, Ballincollig, Buttevant, Ballyvonaire, Fermoy and Kanturk were engaged. From before midnight on 9th March these forces in their armoured vehicles had been moving out from distant posts, armed with rifles, machine-guns, mortars and grenades, and converging on this high, bleak upland on the northern slopes of the Boggera Mountains. Before dawn on the 10th, most of them were being quietly detrucked from unlighted vehicles in a huge ring, taking up their allotted positions in a circle of steel around the unsuspecting columns. They had good information, and this was to be a killing.

It was a well-planned operation, efficiently carried out, and its limited success was attributable to factors inherent in the conditions under which the British forces operated. For complete success it was necessary that the raiding forces should seal off the billeting area simultaneously on all sides, and that no alarm should be raised in the I.R.A. camp before the various detachments surrounding it had taken up positions. Hence the approach under cover of darkness and the detrucking of troops well out from the target. Contact between all the component units of the raiding force was not possible ; each had to adhere to its timetable, irrespective of what other units were doing or of whether they had in fact taken up their position in the ring. It was precisely this aspect of the plan which broke down, and it broke down because Liam, without any exact information of this impending operation, had acted promptly on an intelligence report on the previous day.

Information which he received from Judy O'Riordan in Buttevant post, indicated the probability of large-scale raiding in the Banteer direction on the night of 9th-10th. He had immediately ordered out the Charleville Battalion on a road-cutting task at certain specified points ; this action saved Nadd from being a major disaster. British forces from Buttevant and Ballyvonaire were considerably delayed by trenches on the Buttevant-Mallow road, and at Eel Weir cross, and by broken bridges at Ballyclough and Templemary. An armoured car skidded into one trench. The result was, that when constriction of the British ring began at dawn, one section of the north-western perimeter was still open, some of the Buttevant and Ballyvonaire troops not having arrived. They occupied their positions too late to prevent the escape of most of their intended victims.

Liam was billeted at Patrick McCarthy's, a quarter of a mile north-west of Nadd cross roads. With him were George Power and Maurice Walsh of Mitchelstown. Michael O'Connell, the Assistant Brigade Quartermaster, had left for Lombardstown on the previous night to arrange for the cutting of the road at Eel Weir cross. Tadhg McCarthy, Adjutant of Mallow Battalion, was on duty in the neighbourhood of Nadd cross, with Volunteer Walsh from Ballyclough and two local Volunteers, Dan Scanlon and Dick Dunne. They were the first to observe troops approaching from the South. Visibility was poor, at times bad, as the fog lifted and filled alternately. Tadhg McCarthy and Walsh went immediately to inform Liam and the other brigade officers. They found them already outside the house. Another report of the presence of raiders had reached them.

The British detachment observed at Nadd cross had turned west, evidently with the intention of approaching their objective from the south. Liam now had reports of the presence of troops to the north-east, south and east of his position. Units of the columns in the scattered farm houses were alerted. They and the brigade officers began to move westward across the mountain. At one point a party of British troops infiltrated the position without being observed. Before any warning had reached the house, they came to David Herlihy's. Here, Lieutenant Edward Waters of Mallow Company, Volunteers Timothy Kiely, Joseph Morgan and John Moloney were sleeping. Kiely was a despatch rider of Lombards-town Company, who had come on the previous night with a despatch and stayed. Morgan and Moloney were members of Mallow Company attached to the Mallow Battalion Column.

Moloney, Kiely and Morgan were sleeping in a room off the kitchen on the ground floor. Waters and Herlihy were sleeping upstairs. The arms of Morgan, Moloney and Waters were in the kitchen. The other two were not armed. A section of the Kanturk Column, under Commandant Denis Lyons, had left " the barracks " on the previous day to co-operate with Millstreet Battalion Column in the destruction of Dromagh Castle, which was being prepared for occupa-tion by Auxiliaries. The Castle was burned down on the night of the 9th. Lyons and his party were expected back at " the barracks " on the following morning. When a knock sounded on the door Herlihy, who was up, opened it at once, believing Lyons and his party had returned. British soldiers under an officer stood outside.

They rushed in and overran the house. They hustled the half-dressed occupants into the yard, the officer shouting, " Get out

you —— we'll give you some of your own stuff now." Covered
by the rifles of the raiding party, they were taken to the back of the
house and lined up in a field. The officer, having posted his men,
said : "When I say run —." Morgan and Moloney made a dash for
liberty. Both were wounded, but managed to get away. Waters,
Kiely and Herlihy were shot dead where they stood. Bayonets were
used on the bodies.

The British were now closing in. Fire was exchanged between
some detachments and groups of Volunteers. Liam himself engaged
in one of these exchanges. Garrett McAuliffe reported to him on
the position in the Inchimay direction. One Volunteer who was not
on duty fell a victim to British fire. He was Edward Twomey of
Lacklown Company, a cow testing inspector, who was at the time
engaged on his civil duties. In running across a field he was shot
dead. When Morgan and Moloney escaped from the British firing
party at "the barracks" they were pursued, but by availing of
cover on the mountain they escaped. They became separated, however, Moloney getting as far as Riordan's farmhouse, Inchimay,
before being picked up by four other members of the columns who
carried him on to Cahill's, Kilmacrane, about three miles from
"the barracks." Morgan fell in with Liam Lynch's party and they
went on to Jim Horgan's, Crinaloo, where Liam dressed Morgan's
wound, while Morgan gave him a report of what had happened at
"the barracks." Liam sent scouts to locate the remaining members
of the columns, and, learning that they were at Cahill's, the whole
party assembled there. Here Liam dressed Moloney's wound, and
arranged to have him sent to hospital. Dr. Ryan of Glantane attended
to him.

Reports coming in gave Liam a picture of the extent of the British
operation and its results. Four Volunteers were dead, though one
of them had not been on duty, two were wounded but not too
seriously, and no one had been captured. For the second time within
a month an abnormal and disquieting feature of the British operation
impressed him. His enemies were evidently acting on accurate
information. There was a striking resemblance between what had
happened at Mourne Abbey and what had taken place at Nadd.
But now the mystery was quickly cleared up. A member of the
Kanturk Column, of whom a number of the men had been suspicious
for some time, was missing. He was a man who had served in the
British Army, and who had been with the column about two months.
Subsequent inquiries established his responsibility for the Nadd
operation, and made it clear that he could also have been responsible
for the reverse at Mourne Abbey, as he was in possession of complete
information about the proposed ambush several days before it was

due to take place. Two days before the Nadd raid the ambush at Father Murphy's Bridge had taken place and he had been ordered to parade for it, but instead of doing so he had gone to Kanturk on the pretext of drawing his pension as a British ex-serviceman. Later it was recalled that in his two month's service with the column he had never taken part in an action, always having one excuse or another for absence. In Kanturk on the 8th, he spent some time drinking, and was later seen in the British barracks in consultation with an officer. The local Battalion Intelligence Officer, Michael Moore, a very competent I.O., becoming aware of this, warned local men and sent a despatch to Brigade Headquarters giving the information. The despatch did not reach Liam Lynch or any member of his staff, and it is not entirely clear what became of it in the excitement created by the raid.

If any doubt remained of this man's guilt it was completely dissipated by the evidence which became available soon afterwards. He was identified as having been with one section of the raiding force at Nadd, dressed in the uniform of a Black-and-Tan. He was not seen again. His was an isolated case. Hundreds of men with British Army service served loyally and well in the I.R.A., some of them being foremost amongst the intrepid fighters. He alone stained their fine record by an act of treachery.

CHAPTER 12

CONFERENCES IN THE SOUTH. FIRST SOUTHERN DIVISION FORMED

I swear to you there are blood and brain in Ireland yet as the world one day shall know.
MITCHEL.

IN the early months of 1921, while the conflict was being developed all over the brigade area by the actions recorded in the previous chapter, Liam did not allow himself to become wholly engrossed in the actual fighting. He never lost sight of his own wider responsibilities. The columns were his main offensive arm, but their continued existence and fighting capacity depended in a large measure upon the efficiency of the territorial organisation behind them. With unabated zeal he continued to move through the seven battalion areas, encouraging the maintenence of an alert and vigorous spirit of combat in every unit, perfecting the special services which served the needs of the fighting columns, and constantly repairing the breaches in the officer ranks made by death and arrests.

Movement under the conditions which then existed, particularly in the heavily-garrisoned battalion areas at the eastern end of the brigade, called for constant vigilance. No house was entirely safe from sudden raids at any hour of the day or night, no road was immune from the menacing intimidation of armoured cars, lorry-borne troops, or roving cavalry or cycle patrols, and no area was free of the threat of being at any time completely surrounded and minutely searched. British forces had used bodies of troops numbering up to three thousand to cordon off and search specific areas. In the face of that situation, Liam and his staff continued to move about in every part of the brigade area, if not freely, at least without any disruption of their duties.

He had developed a technique of movement and protection which he enforced rigidly upon himself and upon his officers. He had never gone unarmed since September, 1919, except on visits to Dublin or Cork. From August, 1920, all his officers were permanently armed and under orders to resist capture. At first he carried a revolver only, but in the summer of 1920, he was asking his officers what the public reaction would be to groups of Volunteers going

146

about bearing arms openly. Thereafter he and his staff carried rifles and grenades as well as revolvers. Acutely conscious of his own responsibilities as he was, he would not tolerate officers taking avoidable risks in regard to their personal safety. He set a high standard in this as in other matters.

Before deciding to sleep in a house he inspected the lay-out in the vicinity, checked the security arrangements, and decided the action to be taken in the event of attack. The local company was held responsible for the provision of guards and scouts. In the early days he moved round his area on a bicycle, later he used horse traps and was always accompanied by one or more of his officers. Cyclist scouts were used when moving in this way from one company area to another, each company being responsible within its own territory.

The Blackwater, which cut his whole brigade in two from west to east, did not unduly restrict though it sometimes hampered or delayed his movements. East of Mallow it became dangerous for Volunteers to use the bridges over the river by day or night. To overcome this difficulty boats were extensively used for crossings near Kilavullen and at Careysville east of Fermoy. In 1921 crossings could be made at the latter place only under cover of darkness. The British forces discovered that boats were being used, and on several occasions destroyed a number of them.

An order issued by Liam on 26th June, 1921, after the First Southern Division had been formed, indicates his views on the wider application of part of a protective system which had been in operation in Cork No. 2, and some other brigades for a considerable time previously. After referring to certain recognised routes frequently used by officers in moving through the area, the order went on to direct that :

" Each company on such routes will be provided with a horse, or pony and car, and these will be kept at a point convenient to the route where they can be got quickly. Such animals and cars . . . will be used only on Volunteer work, and the Company Captain will be held responsible for the non-abuse of the service. At least two bicycles in running order, with pumps and repair outfits, will be dumped convenient to the route and reserved for transport work only. One or two men for scouting should always be available."

Despite all precautions, however, there were numerous occasions on which he escaped death or capture by the narrowest of margins. It would probably have been death because he had said frequently, " If I'm taken, I'll never be taken alive." One such occasion occurred at Mount Hiliary on 18th March. George Power, Paddy O'Brien,

Michael O'Connell, and Maurice Walsh were with him. They were moving on foot in daylight. Suddenly the whole area became infested with British troops on a large-scale raiding mission. Liam and Paddy O'Brien were some distance in advance of the others. Maurice Walsh went forward to them and the three moved on to near the top of the mountain where they took cover. From there they were able to observe the movements of the raiders, one party of whom came quite close but did not observe them.

All the time he was thinking nationally. In the most difficult days he never lost his contacts with adjoining brigades, but these contacts tended to become infrequent and unsatisfactory, under the mounting tension of a situation demanding unceasing vigilance, originality and resource in every commander. His life was now an endless labour of planning and movement. But preoccupation with the day-to-day problems of his brigade, did not blind him to the wider aspects of the struggle. He saw in the uneven development of the conflict over the country as a whole, dangers not evident to many at the time. He thought the potential strength of the inactive brigades should no longer be permitted to remain dormant. He feared that unless the fighting was more widely distributed the British forces might in time come to the point of ignoring the quiescent areas and concentrating their superior strength and armament against the few active brigades. In fact, there had commenced at that time, a shifting of the weight of the occupation forces into Munster.

That was, of course, primarily a G.H.Q. responsibility. But it is characteristic of Liam that he should himself take any action within his power which tended to the successful prosecution of the struggle as a whole. When, at the end of 1920, he took the initiative in calling together for consultation officers of the brigades immediately adjoining his own, he was acting in the true spirit of the Army, as well as taking a very shrewd and practical step to co-ordinate the activities of the fighting forces in the South. The I.R.A. was not a highly regimented organisation, part of its strength lay in the wide field open to local initiative for exploitation, its fundamental unity of purpose was inspired by devotion to a well-defined objective, and the general direction of its activities was never in any danger of becoming diverted to lesser ends. Bit by bit the whole organisation had been created, almost had grown naturally, to meet the needs of the situation as it developed. It was unhampered, free, vital, strong. Suitability for its purpose was the prime and constant test applied to every new expansion of its structure. A new situation was developing in the South—and only in the South—the day of attacks on barracks was over, the struggle was developing into larger actions requiring different tactics. If that new situation offered greater opportunities, it presented also greater dangers. New machinery was required to meet it. Here, again, Liam was blazing a new trail.

His most frequent contacts now were with Cork No. 1 and Tipperary No. 3 Brigades. Dan Breen, Seán Treacy, and Denis Lacey had made a number of visits to him; one of which coincided with Liam's arrest in Cork. Later, towards the end of 1920, Dan Breen paid a further visit and there was an informal conference on the general situation in which Seán O'Hegarty and I from Cork No. 1 Brigade, Liam Deasy from Cork No. 3, and Liam and George Power from Cork No. 2 Brigade took part. This meeting took place near Bweeing about eight miles south-west of Mallow.

The first formal conference of officers of the Southern Brigades assembled at William Barry's, Ballylegan, Glanworth, on 6th January, 1921. The visiting officers were the guests of Liam's brigade. Guard and protective duties were undertaken by Glanworth and Ballindangan Companies under the command of Commandant Tom Barry, Glanworth. The manner in which all the brigades concerned responded to the suggestion of a conference illustrates the general position of the commandants of the active brigades vis-a-vis G.H.Q. They were officers who recognised the value of unified command and they were entirely loyal to G.H.Q. But they had by their own initiative and efforts, and with a little more than verbal encouragement from Dublin, developed the fight to the stage it had then reached, and they did not admit that officers of the Headquarters staff, inexperienced in the actual fighting outside Dublin as they were, had any monopoly of the plans or ideas for the general conduct of the struggle. Almost their first decision was to send a summary of their decisions and recommendations to G.H.Q.

The brigades represented were :

Cork No. 1	...	Commandant, Seán O'Hegarty.
		Brigade Adjutant, Florence O'Donoghue.
Cork No. 2	...	Commandant, Liam Lynch.
Cork No. 3	...	Commandant, Charlie Hurley.
		Quartermaster, Dick Barrett.
Tipperary No. 2		Commandant, James Leahy.
		Vice Commandant, Matt. Barlow.
Tipperary No. 3		Commandant, Seamus Robinson.
		Brigade Adjutant, Con Moloney.
East Limerick		Commandant, Denis Hannigan.
		Seamus Malone.

Seamus Robinson presided at the conference and Con Moloney acted as adjutant to it. In discussions lasting two days and most of the intervening night, these eleven officers reviewed all the factors influencing the struggle in their areas. There was complete unanimity in the view that the war could be maintained and extended, and there was broad general agreement upon the lines of action to be undertaken.

Martial law had been proclaimed by the British over the areas of all the brigades represented. Weak R.I.C. posts had been captured or evacuated and subsequently destroyed by the Army, occupied posts and barracks in towns and cities were now held in much greater strength, and generally speaking were so well fortified as to be incapable of capture with the weapons at our disposal. No substantial acquisition of arms or ammunition could be expected from attacks upon them. The R.I.C. had been demoralised, depleted in strength, and diluted by ruffianly Black-and-Tan elements. A new force had appeared—the Auxiliary Division of the R.I.C. Seven of its fifteen companies, each about one hundred strong, were stationed in the martial law area. British military strength had been reinforced, transport augmented, and a large number of armoured vehicles imported. There were fifty-one British battalions in Ireland at this time, and of these 250 to 300 men per battalion were available for offensive action. They had seventy Peerless and thirty-four Rolls-Royce armoured cars as well as large numbers of armoured lorries.[1]

Terrorism and reprisals had become part of the official policy of the Crown forces. But, despite a number of obvious advantages, they were now never free of the threat of attack. Minor actions and the sniping of their posts had a bad effect on morale. Officers and men lived under conditions approximating to a state of siege. Movements between posts and punitive expeditions of all kinds had to be undertaken in strength. Guard and administrative problems arose and accumulated. Normal routine and training had to be abandoned. There was an undercurrent of unease and discontent.

On our side, relatively severe losses had been suffered by deaths and arrests. Movement, except in the cleared areas, was becoming more difficult. The supply of war material was alarmingly small. We were only just beginning to produce efficient grenades and land mines. We had no heavy weapons which would make possible effective attacks on fortified posts. Training was not of a sufficiently high standard and could not be improved generally in the absence of a greater supply of arms. On the other hand, organisation was better than it had ever been, there was an immense reserve of men ready and willing to fight if they could be armed, our Intelligence Services were beginning to show their superiority over those of the

[1] See Macready, *Annals of an Active Life*, Vol. 2, pp. 479-80 and 525-26

enemy. But there were still many phases of the conflict in which we were not deriving the maximum advantage from our opportunities. Our two paramount needs at that stage were more arms, including heavier weapons and an adequate ammunition supply, and a spreading of the conflict to the inactive areas of the country. The morale of the Army was excellent The people, generally, were steadfast and loyal.

The more savagely the British forces operated the machinery of terror, the more effectively the people were drawn together in common suffering and in common determination to resist. Bishops, priests and people, under the spur of tyranny, maintained a resolute attitude of non-recognition to England's claim to hold Ireland by force of arms. " Ireland," George Russell wrote, " had become for the moment all will."[1]

In their Lenten pastorals many of the bishops condemned the outrages committed by the Crown forces, and showed a better appreciation of the true nature of the conflict than had been reflected in some of their earlier pronouncements. His Lordship, Most Rev Dr. McRory put the true position in a sentence :

> " The Government told them they had no quarrel except with a handful of gunmen, but they knew in their hearts, and the whole world knew, that their quarrel was with the whole nation's spirit of liberty which they were doing their best or worst to stifle and kill."

Consideration of the general position in the South resulted in the conference coming to a number of decisions, and making a number of recommendations to G.H.Q. The decisions were well within the competence of any brigade commander ; the recommendations are a complete vindication of the sense of discipline in the assembled officers.

The recommendations included a request to G.H.Q. that the Army should be publicly declared to be on active service ; that a proclamation should be issued to the effect that where hostages were carried by the enemy, his forces, armed or unarmed, would be shot at sight, and that in view of the British proclamation announcing that our men taken prisoner under arms would be shot forthwith, similar action be taken by us against their forces. A request was made for whole-time medical officers for each brigade, to be paid by G.H.Q., for some decisions on discipline, and for the supply of tinned foods for the flying columns. One of the most important recommendations was in the following terms :

[1] *Pearson's Magazine,* U.S.A., 1921

"To offer G.H.Q. (*a*) an unarmed Flying Column of twenty men from each two Brigades, i.e., three Flying Columns of twenty men each, to be armed by G.H.Q. and sent by them to inactive areas; or (*b*) that the six Brigades represented between them arm one Flying Column for similar action. G.H.Q. to see to their quartering and rationing. It is suggested that this Column operate in inactive areas, and as far as possible from enemy active bases."

That recommendation indicates how keenly the assembled officers felt the necessity for spreading the fight, and it emphasises the fact that there was no shortage of fit and trained officers and men, but that there was a shortage of arms. Nevertheless, out of their own limited resources, they were prepared to arm a column of twenty men so that the fight could be carried into the inactive areas.

The decisions made on communications and intelligence resulted from a study of the dispositions of British forces and of the manner in which their lines of communication cut across our Brigade boundaries. Their system of rationing and reliefs for their outposts made it clear that better results could be obtained by us in attacks upon their convoys if a system of rapid exchange of information between our brigades could be established. For example, the headquarters of all British forces garrisoning Kerry were in Cork 2 Brigade area. Normally, ration and relief parties used two main road routes from their headquarters to their Kerry outposts, one via Newmarket and Castleisland, and the other via Mallow-Rathmore-Killarney. From British 18th Brigade Headquarters at Fermoy, again in Cork 2 area, normal lines of road communication to their posts at Clonmel, Cahir and Cashel passed through part of Cork 2, part of East Limerick and part of Tipperary No. 3 Brigade. The headquarters of all forces garrisoning Cork 3 Brigade area were in Cork City, and their lines of communication passed through Cork 1 and Cork 3 Brigades.

To ensure a more rapid exchange of information on these and similar matters, inter-brigade communications were for the first time put upon a regular organisation basis, and arrangements were made for a more rapid exchange of intelligence between the brigades. The decisions included one to make certain roads impassable for the British forces, to order county councils not to repair cuttings made by our forces, and to post snipers to prevent the enemy from repairing the roads himself. It was decided to snipe all enemy posts on one night each week, and to snipe them constantly by day. The derailment of troop trains was considered. It was decided to have at least one dug-out constructed in each company area.

The keynote of the conference was co-operation and mutual assistance between the brigades. The most urgent necessity present in everybody's mind was that of making the conflict more widespread and truly national in scope. This conference had in it the germ of the idea of divisional organisation which emerged three months later. Liam's initiative set the spark to a new train of development. His brigade organisation had done an excellent job of protection and billeting. The conference was held within six miles of two of the strongest British posts in the area, Fermoy and Kilworth.

The second conference of Southern Brigades was held at Mrs. Hickey's, Tubbereenmire, near Glenville, towards the end of the following month. In addition to the brigades represented at Glanworth, the two Waterford Brigades and Mid-Limerick Brigade sent officers to this meeting. Pax Whelan and George Lennon, O/C and Vice O/C of Waterford No. 2 Brigade and Paddy Paul, O/C Waterford No. 1 Brigade were present. The Brigade Commandant, Seán Wall, represented Mid-Limerick. Cork No. 1 and No. 3 Brigades were represented by a larger group of officers because of a project then under consideration in which both these commands were deeply involved. This was a G.H.Q. proposal to import a cargo of arms from Italy. G.H.Q. was aware of the intention to hold this second conference, and the occasion was availed of to make preliminary plans for the reception and distribution of the arms.

This project had been under consideration for some time. In December, 1920, Liam Deasy, Adjutant of Cork No. 3 Brigade, and I had attended a conference at G.H.Q., at which it was the principal subject for discussion. The meeting took place at Barry's Hotel, Gardiner's Row, about 13th or 14th December. The G.H.Q. officers present included Cathal Brugha, Michael Collins, Liam Mellows and Joe Vize. At that time the project was considered to be sufficiently advanced at the Italian end to justify the selection of a landing-place for the cargo, and the sending of an officer with sea-faring experience to Italy, who would return with the vessel and pilot it to the selected landing-place. The expected boat was a four-masted barque with an auxiliary engine, one of a number of ships owned by the Federaciona Della Mara, normally sailing from Genoa in ballast for cargoes of coal from Newcastle. It was intended that after the discharge of the arms she would go on to Newcastle and pick up a cargo of coal in the normal way. Two decisions were made at the G.H.Q. conference, first that the landing-point should be on the West Cork coast, at a point to be selected by Cork No. 3 Brigade in its area, and second that Commandant Michael Leahy, Vice O/C of Cork No. 1 Brigade should proceed to Italy and return with the cargo. Commandant Leahy left Cork for Dublin on the first stage of his journey on 2nd January, 1921.

The Tubbereenmire Conference was concerned mainly with plans for the effective protection of the landing and distribution of the expected arms. Cork No 3 Brigade had by then fixed the landing-point at Myross Harbour, inside Rabbit Island near Glandore. This small harbour had the advantage of being screened from the sea by Rabbit Island, a sufficient depth of water in the channel at low tide to accommodate the type of vessel expected, and three convenient strands to which small boats working from both sides of the ship could ferry the cargo ashore. There was a good local supply of four-oared and six-oared boats, a number of yawls and two or three motor boats.

Nothing could be done, except by way of concealment, to guard against the possibility of interference by British Naval forces. At the time a British sloop paid visits at irregular intervals to Glandore Harbour. It was planned to get the arms ship inside Rabbit Island under cover of darkness. The Tubereenmire Conference worked out plans for the covering of the landing by Cork No. 1 and No. 3 Brigades. Distribution of the arms was to extend northwards to the Limerick and Tipperary Brigades as well as to Kerry. Routes were selected and the construction of dumps along them ordered. Dumps in the vicinity of the landing-place were to be capable of holding the whole cargo, if transference of it out of the area was delayed by enemy activity. G.H.Q. subsequently changed the landing-point to Helvick in Co. Waterford.

The final conference in connection with this proposal was held at Shanacrane, north of Dunmanway in Cork No. 3 Brigade area on 7th May. Neither Liam Lynch nor anybody else present was aware that Commandant Leahy had arrived back in Dublin a few days previously, the whole project having failed. When the news finally reached Liam it was a bitter disappointment.

The next step in the development of I.R.A. organisation followed logically from the first two conferences. It was the incorporation of groups of brigades into a divisional organisation. It was logical, too, that the first division to be formed should include the brigades which had attained the highest standard of organisation and fighting efficiency at the time. The Second Southern and the Fourth Northern were the only other divisions formed before the Truce. The meeting for the formation of the First Southern Division took place at Kippagh, near Millstreet, in Liam's brigade area on 26th April, 1921. Nine brigades were included, three in Kerry, three in Cork, two in Waterford and one in West Limerick. Liam was appointed Divisional Commandant.

He had now undertaken a responsibility far greater than that of any officer outside Dublin, and equalled only by that of two or three

G.H.Q. officers there. He commanded nine brigades comprising 30,620 officers and men. Of these Cork No. 1 Brigade with 7,500 all ranks was the largest. Cork No. 3 was next in strength with 5,270. Cork No. 2 numbered 4,700; Kerry No. 1, 4,000; Kerry No. 2, 3,400; Waterford (two brigades), 2,270; West Limerick, 2,100, and Kerry No. 3, 1,350. The British forces occupying the area were estimated at 21,260, including 18,750 troops, 1,600 R.I.C., 340 Auxiliaries and 570 Marines.

At the meeting, Cork No. 2 Brigade was represented by Liam and Seán Moylan; Cork No. 1 by Seán O'Hegarty and myself; Cork No. 3 by Liam Deasy and Tom Barry; Kerry No. 1 by Andy Cooney;

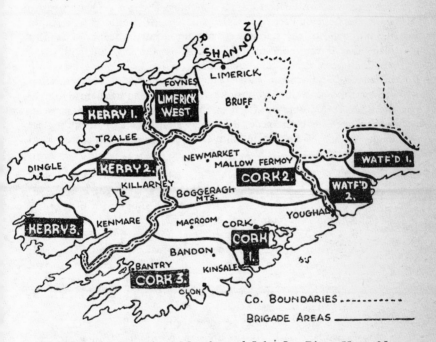

Kerry No. 2 by Humphrey Murphy and John Joe Rice. Kerry No. 3, the Waterford and West Limerick Brigades were not represented.

I had known Liam since 1917. Now I came into continuous and more intimate contact with him on being appointed adjutant to the division. No other appointments were made at the first meeting. Finding a staff for the division was not an easy matter. Liam's own transfer out of Cork No. 2 Brigade made it a hardship to take any other officer from that command. Cork No. 1 Brigade had lost two brigade commanders, Tomás McCurtain and Terence MacSwiney, within the previous twelve months, Cork No. 3 Brigade had lost its brigade commander, Charlie Hurley, killed in action at Ballymurphy, Upton in the previous month, the commandant of the West Limerick Brigade, Seán Finn, had also been killed in a fight near Ballyhahill in March.

Moreover, a proposal was under consideration to divide both Cork No. 2 and Cork No. 3 Brigades, and this involved the finding of two additional brigade staffs of whole-time officers. The division was carried out soon afterwards, the new brigades being numbered four and five—No. 4 consisting of the battalions on the western side of Cork No. 2, and No. 5 those at the western end of Cork No. 3. In the following month, Commandant Joseph O'Connor, Quartermaster, Cork No. 1 Brigade, was appointed Divisional Quartermaster and Commandant Patrick Coughlan, Divisional Engineer. No other appointments to the staff were made until July, when Commandant Liam Deasy was appointed Vice O/C of the division and Commandant Tom Barry, Training Officer.

Ernie O'Malley represented General Headquarters at the meeting for the formation of the division, and read a memorandum outlining the G.H.Q. conception of divisional functions. This document, having referred to the necessity for divisional staffs to obtain a clear understanding of the principles involved in the formation of divisional areas, went on to say :[1]

> " This step marks a very definite advance in our development, and is only being taken by G.H.Q. as areas become fit for it. For one thing, it will make things much simpler for G.H.Q. by diminishing the number of units which come directly in contact with G.H.Q. This will enable far more attention to be given to the main problems of each individual area, and of a much closer co-operation being carried out between the several divisional areas. The machinery of administration will be greatly simplified, and there should be a further pronounced increase in speed and efficiency of working.
>
> " One thing we must lay down emphatically—the Divisional Commandant must rise to his new position. He must not try to run his Division as he used to run his Brigade, if he does chaos will result. A good Brigadier—and only a good one—can keep in close touch with four or five Battalions ; when the number reaches as high as fourteen or fifteen or more, no officer can possibly accomplish the direct personal control of them. To decentralise command, to encourage readiness to assume responsibility, to form machinery suitable for staff work—these are the ways in which a Divisional Staff can best contribute to

[1] See Appendix 2

the general efficiency of the Army. . . . G.H.Q. freely entrusts the Divisional Commandant with a grave and solemn responsibility—nothing less than the absolute military control of two or three counties."

Liam had now, in sober truth, accepted "a grave and solemn responsibility." The Army in three and a half counties was under his command. In territorial area and in numerical strength his division was more than three times the extent of any division subsequently formed. In arms, in trained officers and men, and in fighting experience it was pre-eminent. On its capacity to maintain the struggle the fate of the whole national effort to a large extent depended.

Liam availed of this conference to resume consideration of the aspects of the military situation which had been discussed at Glanworth and Tubbereenmire. An improvement in the arms position, resulting from the expected Italian consignment was then a reasonable hope, which, had it materialised, would have transformed the whole face of the conflict in the south. Now, apart from the agreed necessity for an efficient and rapid development of the slack areas, and the consequent extension of the fighting which would defeat British efforts to concentrate against a small number of active areas, two new phases of British activity demanded consideration and counter action.

The first was the British policy of shooting prisoners of war, with or without the doubtful benefit of trial by drum-head courtmartial. The second was the policy of official reprisals whereby Crown forces arbitrarily selected and destroyed, by fire or explosives, dwelling houses and business premises in the vicinity of the scene of army activities. Executions after trial by military courts had already taken place in Cork, Captain Cornelius Murphy of Cork No. 2 Brigade on 1st February, Captain Seán Allen of Tipperary No. 3 Brigade on 28th February, and five Volunteers captured at the Dripsey ambush, Timothy McCarthy, Thomas O'Brien, Daniel O'Callaghan, John Lyons and Patrick O'Mahony, all shot on 28th February. It was known that prisoners taken at Clonmult and Mourne Abbey might suffer a similar fate. In fact two Clonmult prisoners, Maurice Moore and Patrick O'Sullivan, and two Mourne Abbey prisoners, Thomas Mulcahy and Patrick Ronayne, were executed in Cork two days later—on 28th April. Captain Patrick Casey of 5th Battalion, Mid Limerick Brigade, was shot on 2nd May and Daniel O'Brien of Liscarroll Company, Charleville Battalion, Cork No. 2 Brigade, on 16th May.

The question of attempting the rescue of these prisoners had already been considered by their own brigades, and particularly by Cork No. 1, in whose area they were held. Reluctantly, it had to be admitted that rescue was not possible. The prisoners were held in the military detention barracks attached to Cork military barracks. There all were shot, but their bodies were taken subsequently to Cork Jail for burial.

The counter action to these executions agreed upon at Kippagh was that on a specified date there should be a general attack on Crown forces throughout the Divisional area, irrespective of whether these forces were encountered under arms or not. This action was carried out on 14th May, and although not participated in by all brigades even in the south, it resulted in a higher British casualty list than had ever been the case since Easter Week, 1916. On the question of official reprisals, it was decided to request the sanction of G.H.Q. to the destruction of property belonging to active enemies in the areas where British reprisals had been carried out. It was recommended that this counter reprisal offensive should be sufficiently heavy and persistent either to put an end to British reprisals or clear the country of its active resident civilian enemies. The result of this was that in June G.H.Q. sanctioned a policy upon the lines suggested.[1]

The G.H.Q. memorandum on divisional organisation had recommended the establishment of divisional headquarters in a district comprising as many as possible of the following requirements : " central position, resources of various kinds, thoroughly friendly population, natural defensive strength." The western extremity of Cork No. 1 Brigade area provided all these conditions admirably, as well as being centrally located in the division area. It was decided to ask Commandant O'Hegarty to arrange for accommodation at his discretion in the vicinity of Coolea. In a short time preparations were complete and divisional headquarters was established at the farmhouse of Eamon MacSuibne, Gortyrahilly.

Coolea Company of the 8th Battalion, in whose area divisional headquarters was set up, was one of the largest and best in the Army. Captain James Moynihan had 137 active men on the rolls, and from them guards, scouts and despatch riders were provided for day and night duty. A member of Cumann-na-mBan, Nan Sweeney (Mrs. Jerh. O'Shea, Ballingeary) was appointed to undertake the onerous job of housekeeping for a constantly fluctuating number of officers and visitors.

Cork No. 1 Brigade headquarters was then in the adjoining company area—Ballyvourney. The five companies of the 8th Battalion, Kilnamartyra, Ballingeary, Inchigeela, Ballyvourney and Coolea, were all engaged in protection duties for the two headquarters, and much of the heavy work of communications and guards fell to the Ballyvourney Company, because of its location on the main route most

---

[1] For text, see Appendix 3

likely to be used by the enemy in approaching the area from the east.
The 8th Battalion had cleared its area of enemy forces much earlier.
There was, of course, no secrecy, and no need for secrecy, in this
district. The people were loyal, steadfast and trustworthy. The local
Cumann-na-mBan organisation and the local people co-operated to
ensure that every Volunteer on duty was assured of regular meals.

No word of English was spoken by the old people in the house
where divisional headquarters was set up, and except for the abnormal
amount of cooking, the comings and goings of visiting officers and
despatch riders at all hours of the day and night, and the almost
ceaseless clatter of typewriters, the everyday life of the farmhouse
went on much as it had always done before the demands of guerilla
warfare imported this unfamiliar bustle to disturb its peace.

At the neighbouring farmhouse of Eoin MacCarthaig, where Liam
sometimes stayed, he made the same impression on Eoin's eighty
year old mother that he had made on so many others. Recalling the
" visitors " in a conversation with her gandson, Amlaoib O'Loingsig,
in the winter of 1921, she referred to the tall man, wearing spectacles
who was it seemed in charge.

" Ní féaḋar caḋ é an ainim a ḃí air," she said,
" no éinne mar ġeall air na a cuiḋ ġnóta,
aċ tá fios aġam an méiḋ seo, pé hé féin
nó pé air ġurḃ as ḋo, ḋuine uasal aḃea é."

From this isolated spot lines of communication were quickly
established to all the brigade headquarters and to G.H.Q., by runner
to the points where they fed into the Cork and Kerry brigade communications systems, and thereafter by all the varied means used,
railway workers, lorry drivers, and so on, to their destinations. In a
short time a considerable volume of daily correspondence developed.
The dangers to be anticipated from captured documents, and the
lack of facilities for any except barely essential correspondence, acted
as a constant check on the normal tendency to initiate and accumulate
written orders and directions. That, and the general security practice
of destroying documents, has incidentally resulted in the almost
complete disappearance of any written records of the Division.

Meanwhile, a temporary headquarters had been established at
Michael Howard's, Ivale, Kilcorney, near Millstreet. Captain Maurice
Walsh of Mitchelstown, who had been and continued to be Liam's
principal staff officer, took up duty there. Liam and I began the first
tour of the brigades within a week of the Kippagh meeting. Cork
No. 3, Kerry No. 1, Kerry No. 2 and West Limerick brigades were
visited in a journey partly on foot, in pony-trap, on horse back and
by boat, which lasted fifteen days. Kerry No. 3 Brigade and the

Waterford brigades were not visited on this tour. Conferences of brigade staffs and battalion and column commanders were held in the brigades visited. Every factor influencing the development of the fight was reviewed in detail, organisation, training, arms, intelligence, supply of explosives, communications, security, availability of men and weapons for columns, leadership and control at all formations down to the companies—all these were examined and orders given for such revisions and changes as were found to be necessary.

Effective control by competent officers at every level of command was essential to the maintainence of widespread guerilla action. It could not exist without good organisation, firmly based on efficient companies and battalions. These units had to be ready at all times to reinforce the columns, to provide local protection, to supply intelligence, to arrange billeting and to form a pool of trained reserves. Each command had problems and functions peculiar to itself, but it was in the intelligent utilisation of the situation, created by the pooling of what each could contribute that the best results would be obtained.

The guerilla idea had given us the initiative, and the columns had come to be accepted as the most effective guerilla formations at our command while the arms position remained as it was. That was a situation which might change if more arms became available, or may be lost if our colums were destroyed. Constant vigilance and sound security measures were vital both in action and billets. Clonmult, Mourne Abbey, Dripsey and Nadd were bitter lessons. If activity became reduced to the operations of a small number of columns in the divisional area, their general location would inevitably become known to the Crown forces, who could at any time muster sufficient troops to overwhelm them in a pitched battle. To retain the initiative we had to continue to decide when and where to strike, and our blows should combine the elements of speed, surprise and success. When evasion was essential to survival, evasion was the correct policy.

The maximum number of columns which could be armed should be put in the field in each brigade, every opportunity for improving training should be availed of, a pool of trained officers and men should be ready when more arms became available. The cleared areas had to be maintained and where possible extended. It had to be ensured that Crown forces ventured into these areas only in strength and at their peril. Local initiative should be such that every unforseen opportunity was snapped up on the instant; there should be no time and no area in which the Crown forces would not feel the threat of potential attack.

Under the policy of terrorism being operated by the British, the civil population had been treated more savagely in the areas where the Army was not striking effectively. We had the means of retaliating for the killing of our prisoners, and, as soon as G.H.Q. sanction was received, every command should have its plans ready for counter action to the British policy of reprisals. The full capacity of the organisation should be utilised constantly. Apart from the activities of the columns, sniping and road cutting on a well planned scale were within the capacity of all units.

These were some of the ideas which Liam impressed upon his officers. Out of his talks and discussions, quiet, methodical and imperturbable, hard and undramatic as the realities he was dealing with, there was evoked at these long conferences a vivid sense of his glowing faith and stubborn certitude of ultimate success. The impact of his vigorous personality and his confident grasp of every factor in a complex situation had a bracing effect. He inspired many officers with a new and wider concept of the task and the objective.

CHAPTER 13

COUNTER ACTION TO THE TERROR CAMPAIGN

It is not sufficient to say, " I believe," unless one can also say, " I serve."

PEARSE

THE Glanworth conference had asked for a public declaration that
the Army was on active service. On 30th March, President De Valera
in a press interview, defined the relationship between Dáil Éireann
and the I.R.A., a statement which was in effect similar to that asked
for by the conference.

> " One of our first Governmental acts," he said, " was to take
> over control of the voluntary armed forces of the nation. From
> the Irish Volunteers we fashioned the Irish Republican Army to
> be the military arm of the Government. This army is, therefore,
> a regular state force, under the civil control of the elected
> representatives, and under organisation and a discipline imposed
> by these representatives, and under officers who hold their
> commissions under warrant from these representatives. The
> Government is, therefore, responsible for the actions of this
> Army. These actions are not the acts of irresponsible individuals
> or groups, therefore, nor is the I.R.A., as the enemy would have
> one believe, a praetorian guard. It is the national Army of
> defence."

The defensive role of the Army was well understood by the Volunteers themselves. They were defending the Republic and its government against the aggression of an invader. But the government to
which they gave allegiance was not strong enough to provide the
administrative and supply services available to a regular army, or to
bear the financial burden which a money payment to all ranks would
have involved. As well as risking his life, the Volunteer very often
risked his means of livelihood and put the economic position of his
dependents in jeopardy. These conditions of service were inevitable
because of the nature of the conflict. They bore most severely against
the men on whole-time service, most of whom had voluntarily
abandoned their employments, professions or businesses, and when
the numbers so engaged became substantial, as in the Cork brigades,

a problem was created, the solution of which could not be left indefinitely to the unorganised generosity of the public. It was necessary to distribute the burden more equitably.

Before 1920 the southern brigades received no financial assistance from G.H.Q. In that year and in 1921 a very modest allowance was made to a few officers, but for the large majority of those on active service there was no financial provision of any kind. No one expected any such provision, or thought it possible, but the simple necessities of food and clothing remained.

To provide these, particularly for the columns, each Brigade Quartermaster worked out his own schemes. On the formation of the division, Liam had of necessity to undertake responsibility, not alone for fighting a fourth of the whole military forces of the nation, but also for the administrative and supply problems which a vigorous campaign entailed. While continuing the policy he had operated in his own brigade, of giving officers the maximum of authority and freedom of action and holding them responsible for results, he now set about the achievement of uniformity in the administrative and supply work of the division, and of raising the general standard to that of the most efficient brigades.

To provide funds for the purchase of arms, food and clothing, the method adopted was that of a levy on the whole population of each brigade area, based on the Poor Law Valuation of the individual holdings. This burden fell very lightly on the poorer districts, which had already borne more than a fair share of the cost of feeding the men on whole-time service, and in no case was it an excessive imposition. The levies were cheerfully paid in the great majority of cases. Here and there evasion occurred, but only in rare cases was it necessary to take strong action to enforce payment. Just as he would never countenance the use of the organisation for the private advantage of its members, Liam would not permit its use to penalise opponents in this or in any other matter.

The nine brigades included in his division all had the same type of basic organisation, but in the more recent developments of special services and columns they lacked uniformity. All suffered from the same shortages of arms and explosives. Such arms as were available were in use, their nature and quantity determining the number and strength of columns in any brigade. Generally, the brigades which had been most active were best armed, but their ammunition supply was always precarious. The manufacture of road mines and grenades had not reached a satisfactory standard. Cork No. 1 Brigade had, after overcoming many technical and supply difficulties, set up a grenade factory in the 4th Battalion area, with small auxiliary plants in the city. These were not yet in a position to turn out grenades in any quantity. A small supply of these weapons came from Dublin, but not enough to have an appreciable effect on the conflict.

Numerous factors influenced the manner in which columns were organised in the different brigades, the predominant one being available arms. Rifles, shot guns and road mines were the most suitable weapons in the country districts, revolvers and grenades in the city. Development in Cork No. 1 Brigade had consequently followed a different pattern to that in other areas. In the city, an active service unit of sixteen men, drawn from the two city battalions, working in co-operation with a whole time intelligence squad, and reinforced, when necessary, from the local companies, had been maintaining a vigorous offensive since the autumn of 1920. The brigade had a large column in the field, manned partly from the city and the 7th and 8th Battalions. There were battalion columns in the 4th and 6th and 7th Battalions.

The pattern of development in Cork No. 3 Brigade had been similar to that of the other two commands in the county. A brigade column, magnificently led by Commandant Tom Barry, had fought a number of successful actions, culminating at Crossbarry, where his force of about one hundred officers and men had fought their way out of encirclement by very large British forces after inflicting severe casualties on the enemy, destroying part of his transport and capturing a quantity of arms and ammunition. In addition to the main column, smaller units were active in the battalions, and over the whole area of the brigade, a vigorous and successful campaign was being waged with great spirit and determination.

The County of Kerry had been divided into three brigade areas : No. 1, centered on Tralee, included North Kerry and the Dingle peninsula, No. 2, with Killarney as its centre, covered the middle and eastern portion of the county and extended south to Kenmare, No. 3, a small brigade, comprised the battalions in the isolated south western area centered on Caherciveen. The conflict had developed a little less rapidly in Kerry than in Cork. Although there was con- siderable activity throughout 1920, the attacks on police posts were only moderately successful, mainly because they were made after these barracks had been strongly fortified in the early part of the year. At any time after June, 1920 it required superb organisation, resource- ful planning and a fiercely sustained assault to capture one of these posts in the Munster counties, with the weapons and equipment at the disposal of the I.R.A.

In organisation and leadership the Kerry brigades had now reached a high standard, and their fighting capacity had developed with great rapidity. Brigade columns were operating in No. 1 and No. 2 Brigade, as well as small formations in the battalions. Kerry No. 3, with fewer targets offering in its area, was maintaining a series of minor activities. The largest action fought in the county was at Headfort Junction on 21st March, where in an attack on a train carrying British troops, Dan Allman, the column commander, was killed.

The two brigades in Waterford and the West Limerick Brigade were, at the time of their inclusion in the division, rapidly attaining standards of organisation and development which were not far behind those of the Kerry brigades. Although no actions comparable to those carried out by the Cork or East Limerick brigades had been undertaken, there had been continuous activity, a well sustained series of attacks on police posts, and a few larger actions. Brigade columns were organised in each area, but, even to a greater extent than Cork and Kerry, they suffered from a shortage of arms and ammunition.

In striving for the attainment of the highest standard of fighting efficiency in the columns, and for the widest possible dissemination of the lessons learned in the actions which had taken place—failures and successes alike—Liam issued some orders and memoranda, none of which appear to have survived. They were, however, based on the same principles which he had in mind when issuing similar instructions later. An order in regard to the protection of columns may be quoted :

"When resting, scouts or sentries should be posted on vantage points commanding a view of the whole country about. At night they should be posted on all roads, and should be provided with horns (or other sounders) to signal the approach of the enemy.

When moving, Columns should have advanced and rear guards connected with the main body.

Columns should never move into country until it is first scouted and the O/C has satisfied himself that it is either free of the enemy, or is aware of the exact position he occupies."[1]

Another order, dealing with the organisation and activities of columns, laid down that where a number of units are operating in an area,

"they should keep close touch with one another. This is most necessary both from the point of view of co-operation in operations and of protecting one another from surprise or attack by

[1] Operation Order 2, 22/7/22

the enemy. . . . Each unit while at rest should however provide independently for its own protection.

Each operation, no matter how simple it may appear, should be carefully planned, every detail attended to and all contingencies as far as possible provided against . . .

Before going into action men should have clearly explained to them :

(a) The objective to be achieved,
(b) The line of retreat,
(c) Position of H.Q. and of different sections or units operating.

The strictest discipline on the part of the troops on active service must be insisted on, and any breaches of same should be promptly and sternly dealt with. . . . Officers should set good example in the matter of discipline."[1]

The details of another divisional project were being worked out in May and June. It was the establishment of a divisional training camp at which all brigade officers and column commanders would undergo courses of intensive training. Subsequently the courses were to be continued for other officers, and the whole project visualised the creation of a divisional column for operations in any part of the area. Commandant Tom Barry of Cork No. 3 Brigade was to be Training Officer and was to command the divisional column when formed. The camp was to have been established in the Clydagh Valley, between Rathmore and Ballyvourney, and arrangements for the first course there were almost complete when the Truce caused a change of plans.

A little over two months of exceptionally fine weather intervened between Liam's appointment as divisional commandant and the Truce. It was not favourable to the type of guerilla warfare in which his forces were engaged, and it presented his opponents with the most suitable conditions in which to experiment with a new kind of activity. This consisted of the formation of mobile columns, not very different to our own except that they were lorry-borne, who were taken into selected country districts, dropped at certain points in groups of ten to twenty, under an officer or senior N.C.O., and moved on the roads or across country to a rendevous where they were picked up by their transport. They carried the minimum of equipment and were designed for silent, speedy movement within a prescribed area in which any group attacked could be reinforced quickly by the others. It was a shrewd and intelligent move on the part of the

[1] Operation Order 9, 19/8/22

Crown forces. A variation of their tactics was to lie in ambush in the hope of capturing individual Volunteers, despatch riders, or small groups on the move.

That particular type of activity, while constituting a potential threat to Army communications and a danger to individuals and small groups, was even more menacing in that it was the first step towards giving the Crown forces something of that ubiquity which had been so valuable an asset to the I.R.A., and in that it threatened to restore, in districts now long immune from any incursions, except in force, a sense of perpetual danger. Developed to the extent made possible by the man power and available transport of the Crown forces, this type of activity could to a large extent immobilise our basic territorial organisation, disrupt communications, and add to our losses in men killed and captured. It was, however, inoperable against the columns, and it was too hazardous except in daylight, unless troops had been specially trained.

Satisfied, after his tour of the brigades, that there was no shortage of good fighting material, Liam, on his return to division headquarters, commenced planning for the more widespread development and intensification of the struggle. But three factors combined to defer many of his plans and to alter the type of operations undertaken in the two months before the Truce. The first was the exceptionally fine weather which gave the Crown forces an advantage in the long hours of daylight, which enabled them to undertake extensive sweeps, with large forces, of mountainous areas hitherto inaccessible to them. The second was the failure of the Italian arms mission which threw the division back again on its own meagre resources in arms and ammunition, reverting to the old position in which it had to fight with what it captured from the Crown forces. The third was the necessity for making an effective rejoinder to the official British policy of executing prisoners of war and destroying public and private property as reprisals for Army activities.

The general attack on Crown forces and on their posts, which was agreed upon at the meeting for the formation of the division, was carried out on 14th May. British casualties in Cork No. 1 and No. 3 brigade areas were particularly heavy. Total casualties for that week, fifty-five, including twenty-three deaths, were the highest in any week since 1916. More than half of them were inflicted in the area of the 1st Southern Division. In the week ending 28th May, British casualties were still heavier—fifty-seven, including twenty-seven deaths. In the four weeks ended 28th May, 192 attacks were made on British posts and patrols—the ascertained casualties of the Crown forces during that period being seventy-six killed and one hundred and six wounded.

When G.H.Q. sanction for the destruction of the property of active enemies was received towards the end of May, the British policy of reprisals was answered by a widespread series of burnings of the houses of loyalists. At the time a number of workhouses throughout the area were destroyed. British forces had commandeered and occupied Kanturk workhouse on 31st March, and it seemed probable that, in the heavier concentration of troops now being moved into the south, other similar buildings would also be occupied. Those at Millstreet, Skibbereen, Macroom, Bandon and Clonakilty were destroyed.

While a widespread and vigorous campaign of minor attacks on Crown forces was being maintained, three larger actions took place in the two months before the Truce. The first was at Rathmore, Co. Kerry on 4th May, when a combined force of Cork No. 2 and Kerry No. 2 brigades ambushed a party of police near the village. Eight policemen were killed and their arms and ammunition captured. In reprisal for this action Crown forces set fire to five farmhouses, in the vicinity of the scene of the ambush, four of which, with their entire contents, were completely destroyed. Later they burned down Rathmore creamery and co-operative stores.

On 1st June a cycle patrol of police was ambushed between Castlemaine and Milltown, by Kerry No. 1 Brigade Column, under the command of Commandant Tadgh Brosnan. A district inspector, a sergeant and four constables were killed, and five others wounded. Their arms and ammunition fell into the hands of the attackers.

The largest action against the British forces in the division area, in the last phase of the struggle, took place at Rathcoole, between Millstreet and Banteer, on 16th June, 1921. A combined force of units from the columns of the Millstreet, Kanturk, Newmarket, Charleville and Mallow battalions, under Commandant Paddy O'Brien, attacked a party of Auxiliaries in four lorries. Seven land mines had been laid on the road by the attackers, and in that action three of these were exploded. One was detonated as the rear lorry passed over it, another as the leading lorry reached its position. Both vehicles were put out of action. Their crews suffered casualties and the two remaining lorries were trapped between them. A third mine was exploded as a party of Auxiliaries attempted to outflank the position. The action developed into a long duel. After nearly an hour the Auxiliary machine guns were still in action, and it was clear that the attackers could not achieve a complete victory with their limited ammunition supply. The order for withdrawal was given, the whole force of one hundred and forty men, including protective elements, retiring without casualties.

Although no arms were captured in this action, a reconnaissance party from the column, which returned next day to search the ambush position, recovered 1,350 rounds of ammunition which the Auxiliaries had lost in evacuating the remnants of their convoy in the darkness of the previous night. The action was most creditable to Cork No. 2 Brigade in the circumstances of the time. The successful assembly and dispersal of such a large number of men without loss or casualties was in itself a remarkable achievement.

Seán Moylan had succeeded Liam as brigade commandant, but his term of office in that post was brief. He was captured near Kiskeam in the early hours of the morning of 16th May, and later sentenced to fifteen years of penal servitude. Liam and I, returning from West Limerick Brigade on the night of the 15th and intending to reach the

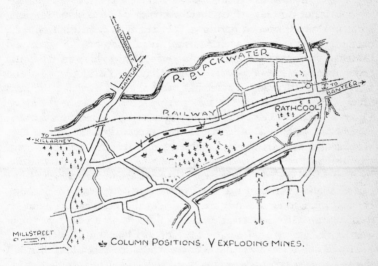

⚓ COLUMN POSITIONS. ⋎ EXPLODING MINES.

Kiskeam neighbourhood during the night, were delayed by a tired horse, and stayed a little further north, near Tuar. We knew nothing of the round-up of the Kiskeam area until next morning. Seán Moylan was succeeded by George Power as brigade commandant, with Paddy O'Brien as vice commandant. Ned Murphy of Lombardstown was appointed brigade quartermaster. In the division of Cork No. 2 into two brigades he took the post of vice commandant of Cork No. 4, and was subsequently appointed assistant quartermaster, 1st Southern Division.

The incident which led to the last official British execution in the south before the Truce, occurred in Cork No. 2 Brigade area. Dan O'Brien, a brother of Commandant Paddy O'Brien of Liscarroll, was captured at O'Donnell's at Aughvrin, near Liscarroll on the morning of 11th May, 1921. Nobody had stayed at O'Donnells for some months previously as it was known that the house was liable to be raided and Commandant O'Brien had in fact put it out of bounds for a time. On the night of the 10th, Paddy arrived there half an hour after midnight. His brother Dan was there and also Jack Regan. They intended to leave after having a meal, but were persuaded to stay as Miss O'Donnell and Miss Regan were leaving very early next morning on a visit to Mick Regan who was in Limerick Jail.

Paddy Sheedy, a member of the battalion column, and Dan Connors, Liscarroll Company, were posted as scouts. In the early morning British troops, detrucking almost a mile from the house, moved in under cover, got inside the sentries and captured them. Approaching the house through the fields the raiders reached the door before anyone inside was aware of their presence. It was about 8 a.m., John O'Donnell opened the door. On seeing the British troops he promptly shut the door again and bolted it. The two O'Briens and O'Regan got out at the back, but about thirty yards from the house came under the fire of a party lining a fence. O'Regan was hit and fell. Dan O'Brien stayed with him, and shouted to Paddy to keep going. Dan O'Brien and Jack Regan were taken, Paddy got away. Dan was taken to Cork military barracks, tried by drum-head court-martial and sentenced to death. He was executed on the 16th.

He had joined the Irish Volunteers in 1917 and had been continuously one of the most active members of the Liscarroll Company. In April, 1920 he had taken part in the attack on Kilmallock R.I.C. barracks, and in August had been arrested and deported to England. He was released soon afterwards and joined the brigade column on its formation. He had taken part in an attack on a police patrol in Charleville early in 1921, and in the fight at Clonbanin in March.

To the officers of the British Court which sentenced him to death this brave man said a few simple words which put the position of the Army in relation to the occupation forces in its proper perspective. " I was," he said, " a soldier of the Irish Republican Army when I was captured, and I expect to be treated as a captured soldier. If I captured a soldier I would not shoot him. You can do as you like with me." Father O'Brien, who attended him on the morning of his execution, imparted the Papal Benediction. He walked to the place of execution continuing to say the Hail Mary which had been interrupted by the final call, and met his death bravely.

Liam arrived back at division headquarters on 17th May and remained until 31st when, with Joe O'Connor, the division quarter-master, who had taken up duty, he set out on a tour of the Waterford brigades. They returned on 14th June and left again three days later on a further round of visits to the brigades. During his first absence

the most elaborate and extensive sweep and search operation undertaken by the British 6th Division was carried out in the mountainous
area enclosed by the circle Kilgarvan, Rathmore, Millstreet, Ballyvourney, Dunmanway, Kilgarvan. It was estimated that several
thousand lorry-borne troops, supported by armoured vehicles and
aircraft, participated in the operation, which began on 6th June.
In a special order of the day General Strickland defined their mission
as that of " seeking out the I.R.A. Columns, bringing them to action
and annihilating them."

It is interesting now to observe how persistent was the conviction
in some quarters that the I.R.A. would revert to the traditional
method of insurrection and take the field en masse. *The Morning Post*
of 31st May, 1921, said :

> " Information has been received from Ireland that the I.R.A.
> is being mobilised . . . present happenings seem clearly to
> indicate that the rebel army means to come into the open. . . .
> In the wild country around the Clydagh mountains, Co. Kerry,
> the concentration of a rebel force is in progress, and at least
> 1,000 are already massed."

This was the area included in the sweep which began a week later,
and it did in fact contain at the time the Cork No. 1 and Cork No. 3
Brigade Columns, Divisional Headquarters and Headquarters of
Cork No. 1 and Cork No. 3 Brigades, as well as the very large number
of Volunteers normally resident in it. There was, of course, no
concentration in the sense understood by the *Morning Post*.

Strickland's order was in Liam's hands almost as soon as it reached
his own brigade commanders. The weather was eminently suitable
for the British mission, but broken bridges and trenched roads
deprived them of rapidity of movement, and the ever present threat
of isolation and destruction of their small parties forced them to
reconnoitre every step of the way. These large scale sweeps presented
no great difficulties to the columns or the staffs, because of their slow
rate of movement. British forces had to bivouac during the short
hours of darkness, and as they moved in a gradually constricting
circle, it was not difficult for men who knew the country to slip
through their lines. Good intelligence and prompt reports, made it
possible to keep all units informed of the progress of the raiding
forces.

Portions of the territorial areas of four brigades were involved,
Cork No. 1, Cork No. 2, Cork No. 3, and Kerry No. 2. Division
headquarters, which was almost at the centre of the enclosed area,
was excellently located to discharge one of its functions in this
situation. Had it not existed there would still have been exchange of

information between the brigades, but there would not have been the same study of the overall picture of enemy movement, which made it possible very early in the week to determine with reasonable accuracy both his general intention and his probable rate of progress. There would not have been the same full and accurate information by each brigade on the enemy's movements in the areas of other brigades. The column and brigade commanders were enabled, as a result of the centralisation of reports to division and the distribution of the resulting intelligence, to plan unhurriedly and deliberately their evasive or counteraction.

While it was probably well within the capacity of either the Cork No. 1 or the Cork No. 3 Brigade Columns to punch a hole in a ring, several considerations combined to recommend evasion as the better policy. The enormous superiority of the enemy in men and weapons, the long hours of daylight, the extremely dry condition of the terrain, the presence of aircraft, the general policy of striking at a time and place of our selection rather than the enemy's, the improbability of any substantial capture of arms or ammunition to counterbalance the expenditure in an action—all these influenced the decision that all forces inside the ring would take evasive action. The whole British operation did not achieve the capture of a man, a weapon or a document. Three unarmed men were shot dead, two of them local Volunteers, and that was the whole achievement. The temper of British regular troops and their attitude to the civil population may be judged from an incident of this sweep. One party of them compelled an old man to carry a machine gun on his back over a mountain, until he collapsed from exhaustion, in the heat of that June day.

Later in the same month, on 23rd and 24th June, a second large scale sweep by Crown forces enclosed an area having its centre at about Millstreet. This operation included much of the terrain covered earlier in the month, but it extended eastwards into the territory of Cork No. 2 Brigade further than the previous raiding had done. Liam and Joe O'Connor, returning from a tour of the Kerry and West Limerick Brigades, arrived at Rathcoole at 4 a.m. on the morning the sweep started. Worn out and exhausted they decided to sleep, although reports indicated they were inside the British ring. Paddy O'Brien, who had also put in a long spell without sleep remained on duty to receive reports. Reluctantly, he felt obliged to wake Liam and Joe O'Connor after a few hours, as the reports indicated raiding parties in strength on all sides. The three officers moved into Kilcorney and remained all day. In the evening, when the positions of the British detachments had been determined Liam and Joe O'Connor moved south to Aghina—and outside the ring. One party of British troops were quite close to them at one stage.

CHAPTER 14

TRUCE TO HOSTILITIES

Ireland is beating down the meanest and cruellest tyranny in Europe.
                                              ARTHUR GRIFFITH.

J UNE, 1921 was a month of exceptionally fine weather. Army
activity on a large scale was restricted, but minor actions continued
to be widespread and persistent. Rumours of efforts being made to
bring about an ending of the conflict were in the air, but neither Liam
nor any of his officers had the slightest official indication that these
efforts were likely to end in a truce to hostilities. On the contrary, it
appeared to them that in view of the uncompromising hostility of
British Government spokesmen to the idea of a free Ireland no
possible grounds existed on which negotiations between them and
the Government of the Republic could take place. The outlook of
the division was one of preparation for a resumption of the struggle
on a larger scale as soon as weather conditions permitted. Confidence
in its ability to maintain the initiative was high, and morale was
excellent.

The difficult question of the capacity of the Army as a whole to
maintain the armed struggle in 1921 is not one that need be discussed
here. But it seems right to put on record what the position in the
1st Southern Division was, without considering in too much detail the
extent to which that position was fully known or correctly appreciated
by the Government. Their evaluation was a long distance one and the
circumstances of the time made close personal knowledge of the
situation by members of the Government difficult. Liam Lynch was not
consulted as to the capacity of his command to continue the struggle
and as he was not aware that it was being weighed in the balance
of probabilities in considering a Truce, he made no representations' on
the matter. The only direct report on the situation in part of the
divisional area made to the President and to some members of G.H.Q.
staff at the time was that made by Commandant Tom Barry of Cork
No. 3 Brigade who was invited to G.H.Q.[1]

The Government had of necessity, to take the whole national
position into account, not merely that of the Army, still less that of
one division, notwithstanding that it was the largest and most active.

[1] *Guerilla Days in Ireland*, p. 179 *et seq.*

Whatever weight was given to the Army position in considering the possibilities of a Truce with the British, and to whatever extent decisions were influenced by the estimation made of the Army's capacity to maintain the struggle, one thing is certain—that the officer commanding the 1st Southern Division was not consulted nor given an opportunity of expressing his views.

I am glad to be able to publish here, with his permission, the following letter from Major General Piaras Beaslai which disposes of the only serious misrepresentation of Liam Lynch's actions in the struggle which has ever been made. I fully accept Piaras Beaslai's assurance that his original statement was made in good faith and under a misapprehension of the facts.

" 82 Lower Drumcondra Road,
Dublin.

" A Chara,   11th October, 1952.

" I was glad to hear that you were writing the life of Liam Lynch. You have all the personal knowledge, capability and access to the necessary sources of information which would enable you to do full justice to your subject.

" You have called my attention to a statement in my book *Michael Collins, and the Making of a New Ireland* to the effect that Liam Lynch and some of his officers, went to G.H.Q. some time before the Truce and reported that, owing to shortage of arms and ammunition and enemy pressure they were unable to continue the fight. You assure me that you can find no evidence of such a visit, and that all those who would be in a position to know deny that any such thing occurred.

" I am not in a position, nor have I any desire, to contradict this. I have full confidence in your integrity, and do not question that you have made every effort to ascertain the truth, and that nobody was in a better position than you to do so. While accepting your assurance, I must be permitted, in justice to myself, to point out what occurred as far as I was concerned.

" I made the statement in question in good faith and on good authority in a book which was published in the year 1926. In that year also the greater part of the text, including this statement, was published serially in the *Cork Examiner*. Some letters appeared in the *Examiner* purporting to correct certain statements with regard to the Cork areas, but nobody raised any question with regard to this particular matter.

" The book had a large circulation, and ultimately went ' out of print.' In all that time nobody told me that this statement was challenged.

"In 1937, when I was asked to write a new abbreviated life of Michael Collins, I naturally repeated the statement in the new book, as a matter of historical interest. Had I any idea that its accuracy was disputed I would certainly not have done so.

"It was not till some years later that I was informed, in a private letter, that the statement was denied by a number of Cork officers to whom my correspondent had been talking. As both my books were then out of print I did not see what I could do about the matter.

"Shortly after I saw Tom Barry's denial. This was the first contradiction which I had seen in print, although, I believe, he was only repeating a statement made by you in an article in *An Cosantoir* in January, 1946. I had not seen the article in question, and nobody had called my attention to it. In any case, it was twenty years after my original book was written, when all the files, notes and records put at my disposal had been returned and dispersed when some of my informants were dead, and when many things had faded from my own and other people's memories.

"I think I cannot be accused of negligence or rashness in this matter. I recorded information which I received with no desire to disparage Liam Lynch or anybody else, but only to show the difficulties the fighting men were up against. I had read in Michael Collin's files a letter from Liam Lynch, in which he asked for 'a few rifles' and said : 'We will soon be in a very hard way for .303, as we had hard luck in captures recently.' At the same time there was a letter from Cork No. 3, saying that they were urgently in need of .303 and adding : ' To a certain extent we are held up by the want of this, and harassed to a terrible extent by the enemy.'

"These statements may have been exaggerations intended to stimulate a greater supply of arms and ammunition, but they had a disturbing effect on G.H.Q. All the authorities I have consulted agree with my recollection that some communication reached Collins at this time which caused him to express a fear that the Cork Brigades would be unable to continue the fight. This was, apparently, the origin of the report which, you tell me, is untrue. I certainly have no wish to publish any erroneous statement, and if I could throw any further light on the matter I would gladly do so. It is not my fault that the question was not raised many years ago.

"With best wishes.

Yours sincerely,
Piaras Beaslai."

The brigades included in Liam Lynch's Division had commenced the fight with about 120 rifles of various kinds, some old and almost worthless, some faulty and inaccurate, and some for which only a few rounds of ammunition were available. The number of modern serviceable weapons was very small. In June, 1921, these brigades possessed 578 modern service rifles, eleven light machine-guns, over 1,000 revolvers and pistols and a large number of shot guns.

Rifle and machine-gun ammunition was extremely limited, but dangerously low as it was, the overall arms position was incomparably better than it had been at the start of the active campaign twelve months earlier. It had been improving progressively during the whole of that period, and while it might be expected to remain static during the summer months, there was no reason to anticipate that it would continue to improve, though, perhaps, at a slower rate, when the shortening days again made more numerous and larger actions possible. The arms position had continued to improve even under the stress of the severest blows the British were able to inflict, and the arms position was the key fact in the whole situation.

That was so because the failure of British Intelligence services had deprived the occupation forces of the ability to use their superior strength effectively. They knew the names and addresses of most of the men they wanted to kill or capture, but they could neither capture them nor identify them if they did.

The efficiency of the units comprising the division had not been seriously impaired by deaths or captures. The structure of I.R.A. organisation made its dependence on good local leadership very evident. Here and there the removal of active officers and men had slowed down or disrupted operations for a time, but the whole organisation was intact, alert, disciplined and showing wonderful resiliency. Losses were small, particularly in relation to the extent of gains. More lives had been lost at the single battle of Ballyellis in '98 than were lost by the I.R.A. in the whole course of the struggle.

The Army was becoming tougher and better inured to hardship; more officers and men were coming on whole-time active service; combat experience was becoming more widespread. Columns could move with considerable freedom, in any part of the area not in close proximity to large garrison posts. They could occupy positions in complete security for much longer periods than in earlier days, often allowing British convoys to pass through in order to engage them at a more suitable time on the return journey. Problems of feeding and clothing the men on active service had been solved. The manufacture of efficient hand grenades and road mines was developing. The whole armed effort was gathering a powerful momentum.

Neither terrorism nor reprisals had broken the morale of the people. No previous armed struggle for freedom had secured the steadfast loyalty and intelligent co-operation of so large a majority of the population. What confronted British rule in Ireland was not merely a poorly-armed guerilla force, but a guerilla force sustained by the disciplined courage and almost incalculable united strength of an awakened people.

Liam Lynch did not possess any accurate detailed information in July, 1921, of the extent to which the national effort had driven the British Government into the inescapable dilemma of deciding upon an all out military conquest of this country or of making peace. What he did know was that in his divisional area his forces held the initiative and felt confident of being able to retain it. The desperate condition to which the British forces in Ireland had been reduced has to some extent been revealed by many authoritative writers since then.

Twelve months earlier the British Government had recognised the fact that if it was to retain its Imperial grip on Ireland, a campaign of reconquest by large military forces was necessary. It was a grim necessity, and it made nonsense of all Britain's professions of high moral principles, and of such catch-phrases as : "We have murder by the throat." Before taking that final step against a small and ancient nation of civilised white people, a step that would have branded his country as infamous even amongst rapacious Empires, the British Prime Minister had another idea. He would try terror. It had always succeeded in Ireland. In a cynical, opportunist experiment the Black-and-Tans and Auxiliaries were loosed upon the country, to murder and maim, to rob and burn and pillage, to browbeat, insult and terrorise, sparing neither age nor sex.

> "Never before," Brigadier General Crozier writes, "had the
> R.I.C. been used so ruthlessly, and at times surreptitiously, to
> destroy and create a new note of anguish in the country."[1]

Terror failed. Worse still, it revolted such a large and influential section of decent public opinion in England, and created such disturbing reactions on British foreign relations in the United States and elsewhere, that no Government dare persist in it. The final alternatives then lay between some kind of settlement and the use of unlimited military force under a reign of martial law.

Macready records that the British Cabinet decided, if a solution was not reached by July, to impose martial law on the whole country, with the exception of six of the Ulster counties, and to reinforce the

[1] *Ireland for Ever*, p. 89

garrison with an additional nineteen battalions and a strong force of marines. This would have brought the British Army strength in Ireland to 80,000 men. 150,000, he thought, would have been essential.[1]

Winston Churchill, then Secretary of State for the Colonies told the British Cabinet :

> " One hundred thousand new special troops must be raised, thousands of motor cars must be armoured and equipped ; the three Southern Provinces of Ireland must be closely laced with cordons of blockhouses and barbed wire ; a systematic rummaging and questioning of every· individual must be put in force."

And if one questions why such forces, with all that is implied in the term " Special troops," and such methods and equipment were necessary, there can be but one answer. It was because the Army of the Irish Republic was an intact, unbeaten force.

The Lord Chancellor, Lord Birkenhead, speaking in the British House of Lords on 24th June, 1921, said :

> ". . . if I must speak frankly I think that the history of the last three months had been the history of the failure of our military methods to keep pace with and overcome the military methods which have been taken by our opponents."

Major J. C. Street (" I.O.") who, as a British Intelligence officer at the headquarters of the British forces in Ireland during the vital period, had unrivalled opportunities of assessing the relative strengths, moral and material, of the opposing forces, writes :[2]

> " A campaign large enough to stamp out rebellion throughout the South of Ireland was an undertaking whose limits no man could forsee, and although the estimates of its cost given at the time by men whose interest it was to dissuade the British public from demanding war were excessive, England recovering from the effects of the greatest war in history was in no position to embark upon fresh military expeditions."

A little later he says :[3]

> " There were only two alternatives, to come to terms with Sinn Féin or exterminate its armed forces."

---

[1] *Annals of An Active Life*, Vol. 2, pp. 561-62   [2] *Ireland in* 1921, p. 4.
[3] *Ibid.*, p. 49

The Irish armed forces were neither exterminated nor beaten in the field. And so, a Truce!

Liam was at Division Headquarters at Coolea when official notification of the Truce reached him on 10th July. He immediately issued the necessary order for the cessation of hostilities at 12 noon next day. This order averted what might have been one of the largest actions of his former Brigade—Cork No. 2.

Some days before the Truce, Commandant O'Brien with eighty officers and men from five battalions columns—Newmarket, Kanturk, Millstreet, Charleville and Mallow—marched into West Limerick and in co-operation with West Limerick units laid an ambush near Templeglantine. The column had been in position for several days without finding a target. Commandant O'Brien, notified on the 10th, that the Truce commenced at 12 noon on the 11th, called his section commanders together and asked for their views about taking up positions on the morning of 11th. All were eager to do so, and the column went into position. At 11.45 the column commander instructed the section commanders to withdraw their sections. At 12.15 the British convoy arrived on the scene, passing some of the dispersing groups on the road. Not a shot was fired.

The Truce wrought changes which penetrated even to the deep foundations of the national movement. After 11th July nothing was, or ever could have been the same no matter how the Truce ended. The most obvious change was that the Army's role of leadership in the struggle was ended and the responsibility for pressing the national demand for Sovereign independence was translated to the field of diplomacy. The Army recognising the rights and functions of a lawfully constituted Government in no way resented this change ; but it expected and had earned the right to expect that the Government would resist any attempt to abate the national demand with the same determination and courage as that displayed by the Volunteers who had fought and died for the Republic.

Nowhere had that right been better earned than in the South. The brigades in Liam's Division had lost 193 officers and men killed twice that number wounded and perhaps 2,000 interned or sentenced to terms of imprisonment. They had in face of these losses and under many other and varied difficulties, continued to strike at the occupation forces so vigorously and persistently that responsible British military commanders were convinced of the necessity for immense reinforcements if their defeat was to be achieved.

Tributes to the fighting brigades of the South came from both sides —from the British the very significant one of a gradual shifting of the weight of their forces into Munster in the last six months of the struggle. In September, 1920, *An tOglac* said :

"If the Volunteers in all areas were as active in guerilla warfare as in certain portions of Munster the enemy would require a very much larger force than he has in Ireland at present to deal with the situation."

In October, referring to the reign of terror then operated by the Crown forces in the West, and pointing out that this was an attempt to regain control and domination of the countryside by the R.I.C., *An tOglac* said :

"In the South the guerilla offensive had been carried out for so long and so vigorously that any attempt by the R.I.C. to regain control of those areas is out of the question, and the enemy can rely only on a big military concentration."

In February, 1921, an appeal was made through the columns of the official organ to the other brigades to ". . . help to relieve the strain on the gallant men in the South against whom the enemy is making a military concentration."

And in March *An tOglac* pays this tribute to the South :

"The Cork Brigades have proved themselves to have reached a level of military efficiency which would make them a match for the most highly-trained soldiers in the world. An example has been set which every Brigade in Ireland should strive to emulate."

The first general effect of the Truce on the Army was a wave of unfounded optimism. In Liam's Division at least, officers and men had for the previous eighteen months concentrated their attention and energies upon the fight to such an extent that all other considerations, personal and national, were excluded. What they witnessed now was the apparent success of their efforts and a promise of the realisation of their hopes. It did not seem to them that England would have agreed to a Truce unless she had decided to evacuate her armed forces from the country, and in their over-simple reading of the situation, evacuation appeared to be equivalent to the establishment of the Republic as a freely functioning state. It seemed almost a miracle, but a very acceptable one.

Liam himself was not much impressed by the general optimism. His earliest reactions were that the point had not yet been reached when England would admit the justice of our full demands, that the negotiations for a settlement would almost inevitably break down, and that the Truce would be of short duration. He did not so much as contemplate the possibility of any settlement on terms which gave

Ireland less than sovereign independence. " We have declared for a Republic, and will not live under any other law," was still his creed.

The general relaxation of the strain under which the people had lived in the two previous years, the termination of curfew and of the prohibition on fairs and markets, the restored facilities for movement, normal trade and commerce, the sense of relief that pervaded the public mind, all combined to create a reaction from the grim events of the war years which had its inevitable effect upon the Army. That effect was intensified because the Army was composed exclusively of citizen soldiers serving voluntarily, whose rights as citizens they did not feel to be in any way restricted by service. They were an integral part of the people and did not have the mentality of a mercenary force. The incipient desire for peace grew with subtle persistence in a very favourable atmosphere as time passed, and it made more difficult any dispassionate assessment of the issues which began to emerge dimly, as the negotiations in London between the Irish and British delegates proceeded.

Liam sought to combat any tendency towards relaxation in his division by the establishment of training camps, a much expanded series of inspections, and the inauguration of a number of courses. He discouraged any tendency on the part of officers or men to come into the open unnecessarily, and for his own part continued to work and travel as unobtrusively as had been his wont in the past. A whole series of new problems arose. Liaison officers had been appointed by both sides to supervise observance of the terms of the Truce. That was one of the ways in which the British had tacitly acknowledged the belligerent status of the Army, and abandoned their long sustained contention, that their forces in Ireland were opposed only by a small group of rebellious civilians. Varying interpretations of the Truce terms, and the provocative disregard of them in some cases by Auxiliaries and Black-and-Tans, resulted in numerous incidents and considerable bickering.

Liam was himself involved in one of these incidents. Division Headquarters had been moved from its war-time location at Sweeney's, Gortarahilly, Coolea, to Patrick O'Sullivan's, Mortonville, Lombardstown, on 21st July. On his way there from Bandon in a car, Liam was held up at Ballinhassig by three lorries of Black-and-Tans on the evening of 18th August. A District Inspector was in charge. He demanded production of a British permit for the use of the car— that being one of the restrictions in force under martial law— restrictions which some over zealous individuals still sought to enforce. Recounting the incident in a letter to Tom, Liam wrote : " I demanded the right as an Irish Army Officer to use my own transport without an enemy permit, as well as they do without our permits." He was however taken to Bandon and detained until 1.30 next morning, when he and his driver were released after a phone message from Dublin Castle. "I enjoyed the time with the Tans and the D.I.," he wrote, "as the Truce feeling prevailed all round. We even discussed the possibility of again meeting them face to face in a clash with arms."

Early in August, Richard Mulcahy, Chief of Staff, visited division headquarters and remained almost a week, during which he inspected units of Cork No. 1, No. 2, No. 3 and Kerry No. 2 Brigades. In the same month President de Valera paid an official visit of inspection. Liam and a number of his officers accompanied the President on a three day tour of the scenes of the principal actions in the division area. At each of these points the columns which had participated were mobilised under arms, and to each group the President spoke, with impressive sincerity, words of congratulation and commendation of which Liam was very proud. They were happy days for him; there was no sign of a break in national unity and the future seemed hopeful. Even England seemed to have suffered a change of heart. When *The Times* could write this it seemed possible that the sword could be sheathed :

> "For good or evil the old Ireland is gone. Instead of it there is a young people with new qualities and also with new defects. Though tested sternly, as undoubtedly it has been, it has given proof of nationhood. None of the efforts that have been made to divide the people . . . have succeeded. On the contrary, they have vindicated the strength of the national ideal."

The Second Dáil assembled in the Mansion House, Dublin on 16th August. It comprised the members elected on 19th May. This election, held under a British Act for the return of members to what were designated the Northern and Southern Parliaments, and generally referred to as the Partition Act, had been, by a Decree of Dáil Éireann, utilised as an election for the Second Dáil and as a demonstration of national solidarity in support of the Republic. The 128 Republican members for " Southern Ireland " were all returned unopposed. Changes in the areas of many of the constituencies brought in some who were not members of the first Dáil, many of whose members, now re-elected, sat for the first time, having been either imprisoned or on active service during the sittings of the first Dáil.

At a private session on 23rd August Dáil Éireann rejected unanimously the British terms of settlement which Lloyd George had sent to De Valera on 20th July. At a public session of 26th August, Eamon de Valera was re-elected President of the Irish Republic.

Nothwithstanding threats of renewed war uttered in the British Houses of Parliament and in the British Press, Dáil Éireann spokesmen reiterated the unabated national demand for Sovereign Independence and emphasised the complete unanimity of its members in support of that demand. So far there was no outward sign of a break in national unity. Members of the Cabinet and the rank and file of Dáil deputies alike all spoke as the representatives of " a separate nation defending itself against the encroachments of a foreign nation." Their task now was to make the *de jure* Republic a *de facto* Republic.

A series of communications between President De Valera and Lloyd George followed, in which the President continued to emphasise that the Irish nation must in the proposed conferences continue to recognise itself for what it was—a separate nation—while willing and anxious to reconcile the differences between the two countries. Lloyd George maintained the British contention that recognition of that position by his Government, as a condition precedent to the conferences, made negotiations impossible. Finally, without surrender of the Irish standpoint, agreement was reached on the formula that accredited delegates from both sides should meet in London to consider "how the association of Ireland with the community of nations known as the British Empire may best be reconciled with Irish national aspirations." On 14th September Dáil Éireann sanctioned the appointment of delegates, and negotiations commenced in London on 11th October. The Irish delegates were, Arthur Griffith, Michael Collins, Charles Gavan Duffy, Robert Barton and Eamon Duggan.

In the period between the Truce and the signing of the Treaty on 6th December, Liam resumed his letters to his mother and to his brother Tom, which except for the very briefest notes on personal or family matters, had been discontinued for almost a year. Although the pressure of work is evident in these letters, he writes now with less restraint than in the days when any letter of his may have fallen into hostile hands, and it is possible to see in his correspondence some reflection of his reactions to the momentous events of these days.

In a letter to his mother on 22nd July, just after the Truce, referring to some fears which she had for his safety and his escapes from capture or death, he wrote :

> " However, I have got through so far, and thank God I am still left alive to help in shattering the damned British Empire. I am living only to bring the dreams of my dead comrades to reality, and every moment of my life is now devoted to same. I never dreamt of having such an opportunity to strike home at England—or at least at the English Government."

In a letter to his brother on 30th August, he says that he is expecting
a call to Dublin in the immediate future, but " should Truce not last
long I of course will not be travelling." After a visit to Dublin in
mid September he felt convinced that national unity on the demand
for Sovereign Independence would be maintained, even if it involved
a resumption of the struggle in arms. To Tom he wrote on the 26th :

> " You may rest assured that our Government as well as the
> Army is out for the Republic and nothing less, and that without
> a rest on our oars either. We are and must be prepared to fight
> to the last for that . . . we have no other authority but to fight
> on—a fight thank God which never for generations seemed more
> hopeful than now. . . ."

He thought it improbable that the Truce would last long, and said
he intended to go to a dance in Mitchelstown, not for amusement,
but to meet old friends, " as I believe that after a few weeks I may
have a poor chance of seeing them again." For the same reason he
intended to pay a visit to his home, which he has said in an earlier
letter to his mother, he was glad had not been destroyed as an official
reprisal. The old homestead, and that deep love for his great-hearted
mother so evident in his letters, called him always, and only a stern
self discipline and a high sense of duty kept him from more frequent
visits. Excusing himself when Tom was home on holidays soon
after the Truce, he wrote : " Somehow I would consider it a national
sin when there is work to be done." His longest term of absence
from duty was two days on the occasion of his brother's ordination
to the priesthood on 11th June, 1922.

He yielded to the call of home in October and had a day's outing
at Ballylanders races. It is evident that he was unimpressed by the
adulation accorded to him, writing, shrewdly enough, to Tom afterwards that perhaps it was due to the peace situation, " but, war or
peace, I'm always the same." One senses something of his utter
indifference to public opinion provided he was satisfied that his own
actions were just and honourable. Groups became vocal during the
Truce whose ostentatious parade of new-found patriotism jarred and
revolted him. In a later letter to Father Tom he lashed out at them.
" I don't give a damn about these people when it comes to praise or
notoriety, and they are making the hell of a mistake if they think I
forget their actions during the war. I remember at one time in the
best areas where it was next to impossible to find a bed to lie on."

With the Army alone he seemed to be completely happy, perhaps
because there he had tested the sincerity of men's faith and the depths
of their convictions. He had not found them wanting. There too

he found an atmosphere, congenial, ingenuous, warmed by human friendship, that was an emanation of a simple conception of unselfish service to the nation, in sharp contrast to some of the things he was beginning to perceive outside its ranks. Conferences at G.H.Q. and in his division, rounds of inspection, plans for the future when the struggle would, as he believed, have to be resumed—these occupied him fully to the end of November. Up to then he was confident that all was well with the cause on which his heart was set.

On 6th December, under Lloyd George's threat of " immediate and terrible war," the Irish delegates signed articles of agreement for a Treaty which disestablished the Republic and partitioned Ireland. British diplomacy had won what British arms had failed to achieve. The dread shadow of disunity fell upon a great national movement. A chapter of heartbreak, bitterness, sorrow and death was opened.

CHAPTER 15

THE I.R.B. AND THE TREATY

While grass grows and water runs there will be men in Ireland to dare and die for her.

DR. O'DWYER, Bishop of Limerick.

FOUR distinct organisations constituted the main structure of the national movement from 1916 to 1921—the Irish Volunteers, which became the Army of the Republic when the Government took responsibility for its activities in March, 1921; Sinn Féin, which engaged primarily in political activities; the Irish Republican Brotherhood, and Cumann-na-mBan. There were youth organisations for boys and girls, subsidiary organisations of a welfare nature, and, after the establishement of Dáil Éireann in January, 1919, various Government administrative departments.

The Irish Republican Brotherhood was the senior organisation. It was a secret, oathbound society, founded in 1858 when John O'Mahony and Michael Doheny, acting on behalf of a group of exiled Young Irelanders in the United States, sent Owen Considine to James Stephens in Ireland with proposals for the foundation of the organisation and promises of support from America.[1] John O'Mahony had been born on a remnant of his family's ancestral lands at Kilbeheny, not far from Liam Lynch's birthplace.

The sole object of the I.R.B. was " to establish and maintain a free and independent Republican Government in Ireland."[2] The unit of organisation was a " Circle," subdivided where necessary into groups of not more than ten. Each circle was under the control of an elected " centre." Circles were grouped to form districts under district centres; a number of these in turn formed a county under a county centre. The whole organisation was divided into eleven divisions, eight in Ireland, two in England and one in Scotland.

The governing body was the Supreme Council, consisting before 1916 of eleven members and after the 1917 reorganisation of fifteen members, one from each of the eleven divisions and four co-opted by them. Under the constitution of the organisation this body met at least once every four months. When not in session all powers and

[1] Luby Papers: Nat., Lib. Ms. 331
[2] I.R.B. Constitution, 1920

186

prerogatives of the Supreme Council, save those of declaring war or altering the Constitution, were vested in an executive of three, consisting of the President, Secretary and Treasurer. The constitution provided for the establishment of a Military Council, subordinate to the Supreme Council. The seven signatories of the Proclamation of the Republic at Easter, 1916, were the members of the Military Council at that time.

The organisation had suffered many vicissitudes in the first half century of its existence, but it never ceased to utilise such opportunities as were presented by the national situation to advance towards the attainment of its object. After the failure of '67 it went into decline and many of the first generation of its members worked and hoped and died without seeing a glimmer of the coming dawn. Not all however. When Tom Clarke returned from America in 1908 and soon afterwards became a member of the Supreme Council, a period of planning and preparation commenced which culminated in the Rising of 1916. Events favoured a forward policy. The foundation of the Irish Volunteers gave the secret organisation its first magnificent opportunity " to train and equip its members as a military body for the purpose of securing the independence of Ireland by force of arms " and of securing " the co-operation of all Irish military bodies in the accomplishment of its objects."[1] The war in which England was so heavily involved provided the most favourable moment in which to strike. The I.R.B. planned the Rising. The Irish Volunteers and the Irish Citizen Army made it possible.

Numerically the I.R.B. was, since the beginning of the century, a small body ; its total membership did not exceed two thousand men in 1916 and a high percentage of that strength was in Dublin. Its influence lay rather in the character, integrity and loyalty of its personnel, in the soundness of its water-tight organisation, and in its genius for working inside and through other organisations. The executions after Easter Week, 1916 almost wiped out the Supreme Council ; its remaining officers and members were amongst the prisoners or internees. A temporary Supreme Council functioned until the sentenced prisoners were released in June, 1917, and in the autumn of the same year the Council was regularly constituted with Seán McGarry as President, Michael Collins as Secretary and Diarmuid Lynch as Treasurer. Even after the reconstitution of the Supreme Council no very active steps were taken for some time to extend or revitalise the organisation. This was due, in part at least, to the fact that a number of responsible leaders, including De Valera and Brugha, had come to the conclusion that no further need existed for a secret

[1] I.R.B. Constitution, 1920

organisation, and that the future of the national struggle for independence after 1916 might well be staked upon the open military and
political organisations. Michael Collins did not take the same view.
He believed the continued existence of the secret organisation to be
essential to the achievement of the Republic, and in this he had the
support of most of the members. In these conflicting views lay the
seeds of subsequent antagonism and bitterness, though they did not
ripen for many a day.

In the South Munster Division there had been a small but virile
organisation since the early years of the century. Though mainly
centred in the cities and towns, it had individual members scattered
over most of the area. In the Volunteer reorganisation after 1916 some
slight extension of membership took place, but as recruitment was a
very slow and careful process, strength was not very much increased.
During the next three years recruiting continued with the same
painstaking caution, although now there were very much better
opportunities of assessing the characters of potential members.
Most of those approached and inducted were Volunteer officers.
No one outside the ranks of the Volunteers was accepted.

Liam Lynch became a member of the organisation late in 1918,
joining the small group which formed a circle in Fermoy. During
the following year he gathered up the scattered threads of organisation
in his area, and organised a district around Fermoy, of which he was
elected centre.

Most of the post 1916 recruits to the organisation were unaware
that any conflicting views existed on the need for its existence. The
mass of the rank and file of the Volunteers had no knowledge of the
existence of a secret organisation in their ranks. That was a delicate
and potentially dangerous situation. The possibilities of misunderstanding were however minimised by the fact that the post 1916
recruits, at least in the south, were almost exclusively Army officers,
and by the traditional policy of the organisation which was to inspire
action by its members through the medium of the other bodies to
which they belonged. The I.R.B. was content to refrain from any
overt military activity as long as its members were pressing forward
its policy in the Volunteers. As the struggle developed, meetings of
circles or districts diminished, and in the last six months before the
Truce the activities of the organisation in Liam's division area were
nominal. Nevertheless it had vitality and significance in that it bound
a group of men into a historic and respected brotherhood which
evoked loyalty of a high order, without undermining in any way the
Army discipline under which they served.

The I.R.B. division designated South Munster, consisted of the
Counties of Cork, Kerry and Waterford. In March, 1921 the Supreme

Council requested Liam Lynch to act as divisional centre in place of Commandant Tom Hales, who had been arrested, until the elections, which were due to take place in the summer. Liam agreed. Thus, a short time before his military command was greatly enlarged by the formation of the 1st Southern Division, he acquired also leadership of the invisible brotherhood within the ranks of his forces in an area almost co-extensive with that of his division. He was then district centre of Fermoy, and had hitherto held no post of heavy responsibility in the I.R.B. Now he was appointed to a position which automatically gave him a seat on the Supreme Council of the organisation which regarded itself as the ultimate custodian of Republican aim and policy.

Between March and December, 1921 the South Munster Division, under Liam's direction, had been reorganised and its membership increased. In the counties of Cork and Kerry the organisation had attained a very high standard of efficiency, in County Waterford, organisation was not completed by the end of the year, but much work had been done. In County Cork total membership was 580. In Kerry 540, and in Waterford 50. This total I.R.B. membership of 1,170 for the three counties may be compared with the Army strength of the same area, which was 31,100.

The biennial elections throughout the whole organisation were due to take place in the autumn of 1921.[1] In March the Supreme Council issued orders for these elections, those in the circles to be completed by 15th June, the county elections by 15th August and those for the divisions by 15th October. This order referred, *inter alia*, to the relationship between the I.R.B. and the Army :

> " In the matter of co-ordinating the military work of the Organisation with that of the Irish Volunteers we have been very successful. In response to the orders issued Organisation men everywhere have shown tact and wisdom in the matter, and to this may be attributed a good deal of the efficiency that has resulted in great military success in the areas where the fighting has been most intense. This is only as it should be, and in strict accord with the desires of the S.C. The military functions of both bodies are similar to each other, the success or failure of one is the success or failure of both."

In fact, since the active campaign commenced in 1919 the I.R.B. as such had not undertaken any military activity in the South Munster Division. Its members were the spearhead of Volunteer activity, and with that position the Supreme Council was quite satisfied.

[1] Article 17 (*a*) Constitution, 1920

But from the moment the Articles of Agreement for a Treaty were signed in London the organisation was galvanised into activity. The Treaty was a matter upon which the I.R.B. undoubtedly had the duty of taking a decision and making its attitude known to its members.

The Supreme Council took a prompt decision. The following note was issued to division and county centres on 12th December :

THE ORGANISATION

THE PEACE TREATY

The Supreme Council, having due regard to the Constitution of the Organisation, has decided that the present Peace Treaty between Ireland and Great Britain should be ratified.

Members of the Organisation, however, who have to take public action as representatives are given freedom of action in the matter.

By Order,
S.C. 12-12-1921.

Liam was present at this meeting—the first which he attended as a member of the Supreme Council. It was held on the night of 10th December. His reaction to the decision is on record in two letters, one written to me on the 11th and one to his brother, Tom, on the 12th. To me he wrote :

" The situation is that I stood alone at the *meeting*[1] I attended, and our Division seemingly stands alone in the Army. G.H.Q. Staff and several others who have done actual Army work are for the Treaty. . . . My belief is that the Treaty will be carried by a majority of the Dáil. The position I have taken up I mean to stand by, even if the whole Division turn it down. On the other hand I do not recommend immediate war as our front is broken—which our leaders are responsible for. Minority in Dáil will fall in and act on decision of majority, the same must apply to the Army or we are lost."

In reference to Michael Collins he wrote :

" I admire Mick as a soldier and a man. Thank God all parties can agree to differ."

To Father Tom he wrote :

" First of all I must assure you that my attitude is now as always, to fight on for the recognition of the Republic. Even if

---

[1] The underlining of the word " meeting " indicated to me that it was an I.R.B. and not an Army meeting.

I were to stand alone I will not voluntarily accept being part of British Empire.

" Whatever will happen here in this week of destiny we must and will show a united front. Thank God that we can agree to differ. Minority of the Dáil will stand by majority no matter what side, the same will apply to the Army. Therefore there will be no disunity as in the past.

" It is only natural that in such a big issue there would be a difference of opinion. The President has a fair backing of T.D.'s, but at the moment, although I am almost certain of the issue, I do not wish to state same. All my Division hold the one view, and that strongly too. Several other southern areas, I know already, are with us in this view. If the Government accept Treaty we shall not, but strike for final victory at most favourable opportunity.

" There is no allegiance asked to the British Empire, only to be faithful to it. At all times, of course, we give allegiance to Irish Constitution. . . . The Governor General would be of our own choice, say for instance Count Plunkett, and he certainly, as only a figurehead, would not be much of a connection for King. . . .

" Even if we must temporarily accept the Treaty there is scarcely another lap to freedom. . . .

" Speeches and fine talk do not go far these days. We have already too much gas, What we want is a definite line of action, and in going along that, to use the most effective means at our disposal. . . .

" Sorry I must agree to differ with Collins—that does not make us worse friends. . . ."

The decision of the Supreme Council that the Treaty should be ratified left Dail deputies who were members of the organisation theoretically free to vote for or against it, but it put those who were against ratification in the position of acting in direct opposition to the wishes of the Supreme Council.

No such doubtful choice was given to other officers and members of the organisation. They were expected to obey the decision of the Supreme Council without question. The organisation demanded absolute obedience from its members ; Clause 20 of its constitution read, in part : " The authority of the Supreme Council shall be unquestioned by members of the Irish Republican Brotherhood."

The South Munster Division received the decision with anger and amazement. And not without reason. At the autumn biennial elections, just before the opening of the London negotiations, Michael

Collins had come to Cork and presided at the division meeting at which Liam Lynch was elected division centre, the position he had held, in a temporary capacity, since March. Collins was then chairman of the Supreme Council. After the elections were completed he spoke that day to the most representative group of officers from the three counties of Cork, Kerry and Waterford which he had ever met in conference since the active campaign commenced two years earlier. All the senior officers of the 1st Southern Division of the Army were present, most of the brigade commanders, and a number of other officers who had taken a prominent and honourable part in the struggle.

They were present as I.R.B. officers, but so closely was the organisation integrated with the I.R.A. in the south, and so completely were they in agreement on methods and objective, that there was not the slightest conflict between their duties in one sphere and the other. The men gathered in that room at Nora O'Brien's, in Parnell Place, were not only the leaders, but were also fully representative of the mind and spirit of both organisations in the area which, as a whole, had acquitted itself with distinction in the struggle.

That Michael Collins had a keen sense of appreciation of that position was evident from a conversation he had with Liam and some other officers just before the meeting. In this conversation he gave, in very general terms, the first indication which any of these officers had heard, that some modifications of the full Republican demand might have to be made in the London negotiations, if a settlement was to be reached, but he did not make any reference to this aspect of the matter when speaking to the meeting.

He said, however, that the officers assembled there had fully earned the right to be consulted before any final decision was reached on whatever terms of settlement were proposed by the British, and that for his part he would do his best to see that they were consulted. That satisfied everybody. But no further communication reached them until the Supreme Council's decision was issued to division and county centres on 12th December, after the Treaty had been signed.

The anxiety and uneasiness with which the organisation in south Munster regarded the absence of any indication of the intentions of the Supreme Council in November and December are reflected in the fact that a number of district boards met and requested a pronouncement from the Council. On the same day that the Council made its decision, but before they were aware of it, Cork City District Board met and called for " the rejection of the Treaty proposals being submitted to Dáil Éireann as being utterly at variance with the principles of the I.R.B. and treason to the Republic established in 1916."

On 7th January, 1922, the Cork County Centre reported to Liam that the whole membership of the organisation in the city and county was unanimously opposed to acceptance of the Treaty proposals. Soon afterwards he had similar reports from the county organisations in Kerry and Waterford. On 12th January the Supreme Council at length issued a statement to the members of the organisation in general. It was a more explicit expression of the policy hinted at by Michael Collins in Cork two months earlier.

" THE ORGANISATION AND THE NEW POLITICAL SITUATION IN IRELAND.

" It has always been the policy of the organisation to make use of all instruments, political and otherwise, which are likely to aid in the attainment of its final end, i.e.,

" ' A Free Independent Republican Government in Ireland.'

" The Supreme Council decided that no action for or against the present peace treaty be taken by the Organisation as such, but issued the following statement to members of Dáil Éireann who were also members of the Organisation.

" ' THE STATEMENT

" ' The Peace Treaty.

" ' The Supreme Council, having due regard to the Constitution of the Organisation, has decided that the present peace Treaty between Ireland and Great Britain should be ratified. Members of the Organisation, however, who have to take public action as representatives are given freedom of action in the matter..'

" By Order,
" S. C.
" 12-12-1921."

" In order to avoid misrepresentation of this statement it may be necessary to draw particular attention to the fact *that this instruction was issued only for the information of T.D.'s who are members of the Organisation and it left those free to act as they wished in the matter of voting for or against the Treaty.*

It is also pointed out that some such situation as that presented on the agreement to the Treaty was obvious from the date of the termination of hostilities, and the agreement to the Truce, and that it would not be expedient for the Organisation to interfere in a situation that may have the result of bringing Ireland nearer to the final end above mentioned. Until the present issues are clearly defined, which cannot be until the draft Irish Constitution can be considered by the Supreme Council, and when the Council may be in a position to judge what use can be made of the new position in the matter of gaining our ultimate aim the sole policy of the organisation shall be to maintain in the Organisation itself, in the Army, and in the nation as a whole, that unity which is so essential to ultimate success, *so that these forces may be availble to support the Republic when the proper opportunity arises.*

Pending the situation that will be created when the Irish Constitution has been drafted :

" 1. The Dáil shall continue to be recognised as the Government of the Irish Republic.

" 2. Members of the Organisation in the I.R.A. shall continue to receive routine military orders through their authorised military officers.

" 3. When the proposed Irish Constitution is published the policy to be adopted by this Organisation will be discussed in accordance with article 35 of the I.R.B. Constitution.

" By Order,
" SUPREME COUNCIL.
" 12th January, 1922."

This document split the organisation from top to bottom. The whole South Munster Division rejected it. Members of the Organisation believed with passionate intensity in the *de facto* existence of the Republic, and they hotly resented that any group of men, even chosen leaders, should attempt to assume the power of destroying what they had sworn to uphold. A meeting of all county board officers and district centres for the city and county of Cork held on 21st January, 1922, passed this resolution :

" That we consider that the statement issued to T.D.'s on the question of the Treaty proposals was utterly opposed to the spirit of the Constitution of the I.R.B. That we consider further that the statement of 12th January from the S.C. (in which the first statement is embodied) is an aggravation of that position. That we hold those members of the S.C. who authorised the issue of both statements did so in opposition to the spirit of the Constitution and that consequently they are unfit to continue as members of the S.C., and that we call on them to resign office.

" We decline to issue this statement of 12th January to the circles in Cork County."

Only a high sense of duty could have driven a group of disciplined officers into such open conflict with their superiors. They acted against a discipline all the more precious to them because it was voluntary and respected, against that almost mystic loyalty which bound them to the Organisation in good times and bad, against their loathing of disunity and with a clear appreciation of the consequences. They so acted because they believed sincerely that a higher duty than any obligations of loyalty to any group of men or to any organisation was imposed on them by their oaths, and that no considerations, personal or national could, without dishonour, relieve them of the obligations they had undertaken.

But if, in the South Munster Division, there was unanimity, it was not so throughout the whole Organisation. Quite frankly members of the I.R.B. were able to salve their consciences with the reflection that acceptance of the Treaty did not preclude a continuance of the fight for the Republic. It was an easy step from that to the very convincing argument of the practical advantages of acceptance— evacuation of British forces, fiscal control, our own flag and army, the opportunity to develop our own way of life, to save the language, to revive industry, to do all the things Sinn Fein had been urging for years. This was a position captured, to be secured and held until we were ready to move forward again. Sophists were not wanting who argued, publicly and privately, that an oath could not bind one to impose a greater evil on the country by keeping it than by breaking it, but members of the Organisation generally took the simpler view.

Another kind of argument which made a strong appeal to some members was that it was the traditional policy of the I.R.B. to " make use of all instruments . . . which were likely to aid in the attainment of its final end," to seize and utilise every position from which the enemy had been driven. These were very comforting theories for those who wanted justification for their honest convictions that it would be lunacy to reject the Treaty, and they are the I.R.B. basis of all the " stepping stone " arguments which became familiar at the time. But they ignored the fact that the whole national position had been changed by the declaration of the Republic in 1916, and by the solemn ratification of it by the people at two subsequent general elections. There, for many, lay the real difficulty. For the first time of crisis in its history the I.R.B. was in the straight-jacket of the Republic.

CHAPTER 16

NATIONAL UNITY IS BROKEN

That is nothing that is quelled by one or two failures, or any number of failures,
or by the indifference or ingratitude of the people or by any unfaithfulness.

WALT WHITMAN.

ON 8th December the Cabinet met. Four of its seven members, Griffith, Collins, Barton, and Cosgrave, were in favour of accepting the Treaty and recommending it to Dáil Éireann; the remaining three, De Valera, Brugha and Stack were opposed to its acceptance.

National unity was broken at the top. No power under heaven could prevent the split from spreading downwards. On the same day the President issued a public statement announcing that he " could not recommend the acceptance of this Treaty either to Dáil Éireann or to the country." " The great test of our people has come," he said. Referring to the Army, he said : " The Army as such is of course not affected by the political situation and continues under the same orders and control." That was much too optimistic a view. The Army, because of its spirit and character, because of the very factors that had made it an efficient weapon of liberation, could not be insulated against the storms of passion and controversy which began to rage around the question of the Treaty. Members of the G.H.Q. staff and some of its officers throughout the country were members of Dáil Éireann. Every Volunteer was a free citizen. His rights to speak and act as a citizen were not abrogated by his army service. Parliament, Army and people were too closely interwoven into the fabric of national resistance to make any isolation of one element possible. The very constituents of national strength in the war years now operated to carry division down to the remotest formations in every organisation working for freedom.

The British Government did what it could to create an atmosphere favourable to the Treaty. The unsentenced political prisoners were released on 8th December, and obvious preparations for evacuation were commenced by British forces.

In the days between 14th and 22nd December public attention was focussed on the debates taking place in Dáil Éireann on Griffith's motion for acceptance of the Treaty and its recommendation to the people. The Dáil had no power to ratify the agreement; that was a function of the people at a general election. But there were two powerful influences at work outside Dáil Éireann which between them had the potentialities of determining the internal situation for war or peace. One, the Irish Republican Brotherhood, was unseen, and its existence almost unsuspected by the majority of the people; the other was the Army. A number of men holding dominant positions in both organisations were in the Cabinet and in Dáil Éireann. Some in Cabinet, Dáil, Army and I.R.B. had already taken a decision as individuals for or against the Treaty, others in all formations of the Army and I.R.B., from G.H.Q. Staff and Supreme Council down to members of companies and circles, were beginning to take sides. No national organisation in the country escaped or could have escaped the contagion.

If there was one organisation which might have been saved from disruption by the Treaty it was the Army. In a normal time it would have remained outside the political arena, but the conditions of the time were not normal, control in the military and political spheres were interlocked, and what was at stake was the success or failure of the greatest bid for Irish liberty in three hundred years.

The Truce had been availed of to improve training and organisation. The policy of forming divisions, initiated in April by the formation of the 1st Southern, was continued during the Truce and at the end of the year almost the whole country had been divisionalised on a territorial basis.[1] Staffs, mostly incomplete, were appointed.

Both the Cabinet and the G.H.Q. Staff had been looking ahead and visualising the two most probable developments. If the negotiations with Britain broke down a new and more ruthless conflict would have to be faced; if there was a settlement and British troops were evacuated the I.R.A. would become a conventional regular Army under the control of Government. In November, before the Treaty was signed, the Army situation had been the subject of consultations between the President and Cabinet and the G.H.Q. Staff. Even then there was an incipient divergence of opinion, a still nebulous, but definite drift towards the formation of two groups along lines which were soon to harden into support for, or opposition to, the Treaty. If that division did not actually have its roots in the earlier differences of outlook on the necessity for reviving and continuing the I.R.B., it certainly followed the same pattern. On one side were those who thought the secret organisation essential, and who had developed it, and on the other those who were opposed to its revival after 1916.

Questions of authority and control were at issue though not openly. President De Valera was not then a member of the I.R.B.,

[1] See Map page 198

neither was the Minister for Defence, Cathal Brugha. Michael Collins was President of the Supreme Council of the secret organisation, a position which had traditionally carried the dignity of President of the Republic. He was Minister for Finance in the Cabinet and Director of Intelligence on the G.H.Q. Staff. In the first capacity his authority was supreme, in the second he was subject to the President,

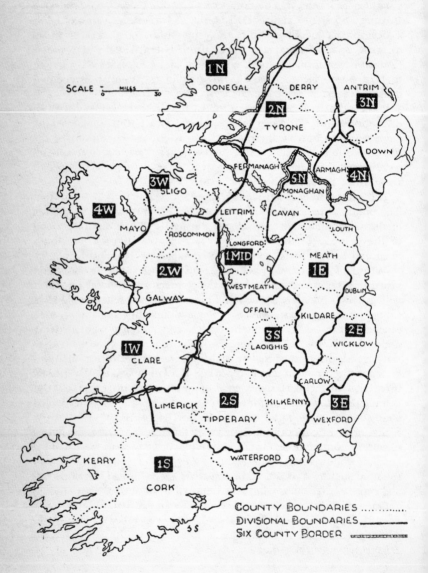

and in the third he was subordinate to the Minister for Defence and the Chief of Staff. Six members of G.H.Q. Staff, Richard Mulcahy, Michael Collins, Georoid O'Sullivan, Owen O'Duffy, Piaras Beaslai, and Liam Mellows, were Dáil Deputies. Three of them, Collins, O'Sullivan and O'Duffy were members of the Supreme Council of the I.R.B. That was a situation in which a major conflict of views on a fundamental issue was bound to create widespread disruption.

What appears to have been developing immediately before the signing of the Treaty was in fact a struggle for control of the Army by men, some of whom at least, foresaw a rift and regarded its occurrence as inevitable in certain circumstances. President De Valera and the Minister for Defence, Cathal Brugha, sought to strengthen the constitutional position by a more explicit expression of the absolute subordination of the Army to the Government—a relationship which had existed nominally since March, but which in the circumstances of the struggle with the British could not be too rigidly enforced. One of the moves in this direction was a decision to issue new commissions to all officers, and to have the oath administered anew to all ranks.

The compact I.R.B. group on the staff, while offering no frontal opposition to these proposals, did not find it difficult to delay their implementation. They controlled most of the administrative machinery of the Army and could direct the manner of its operation without offending against the disciplinary code. The matter of the issue of commissions, for instance, became bogged down in a rather academic controversy concerning appropriate titles for certain ranks. The oath, which was to have been taken by the G.H.Q. Staff immediately after a conference with the President and Cabinet in the Mansion House, on 25th November, was never re-administered to them or to anybody else in the Army.

Commissions were issued to the G.H.Q. Staff and offered to the division commanders. No question of the designation of ranks arose in these cases. Liam Lynch was offered a commission as officer commanding the 1st Southern Division. He knew something of the atmosphere which existed at G.H.Q., he had intimate and friendly relations both with those who were members of the I.R.B. Supreme Council and those who were not, and he had, long before then, reached certain conclusions about the degree of freedom of action essential for the field commanders of a guerilla force. He regarded absolute Cabinet control of the Army with considerable misgiving. Acceptance of a commission would, he feared, create a position in which his freedom to prosecute the struggle would be subjected to irksome and perhaps disastrous restraints. He foresaw a war of savage ferocity if we were compelled to renew the defence of the

Republic; he did not think we had the machinery which would enable any Government to control it in detail, and he feared that whatever military strength existed in the nation would be reduced to near impotence by rigid governmental control. The very essence of Army growth and achievement had been local freedom, guided by a few simple and well understood principles which united all in a varied but common battle for an agreed objective. He wanted to retain for the Army all the advantages that freedom gave if warfare was resumed.

These fears of his may well have been groundless, but it must be borne in mind that he could hardly have failed to be influenced in his outlook then by the memory of his earlier efforts to convince G.H.Q. of the wisdom of an offensive policy. When he wrote to the Chief of Staff, in the first days of December, that he would be glad to be relieved of his command, he was not influenced by any desire to secure release from a post of great responsibility in a new and fiercer conflict, but rather by a reluctance to do something which he believed would restrict the freedom of action of every field commander in such a struggle. The signing of the Treaty transformed the whole situation and Liam did not resign.

Dáil Éireann resumed its sittings after the Christmas recess on 3rd January, 1922, and the vote of the Treaty was taken on the 7th. Sixty-four Dáil Deputies voted for acceptance, fifty-seven against. Two days later President De Valera resigned. He agreed, however, to allow his name to go forward again, and in a vote between him and Arthur Griffith, Griffith was elected by two votes. A new ministry was formed from the pro-Treaty section of the Dáil :

Arthur Griffith	. . .	President
Michael Collins	. . .	Minister for Finance
William Cosgrave	. . .	Minister for Local Government
Charles Gavan Duffy	. .	Minister for Foreign Affairs
Kevin O'Higgins	. . .	Minister for Economic Affairs
Richard Mulcahy	. . .	Minister for Defence
E. J. Duggan	. . .	Minister for Home Affairs

Later five other Ministers were appointed : P. J. Hogan for Agriculture, Joseph McGrath for Labour, Professor Michael Hayes for Education, Ernest Blythe for Trade and Commerce, Desmond Fitzgerald for Publicity.

On 14th January the sixty-four pro-Treaty members met in the Mansion House as the " Southern Parliament." They approved the Treaty and elected a Provisional Government, which under the provisions of the British Act, was to hold office until 6th December,

1922. To this Provisional Government the British authorities formally handed over control on the same day.

Michael Collins became Chairman of the Provisional Government ; its other members were William T. Cosgrave, Eamon Duggan, Kevin O'Higgins, Patrick Hogan, Joseph McGrath, Fionian Lynch, and Eoin McNeill.

An abnormal and complicated position was thereby created in the sphere of Government. Dáil Éireann, the Government of the Republic, still existed and had appointed a ministry notwithstanding that a majority of its members had, by approving the Treaty, taken a step which, if ratified by the people at a general election would undoubtedly disestablish the Republic. The new President was one of the chief supporters of the Treaty and every member of his Cabinet had voted for it. On the other hand a Provisional Government had been formed which complied with the provisions of the British Act. Five of its Ministers were also Ministers in the Dáil Cabinet. The two notable exceptions in this regard were Arthur Griffith and Richard Mulcahy. Neither became a Minister of the Provisional Government at that time.

The anti-Treaty members of Dáil Éireann had asked for an assurance that the Republican position would be maintained in the interval between the Dáil decision on the Treaty and the vote of the people. In regard to the Army, General Mulcahy, the new Minister for Defence, gave a specific undertaking, " the Army," he said, " will remain the Army of the Irish Republic."[1]

Henceforward those Ministers who had undertaken the task of securing ratification of the Treaty entered upon courses of action which were confusing and at times contradictory. In one capacity they acted in conformity with the British interpretation of the position, which was that any Government set up in Ireland was the creation of a British Act of Parliament, and in another capacity they sought to create the impression that the authority which they exercised was derived from Dáil Éireann only. That duality of function was far too complicated to be generally understood in the atmosphere of acutely conflicting views which had developed, and it resulted in the creation of suspicions and antagonisms which began to embitter an already strained situation.

Two interpretations of pro-Treaty policy, although contradictory, are each capable of reconciliation with the position which developed from 7th January onwards. On the one hand Michael Collins and his Provisional Government might be said to be doing, under " the duress of the facts," the things required for compliance with a British

[1] See Appendix 10, note 2

Act of Parliament, but doing them in pursuit of their original aim—
the ultimate achievement of sovereign independence. The Treaty
was admittedly a deviation from the straight road, but the intention
to attain the same goal by a different route, was not abandoned.
Moreover, the advantages conferred by the Treaty made the remainder
of the journey easier and the whole project much less liable to absolute
defeat. If a British Government had no scruples about using its
superior force, actually as it had done, or potentially as it threatened
to do, on a vaster and more ruthless scale, Irishmen, having no such
crude weapons, were entitled to use such diplomatic deceit as might
somewhat redress the balance. They would accept the Treaty, get
the British forces out of the twenty-six counties, and then at the
right moment move forward to complete the task.

The other interpretation was that the pro-Treaty party had abandoned the Republic for whatever advantages they believed the Treaty
gave, but that during the necessarily difficult transition period of the
life of the Provisional Government a facade of Republicanism had
to be maintained, both for the purpose of securing the adherence of
Republicans amongst their own supporters in the national organisations, and of spiking the guns of their opponents. According to this
interpretation it was the Irish people and not the British Government
which was being deceived.

The ardent and very general desire that unity in the national
organisations should be preserved was a factor of considerable
significance. Republicans refused to recognise the authority of any
British Act to set up governmental authority in Ireland, and, perhaps
unrealistically, still regarded Dáil Éireann, a majority of whose
members had approved the Treaty and elected a Cabinet pledged to
support it, as the Government of the Republic. There was always the
hope that the people, who were the final authority, would repudiate
the action of the Dáil at a general election. The pro-Treaty party,
while maintaining with apparently equal earnestness that the Dáil
continued to be the government of the Republic, were taking the
most active measures to create a parliament which would inevitably
destroy it.

The maintainance of Dáil Éireann as the Government of the Irish
Republic and the parade of loyalty to it, was in fact, whether sincere
or otherwise, the master stroke of pro-Treaty policy. The Dáil
became after 7th January the matador's cloak, the quite impotent
focus of loyalty and hope, the facade behind which the Provisional
Government gathered the reins of control into its hands and massed
its strength. In the heroic years the people had made this image in its
own likeness; now, no one wanted to destroy it. If Dáil Éireann
had been extinguished by the vote on the Treaty the issue would

have been much more clear-cut, and many of the subsequent efforts to maintain unity would have taken a different direction.

Despite Republican hopes, time was on the side of the pro-Treaty party. It was purchased by a number of devices, one of the most effective of which was the promise of a Republican Constitution. How such a constitution could be reconciled with an oath of allegiance to a British king and the partition of the country was something that many people were prepared to take on trust.

The subsequent series of events up to the end of June, whether by design or accident, maintained Dáil Éireann as the ostensible national authority, and screened the activities of the Provisional Government. The prolonged Army crisis, the decision of the Sinn Féin Ard Fheis, the continued I.R.B. conferences, and finally the Collins-de Valera pact, which postponed a clear cut decision by the people all tended to foster in many minds the delusion that somehow the national parliament would be preserved as the Government of the Republic, and that out of this welter of confusion the much promised Republican Constitution would indicate a road which the nation could take with honour and in unity. Alas, there was no such road.

One of the most effective arguments used to win support for the pro-Treaty party was that the constitution when it did appear would be one which Republicans could accept. All arguments based on the hope or promise of a Republican Constitution ignored certain fundamental Treaty obligations, and were, as General Mulcahy said later, " finessing a litle too much with honour." To give any reality to the promise of a Republican Constitution as a means of preserving Army unity, it would have been essential that the pro-Treaty party and the Provisional Government (which in fact had no legal power to raise an Army) should have refrained from setting up a separate and rival military force. They did not do so. That was the test of the sincerity of their professions. The very unconvincing rejoinder was that they were maintaining the I.R.A. as the Army of the Republic, even in the service of a Government pledged to destroy the Republic. What emerges is that Provisional Government policy in regard to the I.R.A. was dictated by the fact that a majority of the Army was quite definitely and unchangeably opposed to acceptance of the Treaty.

But, for that majority, opposition to the Treaty was not the simple matter it was for those whose activity was confined to the political field. The looming menace of civil war hung over their decisions, and their forces were later weakened by the withdrawal of those who thought civil war an even worse evil than the Treaty.

The evacuation of British troops and the disbandment of the R.I.C. and Auxiliary forces commenced immediately after control was transferred to the Provisional Government. The British Government, apparently sure that the people would ratify the Treaty at the polls, lost no time in beginning the withdrawal of their forces. As barracks were vacated they were taken over by the local I.R.A. formations. Up to the end of February no question was raised as to the opinion of these local units for or against the Treaty, reliance being placed on the assurance of the Minister for Defence that the Army would be maintained as the Army of the Irish Republic. Even in these transfers the ambiguity of the whole position was evident. British officials regarded themselves as handing over the posts to representatives of the Provisional Government; I.R.A. officers taking over regarded themselves as acting on behalf of Dáil Éireann and the Irish Republic.

It was not until 10th March that the Minister for Defence in a public statement gave this definition of the position :

> " The position of the Army is precisely as stated by me at the Dail meeting on Wednesday, March 1st. It is the Irish Republican Army.
>
> " Its connection with the Provisional Government is that we occupy for them vacated military and police posts for the purpose of their maintenance and safeguarding, the Provisional Government being given an assurance that the troops occupying such posts shall not use their powers to interfere with the expression of the people's will at the pending General Election, and will not turn their arms against any Government elected by the people at the election."

The Minister may well have given such assurances to the Provisional Government, but it is entirely certain that no such assurances were either asked for or given by officers taking over posts throughout the country.

Even two months later, 12th May, 1921, the same Minister in a letter to the O/C Cork No. 1 Brigade[1] with reference to the taking over of the remaining occupied posts in his area, Victoria Barracks, Cork; Ballincollig and Youghal, makes no reference whatever to the two conditions specified in the statement of 10th March. Two of these barracks were amongst the largest British posts in Ireland, and with the exception of Dublin and the Curragh, were the last to be evacuated. The Minister's letter to the O/C Cork No. 1 Brigade sets out in nine numbered paragraphs the conditions under which the brigade would, and in fact did, take over these posts. There is nowhere in them any reference to troops occupying these posts not using " their powers to interfere with the expression of the people's

[1] See Appendix 4

will at the pending General Election," nor is any assurance asked for that they would "not turn their arms against any Government elected by the people at the election." The Army had then split, and Cork No. 1 Brigade was unanimously on the side of the convention which had repudiated the Minister. Its commanding officer, Seán O'Hegarty, was a member of the Executive.

Even as late as May, therefore, the taking over of evacuated British posts did not compromise the position of Army units. They were not thereby committed to support of the Treaty. In the 1st Southern Division, and in some others, there was no alternative to allowing the local units to take over, nor was there any possibility of imposing on them any conditions which included acceptance of the Treaty. Elsewhere it was different.

No unit of the Dublin Brigade was allowed to take over any evacuated British post in its area. Instead, a small but gradually expanding force was built up from officers and men of the brigade, who were known to be entirely loyal to the members of G.H.Q. Staff, who supported the Treaty, and this force was used to garrison evacuated posts. This was done by the Dáil Minister for Defence, and of necessity under Dáil authority, since the Provisional Government had no power to raise a force of any kind; it was done in the name of the I.R.A. and many of these officers and men had been amongst the ablest and most active in the fight against the British. The force thus created was nevertheless a new force—it was the nucleus of the Free State Army. Its creation raised sharply the whole question of Army allegiance.

Throughout the country the same thing could not be done, and local units took over evacuated posts unconditionally. In February, a development in the 2nd Southern Division accentuated the growing threat of incipient disruption in the Army. That division, under the command of Commandant Ernie O'Malley repudiated the authority of Dáil Éireann and purported to adopt an independent attitude in opposition to the Treaty. Early in the month a section of his forces raided Clonmel R.I.C. Barracks when it was about to be evacuated and seized a quantity of rifles and ammunition. On 18th February Liam Forde, Commandant of the Mid-Limerick Brigade of this division issued a proclamation repudiating the authority of G.H.Q. British forces were at the time evacuating Limerick city, which was in the brigade area.

G.H.Q. reacted to this situation untactfully, but from their point of view correctly, by ordering Commandant Michael Brennan of the 1st Western Division, who was known to be in favour of the Treaty, to move detachments from Clare into the city to take over posts being evacuated by the British. Limerick was a strategic position and

they decided it should be held. This was the first time that forces
from one brigade had been ordered into the area of another brigade
to occupy vacated posts. It added fuel to the flame of resentment
against G.H.Q. and it created a menacing and dangerous situation.

There were pro-Treaty elements in the Mid-Limerick Brigade.
Captain Hurley, the brigade quartermaster, began to organise these
as a separate force, with a view to taking over the posts from the
troops of the 1st Western Division. A parade held by him on Sunday,
5th March, was surrounded by anti-Treaty elements who had come
into the city on the previous day from Tipperary, Cork and elsewhere.
Hurley was placed under arrest. Between the 6th and the 10th March
a fairly large number of anti-Treaty units moved into Limerick.
They occupied some hotels and a wing of the mental hospital. Pro-
Treaty troops were in occupation of some evacuated British posts in
the city, British forces were still in occupation of others. The situation
was explosive, feeling ran high, and at any moment a trivial incident
might have created an armed clash which could extend to the whole
Army. The Limerick position threatened civil war. It was, Liam
said in a letter to Tom, " a disgrace to both sides."

A number of persons, including the Mayor of Limerick, endeavoured
to reconcile the conflicting elements and avert an armed clash. They
were not successful. G.H.Q. then asked Liam Lynch to intervene,
and with Oscar Traynor, O/C Dublin Brigade, he went to Limerick
and worked out an amicable solution of the problem.

Averse as he was to publicity, later misrepresentations forced him
to give the facts to the Press in a letter dated 27th April.[1] He wrote :—

> " I have always avoided publicity, but my name has been
> brought forward so much recently that I am reluctantly forced
> to deal with the matter.
>
> Regarding the statement by Beggar's Bush Headquarters to
> the effect that they had done everything for unity in the Army,
> and that the other side had done everything possible to break it,
> I am sure all officers and high command in the Free State forces
> can verify my emphatic assertion that no officer did more than
> myself to maintain a united army.
>
> My activity with O.C. Dublin Brigade in forcing the Limerick
> settlement when all others, including the Mayor of Limerick, had
> failed, is sufficient proof of this, and I am sure that Limerick's
> first citizen will bear out what I say. The M.D. and Mr. Collins
> were present when agreement was reached. In accordance with
> the terms of agreement in that most serious situation, Eoin
> O'Duffy, C/S, authorised me in writing :—

---

[1] *Irish Independent*, 27th April, 1922

(1) To hand over to the charge of the Limerick Corporation the four police barracks, and

(2) To instal a small maintenance party—responsible to myself— in the two military barracks, releasing the occupying troops to return to their areas.

(3) Revolvers taken would be returned. Mr. Griffith tried hard to press the issue in a manner which would have resulted in fearful slaughter in the streets of Limerick.

I was more pleased with my success in securing an amicable settlement of the Limerick situation than with any victory in connection with my activities in the war.

It was a happy consummation for me to see about 700 armed troops on each side who were about to engage in mortal combat, eventually leave Limerick as comrades. It was the Junior officers of the old G.H.Q. staff, who mutinied against the arrangements agreed to by their senior officers in doing the right thing in Limerick, really brought about the present condition of affairs, for I state definitely that it was their action on that occasion which ultimately resulted in a cancellation of the Convention."

CHAPTER 17

THE ARMY CONVENTIONS

The passionate aspiration for Irish nationhood will outlive the British Empire.

MITCHELL

LIAM spent much time in Dublin in January and February, 1922. The full inplications of the Dáil vote in favour of the Treaty were becoming evident, and the consequences it held for the Army were matters for anxious thought and discussion amongst all ranks.

The General Headquarters Staff was divided in opinion. Since the change of Government on 7th January, Cathal Brugha had ceased to be Minister for Defence. Richard Mulcahy held, for a short time, both the Defence Ministry and his former post as Chief of Staff, until the appointment of Eoin O'Duffy to the latter position.

As the staff stood at the change of Government, those in favour of the Treaty were : Richard Mulcahy, Chief of Staff; Eoin O'Duffy, Deputy Chief of Staff; J. J. O'Connell, Assistant Chief of Staff; Georoid O'Sullivan, Adjutant General; Seán McMahon, Quarter-master General; Michael Collins, Director of Intelligence; Diarmuid O'Hegarty, Director of Organisation; Emmet Dalton, Director of Training; Piaras Beaslai, Director of Publicity. Against the Treaty were : Rory O'Connor, Director of Engineering; Liam Mellows, Director of Purchases; Seán Russell, Director of Munitions; Seamus O'Donovan, Director of Chemicals. Opinion in the Army throughout the country, though still fluid and disposed to remain outside the political arena, was beginning to harden on the same general lines as those marking the now inevitable division of opinion in every national organisation.

Immediately after the Dáil vote on the Treaty on 7th January, the senior Army officers opposed to its acceptance held a series of consultations. The policy upon which there was the largest measure of agreement amongst them was that the Army should revert to its original status as a Volunteer force under the control of an elected Executive, and that a convention for the election of this Executive should be held without delay. No convention had been held since 1917, and in the meantime all ranks had sworn allegiance not merely to " the Government of the Republic which is Dáil Éireann," but also to the Republic itself. It was held that the constitutional right of the organisation to hold periodic conventions was not thereby abrogated, and that the best hope of keeping the Army united and faithful to its allegiance lay in the preservation of its democratic and voluntary character. Moreover, the view was strongly held that as Dáil Éireann had, by a majority, accepted a Treaty which disestablished the Republic, the Army was relieved of any further obligations or duty of allegiance to that body.

The group of senior officers sponsoring these views were : Rory O'Connor, Liam Mellows, Seán Russell and Seamus O'Donovan of the G.H.Q. Staff; Liam Lynch, Ernie O'Malley, Joe McKelvey, Tom Maguire, Liam Pilkington and Michael Kilroy, Divisional Commandants; Oscar Traynor and Andrew McDonnell, Commandants of the Dublin and South Dublin Brigades. On 11th January they addressed to the Minister for Defence, Richard Mulcahy, a " request that a Convention of the Army be called not later than Sunday, 5th February, 1922," for the purpose of considering the following resolutions :—

> " That the Army re-affirm its allegiance to the Irish Republic.
> " That it shall be maintained as the Army of the Irish Republic under an Executive appointed by the Convention.
> " That the Army shall be under the supreme control of such Executive, which shall draft a Constitution for submission to a subsequent Convention."

They requested further that preparation for the convention should be entrusted to an equal number of representatives of the Minister and of their body, and they set out a proposed basis of representation at the convention. It was :—

> " (a) All Divisional Commandants shall be ex-officio delegates.
> " (b) Other delegates shall be selected as follows :—
> One delegate selected at a company parade where 30 or less attend ; two delegates where the number is over 30 and under 70 ; three delegates where the number is over 70.
> " These delegates shall attend a Brigade Convention and shall select for the General Convention 5 per cent. of the total number of delegates to the Brigade Convention. In the event of 5 per cent. amounting to a whole number and a fraction, the number of delegates shall be brought up to the next whole number.
> " All Officers and men are equally eligible for appointment as delegates at Company and Brigade Conventions, with the exception of Divisional Commandants, who are ex-officio delegates to the General Convention."

On 13th January the Minister replied :—

1. " That the Dáil as a whole is the elected Government of the
   Irish Republic and that the supreme control of the Army is
   invested in it, and
2. " That the proposal contained in the resolution to change
   the supreme control of the Army is entirely outside the
   constitutional powers vested in the Dáil Executive by the
   Dáil."

The Minister stated that he was making arrangements to meet the
signatories of the letter and discuss the matter with them. This
meeting took place on 18th January. On the same date Rory
O'Connor, as chairman of the " Acting Military Committee, I.R.A."
addressed a letter to Eoin O'Duffy who had been appointed Chief of
Staff in the meantime :

"I am directed by the signatories of the letter of 12th inst.
addressed to Mr. R. Mulcahy, Minister for Defence, to say that
in view of the fact that you cannot see your way to call a convention of the whole Army, that a convention will be called by
the signatories referred to.
"Further that we repeat our desire to co-operate with you
in hastening the evacuation of the country by enemy troops,
but to that end the signatories can only act on orders issued by
you and countersigned by me."

The conference to consider the request for an Army convention
was held on 18th January and presided over by the Minister for
Defence. G.H.Q. Staff, divisional commandants and commandants
of brigades, not yet included in divisional organisation, were present.
Opinion on the matter was divided. It was argued by those in favour
of holding the convention that the Army retained its constitutional
right to do so, even when its members took an oath of allegiance to
Dáil Éireann ; its constitution had not been altered, and now that a
majority of Dáil Éireann had, in approving the Treaty, taken an
action tantamount to the disestablishment of the Republic, the Army
was thereby relieved of any further obligations of allegiance to that
body. Its allegiance was to the Irish Republic only. It could maintain it by no other course than by reverting to the original position
whereby it was under the control and authority of its own Executive.
Against the holding of a convention it was argued that Dáil Éireann
was still, until the people decided otherwise, the elected Government
of the Republic, that the supreme control of the Army was vested in
it and that the Army continued to be the Army of the Irish Republic.

Another argument against the holding of a convention just then was put forward by Frank Aiken, O/C 4th Northern Division. It was that in view of Michael Collins' promise that the constitution would be a Republican constitution, the holding of a convention should be postponed until after its publication, so that, as he said, " we can see clearly whether we have to split, and with whom we have to split." If the convention was held before the constitution was available, he argued, the Army would be divided and its influence on the situation reduced to nil. With two armed forces all over the country it was inevitable that some fool would do something which might start a civil war.

Finally, all with the exception of the O/C 4th Northern Division, agreed that an Army convention should be held within two months from that day—18th January. The Minister for Defence gave a personal undertaking that the Army would be maintained as the Army of the Irish Republic ; and a council of four officers, two pro-Treaty and two anti-Treaty, was appointed to act as a watching and advisory body under the Chief of Staff, as a guarantee that the Republican position would not be prejudiced in any way pending the holding of the convention. It was agreed if any two members of the council regarded any staff proposal as being inimical to the Republic it should not be proceeded with. This council was wholly ineffective, because no decisions of any significance were submitted to it in the two months of its existence.

In view of what happened subsequently two points in connection with this agreement are important. The first is that it was an almost unanimous agreement to hold a convention, representing a decision of both sides, and it would have assembled a convention in which each would have had representation roughly proportionate to its numerical strength in the Army. The second is that no policy or resolutions to be put before the convention were considered or agreed upon at that date. Subsequently it became clear that there was a very wide divergence of view on this matter. The anti-Treaty officers would have put forward resolutions similar to those in their letter of 11th January. The pro-Treaty section would not have opposed the election of an Army Executive *per se*, but would have sought to put its relations with any future government on some definite basis. Probably that could have only one meaning, and the elements of complete disagreement and division into two hostile camps were present all the time, but even in the opinion of the Minister at the time :

" The setting up of an Executive in that way does not in actual fact take the Army away from the control of the Dáil.

It but secures that . . . the work of the Army shall be along lines agreed to, not only by the Dáil, but by its own Executive."

During the next three weeks no acute difficulties arose, and preparations for the convention were being made by the G.H.Q. Staff. Evacuation of British forces was proceeding. By mid February 150 police barracks and 50 military posts had been handed over to the Army and 14,000 British troops had left the country. Among the barracks handed over was Mallow, which Liam had captured in September, 1920, and into which he now moved his division headquarters.

A conference of G.H.Q. Staff, divisional commandants and commanding officers of brigades not included in divisional organisation, assembled in Dublin on 24th February and adopted the basis of representation at the convention which had been proposed in the letter of 11th January to the Minister for Defence. The date for the convention was fixed as Sunday, 26th March. Preparation of an agenda for the convention was deferred to a meeting of the same officers to be held on 15th March. Orders were issued by G.H.Q. to the whole army for the election of delegates to the convention, and as, in accordance with these orders, the selection of delegates was completed by 14th March, the delegates were not instructed to support or resist any particular policy at the convention. The good faith in which Liam's division accepted the situation thus created, and the anticipation that Army unity would be maintained, are evidenced by the fact that a number of officers and men were sent to Beggar's Bush for specialised training, and that some officers were appointed to posts at G.H.Q.

Dáil Éireann had adjourned on 9th January and was due to reassemble on 14th February. The sitting was however deferred to 28th February. The Minister for Defence proposed to ask the Dáil for formal sanction to the holding of an Army convention. Obviously it was not anticipated that the request would meet with any objection. However, on 27th February the Cabinet decided not to bring the matter before Dáil Éireann, but accorded Cabinet sanction to the Minister's request for the holding of a convention. It now appeared that there was a reasonable probability of preserving Army unity, despite the growing expansion of a distinct pro-Treaty force with headquarters at Beggar's Bush Barracks, and the recruitment to it of individual Volunteer officers and men from many parts of the country.

Government sanction to the holding of a convention encouraged Liam and officers like him to redouble their efforts to prevent a recurrence of incidents such as that at Limerick, and to endeavour to work out some solution of the problem of Army allegiance which would avert civil war. The Government's decision had followed immediately upon the very heartening agreement reached at the Sinn Féin Ard Fheis on 21st February, between Eamonn de Valera and Austin Stack on the one hand and Arthur Griffith and Michael Collins on the other.

That agreement preserved the unity of the political organisation at least for a time. It was agreed that the Ard Fheis would adjourn for three months ; that Dáil Éireann would continue to function as it did before the signing of the Treaty, its existing President and Cabinet remaining in office ; that no election would be held during that period ; and that the constitution would be submitted to the electorate at the same time as they were called upon to vote on the Treaty. Dáil Éireann ratified the agreement on 2nd March.

The whole position appeared more hopeful when Liam returned to his division headquarters at Mallow, at the conclusion of his mission to Limerick. His main concern then was to work out with his staff and the senior brigade officers, some policy which would preserve Army unity while keeping the force unchanged in its voluntary character and in its allegiance to the Republic.

His outlook, as always, was national. He was thinking not merely of his own division, but of the whole Army, including the divisions which were wholly inside the proposed six county border, and those which straddled the line of demarcation between the part of Ireland the British were evacuating and the part they proposed to continue to occupy.

He looked to the convention with hope, but saw that if it was to succeed in its main objects some way must be found of reconciling the point of view expressed in the resolution of 11th January with what he knew to be the pro-Treaty point of view—that the Army should in future stand in some clearly defined relationship to any Government elected by the people. That was the kernel of the matter, and he knew it.

He could see the difficulty that any democratic Government would have in accepting the position that the only military force in the country was not in any way under its control ; but he was at all times un-wavering in the conviction that the Army should not in any circum-stances abandon its allegiance to the Republic, nor should it be committed to support of the Treaty. Whether the Army did, or did not, in the changed circumstances owe allegiance to Dáil Éireann, seemed to him a matter of less importance, since he believed that the existing position would be of brief duration, and would end on the day the people voted on the Treaty issue. If they rejected the Treaty there was no problem ; if they accepted it, as he thought they would, the position which would then arise was the one upon which we required an agreed Army policy.

His relations with Michael Collins and Richard Mulcahy continued to be friendly. His sincerity was so obvious, his concern for the nation's welfare and the future of the Army so evident, that no one, however much in disagreement with his views, could treat him with anything but respect. His position in that crisis was a strong one. He commanded a division which represented in numerical strength more than one fourth of the entire Army.[1] In weapons, fighting experience and leadership its preponderance was even greater. It was virtually unanimous in its opposition to the Treaty, and would have supported him in any policy which did not do violence to its fundamental national principles. He never sought to use that position except in what he conceived to be the best interests of the nation.

I travelled to Dublin with him early in March for one of the many conferences he had with the Minister and the Chief of Staff. It extended over several days during which the whole Army position was reviewed in detail in an effort to find some common ground on which the opposing view points could be reconciled.

Although a note of acerbity and partisanship was beginning to appear in public statements, these conferences were not so affected. There was, as there had frequently been in the earlier days, plain speaking, but the predominant atmosphere was one of goodwill and genuine, mutually-shared desire to find a way of preserving in the service of Ireland, untarnished by the stain of civil war, the first Army that had brought her to the brink of success in her long struggle for freedom.

On 15th March the Dáil Cabinet took an action which threw the whole Army situation into confusion, and initiated the chain of events which precipitated the split. Suddenly reversing its decision of a fortnight earlier, the Cabinet decided to prohibit the holding of the Army convention. The reasons for this decision are evident from a note made by the Minister for Defence and subsequently published.[2] This note indicates the terms on which he proposed to put the original request for a convention before the Dáil. It represents the viewpoint of the Minister and those G.H.Q. officers who supported him, but it does not claim to be, and is not, a proposal which had been approved by the conference of officers of both sides which agreed to the calling of the convention on 18th January. Neither is it a proposal which was specifically placed before the subsequent meeting of the same officers on 24th February. It will be remembered that this meeting

[1] See Appendix 5
[2] *Irish Independent*, 24th March, 1922

deferred preparation of an agenda for the convention until 15th March. This note therefore represents nothing more than what the Minister would have wished the convention to do, and which he now believed it would not do, if it was allowed to assemble. In other words, he believed a majority of the Army was opposed to acceptance of the Treaty. As will be shown later, he was right in this view. The text of the note is as follows:

"At the Dáil Cabinet on 15th March, specially discussing the implication of the Limerick episode and the Convention which had been called, the Minister for Defence had to admit to the Cabinet that he could not guarantee that if this Convention was held there would not be set up a body regarding itself as a military government not responsible to the people, and that he had given up hope of having generally accepted for putting before the Convention a resolution:

1. Agreeing to appoint by election from among serving officers a Commission to frame and place before a subsequent Convention to be held after the General Election proposals for associating the I.R.A. with whatever Irish Government was then in authority, and
2. Disclaiming any intention of setting up a Military Government as opposed to any Government elected by the people."

The first paragraph of the Minister's proposed resolution was, at that date, one upon which it may have been possible by good will on both sides to arrive at agreement, but the second paragraph attributed to the anti-Treaty side, by innuendo, an intention which they did not entertain; whatever other solution was found, few if any wanted to set up a military government of the I.R.A.

This decision of the Cabinet was conveyed to the meeting of officers then in session for the preparation of the convention agenda. It immediately terminated their efforts to find common ground for the resolutions to be submitted to the convention. The pro-Treaty group would not, of course, go further in face of the prohibition, and for the anti-Treaty group the time had come to consider their position separately.

The text of President Griffith's order to the Minister for Defence was published on 12th March:

"It is quite evident to the unanimous Dáil Cabinet that at an Army Convention contemplated for 26th March it is proposed to endeavour to remove the Army from under the control of the Government elected by the Irish people, which is Dáil Éireann. Such a purpose is illegal, and you are hereby instructed that the holding of this Convention is illegal."

One may reasonably ask how the holding of a convention was legal on 27th February, when the same Cabinet sanctioned it, and illegal on 16th March. It may be questioned also whether the convention, if held, would have in fact endeavoured to remove the Army from under the control of the Dáil. Certain officers would undoubtedly have endeavoured to do so, but that is not to say that this course would have represented the consensus of opinion in the convention, or that it would be the one decided upon. That there would have been no support for any form of military dictatorship in the convention is sufficiently proved by the fact that when the split became an accomplished fact no effort was ever made to set up such an anomaly, and that during the civil war one of the anxieties of the Republicans was to place themselves under the authority of the Government of the Republic, which they did in the course of the conflict on 28th October, 1922, as soon as the constitutional position became clear.

No one can say now what would have been achieved if the convention had been allowed to meet with the sanction of the Cabinet, and had been allowed to make the attempt at hammering out some policy for the future of the Army. It would have represented the whole Army. It would have met in an atmosphere of freedom in keeping with its spirit and tradition, and it would have had a consequent high sense of responsibility and gravity in its decisions. Every soldierly quality it had won out of the testing years would have urged it powerfully towards preserving unity. Every national instinct which the conflict had sharpened would have turned with loathing from a split in its ranks. Its discipline was not that of a convict prison, it was both a finer and a more spirited thing ; nothing offended against it and infuriated officers and men so much as an unjust or unreasonable order. And to a very large number of officers and men this order, prohibiting the holding of a convention, appeared both unjust and unreasonable. It is to be noted that the Provisional Government, alleged by some to be the only legitimate authority at the time, made no order.

The anti-Treaty officers met and decided to hold the convention on the date originally fixed. They summoned the already elected delegates of the whole Army, irrespective of what views these delegates may have held. The text of the document issued to all units is as follows :

> " Whereas as a result of a unanimous agreement come to at a meeting of G.H.Q. Staff, all Divisional Commandants, Brigade Commandants in areas not Divisionalised, held on 18th January last, a general Convention of the I.R.A. was sanctioned by the

Minister for Defence of the Dáil Cabinet, to be held not later than the end of March;

" And whereas as that agreement has been broken by the acquiescence of the Minister for Defence in the instructions issued by President Griffith forbidding the holding of such a Convention;

" Therefore be it resolved that we, the undersigned members of G.H.Q. Staff and commandants and other officers of the I.R.A. units, hereby call the aforesaid Convention, to be held on the date already determined, viz., Sunday, 26th March, 1922; the representation to be as set forth in the General Order already issued by G.H.Q."

This bore fifty-two signatures.

On 23rd March the Minister for Defence in a letter to Eoin O'Duffy, Chief of Staff, having referred to the solidarity and organisation of the Army, went on to say:

" The calling of the sectional Convention against the order of G.H.Q. Staff breaks definitely, to some extent, this solidarity and this organisation, but it does not and must not break to any degree the brotherhood of those who in the past have worked and borne responsibility together.

" Any officer or man attending the Convention will thereby sever his connection with the I.R.A. O/C's will regard each case for the present as one of suspension, and each case should be reported on separately. In dealing with all such cases O/C's concerned should take the greatest pains to avoid any actions or expressions that would tend to create antagonism amongst those who have been in the Army."

A disaster, worse than any defeat in the field, had struck the Army. A meeting of the 1st Southern Division Council which comprised the senior members of the staff and the brigade commandants, was held at Mallow on 20th March. Liam, who had been in Dublin, hurried back to preside at this conference. Quite unexpectedly the Minister for Defence and the Chief of Staff attended. It is no doubt an indication of the importance they attached to the decisions which the division would make which impelled them to travel from Dublin. The meeting was a long one, and its ultimate purpose became the familiar one of trying to find some means by which the Army could be saved from the abyss towards which the now much accelerated current of events was driving it.

The division, having made its unanimous intention to participate in the banned convention quite clear to the Minister and the Chief of Staff, was willing to explore the possibility of finding some satisfactory method by which the Army would stand in disciplined relationship to whatever Government was elected after the General Election; but there were two points on which it was adamant, first, that the convention should be held (although, in view of the position which had been created by the Government ban, they were willing to consider postponement to a later date than 26th March so that the whole Army may be represented), and secondly, that recruiting for the Civic Guards should cease. The creation of this new peace force by the Provisional Government was an action that particularly angered a large number of members of the Army.

The result is best given in a letter which Liam wrote to the Press on 27th April.[1] He said:

"Instead of meeting the officers duly appointed for the purpose, the Minister for Defence and the Chief of Staff attended a meeting of the 1st Southern Division in Mallow, when differences became acute, but they both left for Dublin before an agreement was reached, as the Council wished to consider the matter further. Eventually it was decided that:

"A meeting of Division and Brigade Commandants with G.H.Q. be held in Dublin, such meeting to select a Council of eight to frame definite proposals for associating the I.R.A. with the new Government elected by the Irish people, and put such proposals before the Division and Brigade Commandants for agreement preparatory to putting them before the Government. Furthermore, there should be no further recruiting for the Civic Guards, and a Convention of the Army should be held to consider the proposals of the Council of eight referred to above.

"The Divisional Adjutant and myself travelled to Dublin by night mail and met the Minister for Defence. The proposed agreement was put before Mr. Griffith and Mr. Collins, who turned down the last two clauses which were ours. We then put the other clauses before the Divisional Council, and it was unanimously agreed not to put them before the meeting that evening of the Divisional Staffs and Brigade O/C's from all Ireland. I was advised not to bring forward these clauses. I knew my ideals then as well as when I fought for them during the war."

That was the point beyond which Liam and his division would not go. Their proposal to let the G.H.Q. Staff and division and brigade

[1] See also statement of Eoin O'Duffy, *Irish Independent*, 26th April, 1922

commandants select eight men to frame proposals for associating the
Army with the new Government, and submitting their recommendations to a free convention, was turned down by Arthur Griffith
and Michael Collins—by the President of Dáil Éireann and the
Chairman of the Provisional Government.

On the same day that the final proposals of the 1st Southern
Division were rejected, Rory O'Connor gave an interview to the
Press. How far his statements represented the views of all the officers
associated with him on the anti-Treaty side of the Army it is now
difficult to say, but it is reasonably certain that they did not accurately
represent Liam Lynch's position.

Having claimed to represent eighty per cent. of the Army which
was against the Treaty, he said, in reply to a question, that there was
then no Government in Ireland to which they gave allegiance. " In
effect," he said, " the holding of the Convention means that we
repudiate the Dáil. If a government goes wrong it must take the
consequences."

> " Our view," he went on, " is that it (the Government) has
> abolished itself—not exactly abolished but it has done something
> it has no moral right to do, and therefore we cannot recognise it
> further. The Dáil, in deciding that the Irish Republic shall go
> into the British Empire, has committed an act of national dis-
> honour that we won't stand."

The convention assembled in the Mansion House, Dublin, on
Sunday, 26th March. The total number of delegates present was 211.[1]
In view of the claims and counter-claims made at the time it is
necessary to indicate what these delegates represented. Because of
the territorial nature of the organisation, and the absence of uniformity
in unit strengths at any level, terms such as division, brigade and
battalion are completely misleading in this connection. In the fact
that the delegates were elected on the basis of company strengths, as
set out in the letter to the Minister for Defence of 11th January and
subsequently adopted, there is the nearest approximation which can
be obtained, both of the actual strength represented by them and the
territorial distribution of that strength. In the autumn of 1921, and
before any substantial number of post-Truce men had enrolled, the
total of all ranks in the Army was computed to be 112,650.[2] Of that
number Liam's division accounted for 33,550, or more than one
fourth. The increase in strength of roughly 3,000 from April, when
the division was formed, was due to the return of prisoners and

[1] See Appendix 6
[2] See Appendix 5

normal recruitment. In March, 1922 there were sixteen divisions, either functioning or planned and one independent brigade (North Leitrim), covering the whole organisation in Ireland.

The method of selection of delegates tended to give a more than proportionate representation to the weaker areas, because where the organisation was weak the companies were small. Many of the companies in the 1st Southern Division had up to 100 members, but in a brigade convention they had no more representation than companies of seventy men. Again, in the weaker areas, any company no matter how small had one delegate at the brigade convention.

It is a fair indication of how the representation worked out to find that the fifty-four delegates from the 1st Southern Division were about one fourth of the total number of delegates who atttended; and, taking the total Army strength into account, it does not appear to be an exaggeration to say that 80 per cent. of that strength was represented at the convention. A few other figures will illustrate broadly the divisions with the next largest representation. The 1st, 2nd 3rd and 4th Western Divisions had thirteen, seventeen, eighteen and twenty delegates respectively; the Dublin Brigade had eight, the South Dublin Brigade six. Either of these brigades had a larger representation than any of the northern divisions. A few delegates from England and Scotland attended.

It is not suggested that all formations which sent delegates to the convention were solid blocks of anti-Treaty opinion; neither would it be true to say that there were no anti-Treaty elements in the formations which refrained from attending. There could have been no such clear cut line of demarcation. Commandant Frank Aiken's 4th Northern Division was endeavouring to maintain a neutral attitude but two delegates from one of its brigades attended with the knowledge and permission of the divisional O/C.

The convention itself was uneventful. Liam Mellows presided and made a statement reviewing the whole Army position from the signing of the Treaty. The following resolution was passed unanimously :

" That the Army reaffirm its allegiance to the Irish Republic :
" That it shall be maintained as the Army of the Irish Republic under an Executive appointed by the Convention :
" That the Army shall be under the supreme control of such Executive which shall draft a Constitution for submission to a Convention to be held on 9th April."

A temporary Executive of sixteen was elected to hold office until the adjourned convention assembled two weeks later. Liam Lynch headed the poll in the voting for this Executive and five other officers from his division were elected to it. The Executive appointed Liam Chief of Staff and headquarters was set up at Barry's Hotel Gardiner's Row.

On 28th March the Executive issued a statement declaring that the Minister for Defence and his Chief of Staff no longer exercised any control over the Army. It called for cessation of recruiting for the force being set up by the Provisional Government still referred to by the pro-Treaty section as the I.R.A. and for an end of recruiting for the Civic Guards. On the 29th it ordered the destruction of the *Freeman's Journal* printing machinery following misleading reports of the convention in that paper.

The Executive ordered battalion parades for Sunday 2nd April at which all units re-affirmed their allegiance to the Republic in the terms of the resolution passed at the convention. A statement giving the background of the conditions which resulted in the holding of the convention and the decisions made thereat was read at each parade.[1]

Official pro-Treaty pronouncements referred to the convention as a " minority convention " stating that the notice calling it was signed by seven commanding officers out of the nineteen separate commands in Ireland. The nineteen commands were probably arrived at by regarding the Dublin and South Dublin Brigades as not divisionalised leaving fifteen divisions three brigades (two Dublin and North Leitrim) and regarding an independent battalion in Derry City as a separate command.

On any basis of computation the description " minority convention " was grossly inaccurate and misleading to the public who had no knowledge of the lack of uniformity in command strengths, a condition of affairs resulting from the G.H.Q. policy of grouping brigades into divisions only when they were considered ripe for that development and of limiting their size to such numbers as it was felt the best local officers could control. At the lowest estimate and without taking into account the representation from other areas, the seven commanding officers who signed the order for the convention represented 71,250 officers and men or more than 63 per cent. of total Army strength.

An official statement issued from the pro-Treaty G.H.Q. on 5th April challenged the representative character of the convention. The following reply[2] was made by Commandant General Rory O'Connor :

[1] See Appendix 7
[2] *Irish Independent*, 8th April, 1922.

" (1) I am challenged by Beggar's Bush to prove that the delegates to the Army Convention expressed the feelings of the Brigades they represented. In reply :—

(a) The objects *inter alia* for which the Convention was called— viz. to consider a motion placing the control of the Army in the hands of an Executive elected by it, was ordered by Mr. Owen O'Duffy to be communicated to officers and all ranks.

(b) By order of Mr. O'Duffy, Company and Brigade conventions were held for the purpose of electing delegates to the General Convention.

(c) It was on these written instructions issued by Beggar's Bush that the local conventions were held.

(d) The matter therefore was fully understood, thanks to the order issued by Beggar's Bush.

(e) The motion referred to above, and which Mr. O'Duffy had in January ordered to be transmitted to all ranks was carried unanimously at the Convention.

(2) Several Brigades, Battalions and Companies which were not represented have since joined.

(3) I am challenged to prove that we have a majority of the Army with us. In reply :

(a) Mr. Mulcahy has proved it. In the official organ of Beggar's Bush it is stated that Dáil Eireann Cabinet had to forbid the Convention being held because the ' Minister for Defence . . . HAD TO ADMIT that he could not guarantee that if the Convention were held there would not be set up a military dictatorship, and Dáil Eireann . . . therefore had but one course open to them, and that was, to forbid the Convention. . . .' (*An t-Oglac* p. 3. Par. E.).

It should be noted that Dáil Éireann did not object to the holding of a Convention as such : but to the defeat which the Minister of Defence foresaw.

(b) If it was thought by Beggar's Bush that they had a majority in the Army, why did they not come over with their adherents to the Convention, and defeat the motion ?

(4) I am challenged to give the names of the delegates attending. Certainly. If the Adjutant General will come to these headquarters, the list will be available for scrutiny and he can satisfy himself that they were "real representatives." They were delegates sent to the Convention in accordance with the orders issued by Beggar's Bush.

(5) I am challenged to produce evidence that the local conventions which selected delegates were held regularly and that ' the system of selection originally laid down was adhered to.' All I can say is that the method of selection, etc., was approved by Beggar's Bush, the orders were issued from there, and the work carried out under its authority.

Several brigade conventions were presided over by officers of Beggar's Bush, who have accepted the Treaty, and when I stated that I wished to preside at the Convention of South Dublin Brigade, I was politely informed that a member of G.H.Q. (who supported the Treaty) would attend. Not a single Republican member of G.H.Q. attended local conventions. Hence Beggar's Bush is in a better position than I am to know whether ' the system of selection originally laid down was adhered to,' or not.

(6) I note that I am considered ' abusive ' in referring to ' I.R.A. acting under G.H.Q.' as the Free State Army. Nothing abusive is intended. I cannot understand these persons who are pledged to destroy the Republic and to establish the Free State objecting to be called Free State.

(7) It is stated that ' there is but one Republican Army in Ireland, and that is the Army taking its orders from G.H.Q., Beggar's Bush.' The portion of the Army taking its orders from Beggar's Bush is about 15 per cent. of the whole. The rest, practically the whole Army, has been suspended, but is none the less Republican. I note that the other ' points ' raised by me are ' irrelevant ' and therefore do not need contradiction. May I say that I raised no point. I replied to a statement issued by Beggar's Bush accusing me of making false statements."

The Army convention re-assembled at the Mansion House on Sunday, 9th April. The number of delegates, 217, was slightly larger than at the first convention a fortnight earlier, a few additional areas being represented. The convention had two main functions, to adopt a constitution, a draft of which had been prepared by the Executive elected at the previous convention, and to elect an Executive to control the Army.

The constitution[1] reverted the Army to the control of an Executive of sixteen elected annually at a convention of the whole Army. It provided that the delegates to conventions would be elected on the same basis as that used in the case of the first convention. The Executive were given power to appoint an army council of seven and a chief of staff, who would appoint his own staff. The constitution declared the objects of the Army to be :

[1] See Appendix 8

(*a*) " To guard the honour and maintain the independence of the Irish Republic :
(*b*) " To protect the rights and liberties common to the people of Ireland :
(*c*) " To place its services at the disposal of an established Republican Government which faithfully upholds the above objects."

The constitution altered the wording of the original oath of allegiance which all volunteers had taken in 1920 by deleting the phrase pledging allegiance to Dáil Éireann as the Government of the Republic. The amended form of oath read :

"I . . . . . . do solemnly swear that to the best of my knowledge and ability I will support and defend the Irish Republic against all enemies, foreign and domestic, and that I will bear true faith and allegiance to the same. I do further swear that I do not, and shall not, yield a voluntary support to any pretended Government, authority or power within Ireland hostile or inimical to that Republic. I take this obligation freely without any mental reservation or purpose of evasion so help me God."

The constitution having been adopted, the convention proceeded to elect an Executive of sixteen under the provisions of Article 4. Any serving Volunteer was eligible for election. The method of election was that the whole convention nominated twenty-five of its members and gave them power to appoint the Executive. Of these twenty-five delegates, five were elected by each of the four groups of provincial delegates meeting separately and the remaining five were elected by the whole convention from a group of twenty delegates, five of whom were nominated by each of the provinces in addition to their primary nominations.

The result of this election on 9th April was that Liam Lynch was elected at the head of the poll, and the fifteen others in the order set out: Liam Mellows, Rory O'Connor, Joe McKelvey, Florence O'Donoghue, Seán Moylan, Seán O'Hegarty, Liam Deasy, Seamus Robinson, Ernie O'Malley, Peadar O'Donnell, Joe O'Connor, Frank Barrett, Tom Maguire, P. J. Ruttledge, Tom Hales.

At the conclusion of the convention the Executive met and appointed Liam Lynch Chief of Staff. An Army council of seven was also appointed, but I have been unable to find any documentary evidence of the names of those who composed it. There is no doubt, however, that it included Liam Lynch, Rory O'Connor, Liam Mellows, Joe McKelvey, and possibly Ernie O'Malley, Seamus Robinson and Peadar O'Donnell.

For three weeks from 26th March, Liam had his headquarters at Barry's Hotel, Gardiner's Row, until the Four Courts was occupied on 13th April.   He began to get a staff together, but his main pre-occupation was with the immense problems created by the split, and the conditions of near chaos which existed in the Army in many parts of the country.   His task was one of extraordinary difficulty.

> " Since the Truce," he wrote to Tom on 18th April, " has been a worse time on me than the whole war.   Every bribe and cunning plan has been put up to us, but thank God we pulled through to take once more free action."   Elsewhere in the same letter he said : " Sad it is to risk having to clash with our old comrades, but we cannot count the cost "

He worked like a galley slave, day and night, without rest and almost without sleep.   The portion of the Army giving allegiance to the Executive had cut itself off from any further share in the arms and equipment handed over by the British to the Provisional Government.   It was without financial resources, it was in occupation of various barracks and posts all over the country, and liabilities were being incurred to traders and merchants.

Very little in the way of arms had been transferred to the section of the Army over which the Executive now ruled, most of the arma-ment received from the British being retained in Dublin in the hands of the new force which the Provisional Government was building up. The only substantial acquisitions of arms which the anti-Treaty forces received since the Truce were those taken in the raid on Clonmel Barracks, 200 rifles and 10,000 rounds of ammunition landed at Waterford in November, and the cargo of the *Upnor* captured on the high seas and brought into Ballycotton Pier on 29th March.

The rifles landed at Waterford had been purchased by G.H.Q. in Germany and were run to Waterford from Bremmerhaven by Charles McGuinness.   The original arrangement had been for a landing at Helvick, but this was changed to Waterford.   The First Southern Division was responsible for all measures concerned with the landing, and the Division Quartermaster, Joe O'Connor, supervised the distribution and security of the arms.

The *Upnor* was a British Admiralty vessel which left Cork Harbour with a cargo of arms, ammunition and other supplies, which were part of the British stores being transferred to England.   She was towing a barge which slowed her considerably.   She was overhauled and captured ten miles off Ballycotton by a vessel commandeered in Cobh for the occasion, and piloted by Captain Jeremiah Collins, a retired master mariner who had rendered earlier service to the

Government in connection with efforts to secure arms abroad during the conflict with the British. The pursuing vessel was manned by a crew of officers and men of Cork No. 1 Brigade.

In organisation and execution, in the secrecy with which the plans were kept, and in the measures taken for security and distribution, this was a brilliant operation, carried out under the orders and direction of the Brigade Commandant, Seán O'Hegarty.

The harbour forts were in British hands, and strong British forces were still in occupation of Cork. They would naturally take effective action if any information about the capture reached them before the cargo was landed and distributed. But there was nothing suspicious about the vessel which sailed out of the harbour after the *Upnor* had gone, and when both vessels arrived at Ballycotton Pier later that night, Cork No. 1 Brigade had isolated the town, arc lamps were ready to light the discharge of the cargo, and sufficient commandeered transport had been mobilised close at hand to ensure rapid and widespread distribution of the captured arms to prepared dumps. The drivers of these vehicles had not the remotest idea of why they had been pressed into service.

On the Pro-Treaty side the Provisional Government, through the Minister for Defence of Dáil Éireann and the Chief of Staff, were gradually building up a uniformed whole-time nucleus of a standing army. Before the March Convention some southern officers had been appointed to positions on the G.H.Q. Staff. These left at the split, but individual officers and men from various parts of the country began to drift into Dublin and join the Beggar's Bush force. Recruitment to it was at that time limited to Volunteers having pre-Truce service.

The Provisional Government had, of course, no difficulty in arming and equipping this force. The British Government was quite ready to transfer to them such arms and equipment as they required. On 12th April, Churchill stated that 4,000 rifles, 2,000 revolvers, 6 machine guns and ammunition had been handed over, and that authority would be given for any further issues that may be required.

Nor was there any dearth of men willing to offer their services. Employment in any regular force offered a measure of security to many, on both sides of the Six County border, upon whom the economic pressure of the war with the British had borne harshly. Nevertheless, there were very many officers and men who, though now in equally dire distress, refused offers of posts which would have given them a much needed security. Instinctively they felt that this was not the same cause they had served with clear consciences and high hearts in the past. The light and joy had somehow gone out of service.

Although the Army had now split into two groups the line of division was by no means clear cut, no great bitterness had developed between officers and men who had known each other in the past and now found themselves on opposing sides, and a considerable number did not give up hope that some settlement would yet be possible. The possibility of reuniting the Army was one of the first matters considered by the Executive, and its members did not regard the door to negotiation as finally closed. On 14th April, Liam Mellows, as secretary to the Executive, sent a letter to the secretary of Dáil Éireann, in which he set out the terms on which the Executive were prepared to agree to reunification of the Army. They were :

1. " To maintain the existing Republic.
2. That Dáil Éireann, as the Government of the Republic, be the only Government of the country.
3. To maintain the Army as the Irish Republican Army under the control of an elected Independent Executive.
4. Disbandment of the Civic Guards, the policing of the country to be carried out by the Irish Republican Army as decided by the Executive of the Army.
5. All financial liabilities of the Army to be discharged and future requirements met by the Dáil.
6. No election on the issue at present before the country to be held while the threat of war by England exists."

This evoked no response. Neither did a wider distribution of the same letter to all Dáil Éireann Deputies on 25th.

The background of the letter from Mellows to Dáil Éireann on the 14th April was a discussion at the convention on the 9th which had been referred to the Executive, and which that body considered next day. It was variously interpreted as a proposal for military dictatorship, a proposal to prevent a general election in the Twenty-six Counties by force, and a proposal to eliminate all four governments then claiming some authority in Ireland—the British, the Northern, the Provisional and Dáil Éireann. What it developed into for practical purposes, and as an issue to be decided by the Executive, was whether the Army should attempt to prevent the holding of a general election in the Twenty-six Counties on the issue of the Treaty. Inextricably associated with it was the whole question of the Army and political situation.

After a long discussion, Seán O'Hegarty proposed :

" That this Executive declares itself willing to meet representatives of Dáil Éireann Cabinet or Beggar's Bush G.H.Q. for

the purpose of discussing Army unification on a basis of non-
interference by the Army in elections."

This was defeated by fourteen votes to two, and Seán O'Hegarty
tendered his resignation, which was not, however, accepted at the
time. The letter sent to the Dáil represented the views of the majority
of the Executive. Liam Lynch was opposed to the idea of a dictatorship,
and there was no support for it. His views on the election were given
in a letter to Tom on 6th March:

> "In the past I made the most of any situation that arose,
> whether granted by the enemy or by any section in Ireland.
> I will do my best at the elections to keep Ireland from handing
> away the Republic or the least portion of her birthright. If we
> fail at the election, I hope to have the Army united under an
> Executive and not giving allegiance to any party or Government.
> If the Army stands together—which I hope it will—we can save
> the country and the Republic. . . . If we can force the Treaty party
> to draw up a Republican Constitution we are A 1 again. This I
> consider quite possible."

That was his hope and the object of his selfless labours in those
terrible days of crisis, darkened by the looming menace of Civil War.
The Army standing together, and a Republican Constitution; who
will dare say now that it was an impossible ideal? Implicit in it is the
fact that he believed the people, for reasons for which he would not
judge them too harshly, were prepared to accept the Treaty. This man
who had fought so gallantly against the British did not want to fight
against his own people. He wanted internal peace. He wanted,
passionately and above all else, to avoid Civil War. But there was a
limit, a point beyond which no bribe or argument could take him.

There was reason to hope that the Constitution when it emerged
would be one which Republicans could accept. The manner in which
that hope was held out to the Army by the Minister for Defence,
after the Dáil vote on the Treaty, will be sufficiently clear from the
statement made by Richard Mulcahy in the Provisional Parliament on
11th September:

> "The point has been raised that a very considerable amount
> of responsibility lies on the people who split the Army, and just
> in connection with that particular point it, perhaps, is worth
> saying what the policy of the Government was with regard to
> the Army, after the passing of the Treaty, and after setting up a
> Ministry committed to seeing that Treaty through. Differences
> arose in the Army. Hot-headed men wanted to pull this way,

that way and the other way, and the great solidarity that was in
the Army, up to that particular point was imperilled. This is the
attitude that, as Minister for Defence at the time, I put forward
to them, and I think that it certainly represented the attitude that
the whole Government adopted toward the Army, although
they might consider as I express the policy now that it was
finessing a little too much with honour.

"The position was that the British were clearing out of this
country. They were evacuating their barracks, and we had an
opportunity of coming from the camps in the country and little
corners in the hills where, during the period of Truce, we trained
for any danger which might again come over the country. We
had the chance of leaving those places, and coming into proper
military barracks, strengthening ourselves within the greater and
more ordered association we could have got in these barracks,
arming ourselves in the way in which we were in a position to
arm ourselves, if we got any particular length of time in these
places, very much better militarily equipped and very much
better militarily organised than we were at any time, even at any
time after the period of truce-training, which we made such full
use of. The Army was appealed to not to raise questions upon
which we could split in that particular atmosphere, but to wait
until there was something definite to decide for or against, until
the Constitution was definitely produced, as it will be in three or
four months. Then when they saw the actual fact of the Constitution, then they would have something before them, on which
they could say : 'We will not have this' or 'Under all circumstances we will have this.' Keeping that policy before them they
would arrive at a particular position with a strength that would be
a very great strength, and with heads that will be clearer. If
there is any number of hearts strong enough to say there is an
element of dishonesty in that Constitution and we will not have
that, then they would have with them as much military strength
as they had in this war, and if there is a voice strong enough
to speak, they will have a weapon if they speak straight and strong
and clear. It may be said that that was finessing with honour,
but I was perfectly satisfied that the situation was not a military
situation alone. I was perfectly satisfied that, given months to
face the circumstances and face the position—that those who had
led the Army would not be blind or mad enough to say, no matter
what better military position they were in, 'We will not have
this Constitution which can and should be got out of that Treaty,
and we will put the people to war,' and I felt absolutely justified
that the putting of that policy before the Army was correct,

and if men split the Army it was men who took a different attitude.
If men could take a more reasonable attitude let us hear what
that attitude could have been."

To the majority in the Army who, in April and May, still believed
that those who accepted the Treaty were sincere in their avowed
intention to extract from it the maximum advantage for Ireland and
to work for the Republic, the advice of waiting for the constitution
could be interpreted only in one way. It would be a constitution
under which a united Army could serve without betraying its
allegiance to the Republic.

A situation of serious potential danger to the whole national effort
developed during April. Neither the Executive nor the Beggar's Bush
Staff were in complete control of their respective forces throughout the
country. Armed clashes had occurred in the course of which eight
had been killed and forty-nine wounded. No one wanted Civil War,
neither side took any steps to prepare for such a catastrophe, yet the
situation was rapidly, and it seemed inevitably, drifting into chaos.

The Executive never fused into an effective unit. It never had a
common mind or a common policy. There was not time. Many
matters, not strictly the concern of the Army, obtruded in discussions,
social theories were aired and debated, projects were considered in an
atmosphere of unreality, stresses developed which weakened the fabric
of authority. Things were done and ordered to be done without the
knowledge of all the members, sometimes without Liam's knowledge.

CHAPTER 18

EFFORTS TO AVOID CIVIL WAR AND PROPOSALS FOR ARMY UNITY

We have declared for an Irish Republic and we will not live under any other law.

LIAM LYNCH.

OF the four main organisations which constituted the national movement, two had still retained virtual unity ; Sinn Fein by postponing a decision on the Treaty, and Cumann-na-mBan by registering a practically unanimous vote against it at a convention held on 5th February. The Army and the I.R.B. were split, but a long series of earnest efforts were made to re-unite them. Although the principal personalities were to a large extent the same, each organisation made re-unification efforts in its own field.

Three I.R.B. conferences were held in Dublin in the early months of 1922, for the express purpose of endeavouring to save that organisation from disruption on the Treaty issue. They were abnormal and not authorised by the constitution, but that was of no significance in the circumstances. They were called by the Supreme Council, and comprised the members of that body, together with the division and county centres of the whole organisation. In these conferences the Supreme Council, the large majority of whose members were in favour of the Treaty, endeavoured to convince the officers of the organisation that the best interests of the cause of the Republic would be served by accepting the position created by the Dáil vote on the Treaty, and maintaining the organisation with its original object.

The first conference took place on 10th January. Here, if anywhere in the distracted ranks of Republicanism, many members thought, some hope of internal peace must lie. On both sides the issue was debated with commendable objectivity and restraint. Those in favour of accepting the position created by the Dáil vote argued that to do so would be in line with well-established I.R.B. policy, that there was nothing dishonourable in advocating such a course, that it was a matter of expediency and not of principle. In their view the country had made a substantial advance towards its goal of complete independence, the people were war weary, wisdom and practical commonsense suggested that the advantages which had been gained should be seized and utilised, and that it would be foolish and irresponsible to commit the Irish people to war again for the difference between the Treaty and the most that could be attained with our present strength.

The other side of the case was presented with equal sincerity. The Republic had been established and ratified by the votes of the people at two elections, therefore no analogy existed between the position of the organisation in any previous crisis and its position now. Acceptance of the Treaty would disestablish the Republic, and for the first time in our history the people would have, by their own deliberate act, accepted foreign domination. The country was being partitioned, Republicans and nationalists generally in the partitioned area were being abandoned to the blind fury of the Orange mob, and to the calculated schemes of Orange politicians to eradicate and destroy them. We were not beaten in the field, we were in a better position to continue the struggle than at any time since 1916; above all, members of this organisation had solemnly bound themselves on oath to maintain and defend the Republic, and should be the last to desert it.

Liam Lynch took a leading part in all the discussions at these conferences. Michael Collins and he were the principal protagonists of the two opposing viewpoints. Admiring and respecting each other, but each apparently immovable in his own conviction, they wrestled with the grim threat of disunity. Each was aware that it had been our fatal weakness in the past, and each was impressed by the appalling fear that it would again prove our undoing.

Liam was one of those who set the distinctive note of these conferences, one of the voices listened to with attention and respect. Clearly divided into two opposed and conflicting sections as this body was, yet some indefinable sense of brotherhood, something deep and strong that had ripened out of intimate association in a great national effort, held the bitter word unspoken, the devouring passions in check. These men wanted above all to maintain a position where they could work together, each group respecting and trying to understand the honest opinions of the other. They failed in that, and no one who loves Ireland can contemplate their failure except with sadness and regret. The first conference achieved no more than an exchange of views and a decision to re-assemble at a later date.

The same body met again at 41 Parnell Square on 18th March. The meeting had been convened for the 12th, but was postponed. Its purpose, as stated in the letter sent to county centres, was that of " dealing exclusively with the attitude of the Organisation to the Treaty." It met now under the shadow of the Cabinet's prohibition on the holding of the Army Convention, and in the knowledge that the convention would be held despite the ban. Michael Collins, who had a large share of the responsibility for the Cabinet's decision, and Liam Lynch, who had a large share of the responsibility for the action which spurned and controverted that decision, met again in an atmosphere which, although strained, was still dominated by the spirit of the organisation. And they were the two men who could have averted the impending disaster, had it been possible to bridge the deep but narrow chasm which separated them.

Collins had decided to accept the Treaty and do whatever was necessary to operate it, retaining his original objective and determined to use every weapon the Treaty put into his hands to achieve complete independence. Lynch had decided that, even if the people accepted the Treaty, the Army should not be committed to it, that the Volunteers should revert to their original status under an Executive, and that there should be a constitution which would enable them to continue in allegiance to the Republic until it could be formally restored. Were these two attitudes so conflicting as to be irreconcilable? It proved so.

The second conference did not produce any tangible results other than a clarification of the relative strengths of the two sections into which the Treaty had divided the organisation. It became evident from the views expressed, that although the Supreme Council itself was, by a large majority. in favour of the Treaty, they would have been quite unable to carry any endorsement of their action at the meeting. A vote of those present would have shown a small majority against the Treaty, but as has been stated earlier, this body had no standing under the constitution of the organisation, except for one specific function unrelated to the crisis which now faced it. While it would have been of considerable value to the pro-Treaty section to be able to claim from the conference an endorsement of their action, there would have been no point in the anti-Treaty section pressing the matter to a division. They could not oust the Supreme Council, and with the Council the power of decision lay.

Moreover, the strongest sentiment was still in favour of trying to preserve unity, and the meeting adjourned without taking any decision other than that the same body should meet again a month later.

On 19th April the adjourned conference met for the last time at 41 Parnell Square. There were twenty-seven present. No record appears to exist of the names, but it is reasonably certain that the incomplete list given here is correct as far as it goes : Michael Collins, Harry Boland, Eoin O'Duffy, Diarmuid O'Hegarty, Michael Staines, Seán O'Murthille, Gearoid O'Sullivan, Martin Conlon, Seán McKeown, Liam Lynch, Humphrey Murphy, Pax Whelan, Florence O'Donoghue, Joe McKelvey, Seán Boylan, Michael Sheehan, Larry Brady, Patrick Mullaney, Tom Larkin.

Two conventions of the anti-Treaty section of the Army, held despite the Cabinet's ban, had taken place since the previous meeting of this body. The Army had split in two. The Four Courts, the Masonic Hall, the Ballast Office and other buildings in Dublin had been occupied by Army Executive forces. Many of the principal. officers on both sides, including the two Chiefs of Staff sat together at this conference.

The chairman asked each person present individually for his views as to whether the position had changed in any material way since the previous meeting. The general opinion elicited by this was tnat the situation had deteriorated, and incidents which had taken place throughout the country led to heated exchanges between some of those present. It was evident that the danger of these incidents developing into a general armèd conflict was in everybody's mind. The atmosphere of the meeting was tense and explosive.

Collins, who could be explosive himself on occasion, was grimly cool and calm. He said that the only suggestion the Supreme Council had to put before the meeting was that the constitution would be available in three or four weeks, and that in it may possibly be found a basis for unity. The Supreme Council's suggestion was that a committee should be appointed by the meeting to consider the con-stitution. This committee could report to the Supreme Council and the council would then summon a further meeting of those assembled to discuss the report. Liam Lynch promptly rejected the suggestion. He said that he could not wait three weeks for a constitution that may not alter the position in any way, unless there was a guarantee that it would be a Republican constitution. Otherwise, he would have to take action.

I suggested that, as the Army situation was the most serious and potentially dangerous aspect of the situation, an effort should be made to find some solution of it which would avoid civil war. I proposed the appointment of a committee of six—three from each side—to try to find a basis of Army re-unification and report back to a further meeting of the body then assembled. This was met with prompt hostility from the pro-Treaty side, but the chairman after a few minutes intervened and said he thought the suggestion might be considered. After discussion, it was decided to form the committee. The views of each person present, for or against the Treaty, were known to everybody else. There was a small majority against, but in the Supreme Council itself an overwhelming majority for the Treaty. The method of selecting the committee agreed upon was that the chairman should nominate one person from each side who would in turn nominate two others, who with themselves would form the committee of six. The chairman named Diarmuid O'Hegarty and myself. O'Hegarty nominated Seán O'Murthille and Martin Conlon,

I nominated Liam Lynch and Joe McKelvey. All agreed to act, and the meeting adjourned.

This committee met next day at 41 Parnell Square. It quickly arrived at the conclusion that a truce to the indiscriminate clashes taking place all over the country would be helpful in creating a better atmosphere in which to discuss re-unification proposals, and exchanged views on terms. In these discussions Liam expressed the view that a truce could be of little service, unless an overall basis of agreement was found. He produced the terms sent to the Dáil by the Army Executive, and interpreted a number of points arising out of them. The pro-Treaty representatives did not think that in their present form these proposals offered a basis for an agreed solution.

The possibility that a constitution acceptable to Republicans would be produced was discussed, but Liam insisted that it was an event too vague and remote to build anything on at that time.

The most important decision of the committee on that day was that, as it was itself representative of a secret organisation and could not announce its existence, it should endeavour to create a committee of Army officers representative of both sides which could issue a public call for a cessation of the conflicts then taking place and for an effort to reunite the Army. It was agreed to recommend that one member of the existing committee from each side be nominated on this new body, so as to keep the activities of both in harmony. The number to constitute the new body was not limited.

At this time Liam held the view strongly, and no doubt rightly, that the whole position created by the Treaty was indivisible, and that any effective solution for any one of the principal organisations, I.R.B., Army or Sinn Féin, was impossible in isolation. Any basis of unity should, he thought, be one which embraced all the national organisations. The simple, but now unattainable, one was that they should reunite in allegiance to the existing Republic and reject the Treaty. All hope of that solution being gone, he looked for some policy which would, without dishonour, avoid civil war.

Four subsequent meetings of this committee were held. The constitution was never submitted to them, nor were they given any indication or draft of the vital articles in it with which they would be primarily concerned. Their efforts to find a basis for Army unity were unsuccessful. The proposal for a Committee of Army officers which could announce its existence also failed. The pro-Treaty side nominated Diarmuid O'Hegarty, Seán O'Murthille Liam Tobin and Martin Conlon. Liam Lynch rejected this proposal on the ground that, while not objecting to these nominees individually or collectively, he did not believe they were in a position to act with any binding authority on behalf of the pro-Treaty section of the Army.

The proposal was considered by the Army Council and on their behalf Joe McKelvey stated at the next meeting of the original committee (from which Liam Lynch was absent), that it was their desire if negotiations were to take place they should be conducted by members of the Army Council on one side and by officers who could speak authoritatively for the other side. The pro-Treaty representatives said that they were prepared to conduct negotiations with anybody on the other side but did not offer to nominate, or have nominated anybody from their side having more authority. At the next meeting the pro-Treaty representatives expressed the opinion of their authorities that a meeting of the prominent officers on both sides would not serve any useful purpose until the constitution was available, and they felt that a better spirit would be maintained if men who had been in the forefront of the conflict which divided them did not come together in the circumstances. They said further that they could not see what could be done until the constitution was ready, except to suspend hostile activities on both sides, a matter which they considered vital and were prepared to discuss with anybody from the other side.

To this Liam Lynch rejoined that without guarantees he could not wait a fortnight for a constitution, that he had already waited too long and that action should be taken. There was a state of affairs in the South, he said, which required to be dealt with at once. He asked from the other side, within two days, a guarantee that they would maintain the independence of Ireland and produce a Republican constitution. In the absence of such a guarantee he saw no point in continuing these meetings. The Republic would have to be maintained and the Free State would not be allowed to come into existence, no matter what sacrifice may be necessary to prevent it. On that note this particular effort ended.

Other groups were active in trying to find some common ground on which both sides could come together. A number of officers who had been amongst the most prominent fighters during the war, and who were now on opposite sides had been meeting and holding discussions. Dan Breen had done much to bring them together and presided over their conferences.

His Grace the Archbishop of Dublin and the Lord Mayor had intervened, and had held a series of meetings at which both sides of the political organisation and the Dáil members were represented. Later the Labour Party joined in these conferences and when their failure was announced on 29th April it looked as if the last hope of peace had vanished.

Those of us on the anti-Treaty side who had been working on peace proposals, considered ourselves free to pursue any other line

that offered the slightest hope of an honourable settlement after the
I.R.B. committee had failed in its mission.   As a result of another
series of conferences in the last days of April, ten officers, five from
each side met on the evening of 1st May and agreed to sign and
publish the following statement the original draft of which was
prepared by Seán O'Hegarty :

> "We, the undersigned officers of the I.R.A., realising the
> gravity of the present situation in Ireland, and appreciating the
> fact that if the present drift is maintained a conflict of comrades
> is inevitable, declare that this would be the greatest calamity in
> Irish history, and would leave Ireland broken for generations.
>
> "To avert this catastrophe we believe that a closing of the
> ranks all round is necessary.
>
> "We suggest to all leaders, Army and political, and all
> citizens and soldiers of Ireland the advisability of a unification
> of forces on the basis of the acceptance and utilisation of our
> present national position in the best interests of Ireland, and we
> require that nothing shall be done that would prejudice our
> position or dissipate our strength.
>
> "We feel that on this basis alone can the situation best be
> faced, viz. :—
>
> (1) The acceptance of the fact—admitted by all sides—that the
> majority of the people of Ireland are willing to accept the
> Treaty.
>
> (2) An agreed election with a view to
>
> (3) Forming a Government which will have the confidence
> of the whole country.
>
> (4) Army unification on above basis.

Dan Breen,	Tom Hales,
H. Murphy	S. O'Hegarty,
F. O'Donoghue,	Seán Boylan,
R. J. Mulcahy,	Owen O'Duffy,
Gearoid O'Sullivan,	Miceal O'Coileain."

It was not to be expected that this effort would be received in an
uncritical spirit by the Army Executive.   Three of the signatories
were members of the Executive, but that body itself was not committed.   Liam was beginning to distrust all efforts at reunification of
the Army, and he had little hope that this particular one would achieve
anything.   A statement was issued from the Four Courts which
expressed the opinion that instead of unifying the Army this effort
would, on the contrary, make for further disunity :

" The Army Council," it added, " has no knowledge of the
agreement said to have been reached by Free State soldiers and
Republicans. Any agreement upon which the Army can be
united must be based upon the maintenence of the Republic.
Attempts to make ' deals ' with individual soldiers cannot result
in unity they can only intensify existing disunion. . . . The
Executive elected by the Army has the duty imposed on it of
directing the conduct of the Army. In that capacity it will deal
with all efforts to reach unity, but it must be realised that unity
cannot be bought at the expense of honour and principle."

However critical or sceptical the Army Council may have been
about the latest call for unity, it was one that could not be entirely
ignored. It was the starting-point of a new effort that ended in the
Pact between De Valera and Collins a fortnight later. On 3rd May a
deputation of five officers representing the signatories to this appeal
for unity was admitted to Dáil Éireann, then sitting at University
College, Earlsfort Terrace. On their behalf Seán O'Hegarty addressed
an assembly which, although now divided on the Treaty issue, was
still strongly Republican in sentiment, and anxiously concerned for
national unity. It was perhaps the only occasion on which Dail
Éireann admitted a deputation to its councils, or on which a person
who was not a member was allowed to address the House on the most
vital question of the day. In a brief speech, sincere and impressive in
its perception of the difficulties on both sides, he reminded a hushed
assembly that the national position, which for some time had been
drifting, was now driving towards disaster. He called upon Dáil
Éireann as the supreme national authority to act promptly, to act with
wisdom and courage, in endeavouring to find a solution which would
save the country from civil war.

Dáil Éireann decided to appoint a committee of ten to endeavour
to find an agreed basis of unity. They were :—

Seán Hales,	Mrs. Tom Clarke,
Pádraig O'Maille,	Harry Boland,
Joseph McGuinness,	P. J. Ruttledge,
Seamus O'Dwyer,	Seán Moylan,
Seán McEoin,	Liam Mellows.

Next day a truce was agreed upon for four days, and at the end
of that period, on 8th May, a joint statement signed by Liam Lynch
and Eoin O'Duffy ordered a continuation of the truce indefinitely,
" with a view to allow the Army and Dáil Committees bring their
work to completion." On the 4th, a joint committee consisting of

Liam Lynch, Liam Mellows, Seán Moylan, Rory O'Connor, Seamus Robinson, Michael Collins, Richard Mulcahy, Diarmuid O'Hegarty, Eoin O'Duffy, Gearoid O'Sullivan and Seán McEoin began consultations. It was agreed that all prisoners held by both sides who were not charged with civil offences should be released forthwith, and that buildings in Dublin, other than the Four Courts, occupied by Republicans should be evacuated. Evacuation of the Four Courts was neither asked for, nor apparently desired, at that stage by pro-Treaty representatives.

Liam was then hopeful that an acceptable settlement would be reached. " There can be unity," he wrote, in a letter to his godmother, Hannah Cleary, " if all forces will uphold the established Republic now as in the past." Having said that the sacrifices of the past few years would be in vain if the Free State was accepted, he went on :

> " At the moment I have hopes that the pro-Treaty people have seen the error of their ways and that they will come to terms that will not let down the Republic. However, we cannot go back to a recurrence of last week, as some other way than Civil war must be found."

On 10th May the Committee of Ten reported the results of their efforts to Dáil Éireann. They had failed to reach agreement except on two principles which had been propounded at an earlier stage by Labour representatives. These were, first, that all legislative, executive and judicial authority in Ireland is, and shall be, derived solely from the people of Ireland ; and secondly, that Dáil Éireann is the supreme governing authority in Ireland. Beyond that point they had failed to find any basis of national unity. Two sets of final proposals were submitted. The anti-Treaty group suggested that the forthcoming election should not be contested, that existing T.D.'s (with some minor adjustments), should constitute the Third Dáil, and that pending the adoption of a constitution a President and Council of State should be the sole Executive. They proposed that an Army Convention, consisting of all the delegates elected to the convention of 26th March be held, and that it elect a representative on the Council of State, who would be Minister for Defence. The pro-Treaty group proposed an agreed election with a view to forming a Government which would have the confidence of the whole country, and made no specific recommendation on the question of how the Army was to be reunited.

Dáil Éireann heard a third report on that day. The five anti-Treaty officers who had signed the appeal of 2nd May were again present. On their behalf Seán O'Hegarty read a report which indicated that they had been called into consultation by the Committee of Ten on 9th May and had endeavoured to find a basis of reconciliation. The formula which they proposed was not, however, accepted by either side, and it was now submitted to the Dáil. Dáil Éireann requested the committee to make a further effort towards unity. Meetings of the committee continued during the next few days, but on the 16th they confessed failure.

On 17th May the reports were debated in the Dáil. Not since the House had divided on the Treaty issue on 7th January, was there so evident as there was on this day a general desire to find some means of bridging the chasm it had created. The idea of an agreed election with a view to forming a Government which would have the confidence of the whole country had made a powerful appeal to both sides. Dáil Éireann requested that De Valera and Collins should re-examine the proposal. On the 18th and 19th they sat in conference at University College, and finally on the afternoon of the 20th they reached agreement and signed a Pact.[1] The whole nation received the news with profound relief. To the Army negotiators it presented an incentive to continue their difficult task and for the first time an apparently firm base on which to build. The character of the next Government could now be visualised.

The main provisions of the Pact had the effect of providing for the Constitution of the Third Dáil, postponing a direct vote by the people on acceptance or rejection of the Treaty, and creating a Coalition Parliament and Government in which both pro-Treaty and anti-Treaty elements had representation roughly proportionate to their existing strengths in the Second Dáil. The Executive to be formed after the election was to consist of the President, and the Minister for Defence, with nine other Ministers, five of them pro-Treaty and four anti-Treaty. Allocation of Ministries was to be a function of the President. The democratic principle was preserved by provisions which made it clear that any group or party could put forward candidates at the general election in opposition to the national-coalition panel, and that if a dissolution became necessary, a general election on adult suffrage should be held.

The British Government became alarmed. The evacuation of troops was suspended, and the transfer of any further supplies of arms or military stores to the Provisional Government was stopped. British forces now occupied in the Twenty-six Counties only the Curragh and certain barracks in Dublin. The military security of these weak forces became a matter of concern to their Government.

The negotiations for Army unity continued into the first week of June. Many proposals and counter-proposals were considered and

[1] For text, see Appendix 10, note 1

discussed, there were various drafts schemes and amendments of them, until the proposals reached final form in three documents, one submitted by Liam Lynch, another by Seán Moylan, which was generally accepted by the pro-Treaty side, and the third, setting out general Army proposals, indicating the personnel of the proposed Army Council and the six principal officers of G.H.Q. Staff, put forward by the pro-Treaty representatives.

Liam's memorandum was as follows :

> " 1. The maintenance of an Irish Republic, meaning that the whole administration of the country shall be conducted by the Government of the Irish Republic.
>
> " 2. That the I.R.A. be maintained as the Army of the Republic under the control of an Independent Executive. Such an Executive to be elected at a Convention composed of the delegates entitled to attend the Convention called for 26th March last.
>
> " 3. A working agreement to be entered into between the Government of the Republic and the Executive of the I.R.A.

That may be said to represent the broad position from which he started in the negotiations and the point of view of the Army Executive as a whole. In the course of the discussions Liam came to accept all the proposals put forward by Seán Moylan in the following memorandum :

PRELIMINARY MEMO.

" All ranks and positions to be as on the 1st December, 1921, except where objection is held to any appointment on the grounds of :

(a) Inefficiency.

(b) The officer being so unacceptable to the particular command that he reasonably cannot be expected to make a success of it.

(c) Re-organisation proposals.

(d) Bad record.

Special cases and appeals to be gone into by the Director of Organisation, and recommendations to be submitted to the staff.

2. Ex-Soldiers of other Armies to be employed ordinarily in a *Training or Advisory* capacity : only those whose record and

character stand scrutiny to be so employed. (This rule not to apply to men who have fought with us).

3. Re-organisation Staff to be appointed under Liam Lynch as D/C/S to re-organise Army, with instructions that all inefficient officers be dispensed with.

4. Divisions shall be recruited and controlled locally.

5. *Appointments* :—Promotions shall be based on War-records, personal character, and ability, and individual records be compiled forthwith under a scheme to be outlined by G.H.Q. Staff.

6. No man to be victimised because of honest political views.

7. The Army ideal to be looked for shall be the training militarily of the youth of Ireland. All men of military age to have an opportunity to be trained as soldiers. The standing Army to be as small as possible.

8. The Training syllabus shall be drafted as much with a view to giving men a Gaelic outlook as to making them efficient soldiers. (A mercenary Army must be avoided).

9. Members of the Army shall not be concerned with maintenance of law and order, except in so far as all good citizens should be.

10. The Committee engaged in finding a settlement basis must take cognisance of the fact that an extremely bitter feeling obtains between both sides in many areas, and that it may be found impossible to get either side to work under the command of officers from the other side. This may be got over by drafting in officers native to the area who are at present serving in other districts."

The third document consists of the General Army proposals and the personnel of the proposed Army Council and G.H.Q. Staff put forward by the pro-Treaty representatives :—

" GENERAL ARMY PROPOSALS.

1. A periodical Convention to elect an Army Council of say seven.

2. Both the Minister for Defence, who shall be appointed in the ordinary way by the Government, and the Chief of Staff, who shall be appointed by the Minister for Defence, shall require the approval by a majority vote of the Army Council.

3. Each member of the Army Council to hold full-time senior Military Appointment attached to G.H.Q. Staff, or to be Commanding Officer of a Division.

4. After a certain period when our Military Schools of Instruction have been properly set up, no person to be eligible for

election to membership of the Army Council without possessing certain defined Military and general Educational qualifications.

5. All appointments to Commissioned Ranks shall be recommended by the Chief of Staff, and confirmed by the Minister for Defence.

6. Divisional areas to be enlarged, and number of Divisions reduced. Both troops in Barracks, and ordinary Volunteer Units to come under the Divisional Command, with the exeption of the Curragh Training establishment, or any of its adjuncts.

FINAL PROPOSALS FOR AGREEMENT.

Army Council.

M/Defence, E. O'Duffy, L. Lynch, Seán Moylan, G. O'Sullivan, L. Mellows, R. O'Connor, F. O'Donoghue.

A Convention to be held when the D/Organisation has satisfied the Staff that the re-organisation of the Army is fairly satisfactorily complete, i.e. that there are fairly stable conditions restored in the Army.

G-H.Q. Staff.

1. Chief of Staff – – –		Eoin O'Duffy.
2. Deputy Chief of Staff	–	Liam Lynch—To be specially charged with re-organisation.
3. Deputy Chief of Staff	–	Liam Deasy—In charge of general training.
4. Adj. General – –	–	Florrie O'Donoghue.*
5. Q.M.G. – –	–	Seán McMahon.
6. D/Intelligence –	–	G. O'Sullivan.*

* May alternate if agreed."

In these prolonged negotiations each side had gone a considerable distance to meet the view-point of the other. The pro-Treaty representatives had conceded the right of the Army to hold periodic conventions. Moreover, these conventions, initially at any rate, were given freedom to elect an Army Council which in effect controlled the appointment of both the Minister for Defence and Chief of Staff, since no officer could hold either of these posts without the approval of a majority vote of the Army Council. The first council of eight members, which as proposed included the Minister, would have given the anti-Treaty side five representatives against three pro-Treaty members. Of the six principal members of the G.H.Q. Staff, three would have been pro-Treaty and three anti-Treaty, but it was generally

understood that Owen O'Duffy would become Commissioner of the
Gárda Siochána (in fact he had tendered his resignation from the post
of Chief of Staff on 22nd May), and that Liam Lynch would succeed
him as Chief of Staff with Liam Deasy as Deputy. That is the
explanation of the abnormal suggestion of two deputy chiefs in the
proposals. Of the five principal staff officers then three would have
been anti-Treaty and two pro-Treaty. Of the Directors of Services
on the staff five would have been anti-Treaty and two pro-Treaty.

It was after a long and anxious consideration that Liam Lynch
accepted this basis of settlement. The negotiations had in fact reached
deadlock before the Pact was signed. It was the prospect which it
envisaged of a Parliament and Government deriving its authority
directly from the votes of the people, as did the first and second Dáil
Éireann, which made possible resumption of negotiations and his
ultimate acceptance of the results. Even in the final stages there were
grave difficulties, and some members of the Army Executive refused
absolutely to accept the proposals at any time. When a new crisis
developed in 7th June, Lynch and Mulcahy were brought together
in a final effort to avert civil war.

Although the fundamental question of acceptance or rejection of
the Treaty appears to have faded into the background in these
documents, it was not so. What had happened was that the whole
situation was coloured by the prospect of a Coalition Government.
The third Dáil could be regarded, if not as the Government of the
Republic, at least as a Parliament freely elected by the people, and not
the creature of a British Act. Under such a Parliament, and under a
Government responsible to it, Liam was prepared to place the Army.

While the Army negotiations were in progress the political situation,
which had appeared so hopeful after the signing of the Pact, underwent a rapid deterioration. Griffith and Collins were summoned to
London and went on 26th May. Griffith remained; Collins returned
almost immediately and signed with De Valera a joint appeal to the
nation to observe the Pact. This was issued on 5th June. On the
13th Collins went again to London, and on his return made the
speech in Cork on the 14th which was clearly a breach of the Pact.
Two days later the General Election took place. The Dáil had
adjourned on the 8th having decreed that the new house, the third
Dáil Éireann, would reassemble on 30th June.

On 12th June the Minister for Defence wrote to the Army Executive
setting out the proposals for Army re-unification. These proposals
were not acceptable to all the members of the Executive and had no
particularly enthusiastic support from any of them. A little earlier,
on the issue of an attempt to forcibly prevent the holding of a general
election, Seán O'Hegarty, Tom Hales and I had resigned. We had

been replaced by Tom Derrig, Tom Barry and Pax Whelan. Now only Liam Lynch, Liam Deasy and Seán Moylan were in favour of the reunification proposals as submitted, and when the Executive met on the 14th the proposals were rejected. The following resolution was passed:

> "That we instruct the officers deputed to meet the Beggar's Bush officers to inform them that:
> (a) Negotiation for Army unification with Beggar's Bush must cease;
> (b) We take whatever action may be necessary to maintain the Republic against British aggression;
> (c) No offensive will be taken by our troops against the Beggar's Bush forces."

On the same day a copy of this resolution was handed to the Minister for Defence by Rory O'Connor and Ernie O'Malley.

The long awaited constitution appeared in the press on the morning of Friday, 16th June—the day of the general election. Voters generally had thus little opportunity of judging how far it fulfilled the promise that it would be one which Republicans could accept. Many did not see it before recording their votes. To Republicans it brought disillusion and bitter disappointment. The detestable oath of allegiance to a foreign king was included. The constitution itself was made subject to the terms of the Treaty. A partitioned Ireland was to become part of the British Empire.

What Liam wrote to his brother that night may well stand as an expression of the ruined hope that saddened many a loyal heart:

> "Well Tom, the situation generally is beyond anything I could any longer hold out hope for. As you often said, I always held out hopes to the last, but really all are blighted now, and as far as I am personally concerned I feel all my life's work has been in vain.
> "Surely this is a terrible way to feel. Would we could even get back all our glorious dead."

With bitter anger in their hearts against the men who had accepted the Treaty and the constitution, and not a little dismayed at the apparent loss of all they had fought for in the previous years of hardship and danger, the Army delegates met at their third convention since the Truce with the British. On Sunday, 18th June the same delegates who had composed the previous conventions assembled in Dublin. The events of the previous week had created an atmosphere in which counsels of moderation had no hope of even a patient hearing. The Army reunification proposals could not have been brought forward under any conditions better calculated to ensure their summary rejection.

At Liam Lynch's pressing request, I moved the adoption of the proposals. Liam and the delegates and members of the Executive who shared his views, although now themselves shaken by the disastrous turn of events, made what was to be their final effort to carry the proposals in the convention and avert civil war. Utter distrust of pro-Treaty promises and intentions was general; no one, for or against the proposals, now entertained the post Pact hope that the separatist elements on the pro-Treaty side were still strong enough to resist further British pressure. In that atmosphere of disillusion and anger the motion for acceptance was debated. Considering the gravity of the issues involved, and how violently disturbed were the minds of the delegates, the debate was conducted with admirable restraint. After it had proceeded for some time, Tom Barry proposed that instead of discussing the proposals any further the convention should consider a motion to resume the war against the British forces in Ireland. Only posts in Dublin and the Six Counties were then occupied by foreign troops. This motion was opposed by Liam Lynch, by Cathal Brugha, by practically all the delegates from the 1st Southern Division and by many others, but was supported by the members of the Executive opposed to the reunification proposals.

On a show of hands it appeared to have been carried, but a poll was demanded with the result that 103 voted for the motion and 118 against. The minority thereupon left the convention and returned to the Four Courts, excluding therefrom Liam Lynch and the members of the Executive who had supported him. The Executive itself was now split, the anti-Treaty section of the Army was split. The convention broke up in gloom and confusion. It had divided not on the reunification proposals, but on the question of a resumption of the war with Britain.

For ten days after this third convention the state of the Army was chaotic. Although never voted upon by the convention the proposals for Army reunification were dead. Without the Coalition Government envisaged by the Collins-De Valera Pact there was no prospect of their acceptance even by a majority of the anti-Treaty section in the Army. Immediately after the general election it was clear that the Pact would not be honoured by the pro-Treaty party, notwithstanding that 73 per cent. of the electorate had voted for the Panel candidates put forward under its terms. Even if the convention had approved the reunification proposals they could not have been made operative in the political atmosphere which developed. The cleavage in the national ranks created by the Treaty, and so nearly closed by the Pact, was now widened into a chasm that no man or party in Ireland was able to bridge for many a day.

CHAPTER 19

THE ARMY IN ULSTER

Oh ! Uladh ! last to bend the knee, awaken
And give these knaves the lie.
Say you stand still unawed, unbought, unshaken,
True to the days gone by.

WILLIAM ROONEY.

THE Army units in the counties of Antrim, Armagh, Down, Derry, Fermanagh and Tyrone had carried on the fight against the British occupation forces under difficulties unknown to their compatriots in the rest of Ireland. Every problem in the organisation, training and arming of Volunteers which had to be overcome in every brigade was intensified a hundred fold in these counties. Republicans were a minority of the population. Their relative numerical strength may be judged from the results of the Parliamentary elections in May, 1921. Of the fifty-two seats in the whole area, Unionists secured forty, Republicans six, and Nationalists, six.

Army organisation was consequently much more widely dispersed than in the south or west, there were blank districts, and only in a few limited areas could the Volunteers command that moral and material support of a majority of the people which was given them in such generous measure in the remainder of the country. Moreover, they had to contend with organised civilian opposition, and this was not exclusively Unionist and non-Catholic. That situation gave the British forces a valuable acquisition of strength which they lacked elsewhere. Support from the civil population is a factor so important as to be sometimes decisive in the kind of guerilla warfare which existed in Ireland at the time. Nevertheless, despite all handicaps, difficulties and limitations, the Army units in these counties had put up a gallant resistance to British rule, and their organisation was growing in strength and efficiency up to the Truce.

The "Northern Government" for these Six Counties came into existence as a result of an Act passed by the British Parliament on 23rd December, 1920, and the elections held under it on 24th May, 1921. This Act provided also for a "Southern Parliament" for the remainder of the country, and for a Council of Ireland composed of an equal number of representatives from each area. The elections for the twenty-six counties to be held on 19th May, 1921, were, by a

247

decision of Dáil Éireann, declared to be elections to the Dáil, and no contest took place in any constituency. 124 Sinn Féin candidates and four Unionists representing Dublin University were returned unopposed.

For six of the nine counties of Ulster there was set up by Lloyd George and his Coalition Government a Unionist and Orange authority even more virulently determined to liquidate the I.R.A. than were the British themselves. Before its establishment the policy of systematic terrorism, directed against the Nationalist and Catholic elements in the population, had been in force. It began on 21st July, 1920, and continued until the Truce a year later, after which it subsided until early in 1922.

The formation of I.R.A. divisions in Ulster created commands some of which were entirely inside the Six County area and others which straddled the artificial boundary. The 1st Northern Division (Donegal and Derry City) was almost wholly outside it ; the 2nd (most of Derry and a large part of Tyrone), was wholly inside ; so was the 3rd (Antrim and North and East Down). The 4th, which was the only northern division formed before the Truce, and which included Armagh, South Down and North Louth, was almost entirely inside the border ; the 5th (Monaghan, part of South Tyrone and part of Fermanagh) had territory on either side but was mainly outside; so was the Midland Division (Longford, parts of Westmeath and Fermanagh).[1] The total I.R.A. strength in the Six County area probably did not exceed 8,500 all ranks.

To these commands the Truce brought only a temporary cessation of hostilities, and the position brought about by the setting up of the Six County Government created for them new problems and difficulties different from any existing elsewhere. It soon became evident that the " Northern Government " had determined to destroy them. In the early months of 1922 Sir Henry Wilson was engaged as Military Adviser and two millon pounds earmarked for whatever measures of repression he might recommend. In March a special Powers Bill was enacted which imposed the death penalty for possession of arms, authorised flogging for certain offences, enabled trial by jury to be suspended and coroners inquests abolished.

The Ulster special Constabulary was rapidly expanded. This force was organised in three classes. " A " class gave full time service and supplemented the Royal Ulster Constabulary; " B " class was part-time and was used mainly for night patrols and raids ; " C " class was a civilian intelligence auxiliary, to which persons had to

[1] See Map, p. 198

belong before they could obtain licences for arms, even shot guns. At the end of March this force was 25,000 strong, and at least 15,000 were armed with rifles supplied by the British Government. Later the number enlisted was increased to 49,000. In addition there were thirteen British battalions in the Six County area, and a force of police comprising the old R.I.C. and the new recruits to that body, now renamed the Royal Ulster Constabulary.

All that build-up culminated in an even more ferocious revival of the ruthless campaign of extermination. From early in 1922 a systematic policy of terrorism, arson and murder was operated by the specials and by the Orange mob against Catholics and Nationalists. Apart from clashes between the I.R.A. and the forces of the Northern Government, large scale intimidation of the Catholic civil population was rampant, particularly in Belfast. Men were driven from their employment, homes were burned down, women and children were subjected to terrorism. All this was designed to drive the Catholic and Nationalist elements in the population out of the Six Counties. It was very effective. In the two years ended June, 1922, 23,000 persons had been driven out, nearly 500 had been killed and over 1,500 wounded. Many of the thousands who left abandoned their employment and their possessions, and sought refuge in Dublin, in the south generally, and even in Scotland. Orange fury reached a peak in Belfast on 23rd March, when Catholic streets were sacked and five members of one family murdered.

In Dublin, both before and after the crisis which split the Army on the Treaty issue, there was general agreement that the policy of terrorism operated by the Northern Government should be countered by every means at the disposal of the nation. For the Army the policy decided upon was that the northern divisions should be reinforced by men and material from other areas, and that it should strike back vigorously at the lawless forces operating in the North. Preparations for action were being made when the first Army Convention was held, and although in the North as elsewhere there were divided opinions and confused councils, and although all the divisions sent some representatives to the convention, the break in Army unity did not affect seriously either their own exceptional problem in the Six County area or the policy for dealing with it.

The position in the North was the sole aspect of national defence on which after the Army split both sides had a common policy which they continued to operate jointly even after two separate Army commands had been set up. Liam Lynch and Michael Collins took a leading part in the formulation and operation of the measures agreed upon. It was decided to send a number of experienced officers from Liam's Division to the North to take charge of some of the divisions and to co-operate with all of them in activities against the forces of the Northern Government.

Seán Lehane, then O/C Cork No. 3 Brigade, was appointed O/C 1st and 2nd Northern Divisions, with Charlie Daly of Kerry No. 2 Brigade, who was already in the area, as Vice O/C. Maurice Donegan, Seán Fitzgerald and Seamus Cotter of Cork No. 3 Brigade were appointed brigade commanders. Other officers from the 1st Southern Division, to the number of about twenty, were included in the party. Others were to follow, including machine gunners. They were to operate from the portions of the Northern and Midland Divisions which were outside the Six County border, mainly from Donegal in the west, and co-operate with Frank Aiken's division in Louth and Armagh in the south east.

Their mission was to make war on the Crown forces in the North, on and inside the border. Donegal was to be a base for those operating from the west. The forces occupying posts evacuated by the British in that county were mainly under the control of the pro-Treaty H.Q. at Beggar's Bush, but arrangements were made at the highest level which provided that here and elsewhere along the border, these forces and those of the Executive would co-operate, and that both would support the Army units in the Six County area, no matter to which side they gave allegiance, in the operations to be undertaken against the Crown forces.

After the split both sections of the Army co-operated in supplying the units going North with arms and equipment. But on the pro-Treaty side one thing was insisted on—rifles or other weapons transferred to the Provisional Government by the British would not be taken into action. It would be embarrassing if some of them were captured and identified. An arrangement was therefore made under which Cork No. 1 Brigade supplied an agreed number of rifles, and these were replaced from the pro-Treaty side by an equal number of weapons handed over to the Provisional Government. Most of the arms for the North came from the 1st and 2nd Southern Divisions.

In the arrangements for this project Lynch and Collins worked together in a spirit of harmony reminiscent of the Tan War days. It was the point at which they touched most closely on a common policy after the Army split. Liam's view was that, apart from the Army's plain duty to defend our people in the North, vigorous development of activity against the Crown forces there, if supported by pro-Treaty leaders and pro-Treaty Army elements in the counties along the border, would be regarded by the British as a breach of the Treaty, and would create a situation in which a re-united Army would again confront the common enemy.

What the pro-Treaty view of the outcome of these proposed activities may have been it is difficult to determine. There is no doubt that the Beggar's Bush H.Q. continued to send arms to the units in the Six Counties which were known to be in favour of the Treaty, and that they co-operated with the Army Executive in plans for a general attack on the British forces in the Six Counties, and for the reinforcement of Army units in the North generally. In the face of that policy, and coterminous with it, it is not a little surprising to find that Michael Collins signed an agreement with Sir James Craig on 30th March, one clause of which provided that I.R.A. activities in the Six Counties should cease. He was not of course in a position any longer to secure complete observance of this clause, since some units of the northern divisions had given allegiance to the Army Executive at the convention held four days earlier.

The policy of vigorous retaliation against the activities of the Crown forces in the North, agreed to by both sides, was clearly one that involved the risk of British re-occupation of the whole country and a renewed struggle whose end no man could foresee. That was a risk which many on that anti-Treaty side were at all times prepared to take. It was a prospect which revolted Liam Lynch less than what he saw as the alternative—civil war. Neither could Michael Collins have been blind to it. For both of them—and it was very evident—there was in this project a clear objective that revived the old bond of brotherhood, a mutually shared desire to strike at the common enemy which was devoid of the heartache attaching to so many of their decisions at the time. They had, each for the other, a regard that went deeper than friendly comradeship—these two men that Ireland could so ill afford to lose who were soon to die tragically on opposite sides in a war of brothers.

But although a common policy in regard to the Six County area apparently existed, and although the continued personal contacts arising from the necessity for co-operation between pro-Treaty and anti-Treaty elements tended to dwarf their differences, it was difficult nevertheless to keep that policy isolated from the predominant issue which divided the whole country and the whole Army. Its effectiveness was jeopardised from its inception by being linked with other aspects of the situation and used as material for propaganda. Richard Mulcahy's charge that "hot headed men wanted to pull this way, that way and the other way" could have been applied to his own headquarters staff as well as to those who opposed him. In a partisan statement issued officially and published in *An tOglac*, from which the *Irish Independent* reprinted it on 26th April, his Chief of Staff, Eoin O'Duffy, made a reference to the arms for this force which was as inaccurate as it was indiscreet. In reply Liam wrote on the following day :

"With reference to the alleged holding up of arms intended for the Northern areas, these are the facts. The C/S and A/G phoned me to forward 30 Thompson guns, 10,000 rounds .303, and also 100 rifles, these latter to be exchanged as soon as could be arranged. The following supplies of arms and ammunition were forwarded within 36 hours; 30 Thompson guns, 8,000 rounds ammunition for T.M. guns, 10,000 rounds .303, 75 rifles.

"I also sent 10 machine-gunners. Any of these supplied, I afterwards learned, did not get to the North, and the gunners after being detained for a week or so at Beggar's Bush, were ordered home to their own areas after all being so urgently required by 'phone for the North. It is very easy to judge where the responsibility lies for the situation which now exists."

What was planned was a general attack on the Crown forces in the Six County area, in which units of the five northern and the 1st Midland Division were to participate. This was to take place early in May. It was postponed on representations being made to Beggar's Bush H.Q. that there was a possibility of capturing a police barracks in Belfast by a ruse. If successful this would have made two armoured cars available to the I.R.A. and these would have been an invaluable asset in the general attack. It was agreed that the attempt to seize the barracks would be made when the first opportunity offered, and that whether it succeeded or failed, the general attack would follow two days later.

The attempt to capture the barracks was made on 17th May, it failed. In accordance with the plan the 3rd Northern Division carried out a series of attacks on 19th May, but it was some days later before the other divisions moved. Some general attacks were carried out by the forces based on Donegal but, lacking active co-operation from the pro-Treaty forces, they were unable to undertake anything more ambitious than raids across the border, sniping of British posts, destruction of block houses and cutting of communications.

The plan visualised the formation of columns, the members of which would remain on continuous active service, and who would be maintained out of funds provided by Beggar's Bush Headquarters. The men were to be paid at the same rate as those serving in the Beggar's Bush force. In the 2nd and 3rd Northern Divisions, which were wholly inside the border these men could not hope to return to their homes after taking up active service. In the other divisions the men were able to move into areas south of the border if too hard pressed.

The Northern Government, apparently nonplussed by the attacks, adopted a cautious attitude and largely confined their forces to

barracks for some weeks. When the attacks were not sustained efforts
to track down and destroy the I.R.A. columns were initiated. These
were particularly thorough in the areas of the 2nd and 3rd Divisions—
Derry, Tyrone, Antrim and Down. When the civil war started the
position of the I.R.A. units in these areas was one of acute difficulty.

An agreement was entered into between the Beggar's Bush G.H.Q.
and the officers of the 2nd and 3rd Northern Divisions that the men
on the run in these areas would go to the Curragh for a period of
intensive training, after which they were to return and continue
operating in the Six Counties. Michael Collins, Richard Mulcahy and
Gearoid O'Sullivan gave these men, through their officers, a very
definite undertaking that they would not be asked to take part in the
fighting in the south. To their credit be it said that this undertaking
was honoured, although later many of the officers and men who had
come from the North joined the Free State Army. They did so of
their own free will.

But none of the 500 men brought to the Curragh for training was
ever sent back to continue the struggle against the Northern Government. Given the prospect of any support from outside the area they
were ready and willing to return, but the outbreak of civil war in the
south ended the possibility of that united support which would have
been essential, and engaged the attention of both parties to it to such
an extent, and so far to the limits of their resources, that all plans for
the North fell to the ground. This phase of I.R.A. activities in the
Six Counties was for all practical purposes ended by the outbreak of
civil war.

The fortnight's training which these men were to undergo at the
Curragh dragged out to three months, and in September the differences
of opinion on the Treaty issue, which had existed here as elsewhere,
came to a head. Some joined the Free State Army, some the Republican forces, and others returned to their homes. Most of the officers
who had been sent to Donegal from the south returned to their own
commands and took up arms against the Free State forces. Seán
Lehane was appointed O/C 3rd Eastern Division. Moss Donegan led
a column in the actions at Limerick and Kilmallock. Charlie Daly
continued in charge of the Republican forces in the 1st Northern
Division. He was captured in November, 1922 and executed at
Drumboe Castle, with Timothy O'Sullivan and Daniel Enright of
Listowel and Seán Larkin of Bellagherty, Co. Derry, on 14th March,
1923.

The position in the 4th Northern Division was unique in the whole
Army. Here, Commandant Frank Aiken had endeavoured from the
outset to keep his division united in any decisions it may make on the
question of the Treaty. When the Dáil Cabinet prohibited the holding

of the Army Convention, he was not convinced that participation in
the banned convention would promote unity, and he took no part in it.
A few delegates from one of his brigades did however, attend with his
knowledge and consent. The majority of the division decided to
remain under Dáil control until the constitution was published.
That decision did not in any way minimise the capacity of the division
to participate in the activities against the forces of the Northern
Government, since this was a policy upon which both sides were in
agreement, and the division had many engagements between January
and June, 1922 in the course of which a number of Specials were killed.

A proposal was made by the Minister for Defence, Richard Mulcahy,
that Commandant Aiken should take charge of all the northern
units of the I.R.A. in their operation against the Six County and
British forces. Commandant Aiken was willing to agree provided
that he was given freedom of action, but this was not forthcoming and
the proposal did not materialise.

The outbreak of civil war created a new situation for the division,
which had 300 men in occupation of Dundalk barracks. On 4th July
Frank Aiken wrote to the Minister for Defence intimating that he
would not fight on either side because in his view a " fight would
only ruin the country without gaining any ground for the Republic."
On the 8th he went to Limerick and saw Liam Lynch. He was unable
to make any impression on the fixed conviction at which Liam had
then arrived—that defence of the Republic in arms was the only
means left of preventing its extinction.

The officers of the 4th Northern Division met on 14th July and
decided to withhold all moral and material support from the Provisional Government unless it gave the anti-Treaty parties, civil and
military, a constitutional way of continuing to work for the Republic.
Frank Aiken saw the Minister for Defence in Dublin and informed
him of that decision. Next morning the barracks at Dundalk was
captured by Provisional Government forces, and he was taken
prisoner. He got parole, went to Dublin again and had another
interview with the Minister for Defence. On returning to Dundalk
he was arrested and imprisoned in the local jail. He escaped on 28th
July, and on 13th August his command recaptured the barracks and
jail from the Provisional Government forces, took the arms and
equipment of the garrisons and thereafter continued to carry on
guerilla warfare on the side of the Republican forces.

CHAPTER 20

CIVIL WAR

The doer is always conscienceless ; no-one has a conscience except the spectator.
GOETHE.

IN the days following the third Army Convention events moved swiftly to a crisis. On 22nd June, Sir Henry Wilson was shot dead in London. His period of office as Chief of the Imperial General Staff had expired in February, and from that date he had acted as Military Adviser to the Six County Government.

The execution of Wilson was carried out by Commandant Reginald Dunne, O/C London Battalion, I.R.A., and Volunteer Joseph O'Sullivan, both of whom were captured and subsequently hanged. The orders upon which they acted have since become a subject of controversy. It can be stated with certainty that these orders did not come from the Army Executive set up in March, from the Executive which succeeded it, or from anybody acting under the orders of these Executives.

In a booklet, *Remembrance*, published by the Association of Old I.R.A., and Cumann-na-mBan, London, it is stated that " the order for his (Wilson's) execution had been given before the Treaty negotiations, and was actually confirmed whilst the negotiations were in progress." A brother of one of the executed men, Patrick O'Sullivan, who was Vice Commandant of the London I.R.A., in a letter to the author, states that the order was given by Michael Collins to Reggie Dunne and never subsequently cancelled. In any event it is clear that Dunne and O'Sullivan were acting upon orders which they accepted as official and therefore legitimate.[1]

The death of this most fanatically anti-Irish Irishman, who had in the preceding two years, as his journals bear witness, used his great authority and his privileged position of constant access to members of the British Cabinet, to initiate and maintain a policy of terrorism, arson and murder by Imperial forces in Ireland, was now made the occasion of a combination of private pressure and public threat before which the Provisional Government quailed.

[1]See correspondence in *Sunday Press* of the 20th and 27th, Sept., 1953 and 4th, 11th, 18th and 25th October, 1953.

The section of the Army Executive in favour of resuming the fight with the British almost had it thrust upon them. On 24th June, Macready, still in command of the remnant of British forces in Dublin, received orders to attack the Four Courts next day.[1] While he prepared to carry out orders the British Cabinet altered its decision, cancelled his instructions, and instead sent an ultimatum to the Provisional Government on the 26th demanding that the occupation of the Four Courts be brought to an end.

Against this insolent demand and against all British threats the leaders of the Provisional Government could have mobilised at a word the whole strength of Republican Ireland. It was the appropriate moment to call for a closing of the ranks, and the means of doing so effectively was in their hands—and in their hands only. Dáil Éireann was to have reassembled on the 30th. Had it been permitted to assemble, had the terms of the Pact been observed and a Coalition Government formed, a reunited Army and people would have stood firm in the face of any threat. But the opportunity was lost. De Valera and Harry Boland waited in vain for the call they expected from Collins and Griffith to nominate their members of the Coalition Cabinet.

Instead the Provisional Government took the fateful decision to form a Government from amongst their own supporters—a sectional Government, but one that satisfied the requirements of the British Act—and to wipe out opposition to it by force. General Mulcahy stated later that the decision to attack the Four Courts was practically taken before the pro-Treaty Deputy Chief of Staff, J. J. O'Connell, was arrested by Republican forces as a reprisal for the arrest of Commandant Leo Henderson, who had been detained by Provisional Government troops while engaged in commandeering transport for the removal of supplies to the North—a project on which both sides were still nominally co-operating.

From the point of view of the Provisional Government the moment seemed a favourable one at which to strike. The 1st Southern Division had apparently broken with the Executive, councils on the anti-Treaty side were obviously divided, they had no plan except the old plan of sitting down and waiting to be attacked. Much of the opposition the pro-Treaty leaders assumed to be truculent bellicosity and nothing more. If the 1st Southern was out, the probability was that a swift defeat of the Executive forces in Dublin would intimidate any resistance in most of the country, or would at least leave it without leadership or coherence.

At 3.40 a.m. on Wednesday 28th June Tom Ennis, on behalf of the

[1] *Annals of an Active Life*, Vol. 2, pp. 652, 653

Provisional Government, demanded the surrender of the Four Courts by 4 a.m. It was refused and at 4.30 a.m. the attack opened. Field guns, borrowed from the British forces, and supervised by British personnel, were used to shell the historic building. The civil war had commenced.

The shelling continued from early in the morning of 28th June until noon on Friday the 30th. Fire had spread to most of the buildings by Friday morning, and by mid-day the position had become untenable. Two of the garrison had been killed and a number wounded. Explosives which had been loaded on trucks for the North blew up and killed a number of a storming party of the attackers.

The Dublin Brigade had occupied a number of positions in the city, and in one of these, a block of buildings on the east side of O'Connell Street, Oscar Traynor set up headquarters. He was, however, unable to give any effective assistance to the Four Courts garrison, and on receiving a report from them on Friday morning, which indicated that resistance could not be continued much longer in the burning buildings, he ordered them to surrender. In the subsequent transfer of the prisoners to Mountjoy six escaped, including Ernie O'Malley, Seán Lemass, Joseph Griffin and Paddy O'Brien, the garrison commander, who was killed subsequently in an action near Enniscorthy. The prisoners included Rory O'Connor, Liam Mellows, Joe McKelvey and Dick Barrett.

The posts occupied by the Republican forces in Dublin could not be held against artillery fire, and it was decided to evacuate them gradually and revert to guerilla tactics. Harry Boland had gone to Mallow on 29th June to seek reinforcements and munitions for the fight in Dublin. The 1st Southern Division sent 900 grenades, but they did not all reach Dublin, and the 2nd Southern sent 110 men, who had marched in as far as Blessington, where most of the South Dublin Brigade was mobilised, before the decision to evacuate the posts in Dublin was taken.

The garrison in the posts in O'Connell Street had been reduced until, on Wednesday, 5th July, only a small group remained under the command of Cathal Brugha. He had reported for duty to the O/C Dublin Brigade on the day the Four Courts was attacked, and Oscar Traynor now sent him an order to evacuate the position. Brugha tried to get the last of his small group out of the buildings and succeeded, but refused himself to leave or surrender. Driven out by the flames in the afternoon he rushed into the street alone and was cut down by machine-gun fire. Two days later he was dead.

Liam Lynch and a number of his officers were at the Clarence Hotel, across the river from the Four Courts, when the attack on that position opened. Awakened by the firing of the eighteen

pounders, they quickly assembled and, without hesitation, decided
to support the men on whom the Provisional Government had now
opened an attack. That decision brought the 1st Southern Division,
as well as the other Republican units throughout the country into the
conflict and ended any possibility that the aggressors would have
an easy victory.

The Provisional Government miscalculated the results which
their action in attacking the Four Courts would bring about. Except
an attack by the British, nothing was more certain to solidify Republican opposition than this crude bludgeoning. There had never
been a complete break between the majority of the Executive in the
Four Courts and the minority in the Clarence Hotel. Early in the
week after the convention, Liam had interviews with O'Connor,
Mellows, McKelvey and other members, and was still trying to devise
some policy on which they could agree. On the night before the
attack he remained in the Four Courts until after midnight, in
friendly discussion with Mellows. How far these talks had taken him
towards a resumption of his post as Chief of Staff is unimportant,
for it is clear that the differences which split the Executive at the convention were being healed, and that any idea of putting into operation the policy on which he had broken with the majority had been
abandoned. It was the wish of every member of the Executive that
he should resume his post, and no doubt he would have done so in
any event.

The attack on the Four Courts evoked in him an immediate
determination to take his place at the head of the forces resisting
this direct assault upon all he had worked for so devotedly and
believed in so passionately. He had undergone six months of almost
intolerable heartache and strain. He had seen every effort to save the
Army from being sucked into the maelstrom created by the Treaty
go down in failure before what seemed to be an implacable destiny.
He had known moments of hope and days of despair. He had worked
through a long series of negotiations and conferences in which dozens
of schemes and plans had been torn to rags by one side or the other.
And the end of it all was failure. Now there was a call to action.
Having made his decision to answer the challenge in arms, he adhered
to it with characteristic stubborness to the day of his death.

A proclamation[1] calling on the Army to resume the fight for the
Republic was drawn up, signed by the members of the Executive
present, and prepared for publication by adding the names of the
members in the Four Courts and of Tom Barry who was in Cork.

A decision was taken that the Southern Division officers present

---

[1] See Appendix 9

would return to their commands, and that Liam would also go south and set up headquarters in the country. Oscar Traynor, O/C Dublin Brigade, took command in Dublin, and began at once to mobilise the Dublin Brigades in support of the men in the Four Courts. He was opposed to the occupation of positions in the city because the Provisional Government forces had artillery and he had not ; he had in fact gone to the Four Courts on the night before it was attacked and advised the members of the Executive there to evacuate the building. He was unable to convince them.

On their way from the Clarence Hotel to Kingsbridge Liam Lynch, Liam Deasy and Seán Culhane were detained by a party of Provisional Government troops under Liam Tobin and taken to Wellington (now Griffith) Barracks. There Lynch and Deasy were interviewed separately by Eoin O'Duffy. In a Provisional Government publication *War News*, dated 22nd July, 1922, it is alleged that at this interview Liam was released by O'Duffy " on giving his word of honour that he disapproved of the policy of the Irregulars, and would not assist them." It is further alleged that he was re-arrested at Castlecomer and again released, " repeating to Colonel Prout that he would not take part in the fight." These charges are unfounded, and are no more than bad examples of the regrettable propaganda material of the time.

Of his interview with O'Duffy, Lynch told Seán Moylan at Kingsbridge immediately afterwards that O'Duffy had merely asked him what he thought of the situation and Liam replied, " I think ye're all mad." It was stated afterwards that Lynch had said he thought the people in the Four Courts were mad, so that his release may have been due to a misunderstanding. On the other hand, O'Duffy may have thought it politic not to detain Liam, believing that the confidence or goodwill thereby shown might have the effect of limiting the spread of civil war to the south. It is significant that O'Duffy did not question Liam Deasy on his attitude to the war, having only a general and friendly conversation with him.

And it is entirely certain that Liam did not give a parole to Colonel Prout, whom he did not even see, or to any other officer at Castlecomer. After their release, Lynch, Deasy and Culhane joined the other southern officers at Kingsbridge, and took a train which did not, however get beyond Newbridge. In an endeavour to find transport to continue their journey most of the group drove to Kilcullen on outside cars, and near there Seán and Con Moylan procured one car in which they returned to Kilcullen and picked up Lynch, Deasy, Culhane and Seán McSwiney. Another group which included Frank Barrett of Clare had got another car.

Con Moylan drove the car in which Liam and the other four officers travelled. They were held up at Castlecomer, by a party of Provisional Government troops under Captain Murphy. Liam did not give parole to this officer or to anybody else, either here or at any time during the journey. In fact he held no conversation with Captain Murphy ; it was Seán Moylan who spoke to him, and obtained from him a supply of petrol and oil for the car.[1] Liam's party left the barracks with a salute from the guard. They arrived at Mallow in the early hours of the morning of the 29th and that day Liam went on to Limerick and set up headquarters there.

The following statement was issued from Mallow on 30th June :

" To all Units :—

Owing to statements in some newspapers and general false rumours among the Army, I deem it necessary that all ranks should know at once the position of Army Command. It is not possible to give a full outline of situation until a more satisfactory army position prevails.

" Army Executive recently differed in the matter of policy which was brought about by the final proposals of Minister for Defence for Army unification. As a result, while remaining a member of Executive, I have not carried on as C/S since Convention of 18th inst.

" Owing to attack on G.H.Q. and other posts occupied by our troops by Dáil Forces, and position created by draft Free State Constitution, I have again taken up duty as C/S since Thursday, 29th inst., with Temporary H.Q. at Mallow. Communications are established with all Southern, Western and Eastern Divisions, and a united plan of action being carried out. Assistant C/S has been detailed to Command Dublin and Northern areas, and I am in constant communication wtih the latter. By this evening we hope to have made rapid progress towards complete control of West and Southern Ireland for the Republic. Latest reports from Dublin show that the Dublin Brigade have control of situation, and reinforcements and supplies have been despatched to their assistance.

" I appeal to all men to maintain the same discipline as in recent hostilities, and not interfere with civilian population except absolute military necessity requires it.

LIAM LYNCH, Chief of Staff.[2]"

Despite six months of talk of the possibility of civil war no one had allowed himself to believe it to be inevitable, and no plans existed on

[1] See also " A contradiction," *Cork Examiner*, 12th July, 1922
[2] J. L. O'D., 1/104/2

either side for conducting it. That was a more serious handicap on the Republican forces than on their opponents. The Executive was ineffective since four of its members were prisoners (Tom Barry had been captured in an effort to get into the Four Courts during the fight), and the others dispersed with their own commands. There was now no Government, *de jure* or *de facto*, to control and direct activities, Liam's staff was altogether inadequate in numbers, and no clear cut policy for the conduct of the war had been determined. A policy decision was of the utmost urgency because Republican forces held a great many posts which had been evacuated by the British all over the country, and they were in practically complete control of the country south of a line from Waterford to Limerick.

Provisional Government forces also held many posts throughout the country, but very few in Munster and Connaught. These forces were totally inadequate for the task which their Government contemplated—the destruction, disarming and imprisonment of the armed forces opposing them. The Provisional Government had the advantage of a definite policy, control of the public purse, and the ability to call upon an adequate supply of war material from Britain.

They took prompt and vigorous action to mobilise both public opinion and physical strength. On 6th July they issued a call to arms which met with a ready response from demobilised officers and men of the British forces, and from youngsters attracted to military service for the first time. Since the majority of the recruits had had some previous training or experience they were thrown into action at once. The original nucleus of old I.R.A. men was almost swamped in the intake of mercenaries in some areas.

There were only two posts in the 1st Southern Division area occupied by Provisional Government troops, Skibbereen and Listowel. These were attacked on 1st July. Listowel surrendered on the same day, Skibbereen on the 4th. That left the area wholly in Republican hands. Of the posts in the Mid-Limerick Brigade Adare and Foynes were captured and the remainder evacuated under an agreement made between Liam Deasy, O/C of the division and Commandant General Donncada Hannigan on behalf of the Provisional Government forces.

Liam Lynch established his headquarters at the New Barracks, Limerick. His forces were also in occupation of Strand Barracks, Castle Barracks, and the Ordnance Barracks. His staff consisted of Ernie O'Malley, Assistant Chief of Staff and O/C Northern and Eastern Command, who had set up a headquarters in Dublin and was operating from there; Con Moloney, Adjutant General; Joe O'Connor, Quartermaster General; Seán Moylan, Director of Operations; Dr. Con Lucy, Director of Medical Services; Seán Hyde, acting Director of Intelligence; Jim Moloney, Director of

Communications ; Seán McCarthy, Director of Publicity and Maurice Twomey, General Staff officer.

Provisional Government forces under Donncada Hannigan, an old friend of Liam's who had brilliantly led the East Limerick Brigade Column in the war against the British, were in occupation of other posts in the city including the Custom House, the Jail, the Courthouse, William Street Barracks and Cruises' Hotel. On Liam's arrival in Limerick, Dan Breen and the Mayor, Mr. S. M. O'Meara intervened to avert a conflict. Lynch and Hannigan met and reached the following agreement, which was signed at 6.30 p.m. on 4th July :

" AGREED

1. Commandant General Hannigan will not at any time attack Executive forces ; Executive forces will not attack Commandant General Hannigan's forces.

2. That Executive Forces will not occupy any post in East Limerick Brigade area.

3. That both sides only occupy their normal number of posts in Limerick City.

4. That there be no movement of armed troops in Limerick City or in East Limerick Brigade Area, except by Liaison Agreement.

5. That Commdt. General Hannigan withdraws any of his troops drafted into Limerick City since Saturday.

6. Executive Communications to be maintained between 1st 2nd and 3rd Southern Divisional Headquarters and Limerick City.

7. This agreement to hold during the period of fighting between Executive forces and Beggars' Bush or until both sides of the Army find a solution of the problem.

8. We agree to these conditions in the practical certainty that National peace and unity will eventuate from our efforts, and we guarantee to use every means in our power to get this peace.

9. This agreement to be put into effect by 12 o'clock to-night."

This agreement represents something of what was in the minds of officers like Lynch and Hannigan, old comrades in the fight against the British but now on opposite sides in civil conflict. Hannigan had in an earlier agreement with Deasy agreed to evacuate the 1st Southern Division area, which was in the main anti-Treaty ; Lynch now undertook not to occupy any posts in Hannigan's old brigade area—East

Limerick. Both still hoped that by limiting the area of conflict some solution of the whole Army problem would yet be found and were prepared to use every means in their power to secure peace.

This agreement however never operated, because another Commandant General evidently exercising G.H.Q. authority summarily cancelled it next day. He wrote to Liam :

"This is to inform you that I arrived here from Dublin this evening with definite instructions from G.H.Q. as to Military operations in this area. Before coming into this area I made arrangements for certain positions to be taken up immediately. On arriving at Cruises' Hotel, I discovered that Commandant General Brennan and Commandant General Hannigan had been discussing terms of agreement with you for some days past.

"I have definite instructions that no such agreement if signed, could be admitted by G.H.Q. and these officers had no authority whatever to enter into such agreement.

"I hear that another meeting between these officers and yourself had been arranged for 8 a.m. to-day. I have instructed them that this meeting is not to take place and that they are to have no further communication with you on this matter. I herewith reserve full liberty of action, and I have made certain dispositions to protect my posts in the City and their communications.

"(Signed) D. A. MacMaghunsa, Commdt. General,
"General Headquarters."

Notwithstanding Commandant General McManus' instructions to the contrary the parties to the agreement came together again next day and in the presence of two prominent Limerick priests signed this new agreement at 1.30 a.m. on 7th July :

"We agree in the interests of an United Ireland and to save our country from utter destruction to call a meeting of Divisional Commandants representing the 1st and 2nd Southern Divisions and the 1st Western Division of the Executive Forces Irish Republican Army and the Divisional Commandants representing the 4th Southern Division and the 1st Western Division and the Mid-Western Command of the Dáil Forces Irish Republican Army. The meeting to be held as soon as Seán McKeown can be got into this area. The Conference to be held in Limerick.

"The Forces now opposed to one another in Limerick City end for all time this fratricidal strife in view of the meeting of Divisional Commandants in Limerick. And as a guarantee of good faith towards a permanent agreement the Divisional Council of the 1st Western Division Dáil Forces I.R.A. agree to hand in their resignations if agreement is not reached at the meeting of Divisional Commandants. The agreement as regards the resignations of the Divisional Councils to be signed by Saturday evening. The buildings to be occupied by the Dáil Forces Irish Republican Army are the Custom House, the Jail, the Courthouse, Cruises' Hotel and William Street Barracks. The troops of the Executive Forces Irish Republican Army be withdrawn to Barracks. No troops in Limerick City to appear in public with arms except by liaison arrangement. A truce now exists between the Executive Forces Irish Republican Army and the 1st Western Division and the 4th Southern Division Dáil Forces Irish Republican Army until the Conference ends between the Divisional Commandants. All outposts to be withdrawn to the agreed centres by six o'clock Friday evening, 7th July, 1922. This agreement takes effect from the moment it is signed 1.30 a.m. 7th July, 1922.

> " LIAM LYNCH, C/S Executive Forces.
> " DONNCADA O hANNAOGAIN, Comdt. Gen., 4th Southern Division.
> " M. BRENNAN, Comdt. Gen., Commanding 1st Western Division."

McManus' reaction to this was slightly more restrained, but still disapproving. He wrote to Liam on the 7th :

> " I have just returned here to find that Commandant Gen. Hannigan and Commandant Gen. Brennan have entered into a signed agreement with you. While absolutely disapproving of this agreement, in order to try and avoid a conflict all over the country, I am willing to allow this matter to go ahead on condition that there is no change in the military position here. I cannot agree to any interference with our present strong military position.
> " While I have great hopes that peace will result from this agreement, I have no power to change the whole military position here, either on my own authority, or on that of any local Commander. I agree strongly that negotiations would have the best results at this stage and I am willing to forego using the advantages I have gained in the military position for an attempt at getting national agreement.
> " D. A. McManus,
> " Comdt. Gen."

This last effort to preserve even a portion of the country from the scourge of civil war failed because the men who controlled Provisional

Government policy had determined to destroy that section of the Army which refused to accept the Treaty. A settlement of the Army situation was not so much desired as a liquidation of its intransigent elements, although the truce cannot have been unwelcome since it gave a valuable breathing space at a critical moment. The agreement had been signed on the day the Provisional Government issued its call to arms.

The idea of a meeting of divisional commandants from both sides in the south did not find favour in Dublin, and the developments visualised in the agreement never took place. Two officers, one from each side, were to go to Dublin from Limerick to convey the proposals to the Provisional Government. Seán McCarthy was detailed by Liam for the mission, but his opposite number was never appointed and the whole project was allowed to lapse. An uneasy peace reigned in Limerick for a few days. At 5.30 on the evening of the 7th the Provisional Government forces at William Street post opened fire on the Ordnance Barracks and the pattern of the conflict in Dublin was repeated.

By mid July the splendid I.R.A. organisation of a year earlier had broken down into three fairly well defined sections—those fighting on the Republican side, their opponents in the Provisional Government forces, and those who remained neutral in the civil conflict. Outside Munster and the counties of Mayo and Sligo, almost all the large military barracks were in the hands of Provisional Government troops, but many of their smaller posts throughout the twenty-six counties were captured by Republican forces in the opening phase of the struggle.

Generally, these small posts were held only for a short time ; in common with those occupied since the British evacuation by anti-Treaty forces, they were abandoned and destroyed when guerilla tactics were adopted. The counties of Cork, Kerry, Waterford, and parts of Limerick and Tipperary constituted the only large block of territory occupied exclusively by Republican forces. Consideration was given to the possibility of holding this area against attack ; something was done about coast defence, and a line running from Waterford to Limerick was regarded as a possible defensive zone in the north. But all such plans were vitiated by two factors—the lack of artillery and machine guns, and the immensely long coast line with its numerous harbours and landing piers. The available forces and armament were entirely inadequate to defend this territory successfully, even if there had been time to organise a defence.

The Limerick–Waterford line, which ran through Tipperary, Golden, Cashel, Fethard, Clonmel and Carrick-on-Suir, held for a short time, and Liam moved his headquarters from Limerick to Clonmel on the 11th. There he was joined by Mr. De Valera, who was assigned to a post on the staff of the Director of Operations. Headquarters moved again on 15th to Fermoy Barracks. De Valera came with Liam, but soon afterwards again returned to Clonmel to work with Seamus Robinson, O/C 2nd Southern Division, in an effort to reinforce the Limerick–Waterford line, which he thought should be held.

A Provisional Government review of the position in the twenty-six counties on 19th July claimed that their forces had control of all Leinster, Monaghan, Cavan, Roscommon, Leitrim and Clare, that they had opposition in Donegal, Sligo, Galway, Limerick and Tipperary and that Republican forces held Cork, Kerry, Waterford and Mayo. They had, on the 13th, created a war council consisting of Michael Collins, Commander in Chief, Richard Mulcahy, Minister for Defence and Chief of Staff, and Eoin O'Duffy, General in charge of the South Western Division.

Any possibility that Liam Lynch's forces would be able to retain control of south Munster was nullified by his opponents use of coastwise shipping to land troops at strategic points. The first landing was made at Waterford on 23rd July. On the following day Provisional Government troops landed at Westport and advanced to Castlebar. On 2nd August a landing was made at Fenit, from which the troops engaged quickly pushed on to Tralee, and in the following days occupied Castleisland, Listowel and Farranfore. Limerick was already in their hands. On 8th August a landing at Passage West, though vigorously opposed, opened the way to the occupation of Cork. Other landings at Youghal, Glandore and Kenmare laid most of Cork and Waterford open to occupation. But it was no more than the occupation of the towns and larger villages ; substantial areas of the country were untouched.

The change over to the type of guerilla warfare with which they were familiar put the Republican forces in a position not dissimilar militarily from that which they occupied in fighting the British. But there were two differences of sufficient weight to be significant. The majority of the people were no longer with them, and their opponents had an intimate and detailed knowledge of their personnel which the British lacked completely. Over 1,000 Republican prisoners in the first month of the war was an indication of this. And there was a third difference, moving below the surface, but inescapable and emerging now and then in strange deeds, heroic, chivalrous or sadistic —this was a war of brothers. It brought out all that was best, and worst, in the national character.

After the occupation of Waterford the line from there to Limerick was subjected to pressure at many points. Golden was taken in a surprise attack, Carrick-on-Suir fell after a three day struggle,

Tipperary had to be evacuated. Broken at many points, the line collapsed. The forces defending it formed in columns and began to harrass the garrisons.

On 11th August Fermoy Barracks was evacuated and burned. It was the last post to be held by Republican forces. Liam walked out into the streets where he had issued his first challenge to British military domination almost three years earlier, once more the leader of a guerilla army without barracks or bases, stores or supply services. The first phase of the civil war was ended.

The change over to guerilla warfare cost the Republican forces time and created a whole series of new problems. Morale, which had been high under conditions of open fighting, suffered in an atmosphere that was new to many who had not served in columns against the British. Truce conditions and Truce training bred a mentality that irked at the absence of regular quarters, normal meals and ordinary amusements. Many men faced the altered conditions with no great enthusiasm. And they felt the hostility of a large section of the people amongst whom they moved.

The reorganisation was carried through during the month of August. Referring to the decision to " split up into columns, operating as far as possible in their own areas," the Adjutant General, Con Moloney, wrote in Bulletin No. 7, under date 5th September :

> " There was very naturally an amount of disorganisation caused for the moment, but things have again righted themselves and very effective work is being done. . . . The whole Army is now operating as during the war with Britain. We have got down again to guerilla tactics and have fallen into our stride."

By September Liam had redirected the energies of his forces into the kind of activity of which he was master. In a long series of orders, directives and memoranda be reiterated the principles he had learned and the theories he had evolved in the hard school of guerilla warfare against the British. His mind had set in its final mould. He would not, or could not, contemplate the collapse of armed resistance to the imposition of the Treaty. He would have continued that resistance if his force had been reduced to a single active service unit. But in fact the position was by no means desperate just then, and he worked with feverish energy to impress his own confident optimism upon his followers and to extract the maximum of efficient performance from his organisation.

He believed that the Republican forces could maintain almost indefinitely the kind of opposition to the Provisional Government upon which they had embarked ; and he believed that this opposition

could be made sufficiently effective to prevent the Government from
functioning, thereby creating a situation in which the attempt to
impose the Treaty would be abandoned, and the sundered elements
of the old movement would come together again to demand a less
humiliating settlement with Britain. If his judgment was at fault
here it was because he failed to give due weight to the power of public
opinion. A large majority of the people wanted the Treaty and an
end of warfare, but just then there was a temporary revulsion of public
feeling against the high handed (and to many minds, illegal) action of
the Provisional Government in launching a military offensive against
Republicans.

Writing in Bulletin No. 9 on 20th September Con Moloney said :

> "The attitude of the civil population towards our cause
> continues to improve as they come to understand our position,
> and the cause we defend, and see the composition of the forces
> opposing us. . . . In very few areas has active hostility been
> manifested to our forces."

In Operation Order No. 9 of 19th August Liam had directed :
"Our troops will now be formed in A.S.U.'s and operate in the
open." Elsewhere he laid it down that the strength of columns
should not exceed thirty-five all ranks, and that where a number of
columns were operating in the same locality they should co-ordinate
their security measures, afford each other mutual protection, and act
in combination when necessary.

Reviewing the position a month later it was evident to him that the
policy of guerilla warfare thus initiated had been reasonably rewarding.
The total number of attacks on Provisional Government forces up to
15th September was 467.[1] Fighting had taken place in everyone of the
twenty-six counties, and the territorial distribution of the actions shows
how the weight of the conflict was once more being borne by Dublin
and the south. The number of clashes ranged from 77 in Cork, 68 in
Dublin, 57 in Tipperary and 50 in Kerry, down to one each in Cavan
and Longford.

Within the previous three weeks damaging attacks had been made
on the posts of Provisional Government forces in thirteen counties—
Carlow, Cork, Galway, Kerry, Leitrim, Limerick, Mayo, Meath,
Monaghan, Offaly, Tipperary, Waterford and Wicklow. In addition
about twenty posts or barracks had been captured outright including
such substantial garrisons as those at Ballina and Kenmare, where the
captured material included four machine guns, 150 rifles, 50,000

---

[1] *Poblacht na hEireann War News*, No. 63, 21st September, 1922.

rounds of ammunition, four motor lorries and large quantities of food and clothing.[1]

The town of Dundalk had been recaptured by the 4th Northern Division on 14th August. Two hundred Republican prisoners were released from the Jail, four Lewis guns and 50,000 rounds of ammunition were captured. The captures of smaller posts had been widespread, yielding a total of 2,000 rifles, twenty-one Lewis guns, thousands of grenades and 200,000 rounds of ammunition. *The Irish Times* commenting on the failure of the Provisional Government forces to make any headway against the Republicans referred to the need for " an infinitely greater number of troops . . . better officers and unlimited transport."

Liam had some reason for optimism. But behind his determination and optimism there was grief and heartache. Writing to Father Tom on 16th September, he said :

> " The disaster of this war is sinking into my very bones, when I count the loss of Irish manhood and the general havoc of Civil War. Who could have dreamt that all our hopes could have been so blighted."

---

[1] *Poblacht na hEireann War News,* No. 63, 21 September, 1922

CHAPTER 21

GOVERNMENT OF THE REPUBLIC RE-CONSTITUTED

*Never to desist from our efforts until we had subverted the authority
of England over our country, and asserted her Independence.*

TONE.

IN the first three months of the civil war the Republican forces were
not subject to any authority, other than that of their own Executive.
Except for a brief meeting of eight of the then available members in
Fermoy on 15th July, the Executive did not meet until 16th October.
Until then Liam had kept the progress of the conflict under continuous
review at frequent staff meetings, but in fact complete control of the
Republican forces may be said to have rested with him, in so far as it
was possible for any one man to exercise authority in the circumstances.

Liam does not appear to have desired any change in this position.
It was his view that nobody on the Republican side had any respon-
sibility for carrying on the war except the Executive. When Mr. De
Valera had expressed to him a desire to meet members of the Army
Executive before their next conference, he replied that the meeting had
not been held,

> " and in any case as the military situation improved considerably
> just previous to it, I did not consider it necessary to hold it. . . .
> I would, however, be only too pleased to have your views, at
> any time on the general situation, and matters arising out of it,
> and they will receive my earnest consideration."

Mr. De. Valera was anxious to urge upon members of the Executive
the advisability of considering whether a military victory was not
merely improbable, but virtually impossible. He had been opposed
to civil war from the beginning of the Army split on the Treaty.
He had then expressed to at least one member of the Executive his
earnest wish that some solution of the Army problem should be found
which did not involve civil war. His public statements at the time, in
which he indicated what the consequences of an attempt to impose
the Treaty would be, were misrepresented as incitements to civil war.
They were in fact warnings of what a calamitous evil it could be.
When it started he reported for duty with the Army, and remained
most of the time between July and September in the south. But he

did not cease to urge upon such of the leaders as he could contact the view that somehow it should be brought to an end—a view not shared or approved of by Liam at the time.

The position of the Republican Dáil deputies elected in June was a peculiar and difficult one. The Dáil, which was to have re-assembled on 30th June, was prorogued to 8th July, then to the 15th, then to 29th, then to 12th August. It did not assemble until 9th September, and by then both Collins and Griffith were dead, and the whole conflict had developed into one of great bitterness. Until the Dáil met the position created by the Collins–De Valera pact was still technically in existence. After 9th September it was clear that the pact was dead, that the body which assembled was not the third Dáil Éireann but the Provisional Parliament set up under the British Act. The Republican deputies decided to refrain from attendance or participation in this parliament.

The question of the relations between them and the Republican forces was in need of clarification. Mr. De Valera favoured a public declaration by the Army Executive of what was in fact the actual situation.

> "The Army Executive," he wrote, "must publicly accept responsibility. There must be no doubt in the mind of anybody in this matter. This pretence from the pro-Treaty party that we are inciting the Army must be ended by a declaration from the Army itself that this is not so."

This was one of the matters which made it necessary to call the Executive together, even though doing so involved considerable risks. Liam issued instructions to have the meeting called.

The sixteen men on the Army Executive on 28th June, 1922 were : Liam Lynch, Liam Deasy, Rory O'Connor, Liam Mellows, Joe McKelvey, Peadar O'Donnell, Tom Derrig, Ernie O'Malley, Tom Barry, Michael Kilroy, P. J. Ruttledge, Frank Barrett, Pax Whelan, Seán Moylan, Seamus Robinson and Joe O'Connor. Ten of these attended the meeting held at Mrs. Nugent's, Poulatar, Ballybacon, on 16th and 17th October. Four were prisoners, Rory O'Connor, Mellows, McKelvey and O'Donnell. Tom Barry, who had been a prisoner, escaped from Gormanstown camp about the end of August. Two members were absent, Michael Kilroy and P. J. Ruttledge, but they arrived after the meeting had terminated and endorsed the decisions which had been made.

Liam Lynch presided. It was decided to co-opt four members to replace those imprisoned, Seán Lehane for O'Donnell, Frank Aiken for McKelvey, Seán McSwiney for Mellows and Con Moloney for

Rory O'Connor. Con Moloney, who was in the vicinity, attended for the remainder of the meetings. Substitutes were named for all members, and ratified by the whole body.

The first day was devoted to a review of events since the outbreak of hostilities, and to the consideration of certain peace proposals mentioned later. In his report Liam stated that it had been decided at the Clarence Hotel meeting after the attack on the Four Courts that each division would operate on its own, as there was no head-quarters outside the Four Courts. It would appear that he must have become convinced soon afterwards that this would not give the best results, because he had created three commands, a northern and eastern, commanded by Ernie O'Malley, a western, under the control of Michael Kilroy, and a southern, commanded by Liam Deasy.

After the evacuation of Fermoy, the Adjutant General, Con Moloney, had established headquarters at Rossadrehid in the Glen of Aherlow; and as he acted also as Adjutant to the southern command both headquarters were there, although Liam did not move into the Glen until about 25th September. With Con Moloney had gone his brother Jim, as Director of Communications, and Maurice Walsh as Staff Officer.

In reviewing the position since July, Liam stated that he had wished to clear the 1st and 2nd Southern Division areas of Provisional Government forces before advancing towards Dublin, but that the long operation in Limerick had delayed this plan. One hundred men from the 2nd Southern and 900 grenades from 1st Southern were sent to Dublin. When the south was over-run by Provisional Government forces the destruction of posts and communications disrupted activities for a few weeks until men settled down to guerilla tactics.

Elsewhere in the documents of the period there is evidence of other difficulties which beset the Republican forces. Except in the 1st Southern Division and in Mayo, strengths were not more than half what they had been in the war against the British; it had not been possible to reorganise completely the remaining forces, and that position had drawn from the Adjutant General a number of sharp reminders. There were too many senior officers with columns and no substitutes had been appointed in their commands; staffs were generally incomplete; unit headquarters were difficult to maintain; the security of communications and documents was a recurring problem. Attempts had been made to establish some civil adminis-tration—a matter to which Liam attached much importance—and to prevent the functioning of the civil administrative departments of the Provisional Government. All these had combined to strain the available resources in strength and organisation to the limit. Casualties had mounted to over three hundred killed or wounded, and there were over 6,000 Republican prisoners in jails and internment camps.

The arms position was satisfactory, apart from the lack of mortars and artillery, and this absence of heavy weapons imposed the same difficulties and limitations on attacks on fortified posts as it had done in the war against the British forces. A few armoured cars which had been captured somewhat redressed the balance. Large numbers of rifles, some machine guns and a considerable quantity of ammunition and grenades had been captured, together with some food and clothing; but in many areas, particularly in the west, problems of feeding and clothing the active service units were becoming acute. All these units were facing a winter of privation and hardship.

How effective the guerilla activities had been in pinning down Provisional Government forces to their posts may be judged from the comments of the special correspondent of the *Irish Times* with these forces in Kerry. He wrote on 27th September :

> " In truth, beyond the occupation of some of the towns the national forces have been able to do little. They are pinned to barracks, and they cannot leave barracks safely in Columns of less than 100 men. Even in barracks they are continually harassed by sniping and occasionally more seriously attacked."

The attitude of the Provisional Government and its military forces towards their opponents was rapidly assuming a character of implacable harshness and cold-blooded violence. Government had fallen into the hands of men who appeared to desire the annihilation of their opponents rather than a translation of the struggle to the political field.

Six days before the Executive meeting, a Provisional Government proclamation was issued giving effect to a decision to set up military courts with power to inflict the death penalty, which had been carried by forty-eight votes to eighteen in the Provisional Parliament on 27th September. On the same date the Irish Hierarchy, meeting at Maynooth, described Republican armed resistance as " morally only a system of murder and assassination of the national forces." Their Lordships hoped that Republicans would take advantage of the Provisional Government's offer of amnesty made on 3rd October.

The official Provisional Government organ, *Free State* in its issue of 7th October said :

> " If prisoners are taken they must not be released until they are incapable of further harm. If executions are necessary they must be carried out with no fear of the chimera of popular reaction."

Casualties amongst Provisional Government forces had not been
light. Up to the middle of September 185 had been killed and 674
wounded. One of the most tragic features of the whole conflict was
the deaths of men on both sides, most of them in the flower of manhood, who had carried the heaviest burdens with magnificent courage
and inspiring determination during the fight against the British.
Cathal Brugha was dead, riddled with machine gun bullets in the
streets of Dublin, where he had, six years earlier fought so gallantly
and almost to the point of death from wounds against the British.
Harry Boland, who had, as he said, gone into the fight, " with a
heavy heart, but yet not without hope," was dead, shot down by
raiding troops at night in a hotel at Skerries, on 30th July, in one of
those darkly confused encounters of the time. Arthur Griffith had
died in Dublin on 12th August, perhaps broken hearted. Michael
Collins had been ambushed and killed at Bealnablath in his native
county on the 22nd of the same month. There were many others.

The prisoners, overcrowded in jails and internment camps, were
subjected to all the petty tyrannies bred by the kind of situation which
existed. Liam had forbidden hunger strikes where political treatment
was granted. All the prisoners taken by his forces had been released
unharmed. Arms in the hands of inexperienced and often indisciplined Provisional Government troops had resulted in much
indiscriminate shooting, and in a number of casualties. Up to the
end of September not less than twenty-two men had been shot dead
either in jails or while in the custody of Provisional Government
forces outside.

On the second day of its meeting the eleven members of the Executive
present turned their attention to the questions of policy which confronted them. The first was whether their forces should, as hitherto,
continue to wage war under the authority of the Executive only, or
whether the Executive itself should sanction and co-operate in the
formation of a Republican Government to which it would give
allegiance, and under whose direction and control Republican forces
would continue to offer armed resistance to the Provisional Government. The second question of policy was to decide what were the
minimum terms of peace which could be accepted.

This was taken first, and after a discussion, recorded in the following
resolution, proposed by Con Moloney, seconded by Seamus Robinson
and passed unanimously :

> (*a*) " That the Army Council be instructed by the Executive
>   to negotiate terms of peace, such as will not bring this
>   country within the British Empire.
> (*b*) That the final decision rests with the Executive."

An Army Council had been appointed at the same meeting consisting of Liam Lynch, Ernie O'Malley, Liam Deasy, Tom Derrig and Frank Aiken. Its functions were defined as those of the Executive when the latter was not in session. Three deputies were appointed to replace any member of the council who became a casualty, and designated one, two and three in the order, Joe O'Connor (Dublin), Con Moloney, Michael Kilroy.

On the question of the constitutional position Mr. De Valera had sent a memorandum to Liam, which he now put before the Executive for a decision. Mr. De Valera wrote :

> " Owing to the suppression of the Second Dáil and the assumption of authority by the Provisional Parliament, it has become imperative, if it be decided to continue the fight, to set up a Government for the Republic.
>
> " The demand for such a controlling authority is insistent from all sides—from our people at home, and from our supporters in America. Such a government is necessary in order :
>
> (*a*) To provide a rallying point and a centre of direction to co-ordinate the efforts in various fields to maintain the Republic.
>
> (*b*) To preserve the continuity of the Republic and prevent the Free State Government from establishing itself as the legal successor of the Second Dáil.
>
> (*c*) To establish a claim to the funds and other resources of the Republic.
>
> " The proper body to set up such a government would undoubtedly be the elected representatives of the people, meeting as the Parliament and the Government of the Republic in Dáil Éireann. The faithful Republicans are prevented from meeting, however, and as the present position has developed from army action and not directly as the policy of the Republican Party, and as there is doubt as to whether the Army would give its whole-hearted allegiance to any other than its own Executive, or the creation of that Executive, it is obvious that the Army must take the initiative in causing the Government to be set up. . . .
>
> " A simple Military Dictatorship is open to a host of objections, whilst a government which would not get the allegiance of the Army would be a mockery. Under the circumstances, the proper course would be for the Army Executive to call on the Republican Members of the Dáil to set up the Government, having arranged with them in advance as regards the personal and the broad outlines of policy. . . . As this would take time, and as very

few of the members are accessible, I have suggested a modification
to the members of the Executive whom I have met, and drafted
a suitable Proclamation."

Having said that the only public policy necessary at the moment
was the policy of maintaining the Republic and the Sovereign Independence of the nation, he suggested that there should be a frank exchange
of views and a very definite understanding between the Army and the
Government on three matters, namely,

> "1. The right of the People to determine freely their own
>   Government, and the relations of the State with foreign
>   States.
> "2. The terms on which the present armed opposition to the
>   Free State (if it continued to have a majority) might be
>   desisted from, and
> "3. The terms, short of a simple recognition of the Republic,
>   on which, if we succeed in establishing ourselves in
>   Nationalist Ireland, we might make peace with England
>   and the Northern Unionists."

In his elaboration of his views Mr. De Valera referred to the terms
set out in Document No. 2 and expressed the view that they represented the utmost which there was any reasonable grounds for
hoping to attain under existing conditions of British and world
politics. If the nation's sovereignty and its territorial integrity could
be preserved he would have been in favour of working the Treaty,
or allowing it to be worked, believing that by such a programme we
could reach without bloodshed the most we could at present reach by
arms. But because the hypothesis was impossible he was forced to
oppose the Treaty. He regretted this because he believed that " with
the national forces unified we could make a success of almost any
programme whilst divided we can scarcely make a success of any."
In the course of the discussion on the whole problem it became
evident that there was an almost unanimous feeling in favour of the
establishment of a Republican Government, members of the Executive
realising that the problem was not solely or altogether a military one,
that even apart from the constitutional position there were practical
aspects in which the authority of a Government, even if incapable
of full or complete exercise, would be helpful. They were, however,
reluctant to surrender the right of saying the last word on the question
of the terms of peace with the Provisional Government authorities,
and they did not surrender it. The following resolution, proposed by
Con Moloney and seconded by Seamus Robinson was passed with
one dissentient :

" That this Executive calls upon the former President of
Dáil Éireann to form a Government which will preserve the
continuity of the Republic. We pledge this Government our
wholehearted support and allegiance while it functions as the
Government of the Republic, and we empower it to make an
arrangement with the Free State Government, or with the
British Government, provided such arrangement does not bring
the country into the British Empire. Final decision on this
question to be submitted for ratification to the Executive."

On 28th October a Proclamation was issued by the Army giving
effect to this resolution[1] On the 25th the available Republican
Deputies met secretly in Dublin, constituted themselves as the
Republican Government and appointed De Valera President. A
Council of State of twelve members was also appointed. On the
following day a proclamation was issued giving effect to these
decisions.

Liam now decided to move his headquarters to Dublin, which
offered certain advantages in the matters of communications and
contacts. Since he came South at the end of June, a line of communication to him from Dublin had been organised and maintained
by Kathleen Barry (Mrs. Jim Moloney), who had done and continued
to do very valuable work as a courier. Since the evacuation of Fermoy
Barracks, he had remained in the 1st and 2nd Southern Division areas,
where he spent some time in his old brigade area, staying at McCarthy's
Creggane, O'Connells, Lombardstown, O'Callaghans, Newtown-
shandrum, and in the Liscarroll and Kilavullen districts.

On 20th September, Kathleen Barry met him at Kilavullen and
accompanied him to Rossadrehid in the Glen of Aherlow. On the
way, they called to his home at Barnagurrahy and had a meal there.
It was the last time Liam saw his mother, or the home to which he
was so much attached. While he was in the Glen, Father Tom paid
him a visit, cycling from Anglesboro. On 14th October, accompanied
by Con Moloney, Moss Twomey and Matt Ryan, he left the Glen and
crossed the Galtees to Ballybacon for the Executive meeting.

On the 19th Liam left McGraths, Ballybacon where he had stayed,
on a slow journey, mostly on foot, via South Kilkenny, South
Wexford, Carlow, and Wicklow to Dublin, where he arrived on
3rd November. Paddy Ruttledge travelled with him, and they stayed
a night at Robert Barton's at Annamoe, where Erskine Childers was
captured a little over a week later.

In Dublin headquarters was established at Tower House, Santry,
the residence of Mr. and Mrs. Michael Fitzgerald and the Misses Nora,

[1] See Appendix 10

Kit and Nan Cassidy. It was a large house, in which a secret room had been so expertly constructed that the most thorough searching failed to disclose it. Here the staff consisted of Liam, P. J. Ruttledge, Tom Derrig, Moss Twomey, Seán Brunswick and Madge Clifford (Mrs. Dr. Comer). P. J. Ruttledge was Minister for Home Affairs, Tom Derrig was Assistant Adjutant General until January, when he became Adjutant General in succession to Con Moloney who had been appointed Deputy Chief of Staff and O/C Southern Command. Maurice Twomey was Chief Staff officer, assisted by Seán Brunswick, who had been wounded and lost an eye in the Four Courts.

G.H.Q. Staff meetings were held frequently at Tower House. The secret room was available to conceal the men, weapons, documents, typewriters and other evidence of the presence of so many persons, but it was largely due to the ingenuity and resource of Kit Cassidy that all rooms could be given an innocent appearance in a few minutes, even in the case of a sudden raid at night, During the whole of the period in which Liam and his staff were the guests of the Cassidy and Fitzgerald families at Tower House, every need and wish of theirs was anticipated with unsurpassed generosity and kindness. The precautions taken for their safety, and in getting visitors into and out of the house, were so effective that no attention was ever drawn to it while Liam was there.

November was a black month as November, 1920, had been in the Tan War. Two days after Liam's arrival in Dublin, and when they had just arranged a meeting, Ernie O'Malley was captured after being seriously wounded in a fight at the house of Mrs. Humphreys, Ailesbury Road, where he had his headquarters. As Assistant Chief of Staff and O/C Northern and Eastern Command, he had held many executive and administrative threads in his hands since July, and in addition to his loss as an intrepid fighting officer his removal confronted Liam with the necessity for a re-organisation of the Command and G.H.Q. Staffs. He confirmed the appointments of the officers on the Command Staff; Seán Dowling, Director of Organisation; Michael Carolin, Director of Intelligence; Michael Cremin, Director of Purchases; Pa Murray, O/C Britain, Robert Brennan, Director of Publicity. Tomas O'Derrig was appointed Assistant Adjutant General at G.H.Q., and Frank Kerlin as General Staff Officer.

The first executions under the Provisional Government's legislation were carried out on 17th November—four lads who had carried no special responsibility and whose only offence it was to be captured armed in defence of the Republic. It was feared that these executions prepared the way for the killing of Erskine Childers, and it was proved to be so. He was shot on the 24th. On the same day, Michael Kilroy, O/C Western Command was wounded and captured.

At the end of the month Frank Barrett, O/C 1st Western Division reported that :

> " As a result of the capture by the enemy of nearly all the best officers in the area the organisation showed very grave signs of collapse, consequently all our energies are directed towards reorganising."

Liam was amazed and shocked by the Provisional Government's policy of executions. On 27th November he addressed a letter of protest and warning to " the speaker of the Provisional Parliament of Southern Ireland," and sent a copy to Thomas Johnson, Chairman of the Parliamentary Labour Party. Having referred to the fact that the Provisional Government had " declared war on the soldiers of the Republic and suppressed the legitimate Parliament of the Irish Nation," Liam went on to say :

> " As your ' Parliament ' and Army Headquarters well know, we on our side have at all times adhered to the recognised rules of warfare. In the early days of this war we took hundreds of your forces prisoners but accorded to them all the rights of prisoners of war and, over and above, treated them as fellow countrymen and former comrades. Many of your soldiers have been released by us three times although captured with arms on each occasion. But the prisoners you have taken have been treated barbarously, and when helpless you have tortured, wounded and murdered them. . . .

> " Next to the members of your " Provisional Government," every member of your body who voted for this resolution by which you pretend to make legal the murder of soldiers, is equally guilty. We therefore give you and each member of your body due notice that unless your army recognises the rules of warfare in future we shall adopt very drastic measures to protect our forces."

On 7th December two pro-Treaty Deputies, Seán Hales and Padraig O'Maille, were fired on in Dublin. Hales was killed and O'Maille wounded. Early next morning four men who had been prisoners since the fall of the Four Courts at the end of June, Rory O'Connor, Liam Mellows, Joe McKelvey and Dick Barrett, were taken from their cells in Mountjoy and executed. Civil War had reached the nadir of desperation and savage hate. Imbrued in the blood of brothers, the Free State came into official existence on 6th December.

In the South, Tom Barry, who had so brilliantly commanded the Cork No. 3 Brigade Column against the British, was organising for a

major blow against the Free State forces. After his escape from
Gormanston, Liam had appointed him Operations Officer, Southern
Command. With a few selected column leaders of experience from
the Cork brigades, and a force from the 2nd Southern Division, he
organised a combined attack on the Free State posts at Callan,
Mullinavat, Thomastown and Carrick-on-Suir on 19th December.
Callan, Mullinavat and Thomastown were captured by the 2nd
Southern Division, led by the Divisional O/C Operations, Bill Quirke.
Heavy resistance was experienced at Carrick-on-Suir, where the attack
was led by Tom Barry but that post also was captured. 215 rifles,
two machine-guns and a large quantity of stores and clothing were
taken. All the prisoners were released, notwithstanding that seven
more Republicans had been executed on the same day.

Tom Barry had plans to develop this offensive northwards by an
attack on Templemore, where he hoped to capture artillery which
would enable him to attack the Curragh and eventually Dublin.
But these plans were frustrated by the rapid change in the situation
in the early months of 1923.

As the year drew to a close the outlook for the Republican forces
was not hopeful, yet men were facing it with great fortitude. This
civil conflict had from the beginning an unhappiness which caused
many a heavy heart; now the executions and the deaths of leaders
on both sides added a note of horror. Liam saw as clearly as anybody
that he, too, may be near to death. It did not alter his views or his
policy, but in what he wrote to his mother from Tower House on
22nd December there is premonition:

> "I do pray," he said in that last letter to her, "that many
> weeks of the New Year shall not pass before the Civil War ends,
> but really I have not much hope of an early ending as our present
> enemy still insists on dishonouring the nation by forcing her
> into the British Empire. If I should happen to be murdered
> by fellow Irishmen I die with an intense love for the national
> Irish people, and on behalf of my comrades of the I.R.A. who
> have stood up to the British Empire for years, sincerely forgive
> the Irish people who unintentionally wish to dishonour the
> nation. . . .

> "Would that England's hounds had tracked me down rather
> than old comrades who have been false to their allegiance.
> Future generations can best judge our actions, and these will be
> proud we so acted at a vital period. At the present, propaganda,
> materialism and war weariness hide the brave sacrifices that are
> being made by our forces."

Con Moloney, who had his finger on the pulse of the South, writing to Liam from the Glen on 4th December, did not encourage him to think military victory possible. The Army, he thought, faced a stone wall, local initiative was dead, and there was a growing danger of relaxed discipline. Liam himself, in reply, said the position in the West was far from satisfactory. But these things left him unmoved in his steady determination to continue the fight. " The loss of leaders and sacrifices from week to week," he wrote to Con Moloney on the 26th, " cannot under any circumstances bring us to lessen our demands." And on the following day in a circular on Peace Moves he wrote : " No terms short of independence can be accepted by Army or Government." ...

From the start of the Civil War he had not lost sight of the fact that Britain was still the primary enemy, and he had given much thought to the possibility of waging war against her on her own ground. In a detailed report to the President and Ministers, dated 30th January, 1923, he said :

> " When the Civil War broke out orders were issued from the Four Courts to wage war on England but owing to disorganisation nothing could be done. At the last meeting of the Executive the matter was again discussed, but though action was very much favoured I was not in a position to recommend it, as we had not a staff in charge and no satisfactory organisation."

Now, however, he felt that his forces in England were sufficiently well organised and equipped to undertake operations in specific areas.

> " I can see no reason," he wrote, " to be put forward against hostilities against the common enemy, even in his own country. He is waging war against us—if anything more desperate than before. All his resources are at the disposal of the Free State Army, including finance, experience, artillery, general supplies, etc."

The rapid changes in the situation at home in the early months of 1923 put an end to the plans he had for operations in England.

CHAPTER 22

PEACE NEGOTIATIONS

The people must hold what we won for them, even if they cannot immediately make progress to freedom.

LIAM LYNCH.

EFFORTS to bring the Civil War to an end began immediately after its outbreak and were continued, by different groups and individuals, up to its conclusion. Broadly speaking, they were all unsuccessful—the end did not come through negotiation.

The manner in which the Limerick agreements were terminated in July, 1922, has been related. Another effort originated from the same revulsion against Civil War between old comrades as that which influenced Lynch and Deasy on the one hand, and Brennan and Hannigan on the other, to agree upon a cessation at Limerick. Major General Emmet Dalton, who had been Director of Training on the pre-Truce G.H.Q. Staff, commanded the Provisional Government forces which occupied Cork City in August, 1922. Through intermediaries he made contact with some Republican officers and put forward peace proposals. Associated with him was Major General Tom Ennis, an old Dublin Brigade officer.

Liam strongly discountenanced these meetings and in writing on 6th September to the O/C 1st Southern Division, who had reported them without comment, he asked:

"Is anyone foolish enough to believe that either of them (Ennis or Dalton) would negotiate without orders of Government? Then why not direct negotiations?"

Liam's view that these officers were acting under instructions was proved correct. In a letter of 29th September addressed by Captain T. C. Courtney, General Dalton's Staff Officer, to Mr. S. P. Cahalane, one of the intermediaries, it was stated:

"Major General Dalton . . . wishes to say that he is acting under definite instructions of the Ministry of Defence, and will make any effort towards ending the present needless strife on the basis of an unconditional surrender."

Any proposals involving unconditional surrender had not the remotest hope of being even considered. Dalton dropped out, but

Tom Ennis and Charlie Russell persisted in the effort. At their request a meeting was arranged and took place between them and Liam Deasy and Tom Barry near Crookstown on 13th October. The proposals put forward by the Free State Officers were reported to the Executive meeting at Ballybacon three days later, but they were not of such a nature as to merit any serious consideration, and they achieved nothing.

In point of time the earliest effort came from representatives of commercial and labour interests and public bodies in Cork City and County. It was made under the leadership of Frank Daly, then Chairman of the Cork Harbour Commissioners. On 17th July a conference assembled at the Harbour Board offices in Cork, at which delegates were present from the public bodies of the City and County, as well as representatives of the commercial and labour organisations in the city. The feelings uppermost in the public mind at the time were expressed by Frank Daly when he said :

> " the situation as you know is an extremely grave one and the future presents an appalling prospect. The outlook is such that all good Irishmen are really heartbroken, and little wonder when they see their country in the actual process of self-destruction, and when they see the loyal comrades and brothers in arms of but yesterday engaged in deadly strife."

The keynote of this conference, and in this it was expressing an overwhelming public opinion, was that Dáil Éireann was the only legitimate national authority in the country and that no body of people had the right to prevent it from assembling, as had been done by the Provisional Government—a body which itself existed only with the sanction of Dáil Éireann. It was to Dáil Éireann, therefore, that this representative conference addressed the four resolutions which it passed. The first was a resolution against war in which the conference declared it was

> " not satisfied that such a disastrous fratricidal strife is unavoidable " and in which an appeal was made " to those who fought so nobly for freedom to consider whether we are drifting towards the greatest calamity in Irish history."

The second resolution demanded :

> " the immediate assembling of Dáil Éireann as the Sovereign body in this country and as the only authority now recognised by both sets of belligerents."

The conference invited the Dáil to assemble in Cork if it should be unable to meet in Dublin, and it requested both sides to guarantee safe conduct and travelling facilities to all T.D.'s.

The third resolution asked for immediate cessation of hostilities. The fourth resolution requested that if the proposal for an armistice proved unsuccessful, Dáil Éireann should immediately exercise its authority and order a cessation of hostilities. Copies of these resolutions were sent to Liam Lynch, and on the following day, 18th July, a reply was sent over the signature of the Adjutant General, to which was attached a long memorandum setting out the attitude of the Army Executive. In this it was stated unequivocally that :

"we shall be pleased that second Dáil should meet at once either in Cork or Dublin. We shall guarantee safe conduct to all members attending this meeting, and if necessary we shall provide an escort for them."

The Army position was represented as one of defence against

"unconstitutional and illegal attack ordered by a group of individuals who are usurping Government and acting as a military dictatorship."

The memorandum stated that the Army recognised the position created by the signing and acceptance of the Treaty, and went on to indicate certain alterations which it would require to have made in the draft Constitution. Willingness was expressed to have an immediate Truce on the same terms as those of 4th May, and for a resumption of the arrangements for army unification.

On 28th July, Frank Daly and Professor O'Rahilly, President of University College, Cork, had an interview with Liam Lynch at Fermoy Barracks and requested answers to two specific questions : Would he agree to cease hostilities if the other side did ; and, in the event of the second Dáil meeting would he recognise its authority. On the following day he replied :

"In answer to your queries last evening I wish to inform you that when the Provisional Government cease their attack on us, defensive action on our part can cease."

If the second Dáil, which is the Government of the Republic, or any other elected assembly carry on such Government I see no difficulty as to allegiance of Army."

The Cork Conference of 17th July had constituted itself a People's Rights Association and had elected an Executive Committee. This committee meeting on 1st August decided to send this reply of Lynch's to Michael Collins, together with two queries :

"(1) Do you agree to arrange such a cessation of hostilities as General Liam Lynch intimates he is prepared to accept.

"(2) Do you agree to call forthwith a meeting of the second
Dáil to be followed by a meeting of the third Dáil, as
previously arranged, and to allow the Sovereign Assembly
of the people to decide on the necessity or policy of a
bitter and prolonged Civil War."

In a reply dated 4th August, Michael Collins acknowledged the
communication which had been delivered by Mr. T. P. Dowdall and
Fr. Tom Duggan.

" This is a time " he wrote, " when above all things there
should be clear thinking on the part of public representatives.
The Government is sending you an official answer as presumably
your communication was meant to be addressed to the Government.

" So far as the Army is concerned I am merely obeying the
orders of my Government and all the general staff and soldiers of
the Army merely carrying out the instructions given in accordance
with such orders.

" This Government has made it fully clear that its desire is to
secure obedience to proper authority. When an expression of
such obedience comes from the irregular leaders I take it there
will no longer be any necessity for armed conflict. When the
irregulars—leaders and men—see fit to obey the wishes of the
people, as expressed through their elected representatives, when
they will give up their arms and cease their depredations on the
persons and property of Irish citizens, there will be no longer
need for hostilities."

Having referred to the form which prisoners taken in the recent
conflict had been asked to sign, and which most of them had refused
to sign, and having inferred from that that these men intended to take
up arms again against the Government he went on to say :

" If this is the spirit which animates Liam Lynch then I am sure
your body will agree that it is very little good endeavouring to
talk about terms."

Having referred to the duties of Government, and to the fact
that the time for face saving had passed, the letter ended on a challenging
and provocative note :

" The choice is definitely between the return of the British
and the irregulars sending in their arms to the People's Government to be held in trust for the people."

On the same day Arthur Griffith as acting Chairman of the Pro-

visional Government replied to the two specific questions put by the
People's Rights Association :

> "(1) The irregulars actions are wrongly described as defensive.
> The existence of an armed body which claims independent
> authority and commits outrages on persons and property
> cannot be tolerated.

> "(2) The functions of the 2nd Dáil came to an end on June
> 30th. The meeting which was to have taken place on
> that date would have been purely formal for the purpose
> of bringing its business to a conclusion. The Sovereign
> Assembly of Ireland is now the Parliament elected in
> June last whose authority the irregulars have flouted."

The letter went on to insist that the military action undertaken by
the Government was necessary to enforce obedience to Parliament,
and that it would cease only when that obedience was unequivocally
given. It went on to define what that obedience connoted—surrender
of arms, restoration of seized property and the furnishing of particulars about bridges, roads and railways which had been mined or
otherwise rendered unsafe.

The tone of these two letters indicated that the Provisional Government had decided against ending the conflict in any way other than
through the absolute defeat and destruction of the forces in arms
against them.

At this time the Republican forces were in a strong position to
negotiate, in fact in a stronger position than at any subsequent time.
They were in almost undisputed possession of the country south of a
line from Waterford to Limerick, and had intact organisation in
Connaught, in Dublin, and in the counties on the eastern seaboard.
Public opinion was not entirely embittered. While many favoured
peace at almost any price, there was a large section of opinion which
resented the virtual suppression of the Dáil, and which, given a lead,
would have taken a far more determined stand against the objectionable
clauses in the Constitution than was being taken by the Provisional
Government. The conditions which civil war created prevented the
Republican political party from giving that lead. An acceptable
constitution would have gone a long way to secure peace and unity,
even then.

On 30th August, Very Rev. Monsignor O'Hagan, Rector of the
Irish College at Rome, then in Ireland, wrote to Richard Mulcahy
with a view to bringing about a cessation of hostilities. The reply
which he received on 2nd September encouraged him to request
facilities for a meeting between Liam Mellows and Rory O'Connor,

then in Mountjoy Jail, with Oscar Traynor and Tom Barry. General Mulcahy replied agreeing to the proposed meeting in Mountjoy, and sent a copy of Monsignor O'Hagan's letter to Rory O'Connor and a copy to Liam Mellows. In a joint reply addressed to Monsignor O'Hagan on the 6th, O'Connor and Mellows, after assuring him that they welcomed " any efforts promising to end this new and unnatural attack on the independence of the country," went on to say :

> " Should you then have any reason to hope from Mr. Mulcahy's letter to you that there is a possibility of a calling off of the Irish element in this attack, you will find the Executive of the Irish Republican Army anxious to do all in its power to allay bitter feelings and promote that peace among Irishmen that is the wish of us all."

Monsignor O'Hagan's letter, and a copy of the reply from O'Connor and Mellows, were sent to Lynch, who was still in the South. In the meantime Dr. O'Hagan had an interview with Ernie O'Malley in Dublin, at which some proposals were put forward. Liam's comment on them was that they " were not worth much consideration by us."

Monsignor O'Hagan's efforts were supported by Rev. Fr. Wall, Broadford, whose brother Commandant Seán Wall had been killed in the fight against the British forces. Writing to Liam on 13th October he said that Mulcahy had declared to Dr. O'Hagan that he was carrying on "a defensive war," and that he was willing to stay his Army if Republicans ceased firing on his men. To this Liam replied (27th October) :

> " This attitude of Mulcahy as to his defensive policy is only quibbling with the situation. What a defensive action to first attack our G.H.Q. and other positions all over the country ! When he ceases to attack us in our efforts to maintain the Republic, then there will be peace."

He went on to say :

> " More definite proposals have since reached us but even these are useless. The fight must go on until there is no question of forcing Ireland into the British Empire, by the enemy, foreign or domestic."

His mind had set in the final mould. Not even De Valera's request, earlier in August when it was clear that territory could not be held, that consideration should be given to the probability that military victory was then out of reach, had any effect in softening his stubborn determination to continue the fight for the Republic as long as he had a man or a gun. He had lost faith in the sincerity of proposals from the Free State side, believed they were part of a general policy to undermine the loyalty of the Army, and was convinced that they were directed primarily at breaking down the solidarity of the Army Executive. And in this period in which only the Provisional Government functioned as a national authority, when Dáil Éireann had its legitimate authority filched from it, and there was still uncertainty as to the capacity in which the Dáil would meet when it was ultimately allowed to do so, he was quite clear that responsibility rested with the Army Executive and not with the Republican party or with the members of the Dáil who were opposed to the Treaty. In the letter just quoted he wrote :

> " Surely Republican party are not expected to face any responsibility as regards this war and I hope they realise this."

Other peace efforts made by Rev. Dr. McGrath, O.S.A., Cork, and by Rev. T. Roche, C.C., encountered the same difficulties and were also unsuccessful. A number of individual ex-members of the I.R.A., who had taken no part in the civil war, made appeals to Lynch and Mulcahy, but these also failed. Sinn Féin had tried and failed.

A peace effort undertaken by an organisation having nation-wide membership was made by the Neutral I.R.A. Association in February, 1923. The body consisted exclusively of men who had pre-Truce I.R.A. service, and who had not taken an active part on either side in the civil war. It had a membership of 20,000, but in the conditions of the time its organisation could not be otherwise than loose. The only purpose of its existence was to make peace ; it sprang up spontaneously in every area in response to an appeal for this purpose. The opinions of its members for or against the Treaty were immaterial, but there is little doubt that the sympathies of the great majority were with the Republicans.

The association concentrated its initial effort on arranging a truce, believing that responsible representatives of both sides, if they could be got into conference in an atmosphere of even suspended hostilities, would have a better hope of working out terms of settlement than anybody else. To that end a communication asking for a truce of one month, and defining the conditions for it, was sent on 16th February to the heads of the opposing forces, civil and military. It was at the same time given to the Press, and public bodies throughout the country were requested to support the appeal for a truce. They did so in generous measure. Neither side, however, accepted the proposals.

CHAPTER 23

THE CRISIS

We die for the truth. Vindication will come.
LIAM MELLOWS.

BY the end of January, 1923, fifty-five executions had been carried
out; many others were pending and the Free State authorities had
introduced the policy of sentencing prisoners to death in numerous
places where Republican activities were taking place, and of sus-
pending the executions coupled with a threat to put them into effect
wherever their forces were attacked. This policy, devoid as it was of
the humanitarian consideration accorded even to criminals, imposed
an additional strain on the convicted men in the prisons and a more
terrible responsibility on their comrades who were fighting outside.
The crisis had come. The Free State Government was imbued,
powerfully and perhaps desperately, by the will to win the struggle,
no matter how ruthless the means; the Republican forces as a whole
had lost that essential moral constituent of success.

Many of them felt that they had made "a bloody protest for a
glorious thing," and that in the physical plane they had failed. It
was evident that military victory was no longer a possibility for them,
and it was becoming equally certain that their opponents were determined to deny them the means of ending the struggle honourably by
negotiation. Realisation of that situation induced a mood in which
they were prepared to continue fighting as best they could, grimly and
doggedly, but without hope. Their strength was being steadily
whittled down; each day increased the lengthening roll of valuable
lives lost; the Church had outlawed them; the people, except a
minority, regarded their fate with indifference.

Many of the responsible leaders saw that situation clearly, amongst
them Liam Deasy. When he was captured, while ill at Tincurry on
18th January, he was already satisfied that the time had come when
armed resistance should cease, and that other means should be utilised
to attain the realisation of Republican ideals. He was a member of the
Executive and the commanding officer of one of the three commands
into which the Army had been divided. He had a very keen sense
of the heavy responsibility which these positions represented; and
his arrest, before he had fully formulated the proposals which he had

in mind for ending the conflict, put him in a position of extraordinary difficulty and strain. The action which he would have taken when free was no longer possible, but so completely had he become convinced of the imperative necessity for some action to terminate the conflict, that he was compelled to avail of the only means his captors left open to him. That was to put his signature to a document drawn up by them in terms which they had dictated and which he could not alter :

> " I accept and I will aid in immediate and unconditional surrender of all arms and men as required by General Mulcahy. In pursuance of this undertaking I am asked to appeal for a similar undertaking and acceptance from the following : E. De Valera, P. Ruttledge, A. Stack, M. Colivet, Domhnal O'Callaghan, Liam Lynch, Con Moloney, T. Derrig, F. Aiken, F. Barrett, T. Barry, S. MacSwiney, Seamus Robinson, Humphrey Murphy, Seamus O'Donovan, Frank Carty, and for the immediate and unconditional surrender of themselves after the issue by them of an order for surrender on the part of all those associated with them, together with their arms and equipment."

Copies of this appeal, together with a long covering letter in which Liam Deasy set out, fairly and courageously, the reasons which impelled him to make it, were delivered to the members of the Government and Army Executive by Father Tom Duggan, who had been nominated as courier by Deasy and called to Dublin for the mission. The Free State authorities did not, however, publish the document immediately. They held it until 9th February, when it was given the widest possible publicity in conjunction with a similar appeal from a number of prisoners held in Limerick.

Liam Lynch's reply to the appeal was in the following terms :

> " I am to inform you officially, on behalf of the Government and Army Command, that the proposal contained in your circular letter of 30th January, and the enclosure, cannot be considered."

The ruthless vigour of the policy of executions initiated in November had continued to mount. On 20th January, eleven prisoners were shot, two in Limerick, four in Tralee, five in Athlone. On the 22nd, three men were executed in Dundalk, and on the 23rd, two in Waterford. On the 26th, two men were shot in Birr, and on the next day two were executed at Maryboro. The struggle was developing, on the Free State side, the ferocity of a vendetta.

Not even the bleak prospect now confronting his forces, barren of hope as it was, not even the terrible cost in blood and sorrow which seared his soul, could alter Liam's determination to continue the struggle in arms. Surrender he would not contemplate or countenance. He was still in Dublin, and his appreciation of the military situation was more optimistic than the facts warranted. An officer of G.H.Q. Staff, Maurice Twomey, in intimate contact with him at the time, writes with reference to his determination to continue the struggle :

> " He could not or would not face the thought of defeat and collapse of Republican resistance to the imposition of the Treaty. The farthest he would allow himself to think in such a direction was that the Free State athorities would be compelled to negotiate with Republicans. Abandonment of the struggle in the field he would not countenance, and I believe this would have continued to be his attitude if he had not been killed. I feel that in no circumstances would he himself, surrender, and that he would never order those under his command to do so."

On 26th January, Liam wrote to Con Moloney that he intended to visit the South " in a few weeks." In these few weeks he spent himself in a fever of activity, in what may be regarded as his last gallant bid to get his forces to make that supreme effort which he believed would compel the Free State authorities to negotiate. From the beginning he had endeavoured to conduct the conflict on the recognised lines of warfare. On 27th September, 1922, he had issued an Order (General Order No. 9) strictly prohibiting any retaliation in kind for the killing of I.R.A. men. Having referred to " some cruel and cold-blooded murders " which had taken place, the order stated :

> ". . . Our troops are strictly forbidden to carry out similar reprisals on the enemy for these murders, and no such acts can under any circumstances be tolerated."

The same order prohibited the shooting of unarmed Free State soldiers, and the use of dum-dum or explosive ammunition. It directed further that wounded enemy personnel should receive proper medical attention; that the Red Cross should at all times be respected, and that where the white flag was hoisted his forces " should accept the surrender, no matter under what circumstances." That order was generally obeyed.

Even in the face of the persistent Free State policy of executing prisoners of war, he continued steadily to resist any departure from the letter or spirit of the order, beyond the taking and holding of hostages. But he took every possible step which he could take to bring home to the authorities opposed to him their grave responsibility for the lawless situation which was developing. He addressed a letter, already quoted, to the " speaker of the Provisional Parliament of Southern Ireland," and sent a copy to the Chairman of the Irish Parliamentary Labour Party. On 1st February he issued the following proclamation :

PROCLAMATION

OGLAIG NA H-ÉIREANN

(Irish Republican Army)

" WHEREAS, the Junta called the ' Government of the Irish Free State,' have suppressed the legitimate Parliament of the nation and usurped the Government, and now, in the endeavour to make good their usurpation and to destroy the Republic, have resorted to the infamous practice of shooting Republican soldiers taken by them as prisoners of war, and have already put to death fifty three Officers and Men in this manner.

" AND WHEREAS, the Army of the Republic is determined that it will no longer suffer its members to be thus dealt with, and the international usages of war violated with impunity,

" AND WHEREAS, The Army Command of the said Junta, have issued a Proclamation announcing that ' Punitive Action ' will be taken by them against other prisoners in their power if the hostages which we have been compelled to take are not set at liberty,

" NOW, WE HEREBY GIVE NOTICE that we shall not give up our hostages, and if the threatened action be taken, we shall hold every member of the said Junta and its so-called Parliament, Senate and other House, and all their executives responsible, and shall certainly visit them with the punishment they shall deserve.

" DATED, this 1st day of February, 1923,

at the hour of noon.

(Signed) LIAM LYNCH, GENERAL,[1]

CHIEF OF STAFF.

" FIELD GENERAL H.Q., Dublin.

On the 10th he sent a formal protest to Richard Mulcahy. Having said that " no case of the violation of the laws of civilized warfare by soldiers of the Republic " had been brought to his notice as Chief of Staff, he set out in detail the breaches by the Free State forces against which he entered his protest. These included the shooting of prisoners,

[1] J. L. O'D., 1/104/3

with or without trial, prisoners taken out of lorries and murdered by the roadside, prisoners tortured in the course of interrogation, wounded and sick prisoners denied proper medical attention, women prisoners ill-treated, herded with criminals and fired at and wounded by their guards. An appendix set out full details of the breaches, with names and dates. At the same time representations were made to the International Red Cross by Art O'Brien, acting as Ambassador for the Government of the Irish Republic, in which the charges in Liam's letter of protest were recapitulated. On 9th February he issued a special message to all ranks :

" Comrades,

" We have reached a supreme crisis in the struggle waged by us in defence of the Republic. Since June last the Army has withstood all efforts to break it by force in the field, and by vile and false propaganda. It is to-day in a stronger military position than at any period in its history.

" Having failed by force to break the morale and spirit of the Army the enemy has resorted to intrigue, and the employment of every base method to accomplish this, and to undermine its discipline, principally through individual officers. Realising, however, the enemy's past record in negotiations for peace—bad faith, broken promises and deceit, you will not be deluded by his present wiles into surrendering the strong position you have so dearly won. The war will go on until the independence of our country is recognised by our enemies, foreign and domestic. There can be no compromise on this fundamental condition. Victory is within our grasp if we stand unitedly and firmly.

" You can confidently rely on the situation being effectively handled by the Government, and H.Q. of the Army Command. The situation can only be destroyed by the ill-considered and precipitate action of individuals. You will, therefore, maintain the strictest discipline, and continue to carry out activities with vigour.

" You will be encouraged in this stand by the glorious sacrifices made for the Republic in the past—the sacrifices of some of Ireland's best and noblest soldiers. Our attitude in this crisis may decide whether or not the object for which they were made shall be achieved.

" When the present struggle was forced on us we realised the terrible consequence only too well, and did our utmost to avert them. Are we now to falter when on the threshold of victory and rob the Nation of the fruits of these sacrifices ?

LIAM LYNCH, CHIEF OF STAFF."

Writing to Con Moloney on the same day he expressed the conviction that were it not for recent events " we would have forced
them to accept our terms within a few weeks." He was unshaken
in his belief that there was no alternative policy for Republicans ;
military resistance to the Treaty had to be continued as long as the
Treaty included Partition and enforced inclusion in the British
Empire.

There were demands for a meeting of the Executive. Liam resisted
them for a time. On 22nd January he wrote to the members of the
Army Council and said that " it was impossible for the Executive to
meet." He asked members of the council to report continuously on
the development of the situation and give their views freely. This,
he thought, would " make up somewhat for meetings " which, even
of the Army Council, he considered dangerous.

Tom Barry and Tom Crofts went to Dublin and saw him on 6th
February. They put the request for an Executive meeting to him very
strongly. P. J. Ruttledge, who was present, was so far convinced
of its necessity that he wrote to the President next day :

> " I consider that we have reached a point when it is absolutely
> essential that Army Executive meet and review the situation and
> decide, when conversant with all circumstances and conditions,
> as to prosecution of war or otherwise."

Barry and Crofts arrived back at 1st Southern Division Headquarters near Ballyvourney on the 9th, and held a division council
meeting at Cronin's, Gougane, on the 10th. In a letter to Liam,
dated 11th, they repeated their request for a meeting of the Executive,
and in this they were now supported by Humphrey Murphy and Seán
MacSwiney—the remaining two southern members who were available. On the 15th they wrote again reminding him that they had not
got a reply. Two days earlier Liam had left Dublin for the South.
He had intended to begin this journey on 9th February, but urgent
matters detained him and he did not leave Dublin until the 13th.
There was a premonition of death in his last conversation with Madge
Clifford when he was leaving Tower House.

In Dublin he was joined by Dr. Con Lucy, Director of Medical
Services, and at Chapelizod Bridge, Commandant Paddy Brennan,
O/C South Dublin Brigade, took them over and arranged transport
and protection for them through Templeogue, Kilbride, Blessington
and on to Ballymore Eustace. From there they travelled via Leighlin-
bridge to Borris, where they were joined by Tod Andrews, who was
then on the staff of the Director of Organisation, John Dowling.
Sometimes on foot, occasionally at night in a car without lights, or
in pony traps, they continued the journey southward.

At Galvin's, Coolrainey, Martin McGrath, O/C 6th Battalion, Kilkenny Brigade, took them over, and via Innistoge they went on to William's, Kilmacow, and from there to Murphy's, Aglish. At Foskin's, Riverquarter, Mooncoin, where they stayed a few days, the 9th Battalion took them over and put them across the Suir in a cot to Henneberry's, Portlaw. From there they went to Sheehan's at Mothel, then to Kennedy's, Clondonnell and across the Gap to Pierre Wall's in the Nire Valley.

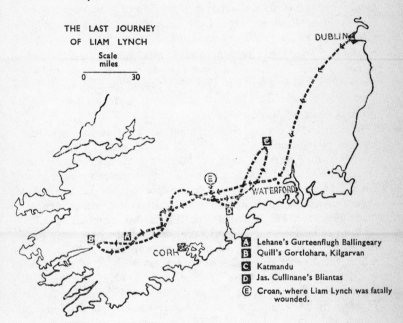

THE LAST JOURNEY
OF LIAM LYNCH

Scale
miles

0 ——— 30

DUBLIN

WATERFORD

CORK

Ⓐ Lehane's Gurteenflugh Ballingeary
Ⓑ Quill's Gortlohara, Kilgarvan
Ⓒ Katmandu
Ⓓ Jas. Cullinane's Bliantas
Ⓔ Croan, where Liam Lynch was fatally wounded.

Through Ballymacarberry they came to David Hackett's near Newcastle. Crossing the flooded Tar River at a ford at night, on their way to Mescall's, Ballybacon, their pony and trap was almost swept away in a high flood and they had a narrow escape from drowning. Passing through Glenaconna and Ballyporeen they arrived at Araglin in Liam's old brigade area on 22nd February. In their ten days journey rain had fallen almost continuously. The long period of confinement at Tower House had lessened Liam's normal physical fitness, but he rested at Araglin only long enough to attend a meeting of Cork No. 2 Brigade Council before resuming his journey to 1st Southern Division Headquarters near Ballyvourney.

He had sent an instruction to Con Moloney to meet him in the Newcastle area on the way South, but Con had been unable to leave the Glen of Aherlow because of extensive activity by Free State forces. Liam now sent Tod Andrews to the Glen, with instructions to follow him to Ballyvourney, and with Con Lucy he resumed his journey. They travelled by Kilworth and Ballindangan, crossed the Blackwater at Killavullen, and went on through Bottle Hill, Ahadillane, Donoghmore, Rylane, Ballinagree, Clondrohid, Kilnamartyra and Reninaree to Lehane's, Gurteenflugh, Ballingeary, where they arrived on 26th February. Except for a short visit to Kerry, in which he was accompanied by Tod Andrews and Humphrey Murphy, to a meeting with Commandant John Joe Rice, O/C Kerry No. 2 Brigade, at Quill's, Gortlohera, Kilgarvan, Liam remained at Lehane's until 17th March.

The 1st Southern Division Council meeting was re-convened at James Moynihan's, Gorthnascorta, Coolea, on 26th February. Liam attended it, and in a letter to Con Moloney on the 28th said it lasted "practically three days." Eighteen officers were present from the division and only three absent.

In reply to the demand for a meeting of the Army Executive, made by four of its members, who were all present at this meeting—Tom Barry, Tom Crofts, Humphrey Murphy and Seán MacSwiney— and endorsed by the divisional council at its meeting on the 10th, Liam said that "he alone was responsible for not calling it." He reminded the meeting that the present Executive had no power to make peace or war, and that the imprisoned members should be released to enable a meeting to take place of the only body having power to make such a decision. "The only terms," he said, "on which the Executive could make peace were those of the October meeting." And once more he reiterated his belief in their ability to continue the struggle. "If he thought we could not carry on successfully he would not allow the war to continue for a moment longer and would put the matter to the Government."[1]

Each of the eighteen officers from the division who were present expressed his opinion on the military situation. With two exceptions, the officers commanding Cork No. 5 and Kerry No. 2 Brigades, Ted O'Sullivan and John Joe Rice, all were of opinion that there was no longer any prospect of military victory. On the other hand, willingness to continue the struggle was expressed by all, but it was emphasised that because of reduced strength, diminished ammunition supplies and general conditions, actions would be on a smaller scale than hitherto.

This conference gave Liam a more realistic appreciation of the position in the South than he had while in Dublin. He knew, and had said, that they were opposed by the heaviest concentration of

---

[1]Quoted from captured documents published in *Irish Independent* of 9th April, 1923

Free State troops in the country; and he had expressed the view that it was mainly against the South the peace offensive would be made.

The relative strengths in the 1st Southern Division area at the time were: I.R.A., 1,270; Free State, 9,000. In the Southern Command area, which included the counties of Cork, Kerry, Limerick, Clare, Tipperary, Kilkenny, Carlow, Wexford and about half of Galway, 6,800 I.R.A. men were opposed by 15,000 Free State troops. In the whole country I.R.A. strength did not exceed 8,000 at that time, and against them the Free State authorities had built up a force of at least 38,000 combat troops. The possession of barracks, armoured cars and artillery emphasised the overwhelming Free State strength.

As he listened to the outspoken opinions of men whom he knew well, and for whose loyalty and fighting qualities he had the highest regard, the conviction was borne in on Liam that a crisis had come, and that however great the risk a meeting of the Executive could no longer be deferred. But he resented what he thought amounted on the part of some officers to a tendency to take action independently of G.H.Q.

In a long letter to Con Moloney on the 29th, the day the conference ended, he said that no vital decision on policy had been taken since the Executive meeting in October, and that he had continually pressed G.H.Q. officers and members of the Army Council to keep him informed of their views.

He thought that the southern officers were not acting through the proper channels. " What they mean by acting on their own views I cannot understand. However, I hope we are now done with it." His determination to continue the struggle remained unalterable. Even after the 1st Southern Division meeting, when the conflict between his views and those of some responsible officers had come to almost open breach, he was still confident that the fight could be maintained and his opponents forced to the point of negotiation. Writing again to Con Moloney on 2nd March he said: " I still have an optimistic view of the situation; if we can hold the Army fast all will be well."

The tragic sequence of deaths and captures continued. Denny Lacy, O/C Tipperary No. 3 Brigade, had been killed at Cloghera in the Glen of Aherlow on 18th February. Now Tipperary suffered another loss. Con Moloney was wounded and captured after a fight in the Glen on 7th March. His brother Jim, I.O., Southern Command, and Tom Conway, O/C Communications, who was wounded, were also taken prisoners. Tom Derrig replaced Con Moloney as Adjutant General, and Liam himself took over the duties of Command O/C temporarily.

In reprisal for the deaths of three Free State officers and two men
in a trap mine at Knocknagoshal, Co. Kerry, nine prisoners were
taken from Tralee jail, roped together and placed over a mine at
Ballyseedy on 7th March. The mine was exploded and eight of the
prisoners killed. On the same date five prisoners were taken from
Killarney to Countess Bridge and similarly treated. Four were killed.
At Caherciveen on the 12th five prisoners met a similar fate in the
same way.

On 2nd March Liam directed the Adjutant General to call a meeting
of the Executive for 9 a.m., on Thursday, 15th in the 2nd Southern
Division area. The venue selected was in the vicinity of Goatenbridge.
Dublin and northern members were to assemble at Rathgormack on
the 14th, western members at the Glen of Aherlow and southern
members at Araglin on the same date. Free State activity made it
necessary to cancel these arrangements and postpone the meeting to
23rd March.

While arrangements were being made for the holding of the
Executive meeting a proposal for the cessation of hostilities was
addressed by His Grace the Archbishop of Cashel, Most Rev. Dr.
Harty, and a number of priests and laymen, to Tom Barry, with a
request that it should be circulated to the I.R.A. leaders. The letter
was issued on 2nd March and in addition to Dr. Harty's bore the
signatures of Canon Ryan, Administrator, Thurles ; Rev. P. O'Leary,
C.C., St. Finbarr's South, Cork ; Rev. Tom Duggan ; Frank Daly,
Chairman, Cork Harbour Board ; T. P. Dowdall and Dr. Tadg
O'Donovan, Cork.

> " To end the present deplorable state of affairs in Ireland, we
> the undersigned appeal to the officers and men of the I.R.A. to
> accept, in the interests of the future of Ireland, the following
> proposals for peace :
>
> (1) The immediate cessation of hostilities by calling off all
>   activities and operations by the I.R.A.
>
> (2) The dumping of all arms and munitions by the Republican
>   forces under the command of the Battalion Commandants,
>   the Battalion Commandants to be responsible that the arms
>   will not be used against the Free State Government or
>   forces.
>
> (3) Subsequent to a general election the arms and munitions
>   to be handed over to the elected Government of the
>   country."[1]

[1] *Irish Independent*, 8th March, 1923

Tom Barry agreed to circulate the proposals. The moving spirit
in this effort was Father Tom Duggan, now Very Rev. Canon Duggan,
President of St. Finbarr's College, Farrenferris, Cork. He had been
associated with nearly every peace effort from the start of the civil war,
and had been indefatigable in striving to find an acceptable solution.
After the issue of Dr. Harty's proposals he continued to urge on both
sides the desirability of peace. On 15th March he saw Liam and many
of the officers of the 1st Southern Division in the area between
Ballingeary and Ballyvourney. Two days later he travelled to Dublin
with Frank Daly and Seán O'Hegarty, where he interviewed Archbishop Byrne and Mr. W. T. Cosgrave, the head of the Free State
Government.

On 17th March Liam left Gurteenflugh on the first stage of his
journey to the Executive meeting, the venue for which had been
changed to Bliantas, three miles east of Ballinamult at the foot of the
Monavullagh mountains. Tod Andrews travelled with him as far as
Araglin. At Carriganimma they were joined by Tom Crofts, Tom
Barry, Humphrey Murphy and Seán McSwiney, and a guard of
officers which included Michael Crowley, Liam Riordan, Peter
Donovan, Ned Fitzgibbon, Seán Cotter and Denis Galvin. A lorry
driven by Michael Lucy, took them to Bweeing; from there Batt
Walsh, Tadg Mullane and Jim McCarthy took them to Jack
O'Sullivan's, Burnfort. O'Sullivan, Dan O'Mahony and John
O'Keeffe drove them in three traps, with Denis Fitzgerald and David
Mulcahy acting as scouts, via Kilavullen, Rockmills and Ballindangan
to near Mitchelstown. Through Araglin they went on to the neigh-
bourhood of Mount Melleray, where they stayed at Seán O'Donnell's,
Knockboy, Hackett's of Moovea and Willie O'Donoghue's of
Crowhill.

On 23rd March the available members of the Executive assembled
at James Cullinane's, Bliantas. The members present were: Liam
Lynch, Frank Aiken, Tom Derrig, Seán Dowling, Austin Stack,
Tom Barry, Tom Crofts, Seán MacSwiney, Humphrey Murphy,
Bill Quirke and Seán Hyde. It was considered that in view of the
vital issues to be discussed the President should be asked to attend,
and on the invitation of the Executive Mr. De Valera attended. It was
the first occasion on which he was present at a meeting of the Executive.

The meeting continued through the 24th, 25th, and 26th March.
Being interrupted by hostile raiding forces on the 25th the members
were obliged to move into the Nire Valley, where the session was
continued and concluded at John Wall's of Glenanore. No minutes
of these meetings are available, and the only written record known
to the writer is contained in captured documents published in the
Irish Independent of 9th April, 1923.

Three points of view emerged in the long conferences :

1. Liam's which was simply to fight on, notwithstanding any losses or disasters, until their opponents were forced to negotiate. He believed they were still quite capable of offering serious resistance to the imposition of the Treaty and that they were in duty bound to do so. There was little unqualified support for that view.

2. The point of view which believed that a continuation of the armed struggle was no longer the best means of advancing the cause of the Republic, and that by negotiation the Free State authorities could be got to agree to certain principles in the sphere of Government which would leave the Irish people uncommitted to the Treaty and Republicans free to advocate and advance their cause without restriction. Specifically, this meant finding some way of making it possible for Republicans to participate in the political and parliamentary life of the nation without taking an oath of allegiance to a foreign monarch.

3. The point of view which recognised that the Free State authorities were not willing to negotiate at all, that the maximum military effort had been made and had failed, and that the war should be ended, because further sacrifices of life would not advance the cause of the Republic. From this point of view a dumping of arms was the most acceptable way of ending armed resistance.

Three significant aspects of the situation were considered in relation to these points of view. First, the heavy losses by death or capture of officers and men ; second, the policy of executions which had been suspended by the Free State authorities in February, but resumed again in March ; and third, the lack of weapons which would enable attacks on posts to be made successfully.

The total strength of the Army was then about 8,000 all ranks. Jails and internment camps held an estimated 13,000 prisoners. Against the 8,000 still in the field the Free State Government could muster 38,000 combat troops. There was no effective answer to the executions policy short of retaliation equally lawless and cruel, and Liam had forbidden any such action. Michael Cremin was negotiating the purchase of mountain artillery on the Continent, but there was no indication that he would be successful.

Two resolutions were considered. Frank Aiken proposed and Seán McSwiney seconded :

" That Government be empowered to enter into negotiations roughly on the basis of principles 1, 2 and 3 of President's memo. dated 9/2/23. Report to be laid before Executive at next meeting."

The voting on this was : for, Frank Aiken, Austin Stack, Seán Dowling, Humphrey Murphy and Seán McSwiney (5) ; against, Tom Derrig, Tom Barry, Bill Quirke, Tom Crofts and Seán Hyde (5). Liam did not vote.

Tom Barry proposed and Tom Crofts seconded :

" That in the opinion of the Executive further armed resistance and operations against F. S. Government will not further the cause of independence of the country."

The voting on this was : for, Tom Barry, Tom Crofts, Seán Dowling, Humphrey Murphy, Seán McSwiney (5) ; against, Liam Lynch, Frank Aiken, Tom Derrig, Seán Hyde, Austin Stack, Bill Quirke (6).

This motion having been defeated by one vote, it proved impossible to reconcile the divergent views held by members of the Executive. This, and the hope that some information in regard to the mountain artillery would soon be available, resulted in a decision to adjourn the meeting for three weeks, to 10th April. In the meantime Mr. De Valera was to endeavour to bring certain negotiations which had been going on through intermediaries to the point where they could be reduced to definite proposals to be put before the Executive.

The members of the Executive thereupon separated with the intention of re-assembling at Araglin on 10th April. The southern members, Barry, Crofts, and McSwiney returned to the Ballyvourney area. Humphrey Murphy went down with pneumonia at Araglin. He was attended to there by Drs. Pat and John Kiely, and brought safely to Cork. Liam, Frank Aiken and Seán Hyde moved northwards towards Callan. On Good Friday, 30th March, they were at Kilcash, where Mick Sheehan's column was billeted. There, the news reached Liam that Matt Ryan, who had been a member of his staff, was killed on the previous day.

Kathleen Barry recalled vividly a talk she had with him in Kilcash on Good Friday. He said there were three courses open to them, to fight on, to surrender, or a third that he would not name, but did not like—which was in fact a dumping of arms. He said that the adjourned Executive meeting would clarify the position. Even then he had an optimistic faith in the ability of the western divisions to continue the fight. That had been one of the strongest arguments he advanced in support of his contention that the struggle could be maintained when Seán O'Hegarty and I saw him for the last time near Ballyvourney three weeks earlier.

On this northward journey Liam visited the house where he had spent the first period " on his keeping " after the action at Fermoy in September, 1919—Kirwan's of Graigavalla. Jerry Kirwan repaired the boots he was wearing, and they are now in the National Museum.

In the townland of Poulacappal, four miles south west of Callan and three from Mullinahone, Jim O'Brien the local battalion engineer, had constructed a place of concealment which was unique in many ways. Some local wag named it " Katmandu " and the name stuck. It sheltered at one time or another during the civil war practically every leader of the Republican cause, including De Valera and Lynch. It defied all efforts to locate it. The efforts were many and thorough, and they were backed by the knowledge that it existed somewhere within the circumscribed ambit of their searches.

" Katmandu " was a little room, about ten feet by five at the end of a cow shed on the farm of the brothers Michael and John Phelan, Poulacappal. The whole building was about thirty feet long and ten wide, with corrugated iron walls and a roof partly of thatch and partly of corrugated iron. Access to the hiding place was from inside the cow shed, so that no tracks led to it from outside, and the entrance was so cleverly constructed in what was apparently the inside of the end wall that it could not be opened except by one who knew the secret.

By an ingenious arrangement of bed boards in two tiers as many as fourteen men were able to sleep in it at the same time. There were twelve in it on one occasion while a long search went on outside. The little hinged table which had been specially made for it, and on which some historic documents were written, is now in the house of Mrs. Anastasia Treacy of Poulacappal, and there also some of the wood work has been built into one of the rooms. On these boards many well-known names had been inscribed, but they are now unfortunately painted over and obliterated.

In the construction of this hiding place Jim O'Brien had the assistance of Jack Gardiner, Pat Egan and Jim Cashin. When Liam availed of its security for a few days in that Easter week of 1923, he worked and had his meals at Gardiners and slept in " Katmandu." The hospitality of the other neighbouring farmhouses, Egan's, O'Brien's, Tracy's and O'Gorman's was always at the disposal of those using the hiding place, and the route of approach to it from these houses was confined to existing well established tracks.

With the very serious position of the Republican forces, as disclosed at the Executive and 1st Southern Division meetings, before him, Liam considered the policy he intended to maintain at the re-assembled Executive meeting. His determination to continue the struggle in the field until his opponents were forced to negotiate remained unchanged, his faith in the policy of armed resistance was still unshaken, but he was heart-sick at the losses and sufferings being endured by his daily diminishing forces. If his responsibility was a grievous burden he took it manfully and never tried to evade it. And he never lost the old habit of turning in his perplexities to Him Who is the source of all guidance. Coming unannounced into the room where he was working one day just before his death John Gardiner found him on his knees saying his Rosary.

With Frank Aiken and Seán Hyde he left " Katmandu " on 4th April on the first stage of the journey towards Araglin. Jim O'Brien brought them to Nine Mile House, and they continued southwards to the Suir, which they crossed west of Carrick. Then via Rathgormack they joined the old route and went through the Gap into the Nire Valley, where they rested on the night of the 6th at Pierre Wall's of Knockaree.

Next day, at Ormond's, Glasha, they were joined by Bill Quirke, Seán O'Meara and Seán Hayes, and about midnight on Sunday the 8th they came into the 6th Battalion area of the 3rd Tipperary Brigade near Goatenbridge. Seán Myles, the battalion vice commandant billeted them at Luby's, Prendergast's and Burke's, Kildongue. Liam was at Prendergast's. Here a despatch rider, Owen McCarthy, brought him a report from Araglin to the effect that a round up of the area was anticipated in a day or two.

Liam decided not to continue towards Araglin next day. He sent the despatch rider back, having instructed him to return next day with a report. On the night of Monday, 9th April it was decided to move to billets about one mile to the east, to Croagh. The Tar river, flowing eastward to join the Suir near Newcastle formed the northern boundary of the billeting area for that night. Off the Clogheen–Newcastle road running parallel with the right bank of the river three minor roads lead southward to the slopes of the Knockmealdowns.

On one of these roads were the farmhouses in which Liam's party was billeted : Liam, Frank Aiken and Seán Hyde at Michael Condon's, Seán O'Meara and Jerry Frewen at James Condon's, and Bill Quirke and Seán Hayes at Bill Houlihan's, which was the house nearest the mountain.

Seán Myles, vice commandant of the 6th Battalion, 3rd Tipperary Brigade, who was in charge that night in the absence of the battalion commandant, Seán Prendergast, posted guards. Michael Condon and Bill Houlihan were on duty at Goatenbridge, Ned Looney and Jim Burke on the Clogheen road. Croagh was at the extreme eastern end of the 6th Battalion area, and the adjoining 5th Battalion posted guards, Tom McGrath and Michael Donnell, covering the approach from Newcastle. The billeting area was adequately protected from the north, east and west ; to the south the Knockmealdown mountains rose immediately behind it.

CHAPTER 24

DEATH OF LIAM LYNCH

When Emmet's epitaph can be written, Ireland will write yours too, Liam.
DE VALERA.

BEFORE dawn on the morning of Tuesday, 10th April the scouts at Croagh schoolhouse saw a party of Free State troops approaching from the Clogheen direction. They were moving silently in two files along the grass margins on either side of the road. Liam and his group were alerted at once and at about 5 a.m. they assembled at Bill Houlihan's, the house nearest the mountains. There they had cups of tea while they waited for other reports. They were not much alarmed. Raids of this kind were an everyday occurrence.

About 8 a.m. a scout ran in to tell them that another column of Free State troops was approaching over the mountains to their left rear. Their line of retreat was threatened. They left Bill Houlihan's and dashed up a glen towards the mountains. At the head of the glen some Free State troops appeared over a rise, and the first shots were exchanged.

In the scheme of Free State army organisation then in operation the area was part of Waterford Command, the commanding officer of which was Major General John T. Prout. He had headquarters at Clonmel. Acting on information to the effect that certain I.R.A. leaders were in the area, he ordered a search of a part of South Tipperary and Waterford to commence at dawn on 10th April. Over 1,000 troops were engaged in the search. Sixty men from Clogheen under Captain Tom Taylor and Lieutenant Laurence Clancy arrived at Goatenbridge at 5 a.m. This was the party which had been observed by the scouts. Captain Taylor's instructions were to drive south east from Newcastle at dawn, with his troops in a well extended formation, across the mountains towards Ballymacarberry where he would link up with another column. Taylor's party marched to Newcastle, extended as it moved up the mountain, and broke into two parts. The section under Lieutenant Clancy observed Liam Lynch's party and opened fire on them.

All the officers in Liam's party carried revolvers or automatics only. None had rifles, so that their fire was quite ineffective at the range except to the extent that it disconcerted the Free State troops. Liam's party continued to move up the mountain, a shallow stream bed, then almost dry, affording them some cover for about two hundred and fifty yards. At the head of it they had to retreat over a bare, coverless shoulder of mountain, where they were in full view of Clancy's party at a range of three to four hundred yards. Heavy fire opened on them in this exposed position; fragments of rock and bits of bog thrown up by the bullets rained around them as they struggled upwards. They had covered about two hundred yards, Liam and Seán Hyde in the rear, when suddenly there was a lull in the firing. For perhaps twenty seconds the still clear air of the morning was soundless, and then one single shot rang out. Liam fell. "My God," he said, "I'm hit."

He had been shot through the body and very seriously wounded. The bullet passed behind Seán Hyde, who was helping him along, and entered just over the hip bone on one side, making an exit wound at almost the same point on the other side of his body. Frank Aiken and Bill Quirke came back to where Liam had fallen. They picked him up and with Hyde carried him some distance, but it was evident that this pained him intensely. Several times he requested them to leave him, but they continued to carry him. Finally he ordered them to put him down and go on. "I'm finished," he said, "I'm dying. Perhaps they'll bandage me when they come up." Frank Aiken took his papers and his automatic. They put a coat over his body, from which life was ebbing slowly, and they left nim.

> "It would be impossible," Frank Aiken wrote, "to describe our agony of mind in thus parting with our comrade and chief. Even in the excitement of the fight we knew how terrible was the blow that had fallen on the Nation and Army on being deprived of his leadership. His command that we should leave him would have been disobeyed, but that the papers we carried must be saved and brought through at any cost. All would be lost if they were captured."

When Lieutenant Clancy reached the point where Liam was lying a soldier covering the now helpless prisoner with a rifle called excitedly that they had captured De Valera. Clancy knew he was mistaken and asked Liam who he was. He said: "I am Liam Lynch, Chief of Staff of the Irish Republican Army. Get me a priest and doctor. I'm dying." Clancy put a field dressing on the exit wound, a stretcher was improvised by tying a soldier's greatcoat to two rifles, and they began the difficult task of carrying him down the steep and rugged mountain side. Only by being kept in a half sitting position could he endure the intense pain. Frequently he had to be rested. He grew weaker and paler every minute.

At the foot of the mountain a jennett and a cart, filled with hay, was procured and in this Liam was placed. Over the rough bye road it was little better than the improvised stretcher. Clancy had disarmed a soldier and sent him for a priest and doctor, but on reaching the road to Newcastle discovered that the young lad had not gone, being terrified of being shot if he encountered an I.R.A. party. In a short time Fr. Patrick Hallinan, Newcastle, came along. He knew nothing of what had happened and when he heard a man was badly wounded he said, " Oh ! thank God I came this way. I was going no place in particular." He attended to Liam on the roadside about 11.30 a.m. It was about 9 when he was shot.

About 1.30 p.m. Liam was carried into a public house in Newcastle, and placed on a mattress with some blankets over him. While there he was attended to by Fr. John Walsh, P.P., of Newcastle and by Dr. Joseph Power. Lieutenant Clancy phoned his headquarters at Clonmel, reported the capture, and asked for a doctor and ambulance. It was 3.15 when they arrived. Liam was taken to Clonmel, where everything possible was done for him. He died at 8.45 that evening.

In Newcastle he had said to Lieutenant Clancy, " when I die, tell my people I want to be buried with Fitzgerald of Fermoy." So little enmity did he bear to those who had shot him that he gave one of his fountain pens to Lieutenant Clancy in appreciation of his humane treatment of him, and said, " God bless you and the boys who carried me down the hill." " Poor Ireland ! all this is a pity. It never should have happened."[1]

When the news of his death was telegraphed to Willie Ryan in Mitchelstown he went immediately, with Mrs. Michael Hyland, to Liam's mother at Barnagurrahy. That great-hearted woman read aright the sorrow in their faces before they had spoken a word. " He is dead, Willie," she said, and then after a little pause : " Thank God he did not let down his comrades." And in the ordeal of the days that followed she carried her grief proudly and kept her tears unshed.

With every mark of honour and respect he was borne from St. Joseph's church, Clonmel to Mitchelstown on Thursday, and on Sunday, despite the deep and bitter sundering of civil war, friend and foe gathered in an immense funeral cortege to follow his remains through Glanworth and Fermoy to Kilcrumper. There he was laid as he wished beside his friend and comrade, Michael Fitzgerald. It was not inappropriate that the bell which tolled for him in Mitchelstown was rung by a woman and a youth, Michael Lynch of Ballinamona.

[1] Quoted from a statement specially written by Laurence Clancy.

The surviving officers and men of the Army he had led so fearlessly could not come to pay a last tribute to their dead chief ; but wherever they were, in jails or internment camps, scattered on the hillsides or in the cities, their hearts were with him at Kilcrumper.

When he died—not yet thirty and without having attained the full development of his character—Liam Lynch had proved himself a man of more than ordinary capacity. But he had no abnormal intellectual gifts and he was not a military genius. It is improbable that he would have chosen soldiering as a career in a free country. He was a good soldier, mainly because he was a good man.

Service to the cause of freedom was predestined for him by the traditions in which he was reared and by his coming to manhood in the years of national resurgence. That service which he gave in such generous measure made self evident and added lustre to the basic aspects of his character—sincerity, gentleness, fidelity, constancy.

Less tangibly, but not less significantly, his personality, the ideals which inspired him, the kind of Ireland he visualised under conditions of freedom he had never known, the fire that was in his blood— all these are symbolic of the spirit which gathered the young men of his day into joyous service to the motherland.

Two kinds of courage enabled the nation to struggle out of bondage —the patient, enduring courage that willed survival in the long years of defeat, and the flashing, buoyant courage that struck manfully, challenging fortune. The latter was Liam's. It was appropriate to his day and generation.

The significance of a man like Liam extends beyond his lifetime. Men of his quality are a minority in every nation, but, after they are gone from us, they become ancestors in spirit to a self replenishing heritage. He enriched that conscious sense of nationhood which is the soul of Ireland. He was in harmony with his time and in harmony with the most durable spiritual forces which have moulded and continue to mould the Irish nation. He was amongst the makers of history.

POSTSCRIPT

Aﬀter the death of Liam Lynch it was not found possible to assemble the Executive on 10th April, but the available members met at Poulacappal on 20th. Some changes of personnel resulted from deaths, captures and illness in the interval. Liam Pilkington replaced Liam Lynch, Tom Ruane, who had escaped from Galway Jail attended as substitute for Michael Kilroy, Tom Sullivan was present as substitute for Seán Lehane, who had been deptuy for Peadar O'Donnell but was captured, Seán O'Meara attended as substitute for Seamus Robinson.

Tom Derrig had been captured at Raglan Road, Dublin with Moss Twomey on 6th April, but his substitute, Michael Cremin, was abroad on the mission concerning mountain artillery. Humphrey Murphy was still too ill to travel to the meeting.

The attendance was : Liam Pilkington, Seán Hyde, Seán Dowling, Frank Aiken, Bill Quirke, Tom Barry, Tom Ruane, Tom Sullivan, Seán McSwiney, Tom Crofts, P. J. Ruttledge and Seán O'Meara.

Frank Aiken was unanimously elected Chief of Staff, and an Army Council of three appointed—Aiken, Pilkington and Barry. The meeting passed a resolution authorising the Government and Army Council to make peace with the Free State authorities on the basis that :

" 1. The sovereignty of the Irish Nation and the integrity of its territory are inalienable and

" 2. That any instrument purporting to the contrary is, to the extent of its violation of the above principle, null and void."

At a meeting of the Government and Army Council held on the night of 26th–27th April at which President De Valera presided, it was decided that armed resistance to the Free State forces should be terminated.

The following Proclamation and special Army order were issued on 27th April :

DAIL EIREANN.

(Government of the Republic of Ireland)

PROCLAMATION

The Government of the Republic anxious to contribute its share to the movement for peace, and to found it on principles that will give Governmental stability and otherwise prove of value to the nation, hereby proclaims its readiness to negotiate an immediate cessation of hostilities on the basis of the following :

1. That the sovereign rights of this nation are indefeasible and inalienable.

2. That all legitimate governmental authority in Ireland, legislative, executive, and judicial, is derived exclusively from the people of Ireland.

3. That the ultimate court of appeal for deciding disputed questions of national expediency and policy is the people of Ireland—the judgment being by majority vote of the adult citizenry and the decision to be submitted to, and resistance by violence excluded, not because the decision is necessarily right or just or permanent, but because acceptance of this rule makes for peace, order and unity in national action, and is the democratic alternative to arbitrament by force. Adequate opportunities and facilities must of course be afforded for a full and proper presentation to the Court of all facts and issues involved, and it must be understood that 1 and 2 are fundamental and non-judicible.

4. That no individual, or class of individual, who subscribe to these principles, of national right, order and good citizenship can be justly excluded by any political oath test or other device, from their proper share and influence in determining national policy, or from the councils and Parliament of the nation.

5. That freedom to express political or economic opinions, or to advocate political or economic programmes, freedom to assemble in public meetings, and freedom of the press, are rights of citizenship and of the community which must be not abrogated.

6. That the military forces of the nation are the servants of the nation and, subject to the foregoing, amenable to the national assembly when freely elected by the people.

We are informed that many in the ranks of our opponents will accept these principles, as we accept them. If that be so, peace can be arranged forthwith.

We hope that this advance will be met in the spirit in which we make it, and that it will be supported by all who love our country and who desire a speedy and just ending to the present national troubles.

As evidence of our own good-will, the Army Council is issuing herewith an Order to all Units to suspend aggressive action—the Order to take effect as soon as may be, but not later than noon, Monday, 30th April.

Dublin,   EAMON DE VALERA,
27th April, 1923.   President.

OGLAIGH NA hEIREANN

(Irish Republican Army)

ARD OIFIG   GENERAL HEADQUARTERS
AT CLIAT   DUBLIN

REF. NO. SPECIAL ARMY ORDER

27th April, 1923

To : C/O's Commands and Independent Brigades

SUSPENSION OF OFFENSIVE

1. In order to give effect to decision of the Government and Army Council embodied in attached Proclamation of this date, you will arrange the suspension of all offensive operations in your area as from noon, Monday, 30th April.

2. You will ensure that—whilst remaining on the defensive—all Units take adequate measures to protect themselves, and their munitions.

CHIEF OF STAFF.

Enc. 1.

GENERAL.

The long expected rebel offensive took place on Saturday. Their action, preceded by thefts of bicycles on a large scale throughout the area, was confined to a number of revolting outrages.

No military skill or courage was shown by the rebels, who evidently find it more profitable to shoot down unarmed men—and women, than to take the field. The appearance in large numbers of pamphlets addressed to the members of the I.R.A. may have acted as a deterrent to many who have not as yet actually committed murder. The recent heavy losses among their leaders, by arrest or decease, had undoubtly (word illegible) their operations, which were probably planned by organisers in their G.H.Q.

There has been no recurrence of counter reprisals by the rebels, who appear to have been stopped by our determination to increase the ratio of destruction indefinitely.

Signed E. P. STRICKLAND,
Major General.
Cork.   Commanding 6th Division.

I.R.A. MOVEMENTS
1st (Mid) Cork Brigade I.R.A.

This brigade has shown more activity during the week. An attack on Midleton police barracks was the first military operation under-taken for some considerable time. A large number of men took part many of whom came from the city apparently on bicycles stolen during the same evening.

The rebels have collected some motor cars and motor cycles during the latter part of the week, also a large number of pedal cycles. These may be used for an operation in the near future.

A concentration of rebels is reported at Inchigealagh again, but information about this area is difficult to confirm.

Information received from several sources goes to show that there is no flying column for No. 1 (Mid) Cork Brigade, and that Hales' column is spoken of as the flying column of both No. 1 and No. 3 brigades. There are a certain number of active service men who go round in small bands, but these appear to spend their whole time attempting to avoid capture. Their numbers when reported by civilians are greatly exaggerated.

No. 4 battalion area (Queenstown, Midleton and Youghal) of this brigade is very unsettled and a small murder gang headed by William Aherne is very active.

No. 5 battalion area (Riverstown) is being plundered by members of the I.R.A. The residents are not reporting these occurrences. This battalion is not otherwise active.

2nd (North) Cork Brigade

2nd Battalion Column is reported to have moved into West Waterford and to be billetted round Kilmacthomas. This seems unlikely but they may have gone there to reinforce the Waterford Brigade Unit, at all events there has been practically no activity in their own area. They are said to have been responsible for the Durrow train ambush.

3rd Battalion has been active in road blocking, and are also responsible for the burning of a motor ambulance at Glanworth and for pulling up the railway line at Ballyhooly. This latter place is now in rather a bad state owing to the release of a number of internees from Kilworth against whom sufficient evidence could not be obtained.

On the night of the 3rd–4th May the A.S.U. of the 6th Battalion were billetted at Gashykinleen, 4 miles N.E. of Kiskeam. On 4th May they moved to the Meeling district, but left hurriedly about midnight in commandeered carts, etc. This may have been the result of a convoy of stores and reliefs, which went to Newmarket on the previous afternoon. They are believed to have returned to the Kiskeam area.

Several of the chief men of the 4th Battalion, A.S.U. were located at Aughrim House, 1½ miles N. of Liscarrol. In consequence, this house was raided on the 10th inst., with the result that Dan O'Brien and John O'Regan were captured. Two men managed to escape and they are believed to be Pat O'Brien and Michael O'Regan.

The remnants of the 5th Battalion A.S. continue to lie low and have not yet been located.

3rd (West) Cork Brigade I.R.A.

During the period under review this brigade was inactive, but on Saturday afternoon they attacked nearly every barracks in their area. These attacks were driven off in every case.

The death of Frank Hurley, Commandant No. 1 Battalion will be felt throughout the brigade.

It is now established that the flying column collects all the best men and material from the two brigades. Hales has always been very loath to leave his own area as he is afraid of being given away by people who are strangers to his men and he dislikes working in a county which is not well known to him. Up to the present there is no direct evidence that he has ever operated outside No. 3 (West) Cork Brigade area.

1st (West) Kerry Brigade

One column is still round Ardfert, Abbeydorney and Lixnaw, but has been comparatively inactive during the past week. Their chief work has been the raiding of Ardfert and Ballyheigue post offices for telephone instruments.

The Duagh Column attempted their anticipated ambush with unfortunate results to themselves, for their leader Jerry Lyons and two others were killed and a number were wounded.

2nd (East) Kerry Brigade

The A.S.U. of the 2nd Battalion are still in the neighbourhood of Castleisland. Members of this gang were responsible for the attacks on police at Farranfore and Castleisland on the 8th inst.

The 3rd Battalion has been active at Lissavigeen and Muckross (east and south of Killarney) in carrying out raids for bicycles and motor cars. A small gang operating to the north of Killarney has made two raids for telephone apparatus and tools at Ballybrack Station.

3rd Kerry Brigade

After a long period of inactivity this brigade carried out several raids for bicycles and cars in Caherciveen last week.

Mid Clare Brigade

Mid Clare Brigade has been inactive and has not been located.

West Clare Brigade has been in the Doonbeg–Cooraclare–Kilmihal area and intended attacking the R.I.C. barracks at Kilkee on the 6th inst. It is now believed to have moved up towards Quilty. Its only activity has been the cutting of roads in the southern part of the county.

The following information re the attack on the Kilrush Barracks on 22nd ult. has been obtained and corroborated :—The attackers comprised about forty men of a flying column from Kerry or County Cork and the Cooraclare Battalion and West Clare Flying Column.

The Kilrush members of the I.R.A. were used as guides, very unwillingly and apparently on point of the bayonet.

Simon Breen's house at Kilmaoduane, Cooraclare was used as the meeting place for arranging the attack.

John Liddy, Michael Hinan and Michael Killoughrey have been living in a dugout in the townland of Clonraddan, which was discovered on the 8th instant. This was large enough to hold six men and apparently a tent had been erected, as a number of tent pegs were found.

Liddy's party were rationed from Cooraclare and obtained money and despatches through a woman who cycles from Ennis to Clonreddan once a week. Willie Haugh is reported to have taken over command of this brigade. One of the rebels who was killed is reliably reported to have been buried at Doonbeg on the 24th ult.

Willie Haugh and twenty others had been living in a dug-out in a bog in Moyasta–Shragh district.

West Clare Brigade I.R.A.

This column is still believed to be north of Scarriff except for a small section under Harry O'Hara of Flagmount, which met at Caher Cross roads during the latter end of the last week. It left in the direction of Feakle. It is now reported to be in the vicinity of the West Limerick Brigade.

Michael Brennan is now reported to be touring County Galway. He is stated to have taken over command of the Galway I.R.A. in addition to the East Clare Brigade. The man he took over from came from Kincarra and was reduced in rank for inefficiency. The above incidents suggest that the I.R.A. are forming divisional head-quarters in certain areas. This is mere conjecture.

Mid-Limerick Brigade

Nothing is known of the movements of this brigade during the last week.

East Limerick Brigade

The large force of rebels reported last week as having been in the Kilteely district, and making for Fedamore, split up into three or four separate columns. One of these columns moved south via Hospital and Ardpatrick where they spent the night, on the 5th instant. At about 13.00 hours on the 6th instant, they were seen in Laurencetown, Kilfinane. Later the same day they were seen in Tankardstown. Another column of rebels estimated about eighty strong was seen on the Drumacummer Railway Bridge north of Bruree. They later moved off in the direction of Castletown Conyers. On the night of the 10th–11th instant, they were in the neighbourhood of Adare, and spent the night commandeering motor-cycles and cycles. Eight of them were surprised during the night near Ballinleenly with a blindfolded ex-soldier prisoner. They ran away and were fired at, one rebel being killed, one wounded and captured and an ex-soldier was recovered. They have not since been located.

One other column is believed to be in the hills between Ballybrosna and Pallas Green.

The civilian killed at Cappawhite during the week has been identified as Seán Wall, Commander of this brigade.

Armed men were seen at the following places during the week :—

Ballyoullane, 2 miles north of Kilmallock.

Ballygubba, 2 miles west of Kilmallock.

West Limerick Brigade

Have remained inactive and have not been located. The column of rebels from County Kerry frequently visit Knockagashel and have recently been in the vicinity of Abbeyfeale.

APPENDIX 1 315

Mid-Tipperary Brigade

The Mid-Tipperary Brigade though inactive is certainly in and around Thurles. James Leahy has been seen in Thurles during the past week. It appears that he has taken to drink, and last time he took charge of an operation was not in a fit state to give an order. James Larkin, Roskeen, James Stapleton and Patrick Kinnane of Upperchurch have left for Kilcommon.

North Tipperary Brigade

The 1st and 2nd Battalions are in the neighbourhood of Nenagh but are not very active. The 3rd Battalion Column is in the hills around Toomevara, and was encountered on the 11th inst. near Toomevara. They left a bicycle and some ammunition behind.

The 4th Battalion has moved from Arra Mountains, and are in the neighbourhood of Dromineer.

The 5th Battalion and 6th Battalion are billeted still in the Kilcommon districts and are inactive.

The 7th Battalion is still in Kings County. Edward Quinlan, the Commandant, has been seen in Shinrone within the last fortnight.

3 (South) Tipperary Brigade

No information has been received.

East Limerick Brigade

The 1st Battalion Column are still in the neighbourhood of Mitchelstown, and it is said that they intend to remain there till the O'Sullivan and Clifford case is finished. They were reported on the 8th instant to be in the Glencurrane area, but were resting and not preparing for any frightfulness. This probably accounts for the fact that the Glen, which is an ideal ambush position, was completely blocked with four stone walls and at least a dozen trees. They have also been located slightly further east in the foothills above Kilbehenney, and on the 11th, four camp fires and a look-out post recently vacated, were found half a mile south of Geeragh Bridge. Two cases of bicycle thefts have also occurred recently in this neighbourhood.

Waterford West Brigade

Patrick Whelan, late Commandant, was not wounded in the Dungarvan ambush, but is now away somewhere in the West of Ireland undergoing a course of intelligence work. The column has not been very active during the past week and is probably in the Comeragh Mountains north-east of Kilrossanty. Mansfield, Commandant, 3rd (Ardmore) Battalion, and six or eight more have been located in an empty house situated in a large wood 2½ miles north-east of Ardmore.

Waterford East Brigade

From reports received there is reason to believe that a column from outside the county has come into Waterford City within the last few days. There is, however, no confirmation except for some vague police reports of strangers. "F" Company (Ferrybank) Waterford City Battalion, mobilised on 10th at the Golf Club House, which is immediately above the goods yard and held up a goods train, while the Dunhill Company 2nd Battalion has been active trenching roads.

Wexford Brigade

An A.S.U. of the North Wexford Brigade has been active and is reported to be moving south. On 7/5/21 they ambushed a police patrol north-east of Gorey, on 10/5/21, a small attack was made on Enniscorthy Police Barracks, and on 11/5/21, a train was ambushed at Killurin. This column is thirty strong and is armed with rifles, shotguns and bombs. A second column, probably of the South Wexford Brigade is in the Campile area, and has so far confined its attention to raiding mails, cutting telegraph wires, etc.

Kilkenny Brigade

Neither the Callan nor the Castlecomer A.S.U.'s have been located definitely, though it is reported that the Castlecomer Column is in the Muckalee area; this is probably correct. Trains have been raided by armed men at Aylwardstown twice within a week but this is the work of local men.

I.R.A. Methods. (2)

(a) Road blocking

It is believed to be the early intention of the rebels in cases where trenches in roads have been filled up, to mine one of such trenches and then fill it up again. They thus hope to blow up military and police lorries passing unsuspectingly over the filled up trench.

The following form of blocking a road has just been reported in the N.R. Tipperary area :—

A single strand of barbed wire is placed across the road at such a height that it will catch the head of a cyclist. This is presumably intended to catch the point of a cyclist patrol operating by night.

(b) Arms and Ammunition

A dump of rebel munitions was discovered under a stable attached to a farm. There were five stables altogether, and each of them had about twelve inches of manure on the floor, which had apparently been there for many months. Each stable was cleaned out by the searching party, and about two tons of manure removed. Eventually, underneath some manure in one of the stables, was discovered some more or less loose earth. This was removed and about two feet below the surface a concrete slab about six feet by three feet with two iron rings was found. The slab was removed and a drop of seven feet was discovered. This was a chamber six feet long, seven feet high and three feet wide; the floor was concrete and the walls built of good quality red brick. There were also some clothing wrapped up in a newspaper, dated 18/3/21, thus proving that the dump had been entered into quite recently.

The rebels are, however, rather giving up the idea of arms dumps, as too many people are bound to know of their existence. Revolvers are now being kept entirely by individuals, and in towns, more attention must be paid to the walls of the back yard.

Whenever a man is seen to run away his track should be closely examined. It will nearly always be found that he has thrown something away.

Rebels in the Waterfall area are said to hide their arms in drain pipes, sunk in the ground upright.

(c) Communications

Every kind of communication is now used for notifying the rebels of the approach of the Crown forces. Post offices and railway telephones are made free use of. The column of smoke from chimneys is now a warning throughout County Cork.

The following method of carrying letters from inside a prison to the outside world has been discovered, and it is quite likely that despatch carriers use the same method. A cord is tied around the waist next to the skin and another tied from this cord between the legs and joining it at the back. The letters are tied to the cords.

Rebels finding that the cutting of the telephone wire has not proved particularly effective, as the wires are usually repaired a few hours after the cutting, have now commenced to saw down the telephone poles. This has been done extensively in this area.

(d) Miscellaneous

It would appear from a document captured in Dungarvan that there is a general order for the I.R.A. to equip themselves with bicycles.

Rebel flying columns are suffering heavily from scabies. In order to cure this disease men are returning to their homes and lying up there for a week or two. It is essential that these men be kept on the move by frequent visits to their homes, thus driving them back to the column.

Two men who raided the post office at Ballinspittle recently, wore Balmoral caps, and entered the post office disguised as Auxiliaries.

3. Anticipated I.R.A. Activities

The thefts of bicycles from all brigade areas, indicates a resumption of activity. This was borne out in and around Cork City, where theft of cycles and cars on Friday were followed by numerous murders on the following day. In some parts of the country, the destruction of roads makes the use of bicycles an absolute necessity, if retribution for murder is to be avoided.

In County Cork the comparative calm of the last few weeks was broken by Saturday's outbreak. No ambushes by flying columns took place, and it is probable that the men who carried out the murders are now in hiding. A period of comparative calm in this area may be anticipated.

Information has been received that the Marine Despatchment at Seafield, Quilty, is to be attacked, and that a hedge which is situated about 100 yards is to be used by the rebels to fire from.

The murder gang in West Clare have decided to assassinate Sergt. Monaghan, Constable O'Keefe and Kelly, R.I.C., Kilkee, for having arrested Michael Roche on 12/4/21.

Information from a fairly reliable source points to the likelihood of the rebels damaging the railway in Limerick County in the near future.

4. GENERAL
16th Infantry Brigade Area

Information from a new untested source in Dungarvan states that the I.R.A. have put a levy on the inhabitants of Dungarvan. Some people have been delivering notices and collecting money. The money is given grudgingly—the inhabitants are becoming very indignant about these collections and only give because they are still terrorised. This method of obtaining money is doing a lot of harm to the S.F. cause in the neighbourhood.

A big drive was carried out by Crown forces in the Kilmacthomas area on the 6th inst. The drive failed to round up the I.R.A. unit which has been operating in the area, yet there is no doubt that it will have a good effect in a part of the country where Crown forces are seldom seen. One old loyalist farmer made remarks to this effect, and said that such a parade of troops would make the hooligans going round the country look very small.

On one man who was arrested there was a printed notice demanding that everyone should subscribe to the I.R.A. funds. The notice contained the usual rebel propaganda, but wound up with the interesting information " that unless the money was forthcoming this area must be given up to the Army of a Foreign Nation."

The editor of the *Waterford Evening News* (a Sinn Féin Organ), has been interviewed during the past week, and a prolonged but friendly discussion ended in his agreeing to present to his readers a fairer and less biassed review of the Irish Situation.

The feeling against the I.R.A. in Enniscorthy, due to their road trenching operations, is steadily growing.

Enniscorthy have arranged a system of weekly conferences between military and police—further a police sergeant has been appointed to furnish a daily account of all intelligence and rumour that comes to the police during the past twenty-four hours.

The state of timidity, which has been such a salient feature in the civil population of Enniscorthy, with regard to its relationship to military is passing, and a bolder outlook is to be seen.

Kilkenny reports that the attitude of the population towards the Crown forces is, on the whole, friendly, especially to the troops, with whom the people often say they have no quarrel. The influx of a number of young English recruits to the R.I.C. who, though not by any means perfect in police work, are more disposed to mix with the civil population, is having a good effect—the R.I.C. are now regarded with more esteem.

A deputation, signed by a number of leading Callan citizens, has been received, asking that the ban on fairs and markets may be removed—this is signed by a number of S.F.'s, and shows the good effect of this proclamation.

An I.R.A. notice, found posted up in Windgap on 6/5/21, is attached as Appendix " B."

Mrs. Potter received on the 8th a parcel containing her husband's diary, will and ring. The diary was completed up to the time of his death, and in one place the D.I. wrote of his being locked in by an old man and woman and a young man. He also said these people were known to Mrs. Potter, which looks as if he had not been taken out of this area. At 11.00 hours, 27/4/21, he wrote of being warned that he was to be executed that same evening at 19.00 hours. Further wrote that his guardians were not at all anxious to kill him, but they had received orders from G.H.Q., I.R.A., which could not be disobeyed.

On 8th inst., a Protestant named Ross was chained to railings of Ballyhooley Church for several hours. This was done because it is stated that he knows who burnt Lord Listowel's house, and the man who did it wished to frighten him into keeping his mouth shut about it.

At Waterford, on the 10th inst., a goods train was held up in the goods yard at 2.00 hours. The driver and fireman were taken off the engine and placed in arrest in a shed. The train was then driven to a bridge about 1½ miles distant. Some barrels of oil, addressed to R.I.C., Kilkenny, were broken open and the oil spilt out, and some bacon for the military was thrown into the river. The train was then backed into the station. Subsequently, the military retrieved the bacon at low tide. Two bicycle shops in Henrietta Street were raided simultaneously by twenty or thirty men, said to be armed, and twenty-three new and second-hand bicycles stolen. A party which was sent out to Ballmacaw found three bicycles under suspicious circumstances and one arrest was made ; one bicycle was found dismantled and carefully wrapped up and hidden in a hedge.

(b) 17th Infantry Brigade Area

The Brigade Mobile Column returned on Thursday, 12th May, after a tour of a part of the brigade area. No armed body of rebels was encountered, but the local company at Aherla was rounded up almost to a man. Frank Hurley, Commandant No. 1 Battalion, No. 3 (West) Cork Brigade, and a prominent leader of the flying column was shot. It is hoped to obtain information as to whether the brigade column made any difference to rebel plans for attack on barracks, and caused them to be postponed.

During the period under review no thefts of any kind took place in the city. The leader of the railway robbery gang was arrested last week actually on his way to one of the stations. His name is Frank O'Sullivan, and he boasts that he took part in the murder of Finbar O'Sullivan and two others.

Several important arrests have been made during the week both by police and military. Men "on the run" from the city are in many cases working on farms at some distance. It is essential that no portion of the brigade area be allowed to become "quiet." It is in these "quiet" areas where the mischief brews.

Reliable information has been received that the rebels intend to attack Kinsale Police Barracks in the near future.

The Berrings Company is becoming active again. This tends to confirm the rumour that an ambush on the Macroom road may be expected shortly.

Parties of rebels are said to be concentrating in the Inchigealagh area again, and are reported to be in possession of two motor cars and to be plentifully supplied with ammunition.

Everything points to the fact that men "on the run" are short of clothes. In the recent cases of robberies of military stores, the boots and clothing were moved in bulk to a convenient shed where they were immediately split up into smaller parcels; and distributed by carts and by hand.

Road communication between Cork and Blarney is completely severed. A patrol of two Rolls Royce cars were able to reach Blarney from the north, but could only get back by driving along the permanent way of the Muskerry Railway.

Apparently reprisals are having the desired effect. The following conversation was overheard during the week: "We should be winning hands down if it wasn't for those reprisals, they are hitting us terribly hard."

(c) 18th Infantry Brigade

A man riding a motor-cycle, No. F.L. 149, was seen on the 5th instant, round the districts of Holycross and the Ragg, commandeering labour for the destruction of bridges and the trenching of roads.

Information has been received that during the week an important meeting of the I.R.A. Officers of high rank was held in the Cappamore district. It is reported that Michael Collins was present.

The people of Caher (south of Loughraney), who have been considerably inconvenienced by the cutting of the bridge there, had a free fight with the people of Killaneens (north of Loughraney), as the inhabitants of the former place accused them of cutting the roads and threatened to go up and cut Killeneena roads. Ballinroan also had the same grievance against the Killaneens people.

In County Limerick the large force of rebels reported last week at Kilteely has been kept on the move. On the afternoon of the 9th instant, they were reported near Bruree, and although large forces of military and R.I.C. converged on that area, they were unable to bring the rebels into an engagement. Finding that we were on their trail they commandeered all motors, bicycles, etc., which they could lay their hands on during the night of the 10th/11th instant, and so made out of that area.

(d) Kerry Brigade Area

The Crown forces have met with successes, both in North Cork and Kerry, the most notable achievement being that of a small patrol of Listowel police who encountered a gang of about eighty rebels and put them to flight after killing their leader and two others and wounding several more. This operation was doubly successful, in that the dead leader has been recognised as Jeremiah Lyons of Duagh, the Commander of the flying column which has been active in North-east Kerry for some time past. Two of the most dangerous rebels in the Liscarroll area have been captured, and at Killarney two men, who have been identified as having taken part in recent ambushes, have been arrested.

During a raid in the vicinity of Tournaboul, about 2½ miles east of Killarney, posters were found, posted on a wall, calling on the people of Ireland to pay their rates promptly to Dáil Éireann, and there were, also, posters forbidding emigration.

A loyal farmer, living near Buttevant, has been forced by the I.R.A. to take a man into his employment against his will.

Information was received by the D.I., Dingle, that an ambush was laid for him outside the town on the evening of the 5th instant. He went to attack it on the following morning but found that the position had been vacated.

It is reported that an ambush was prepared on the 5th instant, on the Castleisland-Abbeyfeale road, Pt. 810. Persons in the vicinity were compelled to remain indoors during the day and traffic was diverted until 18.00 hours, when the ambushers dispersed. The party consisted of about seventy men under the command of Jack Cronin and they were armed with one machine-gun, rifles and bombs.

Information has been received that the I.R.A. in the Brosna districts have a trench mortar, which they intend to use in an attack on the R.I.C. Barracks. This mortar is said to have been brought from Cork.

A round-up, on a large scale, was carried out round Turnaboul, three miles east of Killarney. Eighty-four men were collected and taken to Killarney for further examination. Two of them, Con Lynch and Jeremiah Foran, were recognised as having taken part in recent ambushes and were detained. The remainder were released after being warned about road cutting.

A number of S.F. posters were found on this raid.

On the 9th instant, at 13.30 hours, the typewriter of Mr. Ferguson, Solicitor, Kanturk, was stolen by two men in a very daring and open manner. They drove up to the house, which is next door to the R.I.C. Barracks, and one of them went to the room where the typist was working. He cut the speaking-tube communicating with Mr. Ferguson's office and calmly walked out with the typewriter, whereupon two men drove off in the direction of Mallow. In spite of an exhaustive and immediate search no trace of the trap or men could be found.

On the 9th instant, a party of troops from Tralee, proceeded to Farranfore to carry out punishments for the ambush of three constables. Three houses were destroyed. One officer proceeded to the house of Charles Daly, Knockansoculteens. Posts were placed round the farm and the house was then approached. As the officer entered the house, a man jumped out of the window and ran away. As he refused to halt when called upon to do so, he was fired at and badly wounded. He was found to be John Shanahan, chemist's assistant, son of a chemist in Castleisland. He was wearing a Sam Brown belt, cartridge pouch, and had a 380 revolver loaded with dum-dum ammunition. He had also in his possession a camera and some films, which were found to be those taken from the K.O.R.T. on the 23rd ultimo, when he was held up near Castleisland.

On the 11th instant, a cyclist and M.T. party from Kanturk visited Millstreet to carry out search at the Workhouse and Drishane Castle ; at the later place, hidden in a locked box in a bank were found two revolver holders, a list of all officers of the Millstreet Battalion, I.R.A. (see Appendix B), and other documents and training manuals. Nine wooden dummy rifles were also found in odd places in a quarry. Three men were detained, but owing to there being no female searchers present, the Castle buildings, now a French Convent, could not be searched. It is reported on good authority that rebels often billetted in the place, and it is more than probable in the convent. The Mother Superior is a French woman and harmless, but the Secretary, Sister Beatrice, is an out-and-out Sinn Féiner. The steward of the demense, Jerome McCarthy, is already interned. After finding the list of Millstreet I.R.A. Officers, a visit was paid to the R.I.C. Barracks in the town, but information was given that only two of the men mentioned were likely to be in the town. Of these it was found that Jerh. O'Connor was on his honeymoon, and C. D. Murphy had bolted from his house immediately he saw the M.T. party proceeding to the workhouse.

5. I.R.A. Personnel
(a) 16th Infantry Brigade Area
Broderick, the chemist, is certainly handling Dáil Éireann and prisoners' dependants monies in Fermoy. He took over the job from G. Power, senior.

Mrs. Sweeney (mother of Mick Sweeney, interned), has been receiving 30/- per week from the fund. Broderick made these paymants himself. He is also stated to be collecting money.

One of the Joyce family, a returned hunger-striker, is reliably reported to be staying at the house of a farmer called Burns or Byres, situated on the road between Moore Park and Quinlan Mills.

Pat Whelan, who was relieved of his command of the West Waterford Brigade, is now somewhere in the West of Ireland undergoing a course of intelligence work.

Bennett, railway porter at Mallow, referred to by Lynch in a captured document, as being a safe man for transmission of reports, etc., has gone on a week's leave commencing last Monday. He was reported in Fermoy on Tuesday but left the town in the evening. His whereabouts are not known.

The following are officers of " F " or Ferrybank Company, on the Waterford Battalion :

Michael Norris	... Liar Row.	Captain.
Patrick Carroll	... do.	Lieut.
Thomas Sullivan	... Upper Ferrybank.	Lieut.

They are " on the run."

Two men, William O'Donoghue, and James Kinsella, recently released from Kilworth have gone " on the run."

Robert Nugent of Kilcop was concerned in thefts of bicycles.

The following was discovered in McManna's house at County Kilkenny (Muckalee). A stranger came there for work on 27/4/21. He left them on the following Sunday giving no reason, before 8.00 hours. That was the day the Muskerry Wood ambushers got into position. He gave his name as Patrick Bouningham. Description— age about 50, height, 5 feet 9 inches, greyish hair and grey moustache, decently dressed. Believed to have been working with a farmer called Joe Kenny, Byrnegrove. It seems that this man was a rebel organiser sent specially to prepare the above ambush.

Three brothers, named Shone, living between Coon and Ridge, Co. Kilkenny, are reported to be dangerous rebels.

Mrs. Lucy, of Callan, is the leading local spirit of the Cumann na mBan.

Mrs. O'Gorman, of Burnescourt Castle, is high up in the ranks of the Cumann na mBan. Pat Walsh of Dunmamaggin, recently released after a term of imprisonment at Waterford, has gone on the run.

17th Infantry Brigade Area

John Linnehan is reported to be in command of No. 1 (Mid) Cork Brigade in the place of Seán Hegarty who is in Kanturk at present. This is not confirmed.

Frank McCarthy, 9 Eastview Terrace, Quaker Road, is on the brigade staff.

Tim O'Neill, the new brigade intelligence officer, is sleeping somewhere in the Curragh Road, Cork.

It is reported that all men " on the run " have been housed and fed
at the houses of the following at Dripsey :

    (a) Denis Battens of Knockane, 1 mile north of Dripsey Mill.

    (b) William Murphy of Acres, ½ mile north of Dripsey Mill.

    (c) John Kelleher of Meeshall House, 1 mile north-west of
    Dripsey Mill.

17th Brigade Area

The leading light in the shooting of Sergeant Malliffe and Constable
Ryan in Cork last January is said to be Patrick Murphy. He is to be
found in one of the houses near 25 Blarney Street, Cork, but not
actually at No. 25. He is the son of a Dripsey farmer, named Denis
Murphy, who lives near the National School of the Old Road, Dripsey.

John Crispie, of Cornishal (3 miles north-west of Leap), and
Timothy Donovan, of Foheragh (3 miles west-north-west of
Skibbereen), are reported to be active.

The following address was found written on the wall of a house in
Mount Pleasant, 5 miles north-west of Bandon. It is very likely a house
for men " on the run."

N. Wiseman, 6 Sunday's Well Road, Cork.

(c) 18th Brigade Area

Michael Brennan of Clare is, apparently, Commanding-in-Chief, I.R.A.
in the West. He calls himself Lieut-General of Flying Columns, and
states that it is his job to rouse the West and is confident of his ability
to do so.

The Madigans of Banmore, Moyasta, and Miss Irene Kennedy of
Lisdeen, Kilkee, Co. Clare, are in the habit of harbouring rebels.

Mich. Slattery of Newtown-Shandrum, is Captain of " B " Company,
4th Battalion, Cork Brigade.

Reliable information has been received that altogether fifteen
rebels were killed or died of wounds as the result of Lackally action.

In addition to those already reported killed, the following were
either killed or have since died of wounds :—

Michael Walsh	...	Captain of Spittal Company, 1st Galtee Battalion, died of wounds.
.........Ryan	...	Annagh, Newport, killed.
.........Purcell	...	Shrahane, do.
.........Dea or O'Dea	Pallas,	do.

Martin Deagan, Clonmore, Dovea, is a very active rebel. He is
reported to be in possession of a revolver and goes around that
district turning out trenching parties.

John Casey, Roarstown, Dovea, is a very active rebel. He is believed to have been promoted to commissioned rank in the 1st Battalion, Mid Tipperary Brigade, I.R.A.

Bridie Fitzpatrick, Liberty Square, Thurles, writes to all prisoners in Ordnance Barracks, Limerick, as soon as they arrive there.

John Coots of Spancel Hill, near Ennis, who was acquitted of carrying arms, etc., is an itinerant tailor and also a deserter from the M.G.G. His tailoring is only a cloak, in reality he is a machine-gun instructor to the Clare I.R.A.

John Naylon of Kilfenora, who is serving a sentence for taking rates from a rate collector by threats, was in charge of all the administrative side of the I.R.A., North Clare. If the prison authorities, where he now is, use their influence he might supply some very useful information, although he did not do so when arrested.

Kerry Brigade Area

John O'Connor on whom was found a paper giving the signals between the villages about Kiskeam (as reported in last week's Summary), has now confessed that it was given him about 26th April by Jer. Mullane of Ballybahallagh, near Freemount, to take to John Moylan at Kiskeam on the following Sunday (1st May), when the latter would be found near the cross to the east of the village about 8 p.m.

James O'Connor of Banteer, who was tried recently before a summary court for having a rebel despatch, stated that he used to find letters hidden under a stone in an old lime kiln which he visited twice a week.

Peter Collins, who was arrested during the round-up north of Meelin on the 5th instant, had, apparently, been left behind by the Newmarket Flying Column when they moved from this area before, as he was too drunk to go with them. Philip Curtain had also been left behind as he was ill, but he was not arrested. This man is a lieutenant in the Meelin Company.

The following is an extract from a letter addressed to Martin McGrath, I.R.A. organiser, after his arrest.

"I cannot give you details of my activities, but you know of old that I am ever on the same game."

The writer signs herself "Lena," and gives her address as Loreto Convent, Balbriggan.

Three of the men who took part in the shooting of H.C. Storey and Sgt. Butler at Castleisland, are believed to be Jack Cronin of Ballymacelligott, a man named Lane, and John McCarthy of Brohig. The first two were reported to be in Castleisland on the night of the 7th instant.

An informant, who recently returned from England, observed a man watching the passengers as they were leaving the boats at Rosslare.

He has since seen the man in Cork Station and on the platform at
Headford Junction, and on each occasion he appears to be keeping a
careful watch on the passengers. He has also been seen in Killarney,
and is described as—Tall, fair hair, slight moustache, of well-to-do
appearance.

James Brislane, Commandant of Charleville Battalion, is believed
to have gone to Clare, and one of the Clare leaders is reported to have
taken his place.

In the house of Rev. J. V. Brennan of Castleisland were found a
number of Dáil Éireann Trade Dept. notices. " Importation and
sale of British Goods. Prohibition Order No. 2," dated 14th April.
Also leaflets giving the Belfast Boycott " Blacklist."

6. CASUALTY REPORT

Date	Name	Place

Crown Forces   *Killed*

Date	Name	Place
8/5/21.	Head Constable Storey, R.I.C.	Castleisland.
6/5/21	1 Sergeant, R.I.C.	Newtown.
7/5/21	1 Constable, R.I.C.	Inch.
8/5/21	Constable Sterland	Cork City.
14/5/21	Constable Coughlan	,,
14/5/21	Constable Ryle	,,
14/5/21	Sergeant Coleman, R.I.C. ...	Midleton.
14/5/21	Constable Comyn	,,
14/5/21	Constable Thomas	,,
14/5/21	Private Hunter, K.O.S.B. ...	Berehaven.
14/5/21	Private Chambers, K.O.S.B.	,,
14/5/21	Private McMullen, K.O.S.B.	,,
14/5/21	Constable Briges, R.I.C. ...	Drumcollogher.
14/4/21	I.R.M.A. Gunners	East Ferry.
14/5/21	Constable Kenna, R.I.C. ...	Innishannon.
14/5/21	Major Biggs, D.I.	Newport.
14/4/21	Head Constable Benson, R.I.C.	Tralee.

Wounded

Date	Name	Place
8/5/21	Sergeant Butler, R.I.C. ...	Castleisland.
7/5/21	1 Sergeant, R.I.C.	Inch.
11/5/21	1 slightly wounded	Killurin.
14/5/21	Constable Hayes	Cork City.
	Constable Brookwell, R.I.C.	,,
14/5/21	Constable McDonald	Midleton.
14/5/21	Private Edwards, R.O.S. 3 ...	Berehaven.
14/5/21	1 Constable R.I.C.	Drumcollogher.

Rebel Forces	Killed			Circumstances
5/5/21	Daniel Killourhy	...		Died of wounds received when running away after being called upon to halt.
6/5/21	1 rebel	...	...	At Newtown Cross.
7/5/21	Frank Hurley	...	...	Comdt. No. 1 Battalion No.3 (West Cork) Brigade
11/5/21	An armed rebel (unidentified)			At Clondereen.
10/5/21	John Fox	...	...	At Ballinleenly, Co. Limerick while escorting a blindfolded ex-soldier.
12/5/51	J. Lyons and 2 rebels	...		Kilmorna.
14/5/21	3 rebels	...	...	Carrigtwohill.

Wounded

8/5/21	Pat Walsh	...	...	At Windgap near Dungarvan, refused to halt when challenged.
10/5/21	1 rebel	...	...	When escorting a blindfolded ex-soldier at Ballinleenly, Co. Limerick.
10/5/21	John O'Regan	...	...	Liscarroll.
10/5/21	John Shenahan	...	...	Farranfore.
12/5/21	Several rebels	...	...	At Kilmorna Ambush.
13/5/21	3 rebels	...	...	Drimoleague.
13/5/21	2 rebels	...	...	Tubrid.
14/5/21	4 rebels	...	...	Clonakilty.

7. MUNITIONS CAPTURED

Date	Place			Description
5/5/21	Knocktoosna	...	...	7 rounds, 303; 6 rounds, 450; 1 detonator.
6/5/21	Kilrush	...	...	D.B. gun.
9/5/21	Thomstown, Kilfinane	...		1 maxim gun, German; 1 spare feed block; 1 M.G. flash obscurer; 1 .22 rifle.
9/5/21	Thomastown, Kilfinane	...		3 D.B. guns; 2 bayonets; 1 sabre; 2 trench helmets; 2 mine exploders; large quantity telephone cabling and gelignite; blasting powder; dynamite, 4 short fuse firing; 8 spare cartridges; 30 rounds Mark VII.

Kerry Brigade Area

4 revolvers, 1 shot gun, 61 rounds 303 S.A.A., 28 rounds revolver ammunition, 1 set of leather equipment, 1 signalling telescope.

APPENDIX "A"

A Call to Action

The days of watchful waiting have passed. England is hanging prisoners of war. Shall we stand idly by?

Impatient to act; and mindful of our duty as liberty loving Americans we have organised the Boston Reprisals Commission. We have already placed pickets on the street protesting British atrocities in Ireland. Urging determination against English goods, and favouring home industry. Further we are investigating the mediums of British propaganda.

We have dug the trenches, will you join us in this work? We welcome your assistance.

Have you an auto?   Have you friends who would use their auto or auto-truck in the cause?

Will you picket?

Will you give us one hour of your time?

Can you give us reliable information concerning things of vital importance to Americans' welfare and Ireland's fight for freedom?

Call immediately, Ireland needs you.

Boston Reprisals Commission,
60 Pemberton Square, Room 308, Boston.

APPENDIX "B"

Irish Republican Army Warning

The public are warned not to close trenches, cut up trees, interfere with mines or any way undo the work of the I.R.A. You won't refuse if forced by the enemy. Spies, informers, talkers will be dealt with from this day forward. Women and girls must keep their telephone machines closed when in town and in other public places. Parents will be held responsible for the secrecy of their children when in school, Mass, etc. Look out shortly for a list of spies, informers, talkers in this district. Don't have *your* name on.

Signed,

Officer in charge.

Please tear off and return to:—

Headquarters,
    "I" Branch,
        6th Division.

Your G/18/89/1/2 (Weekly Intelligence Summary) Dated 17/5/21 has been received.

Office No. ....   Signature ....

Copy No. ....   Unit of Formation...................

WEEKLY INTELLIGENCE SUMMARY—6th DIVISION

Distribution List.   Week ending...................

Copy Unit or Formation	Address	Acknowledgment No.	Date
1. General Headquarters	Dublin	....	
2. General Headquarters	Dublin	....	
3. General Headquarters	Dublin	....	
4. 5th Division	Curragh	....	
5. Chief of Police	Dublin Castle	....	
6. Dublin District	Dublin Castle	....	
7. Admiral Commander-in-Chief	Queenstown	....	
8. General Staff, 6th Division	Cork	....	
9. Q.M.G., 6th Division	Cork	....	
10. A.A.G., 6th Division	Cork	....	
11. Law Officer, 6th Division	Cork	....	
12. Senior Divisional Commissioner	Cork	....	
13. Division Commissioner	Cork	....	
14. O.C. 33 Fortress Company R.E.	Cork	....	
15. Division Commissioner	Clonmel	....	
16. 16th Infantry Brigade	Fermoy	....	
17. " A " Company, Auxiliary Division	Innistoge, Kilkenny	....	
18. 1st Brigade, R.F.A.	Kilkenny	....	
19. 2nd Brigade, R.F.A.	Fermoy	....	
20. 31st Brigade, R.F.A.	Cahir	....	
21. 7th Brigade, R.F.A.	Moors Park	....	
22. 1st Battalion The Buffs	Fermoy	....	
23. 1st Battalion Lincolnshire Regt.	Tipperary	....	
24. 25. 1st Battalion Devonshire Regt.	Waterford	....	
26. O.C. Troops	Clonmel	....	
27. 2nd Battalion, The Green Howards	Tipperary	....	
28. 1st Battalion, West Surry Regt.	Kilworth	....	
29. 17th Infantry Brigade	Cork	....	
30. 31st Fire Command	Bere Island	....	
31. C.R.A., 6th Division	Cork	....	
32. 32nd Fire Command	Queenstown	....	
33. 1st Battalion, The King's	Bantry	....	
34. 2nd King's Own Scot. Borderers	Bere Island	....	

Copy	Unit or Formation		Acknowledgment No. Date

35.	2nd Battalion, The Hampshire Regt.	Cork	....
36.	2nd Battalion, S. Stafford Regt.	Cork	....
37.	1st Battalion, Essex Regt.	Kinsale	....
38.	1st Manchester Regt.	Ballincollig	....
39.	2nd Battalion, Queen's Own Cam. Highlanders	Queenstown	....
40.	" J " Company, Auxiliary Division	Macroom	....
41.	" L " Company, Auxiliary Division	Millstreet	....
42.	" O " Company, Auxiliary Division	Dunmanway	....
43.	18th Infantry Brigade	Limerick	....
43.	2nd Royal Scots	Ennis	....
44.	1st Battalion, Royal Warwick Regt.	Newcastle W.	....
45.	2nd Royal Welsh Fusiliers	Limerick	....
46.	Ox and Bucks Light Infantry	Limerick	....
47.	1st Battalion, North Hants. Regt.	Templemore	....
48.	2nd Royal Welsh Fusiliers	Limerick	....
49.	1st Battalion, M.G.C.	Ballyvonaire	....
50.	" G " Company, Auxiliary Division	Killaloe	....
51.	Kerry Brigade	Buttervant	....
52.	1st Battalion, Royal Fusiliers	Killarney	....
53.	2nd Battalion, East Lancs. Regt.	Buttervant	....
54.	2nd Battalion, Royal Regiment	Tralee	....
55.	1st Battalion, Gloucestershire Regt.	Kanturk	....
56.	Cork City Intelligence	Cork	....
57.	Documents Officer, 6th Division	Cork	....
58.	O.C. 136 Battery, R.F.A.	Fethard	....
59.	1st Essex	Bandon	....
60.	" B " Company, Auxiliary Division R.I.C.	Templemore	....
61. 62.	Divisional Commissioner	Limerick	....

APPENDIX 2

The Divisional Idea

It is necessary for divisional staffs to obtain a quite clear understanding of the principle involved in the formation of divisional areas. This step marks a very definite advance in our development, and is only being taken by G.H.Q. in proportion as areas become fit for it. For one thing, it will make things very much simpler for G.H.Q. by reason of diminishing the number of units coming directly in contact with G.H.Q. This will enable far more attention to be given to the main problems of each individual area and of a much closer co-operation being carried out between the several divisional areas.

The machinery of administration will be greatly simplified, and there should be a very pronounced increase in speed and efficiency of working.

At the same time the divisional staffs will have their authority greatly increased. They will now have to decide many matters which formerly were always referred to G.H.Q. If this is not done there is nothing gained by the new arrangement. A study of G.H.Q. Orders and Regulations and Memoranda will enable divisional staffs to form a fairly accurate idea of what is expected of them.

One thing we must lay down emphatically—the divisional commandant must rise to his new position. He must not try to run his division as he used to run his brigade. If he does chaos will result. A good brigadier—and only a good one—can keep in close touch with four or five battalions : when the number reaches as high as fourteen or fifteen or more, no officer can possibly accomplish the direct personal control of them. To decentralise command, to encourage readiness to assume responsibility, to form a machinery suitable for staff work—these are the ways in which a divisional staff can best contribute to the general efficiency of the Army. If a divisional commandant is constantly worrying whether such-and-such a brigadier is doing this or that he will lose his sense of proportion. He will neglect his own proper sphere of activity which is co-ordination ; and he will also undermine the self-reliance of his brigadiers—because if he is always spoonfeeding them they will expect it, and some day when he is not near them they will fail lamentably.

To put it another way G.H.Q. freely entrusts the divisional commandant with a grave and solemn responsibility—nothing less than the absolute military control of two or three counties. Let him, in turn, similarly trust his brigadiers ; if he shows that he considers them equal to their positions it is long odds that they will rise to the occasion. If the brigadiers are suitable and reliable all is well ; if they are not, away with them and replace them by men who are equal to the positions.

The divisional staff should be a body of officers working together like a team, animated by the imperturbable offensive spirit, with a complete knowledge of the divisional area, with a sound military education, and a comprehensive grasp of our present military problems and the war as a whole. Better have the staff only half filled then employ mediocrities.

Divisional administration calls for suitable machinery—a divisional headquarters and a despatch system. The divisional headquarters should be a district comprising as many as possible of the following requirements : (a) central position, (b) resources of various kinds, (c) thoroughly friendly population, (d) natural defensive strength. In this area there should always be one or two members of the divisional staff : it would be a mistake for all the staff to be away from it at the same time. On the other hand two or three of the staff should be always on the move through the divisional area, for only in that way can proper touch with brigades be always maintained. Divisional rounds of inspection and administrative terms at divisional H.Q. should be so arranged that every member of the staff would be frequently on tour, and yet frequently at H.Q.

Communications between divisional headquarters and the several brigades should be established on a clock-work basis. Speed and certainty should be aimed at in this matter at all costs. Thoroughly reliable communications should also exist with adjoining divisions and with G.H.Q. Unless communications are properly established and controlled, the divisional staff is not in a position to carry out its work at all. Communications and despatches are the channels through which the lower grades are reached. Without this the staff is only a head without body or limbs. Hence in even the worst areas of the division, efficient communications must reach.

APPENDIX 3

Irish Republican Army,
General Headquarters,
Dublin.

22nd June, 1921.

GENERAL ORDER

Reprisals

1. Brigade commandants are authorised to answer reprisals against property on the part of the enemy in the following way :—(where a division has been formed brigade commandants will require to receive formal delegation of authority from their divisional commandants).

2. On every occasion on which the enemy destroys house property, or house contents, whether alleging military necessity or not, the following counter reprisals may be taken :—

A. A similar number of houses belonging to the most active enemies of Ireland may be destroyed in the battalion area in which the original destruction takes place.

B. An equal number of houses belonging to the most active enemies of Ireland, may, in addition, be destroyed at that point in the brigade area concerned which may be considered as the centre most strongly occupied by such enemies.

C. The case should be reported to G.H.Q. with a covering statement of what has been done ; and with a view to possible further action.

D. Where the enemy persists in taking counter-reprisals, they may be answered in the same way ; stopping only when the district concerned has been entirely cleared of active enemies of Ireland.

3.   Formal notice shall be served on any person whose house is so destroyed stating clearly that it is a reprisal because of similar destruction carried out by their military forces ; and specifying the particular property for whose destruction it is a reprisal.

4.   In any particular case, or in any particular district in which, in addition to such reprisals it would seem desirable that :—

(*a*) The members of any particular family concerned should be ordered out of the country ; or

(*b*) Have their lands confiscated ;

(*c*) A special report should be submitted.

5.   *For the purpose of such reprisals no persons shall be regarded as enemies of Ireland, whether they may be described locally as Unionist, Orangemen, etc., unless they are actively anti-Irish in their actions.*

6.   No house shall be selected for destruction or destroyed without the personal approval and permission of the brigade commandant.

By Order,
ADJUTANT GENERAL.

APPENDIX 4

To O.C.,   12th May, 1922.
Cork No. 1

A Chara,

The evacuation of the Cork Barracks (Ballincollig, Victoria and Youghal) is desired at the earliest possible moment, and as explained verbally, with a view to this we would be glad to have them handed over for occupation by members of the Cork No. 1 Brigade. I give below an outline of certain understandings that it would be necessary for us to have between G.H.Q. staff and the brigade.

1. That the officers and men of the brigade would undertake to maintain public order.

2. That in the event of a contested election being found necessary in order to secure the terms of the Treaty, they will endeavour, as far as they possibly can, to ensure its being carried out uninterrupted.

3. That after such an election they approach the question of Army unification and control, in the spirit of the document already prepared and generally agreed to by the group of ten.

4. The policing of the area, including the city, to be arranged— the numbers necessary for the work to be agreed with the Chief of Staff. The Government to provide payment at the regular Volunteer maintenance rates for men engaged on this work.

5. Satisfactory fusion of the men who have come over to G.H.Q. within the last three or four months. Difficulties to be got over in a generous spirit and disciplinary matters made bygones.

6. General routine requirements of the G.H.Q. staff should be attended to in the matter of routine orders, expenditure, accounts.
7. A statement of brigade debts to be submitted to the Quartermaster General in the manner required by him, with a view to having the question of payment considered (pre-split debts and post-split debts to be kept separately).
8. The spirit of antagonism to the Civic Guard to be faced (1) with a view to its being overcome by proper understanding, and (2) releasing whatever good material is available in the area for enlistment.

Generally, I am satisfied as a result of our various talks here that all that is wanted is an agreement to work harmoniously and unsuspiciously, and to face any difficulties and suspicions that arise, calmly and in some kind of a detached way.
9. G.H.Q. will be responsible for the equipment and rationing of barrack garrisons to an agreed No.

Beir Beannacht,
AIRE CHOSANTA.

APPENDIX 5

ARMY STRENGTHS AT JULY, 1921.

1st Northern Division	5,000
2nd Northern Division	2,800
3rd Northern Division	1,200
4th Northern Division	2,300
5th Northern Division	2,200
1st Eastern Division	3,700
2nd Eastern Division	5,100
3rd Eastern Division	3,100
Midland Division	6,600
1st Southern Division	33,550
2nd Southern Division	12,500
3rd Southern Division	6,000
1st Western Division	8,500
2nd Western Division	4,000
3rd Western Division	7,700
4th Western Division	8,400
	112,650

For convenience figures are given for divisional areas as planned. Only a few had been formed before the Truce, and the 2nd Eastern (Dublin and South County Dublin Brigades) did not in fact function as a division at any time.

APPENDIX 6

DELEGATES TO ARMY CONVENTION, 26TH MARCH, 1922

1st Southern Division – – – – –	54
2nd Southern Division – – – – –	28
3rd Southern Division – – – – –	10
1st Western Division – – – – –	13
2nd Western Division – – – – –	18
3rd Western Division – – – – –	18
4th Western Division – – – – –	20
1st Northern Division – – – – –	5
2nd Northern Division – – – – –	2
3rd Northern Division – – – – –	3
4th Northern Division – – – – –	2
1st Midland Division – – – – –	2
1st Eastern Division – – – – –	1
Dublin Brigade – – – – – –	8
South Dublin Brigade – – – –	6
Carlow Brigade – – – – – –	2
North Wexford Brigade – – – –	4
South Wexford Brigade – – – – –	5
England – – – – – – –	6
Scotland – – – – – – –	2
Unidentified – – – – – – –	2
	211

Four G.H.Q. officers and eight divisional commandants were ex-officio delegates   –   –   **12**

223

These figures are from a note made by the author during the roll
call at the opening of the convention.

APPENDIX 7

OGLAIGH NA H-EIREANN

General Headquarters,
Dublin.
28th March, 1922.

To All O/C's.

1. You will hold battalion mobilisations on Sunday next, 2nd
April. All officers and men will parade with arms and full equipment.
2. The attached statement which gives the present and recent

situation of the Army and the following resolution passed at the convention will be read on parade :—

    (*a*) " That the Army re-affirm its allegiance to the Irish Republic."

    (*b*) " That it shall be maintained as the Army of the Irish Republic, under an executive appointed by the convention.

    (*c*) " That the Army shall be under the supreme control of such executive which shall draft a constitution for submission to a subsequent convention to be held on the 9th of April."

3. Allegiance shall be re-affirmed to the Republic by the officer in command on behalf of battalion.

By Order,
ARMY COUNCIL.

OGLAIGH NA H-EIREANN

General Headquarters,
Dublin.

(For Transmission to all Ranks).

IRISH REPUBLICAN ARMY CONVENTION

1. It is due to the Army that all ranks should be informed of the position arising out of the approval by Dáil Éireann of the articles of Agreement for a Treaty between Ireland and England, and the justification for calling an Army Convention in Dublin on 26th March, 1922.

The Irish Volunteers by their sacrifices, established the Irish Republic and maintained its Government in power.

2. When the Dáil was formally established the Irish Volunteers were asked to come under its control. This was agreed to, although they were not formally called together to agree.

An oath of allegiance was taken by all ranks of the Army to the Irish Republic and to the Dáil. When the majority of the Dáil (word illegible) carrying into effect of the Treaty meant the disestablishment of the Republic. Consequently four Republican members of General Headquarters Staff, six divisional commandants and two brigade commandants of independent brigades, representing practically all Munster and Connaught, and a large portion of Leinster, requested a convention of the Army. These officers represent, at a low estimate, 75 per cent. of the Army. The object of the convention was to consider the following resolutions :

" That the Army re-affirms its allegiance to the Irish Republic.

" That it shall be maintained as the Army of the Irish Republic under an Executive appointed by the Convention.

" That the Army shall be under the supreme control of such Executive, which shall draft a constitution for submission to a subsequent Convention."

The Minister for Defence refused to call a convention by which the Army would be able freely to express its wishes. In place of a convention, he called a meeting of General H.Q. Staff, and all divisional commandants and commandants of independent brigades. This meeting was held on 18th January, 1922. The Republican officers put forward their reasons for demanding a convention as follows :—

(1) That they had taken an oath " to support and defend the Irish Republic against all enemies foreign and domestic."

(2) That the Dáil, having no moral right to abandon the Republic and having done so, forfeited the allegiance which the Army had given it.

(3) That the Army would not dishonour itself by violating its oath.

(4) That the public undertaking given by the Minister for Defence that he would maintain the Army as the Army of the Irish Republic had not been kept.

(5) That a convention was the only means of establishing unity in the Army.

4. The outcome of this meeting was an Agreement in writing in which the Minister for Defence agreed to call a convention on the 18th March, 1922. It was made quite clear to him that the Republican officers were indifferent as to whether the Dáil agreed to the convention or not. The fact stands out that the Minister for Defence agreed to call the convention.

Particular attention is called to the fact that at this meeting every divisional and brigade commandant agreed that a convention should be held.

Orders were sent out to the Army by G.H.Q. on the authority of the Minister for Defence to make arrangement for the convention. This had been sanctioned by the Dáil Cabinet, but at a subsequent meeting of that Cabinet held on the 15th March, when the Minister for Defence was present, the Cabinet unanimously decided that the convention could not be held : That it was illegal—nothwithstanding that an Agreement existed between the Minister for Defence and the Army.

It is clear that the agreement was deliberately violated and that the intention was, and is, to gain time to establish a paid, uniformed, and equipped force to be the nucleus of a Free State Army whose duty would be to aid in the disestablishment of the Irish Republic.

6. It is only by means of a convention that unity can be established in the Army, general discipline restored, and the present danger of civil war averted. Owing to the resentment caused in the Army by Mr. Griffith's proclamation, the holding of a convention became in the public interest, not less, but more necessary.

7. There is no analogy between the demand made by the Irish Army for a convention and such a demand if made by the Armies of other countries. The Irish Army is a Volunteer Army with full citizen rights and the duty of exercising these rights. Their opposition to the Treaty is not a matter of interference in politics, but a fulfilment of the object for which they voluntarily banded themselves together, surrendered their personal liberty, and offered their lives. This object, to which they bound themselves by oath was to maintain the Republic proclaimed and established in 1916 and solemnly ratified by the National Government on 21st January, 1919.

By Order,
EXECUTIVE OF IRISH REPUBLICAN ARMY.

APPENDIX 8

Oglaig na hEireann

Draft Constitution and Rules

1. The Army shall be known as the Irish Republican Army.
2. It shall be on a purely Volunteer Army basis.
3. Its objects shall be :—

   (*a*) To guard the honour and maintain the independence of the Irish Republic.

   (*b*) To protect the rights and liberties common to the people of Ireland.

   (*c*) To place its services at the disposal of an established Republican Government which faithfully upholds the above objects.

CONTROL OF THE ARMY

4. The Army shall be controlled by an executive of sixteen, which shall be appointed by a committee of twenty-five, selected as follows :—

   Each province elects five delegates.

   Each province nominates five further delegates from whom the whole convention will elect the remaining five. Any serving Volunteer to be eligible to act on the executive. This executive shall have supreme control of the Army, and the executive shall not itself, directly or indirectly, be subordinate to, or be controlled by any other body : Subject to any alterations necessary to put into operation section 3 (Sub-section (*c*) above. Such proposed alterations to be sanctioned by a general convention.

DUTIES AND POWERS OF EXECUTIVE

5. The duties of the executive shall be to define policy for the Army. It shall have supreme control over the Army Council and General Headquarters Staff. It shall not, however, have power to interfere with General Headquarters Staff in respect of purely Army matters, such as organisation, training, method of conducting operations, etc. Ten shall form a quorum at meetings of the executive.

FINANCIAL POWERS

6. The executive shall be responsible for and safeguarding of funds for Army purposes.

EXECUTIVE MEETINGS

7. The executive shall meet at least every two months. In the event of a vacancy occurring on the executive it shall be filled by co-option.

ARMY COUNCIL

8. The executive shall appoint an Army Council of seven, of which four shall be chosen from the members of the executive, and the remaining three may be appointed from outside the executive. Four shall form a quorum at meetings of the Army Council. In the event of a vacancy occurring on the council, it shall be filled by co-option to be approved by the executive.

GENERAL HEADQUARTERS STAFF

9. The executive shall appoint a Chief of Staff, who will appoint his staff.

GENERAL CONVENTION

10. A general convention representative of the whole Army shall meet at least once in each twelve months, and shall elect a committee to appoint an executive as in Section 4, who shall hold office until the next general convention. It shall also receive a report from the Chief of Staff, and a financial statement from the executive.

SYSTEM OF REPRESENTATION

11. The system of representation shall be as follows :—

At a company parade called for the purpose, one delegate shall be elected to attend a brigade convention where the number of men on parade does not exceed thirty men ; two delegates where the number on parade is over thirty and under seventy-one ; three delegates where the number on parade exceeds seventy men ; and an additional delegate for every thirty men over one hundred.

The election shall be by ballot.

Brigade Convention

12. The constitution of the brigade convention shall be as follows :—

> (*a*) The brigade commandant and two members of his staff as elected by the staff.
>
> (*b*) Each battalion commandant and one member of his staff elected by the staff.
>
> (*c*) The company delegates as elected in accordance with the instructions detailed above.

The staff in this connection shall be taken as including the officers commanding special services.

13. The brigade convention shall elect delegates to represent the brigade at the general convention. The number of delegates to be so elected shall be 5 per cent. of the total number of delegates present at the brigade convention. In the event of such percentage resulting in a whole number and a fraction, the nearest whole number will be the number of delegates. The individual delegates so chosen need not necessarily be selected from those present at the convention, but must be active members of the brigade or of the staff of the division to which the brigade is attached.

General Convention

14. The constitution of the general convention shall be as follows :—

> (*a*) All members of the executive.
>
> (*b*) All members of the Army Council.
>
> (*c*) All members of the General Headquarters Staff.
>
> (*d*) All divisional commandants, and two other members of the divisional staff as elected by that staff.
>
> (*e*) The delegates selected at the brigade convention.

Voting at Convention

15. Voting on motions shall be carried out as decided by the chairman of the convention.

16. The chairman of the general convention shall be chosen by the convention.

Quorum

17. The number to form a quorum at a general convention shall be two-thirds of the total number of delegates entitled to attend.

EXTRAORDINARY CONVENTION

18.   An extraordinary convention shall be called if required.

(a) By a two-thirds majority of the executive.
(b) By a two-thirds majority of G.H.Q.
(c) By a two-thirds majority of the divisional commandants, provided they represent two-thirds of the total strength of the whole Army.

MEMBERSHIP OF ARMY

19.   Only such persons shall be allowed to remain in, or shall be admitted to the Army who take the oath of allegiance to the Irish Republic. No person holding any rank in any other Army shall be enrolled in the Irish Republican Army.

20.   The oath of allegiance to be taken by every member of the Army shall be as follows :—

I, ..., do solemnly swear that to the best of my knowledge and ability I will support and defend the Irish Republic against all enemies foreign and domestic that I will bear true faith and allegiance to the same. I do further swear that I do not, and shall not, yield a voluntary support to any pretended government, authority, or power within Ireland hostile or inimical to that Republic. I take this obligation freely without any mental reservation or purpose of evasion so help me God.

AMENDING OF CONSTITUTION

21.   It shall require a majority of two-thirds of the general convention to amend any article of the constitution.

APPENDIX 9

FELLOW CITIZENS OF THE IRISH REPUBLIC

The fateful hour has come. At the dictation of our hereditary enemy our rightful cause is being treacherously assailed by recreant Irishmen. The crash of arms and the boom of artillery reverberate in this supreme test of the Nation's destiny.

Gallant soldiers of the Irish Republic stand vigorously firm in its defence and worthily uphold their noblest traditions. The sacred spirits of the Illustrious Dead are with us in this great struggle. "Death before Dishonour" being an unchanging principle of our national faith as it was of theirs, still inspires us to emulate their glorious effort.

We, therefore, appeal to all citizens who have withstood unflinchingly the oppression of the enemy during the past six years to rally to the support of the Republic and recognise that the resistance now being offered is but the continuance of the struggle that was suspended by the truce with the British. We especially appeal to our former comrades of the Irish Republic to return to that allegiance and thus guard the Nation's honour from the infamous stigma that her sons aided her foes in retaining a hateful domination over her.

Confident of victory and of maintaining Ireland's independence, this appeal is issued by the Army Executive on behalf of the Irish Republican Army.

Commandant General Liam Mellows.
Commandant General Rory O'Connor.
Commandant General Joseph McKelvey.
Commandant General Earnan O'Maille.
Commandant General Seamus Robinson.
Commandant General Seán Moylan.
Commandant General Michael Kilroy.
Commandant General Frank Barrett.
Commandant General Thomas Derrig.
Commandant T. Barry.
Colonel Commandant F. O Faolain (Pax Whelan).
Brigadier General J. O'Connor.
General Liam Lynch.
Commandant General Liam Deasy.
Colonel Commandant Peadar O'Donnell.
P. Ruttledge.

APPENDIX 10

I.R.A. PROCLAMATION

(English Translation)

Last December certain representatives of the nation, yielded to English threats of war, violated their pledge and their oaths and entered into an agreement subversive of the independence of the nation and destructive of its territorial integrity.

Since that time these representatives and their adherents have been engaged in corrupting and seducing soldiers and citizens of the Republic from their allegiance, and, in violation of the constitution of a special decree of Dáil Éireann and of their own express undertakings to maintain the Republic, have suppressed the legitimate Parliament and judiciary, usurped the Government of the State, and now, by the instigation of the English and with English aid, are endeavouring traitorously to destroy the Republic by force of arms, waging illegal war upon it and proclaiming death, exile, or imprisonment to all its faithful citizens, though they are aware, as everyone in

Ireland is aware, that the people desire the continuance of the Republic and that given a free choice they would vote for it in an overwhelming majority.

In these circumstances, in order to preserve the continuity of the independent Irish Government and the better to organise the forces of the Republic in its defence, we, on behalf of the soldiers of the Republic, acting in the spirit of our oath as the final custodians of the Republic, and interpreting the desire of all true citizens of the Republic have called upon the former President, EAMON DE VALERA and the faithful members of Dáil Éireann, to form a Government, which they have done.

Accordingly, in the name of the Army, we hereby proclaim EAMON DE VALERA to be PRESIDENT OF THE REPUBLIC, with Austin Stack, T.D., Seán O'Mahony, T.D., Robert Barton, T.D., Mrs. O'Callaghan, T.D. Count Plunkett, T.D., Mary MacSwiney, T.D., J. J. O'Kelly, T.D., P. J. Ruttledge, T.D., Laurence Ginnell, T.D., Seán Moylan, T.D., Seán T. O'Kelly, T.D., M. P. Colivet, T.D. as COUNCIL OF STATE, and declare such Cabinet as they shall appoint to be temporarily the Supreme Executive of the Republic and the State, until such time as the elected Parliament of the Republic can freely assemble, or the people being rid of external aggression are at liberty to decide freely how they are to be governed and what shall be their political relations with other countries.

On behalf of the Army, we pledge to that executive our allegiance and our support in all its legitimate efforts to maintain and defend the Republic, and we call upon all our comrades and loyal fellow-citizens and upon our kin throughout the world, to join with us in reasserting our ancient right to be a free people and a free nation, owning allegiance to no foreign authority whatever.

Signed on behalf of the Army of the Republic.

Liam Lynch, Chief of Staff.
Liam Deasy, Deputy Chief of Staff.
E. O'Maille, Assistant Chief of Staff.
Con Moloney, Adjutant General.
Tom Derrig, Assistant Adjutant General.
Seán Lehane, O.C., 1st and 2nd Northern Divisions.
Frank Aiken, O.C. 4th Northern Division.
Frank Barrett, O.C. 1st Western Division.
Seamus Robinson, O.C. 2nd Southern Division.
Tom Barry, Operations Staff.
Seán Moylan, O.C. Cork No. 3 Brigade.
P. Whelan, O.C. Waterford Brigade.
Joe O'Connor, O.C. 3rd Battalion, Dublin 1st Brigade.

ARMY EXECUTIVE.

28th October, 1922.

Note 1

The Special Decree of Dáil Éireann referred to in the Proclamation is the following Decree of 20th May, 1922. It was proposed by President Griffith, seconded by Eamon de Valera, signed and supported by Michael Collins and made law without one dissentient voice in the Parliament of the nation. It was endorsed unanimously by the Ard Fheis of Sinn Féin at which delegates from all parts of Ireland were present.

We Are Agreed :—

1. That a national Coalition Panel for this Third Dáil representing both parties in the Dáil, and in the Sinn Féin organisation, be sent forward on the ground that the national position requires the entrusting of the Government of the country into the joint hands of those who have been the strength of the national situation during the last few years, without prejudice to their respective positions.

2. That this Coalition Panel be sent forward as from the Sinn Féin organisation, the number from each party being their present strength in the Dáil.

3. That the candidates be nominated through each of the existing party executives.

4. That every and any interest is free to go up and contest the election equally with the national Sinn Féin Panel.

5. That constituencies where an election is not held shall continue to be represented by their present deputies.

6. That after the election the executive shall consist of the President, elected as formerly, the Minister of Defence, representing the Army, and nine other Ministers, five from the majority party and four from the minority party, each party to choose its own nominees. The allocation will be in the hands of the President.

7. That in the event of the Coalition Government finding it necessary to dissolve, a general election will be held as soon as possible on adult suffrage.

(Signed) EAMON DE VALERA,
MICHAEL O'COILEAN.

20th May, 1922.

Note 2

The express undertakings referred to in the Proclamation are as follows. They were given on 10th January, 1922, in Dáil Éireann after the vote on the Treaty had been taken.

MR. GRIFFITH—The Republic of Ireland remains in being until the Free State comes into being. . . . Whatever position the President occupied, if I am elected I will occupy the same until the people have an opportunity of deciding for themselves. . . . If I am elected I will keep the Republic in being until after the Free State is established when the people can decide for and against. . . . I want the Republic kept in being until the people can have a free election and give their votes.

MR. MULCAHY, MINISTER FOR DEFENCE.—The Army will remain occupying the same position to this Government of the Republic and occupying the same position as regards the Minister for Defence and under the same management and in the same spirit as up to the present. . . . The Army will continue to remain the Army of the Irish Republic.

APPENDIX 11

CORK NO. 2 BRIGADE AND FIRST SOUTHERN DIVISION HEADQUARTERS

1919–20.	Tadgh Looney's,	Burnfort, Mourneabbey.
	Mrs. Mullane's,	Monaparson, Mourneabbey.
1920–21.	Myles McCarthy's,	Creggane, Lombardstown.
	Michael Hallinan's,	Brittas, Lombardstown.
	Jerh. Roche's,	Gortmore, Lombardstown.
	Jerh. Sheehan's,	Mount Hilary, Lombardstown.
	Patrick McCarthy's,	Nadd.
	Eugene Dilworth,	Mohereen.
1921.	Jerh. J. Hallinan's,	Kilcorney, Millstreet.
	Eamonn McSweeney's,	Gortyrahilly, Coolea.
	Patrick O'Sullivan's,	Mortonville, Lombardstown.
	Patrick Murphy's,	Laharn, Lombardstown.
	J. G. Linehan's,	Pallas, Lombardstown.
	Mallow Barracks.	

APPENDIX 12

BRIGADE AND BATTALION STAFFS, CORK NO. 2 AND CORK NO. 4 BRIGADES, 1919–1921

Cork No. 2 Brigade
Brigade Staff, 1919

Liam Lynch	O/C.
Daniel Hegarty	Vice O/C.
George Power	Adjutant and Intelligence.
Thomas Barry	Quartermaster (later appointed O/C, Castletownroche Battalion).

1920

Liam Lynch	O/C.
George Power	Vice O/C.
Patrick Clancy	Deputy Vice O/C,

Maurice Twomey	...	Adjutant and Intelligence.
Jeremiah Buckley	...	Quartermaster, succeeded after his capture by
Patrick O'Brien	...	
Dr. Michael Molan	...	Medical Officer.
Patrick Coughlan	...	Engineer.
Charles O'Connor	...	Assistant Engineer.
Patrick Healy ...	...	Police.

1921

Seán Moylan ...	...	O/C (succeeded L. Lynch when he became Divisional O/C).
George Power ...	...	O/C (succeeded Seán Moylan, captured).
Patrick O'Brien ...	...	Vice O/C.
Daniel Shinnick	...	Adjutant (succeeded M. Twomey, captured).
Maurice Walsh ...	...	Assistant Adjutant.
Ed. Murphy ...	...	Quartermaster.
Michael O'Connell	...	Assistant Quartermaster.
Dr. Michael Molan	...	Medical Officer.
Patrick Coughlan	...	Engineer.
Charles O'Connor	...	Assistant Engineer.
Patrick Healy ...	...	Police.

Cork No. 4 Brigade

(Formed, July, 1921, on division of original Cork No. 2 Brigade)

1921

Patrick O'Brien ...	...	O/C.
Edward Murphy	...	Vice O/C.
Eugene McCarthy	...	Adjutant.
Michael O'Connell	...	Quartermaster.
Tadgh Byrne ...	...	Intelligence.
Charles O'Connor	...	Engineering.
John Barrett ...	...	Communications.
Seán Breen ...	...	Training.
Con Moylan ...	...	Transport.
Patrick Healy	...	Police.

Fermoy Battalion

1919

Martin O'Keeffe	...	O/C (until June, 1919).
Michael Fitzgerald	...	O/C (died on hunger-strike, 1920).
Laurence Condon	...	Vice O/C.
Maurice Twomey	...	Adjustant.
Thomas Griffin	...	Quartermaster.
Patrick Aherne ...	...	Intelligence.

1920

Laurence Condon	...	O/C.
Michael Keane	...	Vice O/C.
Thomas Garry ...	...	Adjutant.
Con Leddy	...	Quartermaster.
Patrick Aherne ...	...	Intelligence (captured).
William Twomey	...	Intelligence.
Daniel Daly	...	Engineer.

1921

Con Leddy	...	O/C (succeeded L. Condon, captured).
Liam Buckley ...	...	Vice O/C
Michael Keane	...	Adjutant.
Michael O'Connell	...	Quartermaster.
Daniel Daly	...	Engineer.
Thomas Cavanagh	...	Intelligence.
James Coss	...	Intelligence.

(Fermoy Battalion, divided, 1921—New formation)

Michael Keane	...	O/C.
Liam Buckley ...	...	Vice O/C.
Patrick Egan	...	Adjutant.
Michael O'Connell	...	Quartermaster.

Mallow Battalion

1919

Liam Jones ...	...	O/C.
Jeremiah Buckley	...	Vice O/C.
Patrick McCarthy	...	Adjutant.
Tadgh Looney	...	Quartermaster.

1920

Patrick McCarthy	...	O/C.
Owen Harold ...	...	Vice O/C.
Tadgh Looney	...	Adjutant.
Michael Nagle ...	...	Quartermaster.
Tadgh Byrne ...	...	Intelligence.

1921

Tadgh Byrne ...	...	O/C.
Edward Murphy	...	Vice O/C.
Jeremiah O'Hanlon	...	Vice O/C (succeeded Edward Murphy, appointed Brigade Quartermaster).
Tadgh McCarthy	...	Adjutant.
Tadgh Looney	...	Quartermaster.
Michael O'Callaghan	...	Intelligence.

John Cunningham   ... ... Column leader and Training Officer.
John Barrett   ...   ... Communications.
Batt. Walsh   ...   ... Police.

Castletownroche Battalion
1919

Patrick Barry   ...   ... O/C.
James O'Neill   ...   ... Vice O/C.
Thomas Palmer   ... Adjutant.
Seán O'Regan   ...   ... Quartermaster.
Patrick Coughlan   ... Engineer.

1920

Thomas Barry   ...   ... O/C.
William O'Regan   ... Vice O/C.
Daniel Shinnick   ... Adjutant.
John Curtin   ...   ... Quartermaster.
Patrick Coughlan   ... Engineer.
Seán O'Regan   ...   ... Engineer.
Patrick Barry   ...   ... Intelligence.
William O'Regan   ... Training.

1921

Thomas Barry   ...   ... O/C (until capture in March).
William O'Regan   ... O/C after March.
William O'Regan   ... Vice O/C until March.
Patrick J. Luddy   ... Vice O/C after March.
Daniel Shinnick   ... Adjutant.
John Curtin   ...   ... Quartermaster.
Seán O'Regan   ...   ... Engineer.
Patrick Barry   ...   ... Intelligence.
David Bernard   ... Training.

Castletownroche Battalion was divided into two battalions in July, 1921—Castletownroche and Glanworth.

Castletownroche Battalion
1921–22

John Lane   ...   ... O/C.
Michael O'Connor   ... Vice O/C.
William J. Griffin   ... Adjutant.
D. O'Regan   ...   ... Quartermaster.
Michael O'Sullivan   ... Intelligence.
John O'Regan   ...   ... Engineer.

Glanworth Battalion

William Kearney   ... O/C.
Richard Smith   ...   ... Vice O/C.

Daniel O'Keeffe   ...   ... Adjutant.
Patrick J. Luddy   ...   ... Quartermaster.
Thomas Lee   ...   ... Engineer.
James Walsh   ...   ... Intelligence.
David Bernard   ...   ... Training.
Patrick Barry   ...   ... Police.

Charleville Battalion

1919

Seamus Brislane   ...   ... O/C.
Denis Driscoll ...   ... Vice O/C.
Jeremiah Moran   ...   ... Adjutant.
James Winters ...   ... Quartermaster.

1920

Seamus Brislane   ...   ... O/C.
Patrick O'Brien ...   ... Vice O/C.
M. Sheehy   ...   ... Adjutant.
James Winters ...   ... Quartermaster.

1921

Seamus Brislane   ...   ... O/C.
M. Sheehy   ...   ... Vice O/C.
Edward Ryan   ...   ... Adjutant.
M. O'Donnell ...   ... Quartermaster.
Eugene   McCarthy   and
   Miss Julia O'Riordan   Intelligence.
Edward Ryan   ...   ... Training.
Denis Motherway   ...   Communications.
Patrick Galvin ...   ... Police.

Newmarket Battalion

1919

Seán Moylan   ...   ... O/C.
Patrick Murphy ...   ... Vice O/C.
William Dwyer ...   ... Adjutant.
Charles O'Reilly   ...   Quartermaster.
   O'Reilly was acting O/C for some months in 1919 during illness of
Moylan.

1920

Seán Moylan   ...   ... O/C.
Patrick Murphy ...   ... Vice O/C.
William Dwyer ...   ... Adjutant.
Patrick McCarthy   ...   Quartermaster (Charles O'Reilly wounded
                         early, 1920).
Seán Nunan   ...   ... Quartermaster (replaced McCarthy in
                         September).

1921

Seán Moylan	O/C (to April, 1921).
Seán Nunan	O/C (replacing Moylan promoted Brigade O/C).
Patrick Murphy	Vice O/C.
William O'Dwyer ...	Adjutant (to 21st March, captured by British).
William Barrett ...	Adjutant (replaced O'Dwyer).
James Riordan ...	Quartermaster.
Jack O'Connell ...	Intelligence.
Liam Moylan	Engineering.
Patrick Dennehy ...	First Aid.
Bernard Columbia ...	Munitions.
Thomas Roche	Police.

Kanturk Battalion
1919

Denis Lyons	O/C.
John O'Connell ...	Vice O/C.
Thomas Riordan ...	Adjutant.
Michael Courtney ...	Quartermaster.

1920

John O'Connell ...	O/C (killed).
Denis Murphy	Vice O/C.
Thomas Riordan ...	Adjutant.
Michael Courtney ...	Quartermaster.

1921

Denis Lyons	O/C.
Denis Murphy	Vice O/C.
Thomas Riordan ...	Adjutant.
Michael Courtney ...	Quartermaster.
James Hayes ...	Intelligence.
Maurice K. McGrath ...	Intelligence.
John McCarthy ...	Police.
Edmund O'Donoghue ...	First Aid.
John Hummerston ...	Engineering.
Daniel Fitzgerald ...	Training.
Michael Keating ...	Transport.
Garrett McAuliffe ...	Communications.

Millstreet Battalion.

Con J. Meaney ...	O/C.
Denis O'Brien	Vice O/C.
Jeremiah Crowley ...	Adjutant.
Denis C. Kelleher ...	Quartermaster.

1920

C. J. Meaney ...	... O/C.
Patrick Healy ...	... Vice O/C.
Jeremiah Crowley	... Adjutant.
Seán Lehane ...	... Quartermaster.
Jeremiah Crowley	... Column Leader.

1921

C. J. Meaney ...	... O/C.
Patrick Healy ...	... Vice O/C.
Jeremiah Crowley	... Adjutant.
Tim Condon ...	... Quartermaster (Lehane captured).
Jeremiah Crowley	... Column Leader.
Michael Galvin ...	... Intelligence.
Comdt. C. J. Meaney ...	... Communication.
Jeremiah Crowley	... Training
Con Meaney ...	... Police.
Seamus Hickey ...	... Engineering.

Lismore Battalion

(Attached to Cork No. 2 Brigade late in 1921)

W. Power ...	... O/C.
L. Cody ...	... Vice O/C.
W. Fitzgerald ...	... Adjutant.
J. Ormond ...	... Quartermaster.

Byrne, Sir Joseph, 67.
Byrne, Tadgh, 72, 136.

Cahalane, S. P., 282.
Carrigtwohill, R.I.C. barracks captured, 67.
Cashin, Jim, 302.
Carey, Michael, 91.
Carty, Frank, 290.
Carson, Sir Edward, 6.
Carolin, Michael, 278.
Casey, Margaret, 2.
Casey, Patrick, 157.
Castlemaine, Ambush at, 168.
Cavanagh, Tom, 46.
Chamberlain,. Joseph (quoted), 38.
Childers, Erskine, 277, 278.
Churchill, Winston, 81, 178, 226.
Clayton, Co. Inspector, R.I.C., 57.
Clancy, Patrick, 76, 94, 97, 105.
Clancy, Laurence, 304, 305, 306.
Clarke, Tom, 5, 187.
Clarke, Mrs. Tom, 238.
Cleary, Hannah Condon, 4, 239.
Clifford, Madge (Mrs. Dr. Comer), 278, 294.
Clonbanin, ambush at, 139, 140, 170.
Colivet, M., 290.
Collins, Capt. Jeremiah, 225.
Collins, Michael, 35, 61, 78, 86, 116, 120, 153, and I.R.B., 187, 188, 192, 193; 2nd Dail, 200; and Treaty, 196; Chairman, Provisional Government, 201, 219; Director of Intelligence, 116, 208; and Army re-unification efforts, 237; and Pact, 238, 240, 244, 271; and action in the North, 249, 253; War Council, 266; and efforts to end Civil War, 284, 285.
Condon, William, 4.
Condon, Larry, 22, 50, 56, 97.
Condon, James, 303.
Condon, Michael, 303.
Cooney, Dan, 54.
Cooney, Andy, 123, 155.
Conlon, Martin, 233, 234, 235.
Connors, Dan, 170.
Considine, Owen, 186.
Conscription, threat of, 21, 22, 23, 23, 24, 25.
Conventions, Army (1917), 15; 209; basis of representation at, 209;

agreed to, 211; sanctioned by Cabinet, 212; prohibited, 214; held, 219; representation at, 219; resolutions passed, 220; Executive elected at, 220, 221, 224; pro-Treaty attitude to, 221, 222, 223, second held, 223; Constitution adopted at, 224; third held, 245, 246; North represented at, 251.
Conway, Tom, 297.
Cork, Grammar School, raid for arms, 29.
Cosgrave, William T., 196, 200, 201, 299.
Cotter, Laurence, 91.
Cotter, Seamus, 250.
Cotter, Seán, 299.
Courtney, T. C., 282.
Couglan, Thomas, 97.
Coughlan, Patrick, 156.
Craig, Sir James, 251.
Creedon, Eamon, 136.
Creed, M., 97.
Creedon, Siobhan (Mrs. Seamus Langford), 117, 135.
Cremin, Michael, 278, 308.
Cremmins, Tim., 108.
Crawford, Tom, 92.
Cranitch, Matthew, 2.
Crofts, Tom, 294, 296, 299, 301, 308.
Crowe, Maurice, 92.
Crowley, Tadhg, 61.
Crowley, Michael, 299.
Crowley, Jeremiah, 131.
Crossbarry, Ambush at, 164.
Crozier, Brig.-Gen., 69, 177.
Culhane, Seán, 259.
Cumann-na-mBan, 16, 107, 159, 231.
Cumming, Col. Comdt. R. H., 133, 141.
Cunningham, Jack, 135, 136.
Curtin, Owen, 77.
Curfew, 106.

DAIL EIREANN, First assembled, 36; suppressed, 66; Second 182; debates on Treaty in, 196; vote on Treaty, 200; Ministry, 196, 200; Cabinet split on Treaty, 196; Deputation of Army Officers to, 238; work of re-

Grammar School, Cork, raid on
29, 44.
Greenwood, Sir Hamar, 66, 81.
Griffin, Tom, 47, 52, 137.
Griffin, Joseph, 257.
Griffith, Arthur, 15, 183, 196, 200,
213, 215, 219, 244, 256, 271, 274,
285.
Guerilla Warfare, 45, 50, 68, 69, 70,
71.

HALES, TOM, 35, 122, 123, 189, 224,
237, 244.
Hales, Seán, 238, 279.
Hallinan, Rev. Fr., 306.
Hallina, Attie, 58.
Harold, Owen, 52, 57, 99, 101.
Harris, Patrick, 91.
Harte, Pat, 35.
Harty, Most Rev. Dr. 298.
Hayes, Seán, 303.
Hayes, Professor Michael, 200.
Headfort Junction, ambush at 165.
Healy, Patrick, 72, 97, 100.
Healy, John, 97, 100.
Hegarty, Dan, 36, 52, 57, 60.
Henderson, Leo, 256.
Herlihy, David, 142, 143, 144.
Higginson, Brig. Gen., 111.
Hogan, Seán, 46.
Hogan, John Joe, 52, 56.
Hogan, Patrick J., 200, 201.
Holmes, Div. Commissioner, R.I.C.,
131.
Houlihan, Bill, 303.
Hunger Strike, Cork, 58, 92.
Hurley, Charlie, 149, 156.
Hyde, Arthur, 3.
Hyde, Dr. Douglas, 3.
Hyde, Seán, 261, 299, 301, 303, 305.
Hyland, Maurice, 46.

INTELLIGENCE, I.R.A., 75, 76, 111,
115 *et seq.* British, 114 *et seq.*
I.R.B., 5, 15, 17, 43, 87, 114, 186
et seq. strength 187; in South
Munster Div., 189; and Treaty,
190; Supreme Council, 187, 190;
conferences of, 203, 231 *et seq.*
Irish Volunteers and I.R.A. ; formation, 6; strength (1914), 7;
(1918), Cork County, 27; Cork
No. 2 Brigade (1919), 36; 1920,

49; 1st Southern Division (1921),
155, 189; total Army strength
(1921), 219; in Six County area,
247; organisation, 16, 24, 71,
83; arrests, 17, 27; public
parades, 17, 19, election of officers,
19; proclaimed, 26; refusal to
recognise British Courts, 27;
morale, 31, 55; and Sinn Fein,
32; and 1918 General Election,
32, 33; formation of Cork
Brigades, 35, 36; public reaction
to activities of, 41, 54, 55; discipline, 42, 44, 216; casualties,
179; suppressing crime, 63 *et seq.*;
police, 63 *et seq.*; in contrast to
previous revolutionary forces, 70,
73; training, 71, 73; special
services, 95, 116; Conferences,
149, 150, 153, 155, 157; formation of Divisions, 154, 156; counter action to executions and
reprisals, 157; under Government
control, 162, 196, 199; levy for
arms, 163; development of
Columns, 97, 98, 164; First
Southern Division and Truce, 173;
effects of Truce, 179, 180, 181;
new Commissions, 199; taking
over of British posts, 204, 205;
position after Treaty, 204, clash
at Limerick, 206; G.H.Q. Staff
and Treaty, 208; Army Council,
224, 274, 275; Executive proposals for unity, 227, and General
Election, 228; officers appeal for
unity, 237, 238, 244; re-unification proposals, 241 *et seq.*; rejected by Executive, 245. I.R.A.
in Ulster, 247 *et seq.*; policy in
North after split, 249. Army
Executive, members in June, 1922,
271; meeting in Fermoy, 270, at
Ballybacon, 271, at Bliantas, 299,
300, 301.

JOHNSON, THOMAS, 279.
Joyce, Ellen, 2.

" KATMANDU," 302, 303.
Keating, Geoffrey, 1.
Kelly, Mary (Mrs. Jeremiah Lynch),
1, 2, 4, 306.